DICTIONARY OF
MARINE INSURANCE TERMS

DICTIONARY OF MARINE INSURANCE TERMS

By

ROBERT H. BROWN
A.C.I.I., M. Inst. A.M.

Lecturer in Marine Insurance at
The City of London Polytechnic.

Examiner for
The Institute of Chartered Shipbrokers
The Institute of South African Shipbrokers
The London Chamber of Commerce

Tutor for The Chartered Insurance Institute.

WITHERBY & CO. LTD.
5 PLANTAIN PLACE, CROSBY ROW
LONDON SE1 1YN

Published in 1962
Reprinted 1963
2nd Edition 1964
3rd Edition 1968
4th Edition 1975
WITHERBY & CO. LTD.

MONUMENT
SERIES

PRINTED IN GREAT BRITAIN BY
NORTHUMBERLAND PRESS LIMITED
GATESHEAD

FOREWORD

Marine insurance has a terminology all its own. This is not surprising when one considers the origins, the antiquity and traditional history of marine insurance, together with the entrenched conservatism of marine underwriters. It is not merely that archaic words and expressions, such as, bottomry and respondentia, have been retained (there is still sentiment in our business), but underwriters have been prone to misuse the language. For instance, by preferring " cancelment " to " cancellation ". Then for the layman some words have a meaning different from their ordinary or dictionary meaning. An etymologist could have good fun tracing the derivation of marine insurance words, such as, " average ". Here we have a word which even means something different according to whether it is used in marine or fire insurance. There is some authority for saying that in marine insurance this word is derived from the French " avarie ", so it has no connection with " average " in its ordinary sense.

Mr. Brown's book, however, is not concerned with such intellectual exercises. Marine insurance impinges on every branch of shipping practice, and on all those commercial activities concerned with the sale, transport and delivery of goods by sea, land or air. Consequently, a variety of people are from time to time confronted with strange marine insurance expressions. For them Mr. Brown's dictionary should be a boon, as the simple alphabetical arrangement, and the concise definitions, make it an easily consulted work of reference.

HAROLD A. TURNER

Marine Underwriter
The Motor Union
Insurance Co. Ltd.
1962

AUTHOR'S PREFACE

For many years it has been apparent that the rapid expansion of the Marine Insurance Industry has resulted in specialisation which tends to restrict the knowledge of the individual. A wider understanding of Marine insurance terms and abbreviations should therefore be readily available in every office in which Insurance plays a part. With the foregoing in mind I have written this book in the belief that it will be of assistance to all those in the Insurance Industry and in Commerce who are concerned with Marine Insurance, particularly Overseas Agents, Bankers, Shipping Merchants and Shipbrokers. It is hoped that reference to a particular term will prevent misunderstanding and so save time and money.

Whilst endeavouring to incorporate every term and abbreviation of importance, including many shipping and commercial terms, it has been necessary to limit each definition because a full explanation would result in a volume of formidable proportions. Nevertheless great care has been taken to ensure that no essential point has been omitted.

July 1961

AUTHOR'S PREFACE TO 2nd EDITION

The constant changes in the Commercial and Shipping worlds are reflected in the practices of Marine insurance. In an attempt to keep pace with these changes it has become necessary to revise this dictionary and whilst doing so I have taken the opportunity of extending the coverage by inserting a number of additional terms which I feel may be beneficially included. While acknowledging the practical assistance of Sydney M. Monk and Irvine J. Banyard in the first edition I would also like to acknowledge the continued assistance of Mr. Monk in the revision and the help from many friends and colleagues, engaged in the practice of Marine insurance in the London market, who have kindly offered contributions and suggestions. I would particularly like to thank the Information Department at Lloyd's for their ready co-operation, also Desmond Baker, A.C.I.I. for his valuable assistance.

London   R.H.B.
March 1964

AUTHOR'S PREFACE TO 3rd EDITION

In revising this book for the 3rd edition I have taken the opportunity to incorporate many new entries also to make various amendments.

I am most appreciative to those critics and friends who have contributed suggestions for amendments and fresh entries. This has proved so beneficial in the improvement of this work, that I would like to invite any other reader, who feels he may have something to contribute, to contact me through the publishers.

London   R.H.B.
August 1968

AUTHOR'S PREFACE TO 4th EDITION

The continued demand for this book justifies my belief that the terminology of marine insurance should be readily available to all those engaged in business relating to this subject. With the help of many friends and colleagues in the London shipping and insurance industry I have been able to add further to the collection of terms, whilst updating some of the information already recorded. Since 1968 marine insurance conditions have been the subject of close scrutiny by Underwriters and inevitable changes have followed, particularly in the field of hull insurance. These changes are incorporated in this revision.

London   R.H.B.
14 August 1973

A

A1

This term is used generally to denote first class quality. It actually derives from the highest classification entry in Lloyd's Register which is ✷ 100 A1 and which applies to steel vessels constructed in accordance with Lloyd's rules and under Lloyd's surveyors' in-spections. The vessel remains so classed as long as she maintains the standard required by periodic surveys. For specific details refer to Lloyd's Register of Shipping. The notation A1 alone is used for vessels within sheltered waters.

A1 Conference clauses

An American form of clauses in respect of shipments of frozen and/or chilled meats and/or other frozen goods.

a.a.

Slip abbreviation for " after arrival ", (which see). Also shipping and chartering abbreviation for " always afloat ".

A.A.M.S.

All American Marine Slip. A U.S. insurance syndicate special-ising in high risk exposures (e.g. pollution liability).

A. & C. P.

Shipping abbreviation. Anchors and chains proved.

AB

American Bureau of Shipping.

Abdnt.

Abandonment.

Abandonment

This is the condition precedent to a constructive total loss. In order to claim a constructive total loss the assured must tender reasonable notice of abandonment to the insurer. He may do this by word of mouth or in writing or both. If the insurer accepts a valid abandonment he is liable to pay a total loss under the policy even if it is proved later that the loss was proximately caused by a peril not insured against. To prevent this the insurer usually rejects the notice of abandonment and agrees to place the assured in a position as though a writ had been issued against the insurer. This situation pertains until it has been proved that the loss is proximately caused by a peril insured against. The purpose of notice of abandon-

1

ment is to enable the insurer to take any steps he thinks fit to prevent a total loss and must therefore be given with reasonable diligence. Any such steps taken do not mean the insurer waives his right to reject abandonment (see " Waiver Clause "). Notice of abandonment need not be given when it can be of no use to the insurer, nor need it be given by a reinsured underwriter to his reinsurer. The insurer may waive notice. Once the insurer pays a total loss he is entitled to take over the proprietary rights to whatever may be left of the property and to dispose of it as he sees fit, retaining the proceeds.

In the French shipping market the term " abandon " is used to illustrate the abandoning of the ship and freight to satisfy a claim for liability against the shipowner in respect of injury caused by the master or crew, where such liability exceeds the value of the ship and the freight.

Absolute Warranty of Seaworthiness

A warranty must be strictly complied with. An absolute warranty of seaworthiness means that the vessel must be seaworthy in all respects at the commencement of the voyage and no loophole is allowed to the shipowner where the unseaworthiness is outside his control. British bills of lading do not have an absolute warranty of seaworthiness and provided the carrier exercises due diligence to provide a seaworthy ship he cannot be held liable by the cargo owner for damage to the cargo resulting from unseaworthiness of the ship. There is no absolute warranty of seaworthiness in a time policy, but if the shipowner knowingly sends the ship to sea in an unseaworthy state the insurer is not liable for loss due to the unseaworthiness.

Ab initio

From inception *or* from the beginning.

A/C

Account.

Acc.

Accident.

Acceptance

The insurer signifies acceptance by initialling the slip at which stage the contract is concluded between the insurer and assured.

Accessories Clause

Concerns insurance of vehicles. No claim is allowed for loss of loose or spare parts and/or accessories unless they are lost or stolen with the complete vehicle.

Accidents in Loading

In a hull policy damage to the hull or machinery directly caused by accidents in loading, bunkering or discharging is covered by the " Negligence " Clause, sometimes called the " Inchmaree ", " Additional Perils " or " Latent Defects " Clause.

Accommodation Line

See " Oblige Line ".

Accounting Year

An Accounting year refers to the Calendar year in which premiums are entered into Account Books irrespective of the attaching dates or years of risks for which the premiums are received. It is used particularly in Excess of Loss Treaties whereby the earned premium on a Treaty is calculated as a percentage of the Original Premium Income entered into the Reassured's Account Books in the year of the period of the Treaty. By using this method the Earned Premium on the Treaty is calculated as soon as the annual accounts are completed and no further adjustment is necessary. It is also used in Lloyd's underwriters' accounts to assess the annual premium income and so maintain the principles regarding Lloyd's underwriters' accounts.

Account Sales

When goods have been sold the details are entered on this document. The document is in constant use in connection with marine insurance claims.

A.C.I.I.

Associate of the Chartered Insurance Institute. A professional qualification awarded by the Chartered Insurance Institute to successful examinees. One is not permitted to sit for the Examination without first producing to the Examination Authorities proof of a satisfactory educational standard. An Associate may sit for the Examination to qualify as a Fellow. (Detailed information can be obtained from the Chartered Insurance Institute, 20, Aldermanbury, London, E.C.2.)

Act of God

When a misfortune occurs which could not have been prevented by reasonable precautionary measures this is termed an Act of God.

Actual Total Loss

An actual total loss can occur in three ways. (1) Where the subject matter is completely destroyed. (2) Where the subject matter ceases to be a thing of the kind insured. (This is termed " loss of specie "). (3) Where the assured is irretrievably deprived of the subject matter, although it has retained its specie. A missing ship is deemed an actual loss when it has been posted as "missing" at Lloyd's.

A.C.V.
Air Cushion Vehicle (Hovercraft).

A.C.V. Form
A Lloyd's form designed to cover risks incurred by hovercraft operators. There are three forms published by Lloyd's. A.C.V. No. 1 covers the hull of the hovercraft. A.C.V. No. 2 is a Returns Clause (L.P.O. 77), for use with A.C.V. No. 1. A.C.V. No. 3 covers liabilities. (See "A.C.V. Form (Hull)" and "A.C.V. Form (Liabilities)".)

A.C.V. Form (Hull)
A Lloyd's policy form (A.C.V. No. 1) designed to cover physical damage to the hull of the insured hovercraft whether it is on ground, or water or hovering; excluding wear and tear, mechanical breakdown, etc. Also excluded are theft, burglary or larceny by servants or others under the control of the assured, strikes, etc. and war risks. The provisions of the M.I.A. (1906) apply to the insurance and many standard marine insurance clauses are incorporated. The vehicle must not be driven other than by the person named in the schedule. The schedule, also, specifies the insured value, a deductible to be applied to partial loss incurred when the A.C.V. is hovering and another deductible to be applied to partial loss incurred whilst the A.C.V. is not hovering. The sue and labour clause has a limit of 25% of the insured value and any claim for sue and labour is reduced by underinsurance. If the insurer agrees to allow lay up returns the form L.P.O. 77 is attached to the policy. (See "Returns Clause (A.C.V.)".) The policy is subject to the "Ingestion Clause". Liabilities are insured on a separate policy. (See "A.C.V. Form (Liabilities)".)

A.C.V. Form (Liabilities)
A Lloyd's Policy form (A.C.V. No. 3) designed to cover amounts paid by the assured in respect of legal liability incurred during the operation of a hovercraft. The cover is expressed in three sections but in no case covers liability in respect of members of the assured's family or members of the crew of the hovercraft or the servants or agents of the assured.

Section I covers third party liability, including removal of wreck expenses, loss of life and personal injury. Section II covers, subject to a £25 deductible and a limit of £250 each person, liability to passengers for loss of life, personal injury and damage to or loss of baggage. Section III covers, subject to a £10 deductible, liability to cargo owners for loss of or damage to cargo from any external cause. This section excludes passengers' luggage. The general conditions and exclusions can be found in the policy form.

A.C.V. 1
See " A.C.V. Form (Hull) ".

A.C.V. 2
See " Returns Clause (A.C.V.) ".

A.C.V. 3
Lloyd's Air Cushion Vehicle Policy (Liabilities)—See " A.C.V. Form (Liabilities) ".

A/d
Shipping abbreviation relating to credit terms and bills of exchange. " After date ".

Addendum
A document, attached to a policy, reinsurance treaty or any other insurance contract, which amends or alters the conditions of the insurance.

Additional Damage Clause
A form of the Inchmaree Clause used in the I.F.V.C. Certain claims under this clause are subject to the deductible expressed in the Machinery Damage Co-insurance Clause.

Additional Expenses—Strikes
Additional expenses incurred by the cargo assured when the carrier exercises a liberty granted by the contract of affreightment and either over-carries the cargo or discharges it at a place other than the destination due to strikes, riots, civil commotions, lockouts or labour disturbances. These expenses are not recoverable under the strikes cover of the ordinary marine policy, but a special insurance may be effected separately. There is no ready market to accept the risk once a strike has commenced in a particular area so many cargo owners prefer to effect an overall cover on all their shipments during a period of (say) 12 months, thereby ensuring cover when a strike occurs.

Additional Expenses—War Risks
A clause used on Cargo Policies in wartime which covers additional expenses occasioned by frustration, arrests, restraints, detainments, hostilities or warlike operations. It does not cover physical loss of part or whole of the cargo or any additional expenses recoverable under the ordinary marine or war policies or which in the event of underinsurance would be recoverable if the cargo was fully

insured. The insurer would not be liable for expenses incurred after 12 months from the date of discharge, nor for warehousing expenses exceeding 6 months after discharge.

Additional Perils

Perils specified in a policy in addition to those already printed in the S.G. policy form. It is customary for a hull policy form to be extended by the addition of certain perils, e.g. negligence. (See " Negligence Clause ".)

Additional Premium

When an insurance has been accepted by the insurer and the premium agreed, the addition of any further liability to the insurer incurs an additional premium. The term is also used when the insurer agrees a basic pemium for the basic conditions of the insurance and at the same time agrees to extend the basic conditions subject to the payment of an additional premium. An additional premium is normally added to the basic premium on a cargo insurance when the carrying vessel is over 15 years old and/or is unclassed. (Ref. " Classification Clause ".)

Additional Premiums—Reinsurance

Where the terms of an original insurance are altered or the amount insured increased, whereby an additional premium is attracted such additional premium, or a proportional part thereof, is equally payable by the original insurer to his reinsurer provided that the reinsurer agrees to accept the amendment or increase in amount. A pro rata additional premium follows automatically where the terms of the reinsurance are based on the O.N.R., but where a special rate has been agreed for the reinsurance an additional premium rate has also to be agreed, this latter particularly applying where the reinsurance is effected on limited terms. In the London market it is customary for reinsurance additional premiums on hull T.L.O. (or similar reinsurance) terms to be paid on the basis of half the rate charged on the original policy, provided of course the original insurance is not itself on limited conditions. In some cases the original insurance is on T.L.O. conditions, including such additional risks as salvage charges and sue and labour, in which case a plain T.L.O. reinsurance will attract an additional premium based on 75% of the rate charged on the original insurance.

Additional Strikes Expenses

See " Additional Expenses—Strikes ".

Adjustable Premium

When a basic or deposit premium is paid at inception, subject to details of the final amounts to be covered being advised at a later date, the premium is adjustable at expiry of the policy if the slip so provides.

Adjuster
See " Claims Adjuster " and " Average Adjuster ".

Adjustment
See " General Average Adjustment ".

A dk
Notation in Lloyd's Register meaning " Awning deck ".

Ad Val.
Ad Valorem. An expression used to state that the value of the goods or interest is to be taken into account.

Advance Freight
Freight paid in advance is, in practice, deemed to have been earned and is therefore not returnable in the event that the carrier fails to deliver the goods at destination. The owner of the cargo has an insurable interest in advance freight and can include it in the insured value of his goods. (See " C.I.F." or " C. & F.".)

Advance Premium
American expression denoting deposit premium.

Adventure
Means the period during which the subject matter is exposed to peril whether insured or not.

Advice Cards
Entries processed at Lloyd's Policy Signing Office are advised to Lloyd's Data Processing Services where advice cards are issued to be forwarded to the subscribing Lloyd's syndicates. The advice cards for accounting entries are hole punched so that they can be used in mechanical accounting systems. The advice cards for non-accounting entries are unpunched. Each card bears printed details of the entry to which it relates so that it can be read visually. (See, also, " Tabulations ".)

A.F.
Shipping abbreviation. Advanced freight.

Affiliated Companies Clause
An American clause for attachment to hull policies whereby the term " assured " embraces affiliated companies of the Assured in whatever capacity they are operating. The insurer, by the clause, waives rights of subrogation against the affiliated companies. An

affiliated company has no greater rights under the policy than the owner of the vessel. The term "Assured" in the "Inchmaree" clause does not include charterers, other than bareboat charterers, under the clause.

Affreightment
See "Contract of Affreightment".

A.F.I.A.
American Foreign Insurance Association.

Aft
Towards, at or near the stern of a ship.

After Arrival
The abbreviation "a.a." may be seen in a broker's slip providing cover for a specified period after arrival. The period specified commences, in the case of cargo, when the goods arrive at their destination as designated in the policy. In the case of a voyage hull policy the period specified commences from the expiry of 24 hours after the vessel safely arrives and anchors at her destination port.

After Body
The part of the ship which lies aft of amidships.

Aft peak Tank
See "Peak Tanks".

After Peak Tank
See "Peak Tanks".

Agents
See "Lloyd's Agent", "Underwriting Agent" and "Institute Agent".

Aggregate Stop Loss
This is a wider application of the ordinary Stop Loss Treaty in that it applies to the entire portfolio of one branch of the Reinsured's activities. (See "Stop Loss Treaty".)

Agreed Returns
Returns of premium payable to the assured in accordance with an agreement in the policy.

Agreed Value
See "Valued Policy".

A.G.W.I.
Atlantic, Gulf, West Indies limits.
(See "Atlantic, Gulf, West Indies Warranty".)

A/H. (Europe)
Abbreviation used to denote that the range for ports of arrival, or departure as the case may be, is limited to those ports on the European Coast between Antwerp and Hamburg.

a.h.
Shipping abbreviation. Aft hatch.

AHAB form
An American fishing vessel insurance form, limiting the vessel to the area between 35° and 46° N. lat. in the Atlantic Ocean west of 50° E. long. (The navigational limits may only be broken to take on bait and/or supplies.)

A.H.F.
American Hull Form.

A.H.F. D.A.
American Hull Form, deductible average.

Air Cargo Clauses
The Institute Air Cargo Clauses (All Risks). These Clauses published on 15th June, 1965 exclude sendings by Post but otherwise cover goods against " All Risks " as provided by the ordinary I.C.C. (All Risks). The 60 day limit in the Transit Clause of the I.C.C. is reduced to 30 days under the Air Cargo Clauses. The Change of Voyage Clause is substantially the same but is called the " Change of Transit Clause " in the Air Cargo Clauses. The F.C. & S. Clause has been suitably amended to apply to aircraft.

Air Cushion Vehicle
Hovercraft. (See " Hovercraft " and " A.C.V. Form ".)

Air Pipe
A pipe in a ship, leading from the top of a tank to the upper deck which allows air to escape as the tank is filled with fuel, water, etc.

Air Sendings
Cargo in transit by air. On 15th June, 1965 a set of Clauses was published to cover air sendings on " All Risks " conditions. This set of Clauses is entitled " Institute Air Cargo Clauses (All Risks) ".

A.I.T.H. Form
American Institute Time Hull form of policy. The American equivalent of the Institute Time Clauses, hulls, with variations. Sometimes referred to as the American Hull Form or A.H.F.

Alexandria Cotton Tariff

A set of Institute clauses in respect of Egyptian cotton, the issue of which was discontinued in July 1961. Under the clauses the assured has the option of covering fire and/or exposure to weather prior to shipment, with the premium adjusted accordingly. The policy pays average subject to a franchise of 3% each bale or on the whole, and covers cost of pickings. It contains "not to inure" (see "Benefit of Insurance") clauses in respect of other marine and war policies or bailee's policies.

Alien Enemy

It is illegal to trade with an enemy, so it follows that an insurer cannot undertake to indemnify an alien enemy in event of loss. If a policy is effected on behalf of an assured who later, during the currency of the insurance, becomes an alien enemy the insurance cover is automatically suspended.

All E.R.

All England Law Reports.

All Other Perils

This appears after the specified perils in the ordinary marine S.G. policy form. It must not be taken in its strict literal sense for the legal maxim "Ejusdem Generis" (meaning "of a like kind") must apply. It embraces only perils similar to those specified, which means that it only includes maritime perils or perils which may happen at sea and are incidental to a sea voyage.

All Others

See "Short Tail". With the introduction of "terms of credit" in the London market this term has fallen into disuse.

All Risks

This is a term to denote the conditions covered by the insurers It is *not* to be construed as meaning that the insurance covers each and every loss. It only covers RISKS. A "risk" is something which may arise as a fortuity but it does not include an inevitability. In cargo insurance the term embraces all fortuitous losses occurring during the currency of the insurance. In addition to the ordinary marine perils it includes extraneous risks. A cargo "all risks" policy always specifically excludes losses proximately caused by inherent vice in the subject matter insured and by delay. In practice there is no franchise in an "all risks" policy. Sometimes the hull policy on Institute Time Clauses (Hulls) terms is called the "all risks" Policy but this is purely a means of identifying the policy when comparing it with other policies issued on more restricted terms.

All Risks Whatsoever
This is not the subject of a specific standard set of conditions. It is a term used to provide wider cover than that granted by the term "All Risks". Nevertheless, it is still subject to the limitation of the expression "risks" and a fortuity must occur before a loss is recoverable. The wording does not specifically exclude inherent vice and delay but for losses proximately caused by these perils to be recoverable it would be necessary to prove that they were not inevitabilities.

alt.
Altered.

Alteration of Port of Departure
When the vessel sails from a port other than that specified in the policy, if it be specified, the risk does not attach. (Ref. Marine Insurance Act 1906—Sect. 43.)

Always Open
A term used in the placing of open covers; it means that the insurance remains continuous from the date of inception until notice of cancellation has been given by either party and such notice has expired.

Am.
American.

Ambiguity
The policy is the instrument of the insurer and any ambiguity therein shall be construed to the benefit of the assured, except where it can be shown that the intention or usage is clear despite the ambiguity. (See "Construction of Policy".)

Amended Running Down Clause
This clause was introduced on 1st October 1971 for attachment to the I.T.C.—Hulls (1/10/70) to clarify the insurer's position in connection with liabilities incurred by the owner or manager of the insured vessel regarding pollution and contamination consequent upon collision. The clause is identical to the collision clause incorporated in the I.T.C. except that there are five exclusions (a) to (e) specified at the foot of the clause as opposed to four exclusions (a) to (d) in the I.T.C. Collision Clause. The additional exclusion, inserted at (c), is "pollution or contamination of any real or personal property or thing whatsoever (except other vessels with which the insured vessel is in collision or property on such other vessels)". It will be noted that although the clause clearly excludes liability incurred for contamination or pollution it does

not exclude these where the damage caused is to the other ship or property on the other ship.

American Bureau of Shipping

This is an American classification society. A vessel fully classed with the American Bureau is entered in the American Register as ✠A.1. Lloyd's Register denotes such a vessel with the abbreviation AB. (See "Classification Clause".)

American Cargo War Risk Reinsurance Exchange

An association of American marine insurance companies who group together to reinsure war risks on cargoes. Based in New York, the association enables war cover to be offered during wartime.

American Foreign Insurance Association

A group of American Insurance Companies who offer consolidated facilities for the writing of insurance business outside the U.S.A.

American Hull Form

This is the standard set of clauses approved by The American Insurance Institute for general market use. It is based on the conditions in the Institute Time Clauses (Hulls), but has several differences, particularly in respect of the Collision clause which provides for a four-fourths liability; also the disbursements warranty which allows 25% of the insured value to be insured on disbursements.

American Hull Insurance Syndicate

An association of Insurance Companies writing Hull insurance business and issuing a combined company policy.

American Institute of Marine Underwriters

Similar to the Institute of London Underwriters the American Institute exists to co-ordinate the use of technical clauses, standard policies, forms and procedure and for discussion on common problems among American marine insurers.

American Institute Time (Hulls) Clauses

See "American Hull Form".

American Port Risk Clauses

A set of hull clauses based on risks following the American Hull Form but in respect of port risks.

Amer T.L. & Exs.

American Disbursements Clauses including Excess.

American Trust Fund

See "Lloyd's American Trust Fund".

Amidships
The part of a ship which is midway between stem and stern.

A.M.L.
Absolute Maximum Loss. A reinsurance term.

Amount Made Good
See " Made Good ".

Am.T.L.O. & Exs.
American T.L.O. Disbursements Clauses including Excess
Liabilities.

Anchor Laying Tug
See " Suitcasing Anchors ".

Anchor Policy
A Lloyd's Policy form. So called because the Lloyd's symbol
on the policy contains an anchor.

And Arrival
This expression may be found in the Returns Clause in the Institute
Time Clauses and similar sets of clauses. Its meaning is that before
returns of premium are payable to the assured the policy must have
expired with the vessel safely " arrived " (i.e. not in peril and safely
arrived at a port). The term is derived from the maritime expression
" arrived " which means that vessel has arrived at a port and is
ready to discharge or load as the case may be.

and/or
Embraces both an addition and an alternative, e.g. " Rail and/or
Road ". The goods may go by rail and road or alternatively they
may go by either rail or road.

Annual Audit
A test of solvency applied to the accounts of a Lloyd's syndicate
or an Insurance Company once a year. The annual audit is conducted at Lloyd's under the auspices of Lloyd's Membership
Services Group. The Company audit is conducted by appointed
auditors and the results are published annually. Lloyd's accounts
are published annually, also, but three years in arrears. (See " Three
Year Accounting ".)

Anticipated Freight
Freight which the shipowner expects to earn over a period of
time but which he will lose if the ship becomes a total loss. This is
the insurable interest of the shipowner, but he is limited to the

amount he can insure under this interest by the disbursements warranty in the hull policy.

A/o
Account of.

A.O.A. *or* **a.o.a.**
Any one accident.

A.O.B. *or* **a.o.b.**
Any one bottom.

A.O.L. *or* **a.o.l.**
Any one loss.

A.O.O. *or* **a.o.o.** *or* **a.o.occ.**
Any one occurrence.

A.O.R.
Any one risk.

A.O.S. *or* **a.o.s.**
Any one steamer.
Any one sending.

A.O.V. *or* **a.o.v.**
Any one vessel.

A.O. Voy
Any one voyage.

A.P.
Additional premium.

Appd.
Approved.

A.P.L. *or* **a.p.l.**
As per list.

Apparent Damage on Discharge
Where damage to cargo is apparent on discharge immediate notice of the damage must be given to the carrier. If the damage is not apparent, notice must be given within 3 days.

Application for cargo insurance
Used in the American market, this is a standard form of application for cargo insurance. It is similar to the proposal form in non-marine insurance.

Application for hull insurance
Used in the American market, this is a standard form of applica-

tion for insurance on a ship. It is similar to the proposal form in the non-marine market.

Apportionment of Valuation

Where the subject matter insured has apportionable parts under one valuation the value may be apportioned in like parts for the purpose of assessing total loss of part and application of the franchise, if any. With cargo the value may, if practicable, be apportioned over each package or series of packages or each craft load or similar apportionment. Such valuation apportionment must be agreed when the insurance is placed and be specified in the policy.

Approved *or* **Approved or Held Covered**

In cases where an insurer is asked to accept a cargo risk when at that time the carrying vessel is unknown it is usual to warrant that the vessel shall be " approved ". The term indicates that the carrying vessel must be fully classed in Lloyd's Register, or one of the other accepted Registers, and must be not over 15 years old (liners other than warbuilt tonnage are acceptable up to 30 years old). If the warranty is extended with " or held covered " vessels not coming within the required category are acceptable but subject to a reasonable additional premium to be agreed. The term is generally used in open covers, open slips and floating policies.

A.P./R.P. Pool Scheme

An internal procedure operated in the Lloyd's market whereby payments of premiums or return of premiums are not allocated over the subscribing syndicates unless the payment exceeds £2.00 or U.S. $5.00 (Canadian $5.00), on the average, each syndicate on the risk. Such amounts are paid into or out of a pool account.

A.P./R.P. Waiver Scheme

Application of the Reinsurance Waiver Clause (which see).

APT.

Aft Peak Tank. Lloyd's Register abbreviation.

A.R.

All Risks.

Arbitration

Courts of Arbitration are convened to enable disputes in marine matters to be settled without recourse to the ordinary courts. It is usual for each of the disputing parties to select a representative and for the two representatives jointly to agree on a third arbitrator. Arbitration clauses always appear in Reinsurance Treaties, Contracts, Charter Parties and similar agreements. It is also usual for salvage disputes and awards to be settled by arbitration. When the dispute has been settled and an amount is agreed to be paid to one of the parties by the other, this amount is called an Arbitration Award.

Arbitration Award
A payment made to one of the parties involved in a dispute which has been settled by arbitration.

Arbitration Clause
A clause in a treaty, contract or similar agreement, which provides that all disagreements or disputes be settled by arbitration instead of going to a court of law.

Ardency
A quality in ship design that makes the vessel head into the wind.

Arranged Total Loss
See " Compromised Total Loss ".

Arrd.
Arrived.

Arrests
By " arrest " a ship may be detained because of some infringement of regulations either port or national. When a maritime lien is to be exercised the ship may also be " arrested ". Such a lien may arise when the ship is the subject of a salvage award. Under Australian law a ship may be so detained until the courts have been satisfied regarding any dispute concerning cargo carriage, unless a guarantor resident in Australia is declared. Arrest may also arise in the event of collision disputes. The policy does not cover any of these. (See " Arrests, Restraints and Detainments ".)

Arrests, Restraints and Detainments
The full term is " Arrests, restraints and detainments of all kings, princes and people, of what nation, condition or quality soever " and is to be found among the perils specified in the standard marine S.G. policy form. It refers to political or executive acts and does not include any loss caused by ordinary judicial process or by riot. It, therefore, does not cover arrests where they are incurred by local infringements of regulation (see " Arrests "). Nor does it include war losses. The loss usually occurs by reason of an embargo imposed by a ruling power in a country. It does not ordinarily include confiscation as the criterion is that the property is arrested with the ultimate intention of release, although such a loss may come within the term

where the property has been confiscated but it is the intention to reimburse the owner with the value of the property in due course. (See also " Pre-emption ".)

Arrived Damaged Value
See " Arrived Sound Value ".

Arrived Sound Value
Refers to cargo which is the subject of a claim. A comparison of the estimated arrived sound value and the actual arrived damaged value shows the difference as a percentage of the estimated arrived sound value for the purpose of arriving at the percentage of depreciation. (See " Gross Value ".) The percentage is applied to the insured value to arrive at the claim. " Arrived " means arrived at the destination named in the policy, but may include an intermediate place if the adventure on the cargo is terminated there. (See also " Salvage Loss ".)

Arr. T.L.
Arranged total loss.

Artificial Harbour
It often occurs that for economic reasons a harbour is needed in a position where no natural harbour exists. An artificial harbour is then built with piers and/or moles to protect the harbour from the open sea.

A/S
After sight, reference shipping documents.
Account Sales, reference claims documents.

a/s
Alongside.

As agreed L/U
As agreed by the leading underwriter. A provision agreed by all insurers in an original slip or open cover whereby the other insurers agree to accept the specified conditions or terms when agreed by the leading underwriter. The agreement may be in respect of a vessel to be declared later, or the date of attachment, or an additional premium in event of a certain circumstance arising, or similar.

as &/or as
An expression in common use in reinsurance. Its purpose is to protect the reinsured in the event of a mis-statement in the reinsurance instructions. Its effect is to advise the reinsurer that the information stated is as shown in the original insurance, but in the event

of variation the reinsurance covers any additions or differences in the original insurance.

As Expiry

When a renewal of a slip is effected on the same terms and conditions as the expiring insurance it is common to use the expression "as expiry" to save work in preparing detailed wording on the renewal slip.

as is—where is

Term used in ship valuation. The value to be calculated on the vessel, in whatever condition she happens to be and at the place where she happens to be at the time of the valuation.

A.S.F.

Associate of the Institute of Shipping and Forwarding Agents. The title of this Institute is now "The Institute of Freight Forwarders". An Associate Member (replacing the old A.S.F.) is designated A.M. Inst. F.F.

As may be paid thereon

Part of the reinsurance clause, this has been interpreted in law as meaning that the reinsurer is only liable for those losses for which the original insurer was legally liable under the original policy. This does not include "ex gratia", "compromised" or "without prejudice" settlements.

As orig.

As original. An agreement on a reinsurance whereby the reinsurers agree to accept the same conditions as accepted by the original insurer.

As per List

The abbreviation "a.p.l." appears on a broker's slip when it is necessary to advise the insurer that the vessel has either sailed or is due to sail and the broker is unable to state the exact sailing date at the time of placing. The term means that the insurer will find the sailing date in "Lloyd's List" and that the entry therein shall be accepted as the sailing date under the insurance.

Ass.

"Assisted into". A hull insurance term regarding towage etc. of a ship into port of refuge.

Assailing Thieves

Persons, other than the ship's officers, crew or passengers, who engage in theft from a vessel.

Assd. *or* **ASSD**
Assured.

Assignee
Is the person to whom the interest or beneficial rights under a policy have been assigned. An assignee acquires no greater rights in a policy than the assignor had, so that if the assignor is guilty of misrepresentation by which the insurer may avoid the contract, the insurer may equally avoid the contract after it has been assigned.

Assignment Clause
This clause appears in the Institute Time Clauses (Hulls) and most other sets of hull clauses. It provides that in the event of assignment of the policy being required such assignment must be by specific endorsement and dated. Further the clause provisions shall be subject to the limitations placed on the assured by the Sale of Vessel Clause which is also in the Institute Time Clauses.

Assignment of Interest
When the rights in a property which is the subject of marine insurance change hands the insurable interest therein is assigned by implication. It is not to be implied that the rights in the policy are automatically assigned at the same time.

Assignment of Policy
A marine policy is freely assignable to any person who has an insurable interest in the property at risk. The policy may be assigned either at the time the interest passes or before. It cannot be assigned *after* the interest passes because a person who has no insurable insurable interest has no valid policy to assign. In practice, agreement is made or implied to assign the policy before the interest passes.
A cargo policy is assigned by endorsement and passed to the assignee. Hull insurers on the other hand prefer not to allow free assignment and by the " Assignment Clause " and " Sale of Vessel Clause " in the Institute Time Clauses they prevent assignment unless they agree to the transfer of the policy to the new assured.

Assignor
Is the person who assigns his interest or beneficial rights under a policy to the assignee.

Assured
The assured is the person who, having an insurable interest in the property at risk which is the subject matter of the insurance, effects an insurance in respect thereof. (See also " Insurable Interest ".)

Assurer
The assurer is the person or Company who holds himself liable to compensate the assured in the event of a loss to the insured property proximately caused by a peril insured against.

A/T
Grain trade abbreviation. American Terms.

At and from
This refers to attachment of risk and when a voyage policy on the ship contains the expression it means that the risk attaches when the vessel arrives at the place named in the policy in good safety. The risk still attaches even if the ship is covered by another policy at that time. (See " Double Insurance ".) If the ship is already at the place in good safety when the contract is concluded the risk attaches immediately.

Athwartship
Means the same as transverse (which see).

A.T.L.
" Actual Total Loss ". The same abbreviation is commonly interpreted as " Arranged Total Loss " although this should be shown as " Arr.T.L.".

Atl.
Atlantic coast ports. Applies to Canadian and/or U.S.A. voyages.

Atlantic, Gulf, West Indies Warranty
A trading limitation which warrants the vessel shall be confined to trading between ports and/or places on the Atlantic Coast of the U.S. (including ports and/or places in the Gulf of Mexico) and/or ports and/or places in Mexico and/or Central America and/or West Indies and Caribbean Sea as far south as Demerara. It is usual to extend the southern limit to Paramaribo

att.
Attached.

Attachment Date
The date on which a risk attaches. In practice, at Lloyd's, the leading underwriter enters the month the risk attaches on the broker's slip. This gives a basis for assessing the period of credit allowed for premium payment. (See also " Deemed Attachment Date ".)

Attachment of Interest
The Assured need not have an insurable interest at the time of

effecting the insurance but in order to claim under the policy he must have an insurable interest at the time of loss and he must have some expectation of acquiring such interest at the time of effecting the insurance. An assignee taking over a policy or acquiring an interest after inception of the risk may have the benefit of the assignor's interest in respect of loss by the insertion in the policy of the expression " lost or not lost ". Insurable interest attaches as soon as the assured is in a position where he may lose by reason of an accident to the property at risk.

Attachment of Risk

This refers to the attachment of the risk and commencement of underwriters' liability. If the risk fails to attach the assured is entitled to a return of premium based on failure of consideration as provided by the Marine Insurance Act, 1906.

Cargo—On the plain form of policy the risk attaches as the goods are loaded on board the overseas vessel (no craft risk to the vessel is covered). If the transit clause is attached to the policy the risk attaches when the goods leave the warehouse or place of storage at the place specified in the policy for the commencement of transit.

Hull—On a voyage policy the risk attaches " at and from " the place specified in the policy. On a time policy the risk attaches on the date and time specified in the policy.

Attachment Slip

When it is necessary to obtain the insurer's agreement to an alteration, amendment or addition in an original slip, such agreement is presented to the insurer on an attachment slip, attached to the original slip.

Attestation Clause

The wording appearing in a marine policy whereby the insurer states that he is " contented " and promises to bind himself for the true performance of the terms of the policy. This may be followed with a form of receipt for the premium, but Company policies generally omit the receipt part. The attestation clause in the Lloyd's policy has been changed recently to show that the names of the Underwriters subscribing the policy, as referred to by the Syndicate numbers contained in the policy, are retained at Lloyd's Policy Signing Office. Previously a sheet of flimsy paper attached to the policy bearing the names of subscribing Underwriters (see also " Name ").

AUD.

Audit classification (which see).

Audit Category
See " Audit Classification ".

Audit Classification
Lloyd's underwriters are required to submit statistics to the Department of Trade and Industry in separate classes of business. The audit code allocated to a branch of business (e.g. T = Time, W = War risk only—hull, B = Time T.L.O.) is shown on the placing slip by the leading underwriter. It is the responsibility of the broker to see that the slip is so coded and to copy the code onto the premium advice note so that it can be incorporated in data processing.

Audit Code
See " Audit Classification ".

Australian Sea Carriage of Goods Act 1924
An Act to give force of law to the rights, obligations and immunities of carriers of goods in respect of bills of lading on shipments from Australia to other Australian States or to outside Australia.

Auth R/I
Authorised reinsurance. A term used in relation to syndicate reinsurance.

Automatic Termination of Cover Clause
This clause is used in war and strikes risks insurances in respect of hulls and hull interests. It appears in all sets of the relevant clauses used for these interests and is intended to terminate the insurance automatically in event of the outbreak of a major war. The rate of premium charged by the insurer during peacetime is relatively low and is intended to contemplate only those accidental or incidental losses proximately caused by war perils which may still occur even in peacetime. It is not the intention of the insurer to cover the very heavy risks of a major war and, in any case, certainly not at the rate of premiums charged.
The clause provides that if a hostile nuclear detonation takes place at any time, anywhere, the insurance terminates immediately and it does not matter whether or not the vessel insured is involved. The insurance will also terminate automatically if there is an outbreak of war (with or without declaration) between any of the countries specified in the clause. The specified countries are U.S.A., U.K., France, U.S.S.R., and the Peoples Republic of China. If the vessel is requisitioned, either for title or use, the insurance is automatically terminated.
If any of the above circumstances arises before attachment of a

policy, in respect of which the contract has been concluded (see " Conclusion of Contract "), the policy does not attach.

Aux.
Auxiliary.

Aux. B
Auxiliary boilers. Lloyd's Register notation.

Auxiliary
Seldom seen in these days when sailing vessels have been superseded by mechanical propulsion. The abbreviation " Aux " may be seen on slips and policies to denote that a sailing vessel is fitted with an auxiliary engine. If the vessel is registered the entry will bear the abbreviation.

Auxiliary Yacht
A sailing boat used for private pleasure purposes and being fitted with both sail and mechanical propulsion.

Av.
Average.

Av. Disbt.
Average Disbursements.

Average
This is the marine insurance term for a partial loss. (See " particular average " and " general average "). Particular charges are not to be included when calculating average.

In non-marine insurance the term " subject to average " is used in which case it means that in the event of a claim arising and it being proved that the amount insured is less than the true value the assured must bear his proportion of the loss.

Average Adjuster
An average adjuster is an expert in loss adjustment in marine insurance, particularly with regard to hulls and hull interest. He is more particularly concerned with general average adjustments. He is usually appointed to carry out general average adjustments for the shipowner on whom falls the onus to have the adjustment drawn up. His charges and expenses form part of the adjustment.

Average Agent
Person engaged in assessment of cargo claims, surveys and treatment of damaged goods.

Average Bond
Sometimes referred to as " General Average Agreement". When

a general average act occurs the carrier has a lien on the cargo whereby he may prevent the consignee from taking delivery until payment of a deposit has been made into a trust fund set up by the shipowner and average adjuster pending the final adjustment of the general average and eventual allocation of the fund to the parties due to benefit thereby. Alternatively the shipowner may agree to discharge his lien on production of an underwriter's guarantee of the eventual contribution due by the cargo assured. At the time of payment of the deposit or production of the guarantee the consignee will be required to sign an average bond, or agreement. By this bond, or agreement, the consignee agrees (1) to abide by the decision of the average adjuster (2) to the carrier drawing upon the general average fund immediately, subject to the average adjuster's agreement, in respect of general average disbursements, instead of waiting until the final adjustment has been drawn up, and (3) to be liable for the proper proportion due in respect of his general average contribution. It is customary for the average bond or agreement to be countersigned by a guarantor or the consignee's or cargo owner's bankers. The term " bond " in this context sometimes causes confusion because in the American market it is used to describe an " Average Guarantee ".

Average Clause

Appears in most sets of cargo clauses and deals with the matter of the franchise. Where no average clause is in the policy the franchise specified in the memorandum, at the foot of the policy form, applies.

In non-marine insurance the average clause provides that comparison shall be made between the amount insured and the insurable value and any claim to be reduced in proportion to any under-insurance.

Average Disbursements

See " General Average Disbursements ".

Average Disbursements Clauses

There is no standard set of Institute clauses covering average disbursements but there are several sets of clauses in general use in the market. The shipowner who incurs expenditure in connection with a general average act or as salvage charges is entitled to recover a proportionate part of such expenditure as average disbursements in the general average or salvage adjustment. Such recovery is dependent on the value of the property which arrives at its destination, in the case of general average, or is saved, in the case of salvage. Where the contributing interest is lost there can be no recovery from that interest, hence the shipowner has an insurable interest both in the total loss of a contributing interest and in the reduction in value of such interest, the latter often being called diminution of value. All sets of clauses cover the total loss of the contributing interests whether cargo, ship or freight, from specified perils. In addition, some sets of clauses also cover loss of average disbursements resulting from diminution in value, but insurers do not readily accept such clauses, preferring what are known as the S.A. clauses which do not cover losses based on diminution in value.

Since the interest is closely allied to cargo it is customary for the clauses to contain the usual cargo clauses " craft etc.", " deviation " and " seaworthiness admitted ". It is also customary for the insurer to admit insurable interest and to waive the benefit of any other insurances which may be in force on the same interest. All risks are covered at the port of discharge and during transit of the cargo to its final destination; the perils also include all risks incidental to navigation or management of the ship, also negligence, default, incompetence or error of judgement of persons operating the vessel, employees of the shipowner and those concerned with loading or discharging the vessel, including port authorities. Further perils included are explosion, bursting of boilers, latent defects and breakage of shafts, earthquakes, volcanic eruptions, floods, storms and all other causes of loss however they arise. So far as the ship is concerned the risk thereon ceases on discharge of the cargo but may be extended, at the insured's option, for 30 days after arrival of the vessel at the destination port. Advanced freight can also be considered as an insured interest, being treated as increased value of the cargo if the insured wishes.

Average Guarantee
See " General Average Guarantee ".

Average Irrespective of Percentage
Partial loss is payable without reference to the franchise.

Average Payable on each Package
Usually this is followed by " or on the whole ". It refers to the franchise. Where a large shipment of cargo is involved under one valuation the value may be apportioned (see " Apportionment of Valuation ") and the franchise applied to the apportioned part. The assured has the option of applying the franchise to each package separately (see " Series ") if the claim is not sufficient to attain the franchise percentage when applied to the value of the whole.

Average Statement
Statement prepared by the Average Adjuster giving details of

contributory values, general average losses and expenses.

Average Unless General

Particular average. That is, partial loss other than general average loss.

Average Warranty

An express warranty in a policy stipulating the franchise or excess applicable to partial losses under the policy.

Avoidance

The aggrieved party may avoid a voidable contract. The insurer may avoid the contract, that is, he may consider himself discharged from liability from inception in the event of non-disclosure or misrepresentation of a material fact or in the event of a breach of the utmost good faith. He may also avoid the contract if the voyage under a voyage policy is not commenced within a reasonable time. In the event that the underwriter successfully avoids the contract he must return the premium to the assured except where there has been fraud or illegality on the part of the assured or the risk has already attached. (See " Voidable Policies ".)

B

Bacat

Barge aboard catamaran. A short sea service vessel designed to carry cargo in barges between U.K. and the Continent.

Back Freight

Extra freight charged for a return trip or overcarriage when goods are rejected by the import authority or the consignee. Back freight is generally chargeable to the shipper and he has an insurable interest therein. The shipper may not be charged the back freight if it results from a fault of the carrier.

Back Letter

A letter of indemnity in connection with a " dirty " bill of lading.

Backstay

A wire stay fitted as a support to the aft side of a mast. (See also " Forestay " and " Triatic Stay ".)

Bacterial and Salmonella Contamination Clause

This clause is used in insurances covering foodstuffs (particularly desiccated coconut). The insurer agrees to pay the difference between the insured value and the residual value in the event that the shipment is condemned by the importing authorities as being unfit for human consumption as a result of bacterial and/or salmonella contamination. The clause provides, also, for the insurer to pay the cost of heat treatment or other measures incurred to make the insured food fit for human consumption.

Bailee

Usually this is a carrier of the goods or his agent. It is the person who is responsible for the goods during the transit but who has no rights in the goods. The bailee has an insurable interest in his liability in respect of goods in his charge.

Bailee Clause

This clause appears in the Institute Cargo Clauses and in most other sets of cargo clauses. The Marine Insurance Act 1906 in section 78 states that there is a duty on the assured and his agents, in all cases, to take such measures as may be reasonable for the purpose of averting or minimising a loss. The Carriage of Goods by Sea Act 1924 provides that the shipowner issuing a contract of affreightment in accordance with the Act cannot have a " benefit of

27

insurance " clause therein, but this does not prevent other bailees from inserting such clauses in their contracts to absolve themselves from liability in the event of damage to cargo in their care. To ensure that the assured takes reasonable steps to protect insurers' subrogation rights the " bailee clause " provides that the assured must take all reasonable steps to prevent the bailee from avoiding his liability for damage to the goods.

Balance Settlement

An arrangement whereby premium entries and claim entries are balanced at the end of an agreed period (say, monthly), and settlement is made on the difference.

Balance Settlement Scheme

See " B Scheme ".

Balancing Charges

A form of insurance to reimburse the shipowner for tax for which he may find himself liable on the money he receives from insurance if his vessel becomes a total loss or suffers a major casualty. The tax is calculated on the difference between the book value of the ship and the insured value, which difference is considered to be profit as the insured value is usually considerably higher than the book value. The shipowner has no liability for the tax if he elects to spend the insurance proceeds on a new ship.

Ballast

Material carried in a vessel to ensure stability when the vessel is without cargo, or with only a small amount of cargo. A vessel is said to be " in ballast " at such times. The passage is called a " ballast passage ". A ship proceeds in ballast when she is en route to another port for the purpose of picking up cargo.

Ballast Passage

A ballast passage occurs when the vessel is on a passage from one port to another without cargo.

Baltcon

Accepted code name for the Scandinavian and White Sea Coal Charterparty.

Baltic Ice Clause

A clause which provides that only a proportion of any loss, including general average contribution and salvage, shall be paid by the policy if arising from ice in the Baltic north of 56° N. lat. It is warranted by the assured that the balance is uninsured. The proportion varies between 70% and 80% depending on the age of the vessel.

Baltic Ice Warranty

One of the standard Institute warranties. It provides, on hull policies, that the vessel shall not be in various parts of the Baltic during icing. The prohibited areas and dates are specified in the clause. Single round voyages may be undertaken by prior agreement with the insurer and subject to an additional premium.

Baltime

Accepted code name for Baltic and White Sea time charterparty.

Bank Urgent

A policy required to be signed urgently because it is needed for deposit in a bank as part of the credit system of payment for goods.

Bar.

Barrel.

Bareboat Charter

Under this form of time charter the charterer hires the vessel and pays all expenses incurred during the period of the charter.

Barge

Either dumb or powered, barges are mainly used for bulk cargo carriage, but are also used for the carriage of goods from ship to shore or vice versa and for onward carriage where the overseas vessel cannot navigate due to the shallow draught required. A dumb barge is one without means of propulsion and it is usual for such barges to be towed individually, or in strings, by powered barges or tugs.

Barge Retentions

Special retentions of premium for port risks when lay up returns are allowed under insurances on barges, lighters and similar. These retentions are specially agreed and are not subject to a scale.

Bar Keel

A ship's keel that is a solid (rectangular in section) steel bar. The garboard strakes (forming part of the ship's bottom) are fastened to the keel.

Barratry

One of the insured perils in the policy form. Barratry is any act by the master or crew which is detrimental to the interests of the owner but is without the privity of the owner. The term may also be applied when the act is detrimental to the interests of a charterer or a cargo owner. Provided barratry is an insured peril the insurer is not discharged from liability in event of the vessel being delayed or deviating due to barratry.

Basic Rate

Rate of premium applied to a standard set of circumstances. The rate may be increased or reduced according to alteration of the circumstances.

Basis of Valuation

Declarations under an open cover must not exceed the limit any one vessel as provided by the cover. Subject to this, shipments may be declared even after loss provided the shipments come within the scope of the cover. To protect the insurer regarding the declared value of such late shipments a clause is inserted in the open cover defining the basis which shall be used to reach the acceptable insured value. The basis normally includes the prime cost of the goods plus insurance charges, freight and a fixed percentage representing the profit to the seller.

Battens

Cargo battens are used to keep cargo from touching the sides of the vessel when stowed in the hold. The term may also be used in carriage of timber, battens then meaning narrow lengths of timber.

B.B.

Shipping abbreviation for " below bridge ". Can also mean " Bill Book ".

B.B. Clause

Both to blame collision clause.

B/D

Bank Draft.

Bd.

Bond.

B.D.I.

Both days inclusive.

Bdls.

Bundles.

B'down

Breakdown.

B.D.S.

Broker's Daily Statement.

Bds.

Boards.

Beam

A section constructed transversely in a ship to support the deck plating.

Beam Knee

A connection joining a beam to the frame of a ship.

Beaufort Scale

Beaufort windscale and sea disturbance table. A generally accepted scale giving interpretation by name to varying degrees of wind force. Ranges from " Calm " or " Force O " being a wind of less than one knot to " Hurricane " or " Force 12 " being a wind of 64 to 71 knots. According to the scale a " Gale " is " Force 8 " being a wind of 34 to 40 knots with waves of 18 ft. average, maximum about 25 ft.

B/E

Bill of Exchange.

Benacon

Accepted code name for North American Atlantic wood Charter-party.

Benefit of Insurance

In cases where it is possible that the insured property may be in the hands of a person other than the assured, such as a bailee, the other person may insist in his contract that he has the benefit of any insurance on the property. By this the other person divests himself of any financial responsibility for damage to the property from an insured peril. This may affect the insurer's rights of subrogation so no insurer will readily agree to a " benefit of insurance " clause in a contract of carriage. In fact, where an insurer anticipates this possibility he will usually insist on a clause in the policy preventing the benefits under the policy accrueing to any person other than the assured or his assignee. (See " Not to Inure Clause ".)

Benefit of Salvage

See " Without Benefit of Salvage "

Berm.

Bermudan. (Which see.)

Bermudan

A term used in yacht insurance. Classes of sailing vessels are readily recognised by the rig of the sails. The term " Bermudan " is used to describe the rig of the sails which in this class is a single triangular sail fitted to the mast without spars.

Berthage
A charge made by the Port Authorities for the use of a berth.

Beyond Control of the Assured
The cargo assured is deemed to have control of the insured property in so far as he has control of the persons in charge of the property. In practice the insurer agrees that the cargo owner shall not be prejudiced if he signs an agreement which contains a clause absolving the other party from liability in the event of loss of or damage to the property whilst in the other person's care.

The shipowner may claim that the circumstances are beyond his control, if neither he nor the master has any control over them, as one of the excuses allowed by the M.I.A. as justification for delay or deviation.

b.f.s.l.
Being full signed line. (See " Full Signed Line ".)

b.f.w.l.
Being full written line. (See " Full Written Line ".)

B/G
Bonded Goods.

Bg.
Bag *or* brig.

Bge.
Barge.

B/H (Europe)
Bordeaux-Hamburg range.

b/h
Bulkhead.

B.I.A.
British Insurance Association.

B.I.G.
British Insurance Group.

Bilge
A drainage space in a ship. The bilges are located at the lowest part on each side of the ship (i.e. at the curved portion which lies between the side shell plating and the bottom shell plating). Surplus water in the ship is drained into the bilge tanks from which it is pumped out of the ship.

Bilge Keel
A fin fitted along the bilge strake. Its purpose is to reduce roll in the ship.

Bilge Strake
The shell plating on the hull at the bilge.

Bilge Water Damage
Damage to cargo caused by overflowing of waste pipe water or water from the bilges of the vessel. This comes within the term "fresh water damage" which is an extraneous risk.

Bill of Exchange
A document issued by a buyer to a seller authorising him to draw on the buyer's bank the price of the goods on a fixed date or when the goods have arrived. The bank requires this as one of the documents when lending money to the seller as an advance on the purchase price of the goods.

Bill of Lading
A shipping document prepared by the shipping agent and containing a complete description of the goods to be shipped. The carrier signs the bill of lading, but will qualify it if the goods are unsound or improperly packed. He may refrain from qualifying the bill if the shipper is prepared to give him a letter of indemnity to protect him from liability for damage to the goods. An unqualified bill is called "Clean" and a qualified bill is called "Foul", "Dirty" or
Unclean". A "Clean" bill is only prima facie evidence that the goods were sound when shipped. A bill of lading may be "Shipped" or "Received for Shipment".

Bill of Lading Clause
A clause which at one time appeared in the Institute Cargo Clauses with the intention of protecting the cargo owner in the event of loss of or damage to, the cargo by the misconduct or wrongful act of the carrier or his servants, where the carrier has contracted out of liability by the clausing of his bill of lading. Provided the loss is proximately caused by an insured peril the Marine Insurance Act does not exclude it, even though the misconduct or wrongful act of the carrier or his servants gave rise to the loss. The clause was omitted from the Institute Cargo Clauses when they were republished on 1st August 1958.

The section of the Bill of Lading Clause relating to misconduct or wrongful act of the carrier was retained by being inserted in the "Seaworthiness Admitted Clause" (which see).

Bill of Lading Freight

Freight paid by the shipper to the carrier for the carriage of goods. A charterer who hires the ship may charge bill of lading freight to his shipper, but himself pays "chartered freight" to the shipowner for hire of the ship. Bill of lading freight is generally paid in advance and agreed non-returnable in the event of non or short delivery. The cargo owner, therefore, has the insurable interest in bill of lading freight and he merges this in the value of the cargo.

Bill of Sale

In marine business this is the document used to denote the legal purchase of a British vessel. The purchase is registered by means of the bill of sale.

Bill of Sight

When goods arrive at Customs without documents or available knowledge of full details the Customs Authorities require that the importer completes a bill of sight before he can obtain release of the goods.

Bill of Store

When British goods have been exported and are being reimported they are subject to the same conditions and restrictions as are foreign goods unless a bill of store is completed for the Customs authorities within a stated period.

Binder

American expression for an agreement to insure. It contains the details of the insurance and is used in the same way as the "slip" in the London Market between the time of acceptance by the insurer and the closing of the policy.

Binding Clause

A clause in the S.G. policy form whereby it is agreed that the " .... policy shall have as much force and effect as a .... policy .... made in .... London ". The term also applies to the list of contracting parties in a reinsurance treaty contract; in the latter case it sets out the extent of each subscriber's liability.

Binnacle

The stand that holds the compass in a ship.

Bitt

Another term for a " bollard ".

Bkge.

Breakage. It is common for the same abbreviation to be seen on a slip to denote " brokerage ".

Bkt.
Basket.

B/L
Bill of Lading.

Blanket Insurance
A non-marine American expression describing a combined risk under one insurance.

Bldg.
Building.

Blocking
Another word for " caking ". Occurs in goods such as sugar and shellac. It is usual for the insurer specifically to exclude this risk.

Block Policy
A policy used primarily for inland transit risks on cargo. It covers a number of small sendings subject to a limit for any one sending or conveyance. No declarations are made and a lump sum premium is paid in advance. The policy is for a period and is subject to a cancellation clause.

Blow Out
Peril encountered in offshore oil-drilling rig insurance. Occurs when pressure below the sea bed exceeds the drilling column pressure and literally blows out the column.

Bls.
Bales *or* Barrels.

Blue List
Lloyd's Shipping Index.

Blue Peter
A blue rectangular flag with a white square in the centre. The flag is displayed to indicate that the ship is ready to proceed on a voyage.

B.M.
Bermudan, (which see.)

B.M.U.
Bermudan, (which see.)

b.m.
Shipping timber trade abbreviation for " board measure ".

B.N.A. Warranty
See " North American Warranty ".

B.o.
Sale contract abbreviation. " Buyer's option ".

Board of Underwriters of New York
The representatives of the Board, called " correspondents ", act in a similar way to Lloyd's agents with regard to American marine insurance companies in collecting details of losses to cargo.

Boat
A small craft or pleasure vessel. The term embraces a range from a small canoe to a large motor yacht. Generally, the term is used for private pleasure craft such as yachts for which there is a specialised insurance market. Because boats are used, in the main, by amateur seamen the third party risk is probably more prevalent than it is with professionally handled vessels and, further, limitation of liability based on tonnage would be impracticable, so adequate cover is required for such liability (usually about £25,000 any one accident) in addition to cover for loss of or damage to the boat itself. Another peculiarity in the insurance of boats is that many of the craft are often in transit overland which additional hazard must be considered. An underwriter is also concerned whether the boat is being used for racing, which increases the risk, and whether it is laid up on land or safely moored during the winter or when there is likelihood of damage to the insured craft by inclement weather.

Boatswain's Chair
See " Bosun's Chair ".

Bollard
A post fitted to the deck of a ship for the purpose of securing ropes and/or cables for towing or holding purposes. Sometimes termed " bitt ".

Bollard Pull
A basis for measuring the power of a tug or for determining the strain on a tug when towing.

Bona Fide
Made in good faith.

Bond
An agreement to make a payment of money by a certain date or upon request.

Bonded Goods

Goods, on which duty has not been paid, held in bond either by the Customs or in a bonded warehouse. Goods which are only in the port for transhipment are held in bond. Bonded value means the value of the goods whilst in bond and may be used in place of the gross value where bonded goods are damaged and the subject of a claim.

Bonded Values

Used in claims adjustments and general average adjustments on bonded goods.

Bonding Company

See " Surety Company ".

Bond Premium

See " Surety Company ".

Booby Hatch

Covered opening leading below or between decks.

Boot Topping

A protective composition which is painted on the hull of a ship between the light and load waterlines. This can, usually, be recognised as a broad band painted round the ship. The area below the boot topping is the " bottom ". (See " Scraping the Bottom ".)

BORD *or* **Bord**

Bordereau.

Bordereau

Plural Bordereaux. A French word in common use in the insurance market. A schedule or list. It is used a great deal in reinsurance and treaties where details of the month's or quarter's underwriting entries by the original company are submitted on bordereaux.

Bosun's Chair

Boatswain's Chair. A wooden seat fitted to ropes. This is used to hoist or lower a man up or down a mast or over the ship's side.

B.O.T.

Board of Trade. (Now renamed " Department of Trade and Industry ".)

B.O.T. Code

A code entered in documents submitted to a signing office to enable the data processing services to prepare statistics for submission to the Department of Trade and Industry. The term "D.T.I. Code" means the same.

B.O.T. Coding Card

A coding table issued by Lloyd's Central Accounting Office under reference No. 565. It shows numerical codes for use in preparing statistics in respect of various classes of business insured at Lloyd's, divided as between U.K. business and business from various monetary areas. The statistics are used in a form of return to the Department of Trade and Industry.

Bottom

A vessel or ship. It is also used to describe the underside of a vessel below the boot topping.

Both to Blame Collision Clause

In marine insurance this clause is referred to in the Institute Cargo Clauses where it is stated that the assured shall not be prejudiced by reason of signing a contract of affreightment containing the "Both to Blame Collision Clause". The clause in the contract of affreightment protects the carrier who has indirectly paid part of the collision damage to his own cargo by reason of the operation of some foreign laws. Under American law, two ships in collision where both are at fault are held equally to blame. The cargo owner suffering damage consequent upon the collision is entitled to claim against either or both vessels to recover his loss. The carrier developed a practice of inserting a clause in the contract of affreightment whereby the cargo owner is prevented from claiming against his carrier, leaving him no alternative but to claim 100% against the other, or non carrying, vessel. The other vessel being then permitted, by American law, to apply the carrying vessel's proportion of blame to the amount claimed by the cargo owner and to include this proportion of the amount claimed in his collision claim against the carrying vessel. The carrying vessel would be obliged to pay this, and, since the collision clause in his insurance does not extend to cover liability for damage to cargo in the insured vessel, he cannot claim reimbursement from his own insurers. To protect himself he inserts the "both to blame collision clause" in the contract of affreightment whereby the cargo owner is required to reimburse the carrier for the amount paid by the carrier in the above detailed circumstances. By this procedure the cargo owner, in the absence of insurance on the cargo, has no means of reimbursement for his loss. If his cargo is insured under the terms of the Institute Cargo Clauses, however, he would be able to recover his damage loss from his insurers even though the insurers' subrogation rights against the carrier or the other vessel are defeated by the effect of

American law and the both to blame collision clause. American courts have challenged and invalidated the " both to blame collision clause ". Nevertheless insurers maintain the reference to the clause in the Institute Cargo Clauses to protect the assured in the event of the same situation arising under any other foreign laws.

Bottomry

Only of academic interest today, the term applies to money borrowed by the master of a vessel on the security of the ship and freight for the purpose of completing the voyage. When the vessel completes the voyage the money is repayable with interest, but if the security is lost the loan is considered discharged. The lender obviously has an insurable interest in the loan.

Bottomry Bond

The promise or pledge signed by the borrower in a bottomry loan.

Bouquet of Treaties

This refers to several reinsurance treaties offered together by a ceding Company in respect of all its branches of insurance (Fire, Life, Accident, Marine etc.). This method enables a Company to place all its treaties where individually a particular branch may show a loss to the reinsurer, but overall the " bouquet " shows a profit. Obviously, a bouquet of treaties is only acceptable to a re-insuring Company which covers the same branches of insurance offered.

Bow Stopper

A control used to check the chain cable when the anchor is being lowered.

Bow Thruster

A small propeller, positioned at right angles to the bow of the ship, which is used for manoeuvering the vessel over a small area.

Box

Position in the Underwriting Room at Lloyd's occupied by the desk and seats of an underwriter and his assistants.

B.p.

Shipping and/or Shipbuilding abbreviation. " Bills payable ".

Bq.

Barque.

B.R.

Builders' Risks.

BR

Lloyd's Register notation meaning Boiler room.

B/R
Bills received or receivable. Ship construction abbreviation.

Brand Clause
Provides that where a brand or trademark constitutes a guarantee by the name of the manufacturers or producers any salvage value in event of loss shall be assessed after the brand or trademark has been removed.

Breach
Failure to comply with the warranties or conditions of a policy.

Breach of Condition
When a condition of the insurance is broken by the assured the insurer may avoid the contract from inception.

Breach of Contract
Where one of two parties to a contract breaks one of the conditions of the contract whereby the aggrieved party suffers a wrong or injury, the aggrieved party has the right to sue for damages for breach of contract. The marine broker being the agent of the assured, there is an implied contract between the agent and his principal, so that if his principal suffers a wrong or injury due to the broker's negligence the broker may be sued for damages in respect of breach of contract under the law of agency.

Breach of Good Faith
See " Good Faith ".

Breach of Warranty
Whether or not it affects a claim on the policy the assured must literally comply with a warranty in the policy. In the event of breach of warranty by the assured the insurer is, automatically, discharged from all liability as from the date of the breach; but he remains liable for insured losses occurring prior to that date. Repair of the breach before a loss occurs does not change matters The insurer may waive the breach if he wishes and sometimes, in practice, holds covered breach of certain warranties. Non-compliance with a warranty is excused when, by reason of change of circumstances, the warranty ceases to be applicable to the policy. It is also excused where compliance would entail breaking the law. (M.I.A. 1906, Sects 33–34).

Breach of Warranty Clause
A clause in the Institute Time Clauses (Hulls) which provides that breach of warranty as to cargo, trade, locality, salvage services or date of sailing shall be held covered, subject to notice to under-

writers immediately on receipt of advices, acceptance of amended terms of cover and an additional premium if required. In the absence of this clause a breach of such warranties would discharge the underwriters from liability from the date of the breach.

Breakage

Ordinary breakage is considered to arise out of negligence and is not contemplated as an insured marine peril by the insurer when assessing the premium rate. For this reason ordinary breakage, which occurs on fragile goods such as glass, china, asbestos sheets and earthenware, is excluded from the policy by the Marine Insurance Act (Section 55 (2) (C)) unless the policy specifically includes " breakage ". Obviously a high rate would be charged by the insurer to include the risk on fragile goods.

Breakage of Shafts

The mere breakage of a shaft in a ship without the operation of an insured peril does not entitle the assured to claim under the policy. It is considered that the breakage, without the assistance of an outside agency, is caused by a latent defect. The " Inchmaree " clause in the standard hull clauses provides, however, that damage to any other part of the vessel directly caused by the breaking shaft is covered by the policy, subject to the policy deductible.

Break Bulk

Method of carrying cargo. Sometimes termed " conventional carriage ". It is carriage of goods other than by unit carriage (e.g. containers). Generally, the term is applied to goods that have been carried to a certain point by container, or some other form of unit carriage, and have been removed from the container for onward carriage. (See also " Groupage ".)

Breakdown Clause

Applies to either refrigerating or propelling machinery in a vessel as specified in the clause. The clause attaches to policies covering goods which are subject to deterioration due to non-refrigeration and/or delay. It provides that the insurer shall be liable for any deterioration proximately caused by breakdown of machinery but only when the breakdown period exceeds 24 hours or some other specified period.

Breakdown of Nuclear Installation

Provided the policy is subject to the Inchmaree Clause, where a ship is fitted with nuclear power any loss or damage to the hull or machinery directly caused by breakdown of the nuclear installation is covered under the policy, but the damage to the installation itself is not covered unless the breakdown was proximately caused by an insured peril.

Breaker

A wooden cask for holding fresh water. A wave on the point of breaking.

Breaking Out

The practice of removing the legs of a "jack up" from the sea-bed. (See "Jack Up" and "Spudding".)

Breakthrough Clause

A reinsurance clause relating to Canadian business. The re-insurer agrees to pay any claims due, to the reinsured, in event of the insolvency of the reinsured, but subject to a deduction there-from of the premium due to the reinsurer.

Break up Voyage

When a ship is sold for breaking up it is usual to insure her, on her voyage to the breaker's yard, only against total loss and cost of repairs to enable her to complete the voyage. In some cases low value cargo may be carried on the break up voyage and, since the vessel is sailing to the breaker's, the cargo is often scrap metal. There is no question of the vessel not being seaworthy for the voyage, since this is compulsory, but the insurer is wary of break up voyages because of the moral hazard where the owner may not care whether the vessel is lost since it is sold for break up. Care is exercised by the insurer to see that the insured value of the ship is no greater than her break up value.

Breakwater

A fitment on the weather deck of a ship to cause shipped water to flow off the bow.

Breasthook

A plate bracket (triangular in shape) that joins the port and starboard stringers at the stern of a ship.

Breeches Buoy

A lifebuoy fitted with canvas breeches. This is used to carry a man by cable or rope from ship to shore, or vice versa, or from ship to ship, usually in conditions when transfer by small boat is not advisable.

Bridge Policy

American inland marine policy insuring bridges of all kinds over rivers etc.

British Capture Clause
The customary title for the "United Kingdom and Allies Clause".

British Corporation
This is a British Classification Society. Steel vessels up to 15 years old and fully classed with this Society are acceptable to insurers as carriers (liners other than war built tonnage, are acceptable up to 30 years). Vessels registered with the British Corporation may also appear in Lloyd's Register with the notation BS shown. The cypher to denote full class in the British Corporation is BS*.

British Insurance Association
An Association for the furtherance of British insurance company interests, a great deal of its work being in respect of publicity.

British Insurance Group
A group of British Insurance Companies engaged in underwriting business in Japan and issuing a joint policy.

British Maritime Law Association's Agreement
See "Gold Clause Agreement".

Brkge.
Breakage *or* brokerage.

Brl.
Barrel.

Brok.
Brokerage.

Broker
A marine insurance broker is held in law to be an expert in the law and practice of marine insurance. He is expected to know all that it is possible to know about his business and to use this knowledge to obtain the best possible terms for his principal. He is the agent of the assured and not of the insurer. He has no obligation to the insurer other than that of good faith. He does not guarantee the solvency of the insurer and has no legal responsibility for claims or returns of premium. If he is negligent in his duties to the extent that the assured is prejudiced, the assured may sue him for damages. Once he has placed an insurance the broker is responsible to the insurer for the premium whether or not he has received it from the assured. (See "Broker's Lien".)

Brokerage
Commission which the broker is permitted to deduct from the gross premium before passing it to the insurer.

Brokers' Association
See " Lloyd's Insurance Brokers' Association ".

Broker's Cancellation Clause
Used in hull insurance the clause protects the broker in the event of non-payment of premium on a time policy. It gives the insurer the right to cancel the policy at the broker's request but only in the event of non-payment of the premium by the assured.

Broker's Cover
See " Master Cover ".

Broker's Daily Statement
Items submitted to L.P.S.O. by a broker are allocated a signing number and date. When the interested syndicates are advised of the entry the details are incorporated in a daily statement. Although its title includes the word " Daily " the broker's daily statement is issued to brokers daily only for certain types of insurance. Generally, the B.D.S. incorporates an accumulation of entries over a period of, say, three days. (See also " M.T.E. ".)

Broker's Lien
When a broker has placed an insurance he is responsible to the insurer for the premium whether or not he has received it from the assured. To protect him from non-payment he has a lien on the policy whereby he may retain the policy until he has received the premium, or any outstanding premium, from the assured. The lien is valuable because the assured cannot obtain a claim from the insurer without presenting the policy; or he may require the policy in order to obtain credit from a bank. The lien does not operate where the premium is due to the broker from a sub-agent or another broker.

Broker of Record
A licensed insurance broker in the U.S.A. designated by the assured.

Broker's Pseudonym
An abbreviation, allocated to a Lloyd's broker by L.P.S.O., which the broker quotes on all documents submitted to L.P.S.O. L.P.S.O. and L.D.P.S. quote this on all documents submitted to the broker.

Broker's Slip
A term used in a Signing Office to indicate the slip submitted by the broker for signing and/or accounting purposes. Such slip can be the original slip or an off slip. (See also " Signing Slip ".)

In the London market a broker's slip must be in a standard format.

Bruising
Peril mainly affecting painted products such as motor cars when carried uncrated. It is usual to exclude this peril unless the premium is loaded to cover the risk.

B.S. *or* **BS**
See " British Corporation ".

B.S. *or* **b.s.**
Boiler survey (ship).

B/S
Bill of Sale.

B/s
Bales or bags.

B Scheme
Balance Settlement Scheme. An accounting procedure at Lloyd's whereby premium and claim entries in one month appear in a balance settlement in the same monthly settlement statement; otherwise the claims will, probably, appear a month later than the premium.

B.S.I.
British Standards Institute.

Bs/L
Bills of lading.

B.S.T.
British Standard Time.

B/St
Bill of sight.

b.t.
Shipping abbreviation reference chartering. Berth terms.

btm.
Bottom.

B to blame
Both to blame collision liability.

Builder's Certificate
A document, issued by the builder of a vessel, which must be presented as proof of entitlement to register the ship.

Builders' Risks

Insurance on vessels under construction. The standard clauses used in the London market are the "Institute Clauses for Builders' Risks" (which see.)

Bulk Cargo Carrier

Vessels employed exclusively in carriage of bulk cargoes. The term is generally used for coke or coal carriers.

Bulkhead

A ship is divided into sections by bulkheads which are steel walls built transversely across the vessel. Some vessels also have longitudinal (bow to stern) bulkheads. In most cases they are watertight and fitted with watertight doors.

Bulk Oil Clauses

A set of clauses designed for carriage of oil and similar in bulk. They cover all risks whatsoever from the time the oil leaves the tanks at shipment until discharged into tanks at destination. Shortage, leakage and contamination are excluded, except as below, unless caused by or arising out of a marine peril or forced discharge. Contamination due to stress of weather is covered. Loss or damage including contamination, shortage or leakage are covered if due to bursting of boilers, breakage of shafts, latent defect in ship or machinery or fault in navigation or management. Delay, deterioration or loss of market are not covered. The Insurer waives his subrogation rights against the ship, except in general average.

Bullion

Gold or Silver valued by its weight, ignoring its coin value.

Bulwark

A plating wall constructed at the side of a weather deck for the protection of persons using the deck.

Bumbershoot

An American slang term which is gradually coming into use in the London market. It is, in effect, the equivalent of the non-marine insurance term "umbrella cover".

A bumbershoot cover provides a general liability coverage of a marine nature. It is essentially marine and is a coverage in excess of any other existing underlying insurances. Nevertheless, its scope can be extended to cover an insured's liability which is not already insured elsewhere.

Bunkers

A term used for fuel on which the ship is run. It derives from the storage space for the fuel which is called a "bunker".

Bureau

Term commonly used to denote the policy signing office, whether Lloyd's or the Institute of London Underwriters.

Bureau Sheet

A term previously used to indicate the form submitted to a signing office with the policy and slip. In 1970 this form was withdrawn from use and replaced by the " premium advice note " (which see).

Bureau Veritas

This is a French Classification Society. Steel vessels up to 15 years old and fully classed with this society are acceptable to insurers as carriers (liners other than war built tonnage, are acceptable up to 30 years). Vessels registered with the Bureau Veritas may appear in Lloyd's Register with the notation BV shown. The cypher to denote full class in the Bureau Veritas Register is ✠ 3/3 L1.1.

Burning Cost

This is the estimated net cost, in theory, to Reinsurers under a Treaty when the Treaty is put forward for quotation on a new basis as in the case of a Surplus Line or Quota Share Treaty being converted to an Excess of Loss Treaty.

To arrive at the rate to be charged the total of all claims which would have been settled over the previous years (five years if possible) if the Treaty had been on the Excess of Loss basis is calculated as a percentage of the Ceding Company's net premium Income. This is known as the Burning Cost. The percentage is then increased sufficiently to arrive at the rate which should be charged for the Excess of Loss Treaty to give the Reinsurer a reasonable profit.

Burning Ratio

A ratio arrived at by comparing losses with amount insured. The term is generally to be found in Treaty reinsurance.

Burnt

The term means that the vessel must be substantially burnt before the franchise warranty is broken. It is only in cargo franchises that the expression " burnt " appears and it is one of the major casualties which break the franchise. In view of its interpretation, loss of or damage to the insured cargo attributable to fire is recoverable under the policy without reference to the franchise.

Bursting of Boilers

See " Latent Defect ".

Butt Strap

A metal strap joining two parts of a ship that are butt ended (e.g. the connection holding two plates that do not overlap).

Buyer's Interest

The insurable interest of the buyer of insurable property. The term is generally restricted to "goods". The interest attaches as the buyer acquires title to the property. A buyer who is aware of a loss before his interest attached may not insure in respect of that loss. If he is unaware of a loss he may insure on a "lost or not lost" basis and recover in respect of the loss. Without this term he cannot claim for the loss even though he was unaware of it when he effected the insurance. The buyer may have the policy assigned to him, in which case he has the benefit of the insurance for a loss which occurred prior to the attachment of his interest, provided it would have been recoverable under the policy if it had not been assigned.

C

Cable Length
Approximately 600 feet.

Cable Ship
Specialised vessel used for cable laying, fitted with heavy cable laying drums fore and aft and the hull consisting almost entirely of cable carriage tanks. Special flexible machinery is required for the cable winding.

C.A.C.T.L.V.O.
Compromised and/or Arranged and/or Constructive Total Loss of vessel only.

C.A.D.
Cash against documents.

Caisson
A watertight chamber. A caisson is used when the foundations of piers and bridges are being constructed. Caissons are also used in raising wrecks and in the entrances to dry docks.

Caking
Soluble commodities such as sugar and shellac may cake around the inner sides of the bag.
The policy does not cover this risk, which is generally caused by water absorption from the air, unless it can be proved that the loss was proximately caused by an insured peril. It is usual for the insurer to exclude the risk of caking.

Canadian Trust Fund
See "Lloyd's Canadian Trust Fund".

Canadian Water Carriage of Goods Act 1936
An Act to give force of law to the rights, obligations and immunities of carriers of goods in respect of bills of lading on shipments from Canada to ports in or outside Canada.

Canc.
Cancelled.

Cancellation
If the risk does not attach and the subject matter is not imperilled the insurance is cancelled automatically. Once the subject matter has been imperilled cancellation can only be effected by agreement

between both parties, except where one of the parties is at fault in circumstances where the aggrieved party is entitled to avoid the policy. (See "Cancellation Clause", "Automatic Termination of Cover", "Sale of Vessel Clause" and "Cancelling Returns.")

Cancellation Clause

This clause is used in most forms of period insurance. Its purpose is to protect the interests of either party to the contract in the event that one of them might be unreasonably prejudiced by the continuation of the contract. Open covers always contain a cancellation clause which usually provides for 30 days notice to be given. In the case of war and strikes risks the notice period is 7 days and on strikes risks concerning shipments to or from the U.S.A. the notice period is 48 hours. (For hulls see "Sale of Vessel Clause" and "Cancelling Returns".) The cancellation clause in Treaties usually provides for 90 days notice. Upon receipt of a notice of cancellation the broker should notify his principal and at the same time, in practice, he approaches the insurer with details of the ratio between claims and premium income in an endeavour to have the notice withdrawn. Where notice of cancellation is given on a cargo cover all shipments which have commenced transit prior to the expiry date of the notice remain covered by the insurance within the terms of the transit clause. Shipments which have not commenced transit before expiry of the notice do not attach to the cover.

Cancelling Returns

When an insurance is cancelled by reason of failure of consideration the assured is entitled to a return of premium if the premium has already been paid. The assured is also entitled to a return of premium if the policy provides for such return in the event of cancellation and the policy is cancelled for the reason specified in the policy. No return of premium is due in respect of cancellation of open covers or treaties, nor where the insurance is cancelled by the insurer through fraud or illegality on the part of the assured. Hull clauses contain provision for automatic cancellation in event of change of ownership with a pro-rata daily net return of premium; also they provide for mutual cancellation with a pro-rata monthly net return for each uncommenced month. It is usual for hull returns to be paid on a net basis to the assured, so that the broker is enabled to retain his brokerage to recompense him for the work involved.

Cancelling Returns Only

A provision used in hull reinsurance, but less frequently in direct insurance, providing that no return of premium other than that allowed for cancelling the policy will be payable. A reinsurer may not wish the detailed work of lay-up returns, particularly in hull interest policies covering T.L.O., and may prefer to reinsure on a " cancelling returns only " basis. On direct hull insurances the insurer may agree to a " cancelling returns only " provision if the policy is on " limited terms " and he will usually allow a reduction in premium in this respect. The insurer is not always prepared to agree to reduce the premium under a direct insurance on " full terms " if the assured requests a " cancelling returns only " provision. It is customary for direct hull insurances on " full terms " to provide for " full returns ". The abbreviation for " cancelling returns only " is " C.R.O."

Cancelling War Risks
See " War Risk Cancellation ".

C & D
Transport abbreviation meaning " Collection and delivery ".

C & F
Cost and freight. Sale term relating to goods in transit. This is the same as C.I.F. (which see), except that the seller does not arrange insurance for the buyer.

C & I.
Cost and Insurance. Sale term relating to goods in transit. The seller does not pay the shipping charges, leaving the buyer to make his own arrangements. The seller, nevertheless, does arrange the insurance and includes the premium in the purchase price.

C and/or J
China and/or Japan.

Capacity
The maximum amount of liability in the aggregate that an insurer can accept without risking insolvency.

Capacity Plan
A ship's plan to indicate its loading capacity. (See also " Metacentre, Transverse ".)

Capstan
A revolving drum or post with a vertical axis. A capstan is fitted to a ship to assist the crew in hauling lines and cables. Today, a capstan is operated mechanically.

Captain's Protest
When a ship has been involved in an accident or the cargo has suffered damage the Captain signs a declaration giving full details

of the accident and damage. This is called the Captain's Protest.

Capture and Seizure

Synonymous with a war peril these risks are excluded from the policy by the F.C. & S. clause.

Careen

To lean a ship over to one side to repair the keel. This is only practical with relatively small craft. To heel over.

Cargo

Goods and/or property and/or merchandise carried by a vessel for the purpose of earning freight. (See, also, " Dock Work ".)

Cargo All Risks Clauses

The Institute Cargo Clauses (All Risks). The standard cargo clauses used in the marine market on cargo policies covering total and partial loss, irrespective of percentage. The clauses are identical with those enumerated in " Cargo W. A. Clauses " with the exception of clause number 5. This clause is called the " All Risks Clause " and provides that the policy covers all loss or damage proximately caused by a fortuity. It excludes the perils of delay and inherent vice or nature of the insured interest.

Cargo Clauses

Most cargo is insured on Institute Cargo Clauses of which there are three sets. (1) W.A. (2) F.P.A. (3) All Risks. These sets of clauses incorporate the same clauses 1 to 4 and 6 to 14 but Clause 5 is different in each set of clauses. The clauses which are common to all three sets are detailed under heading " Cargo W.A. Clauses ". There are in addition to the Institute Clauses also a number of trade clauses in use in the marine market.

Cargo Declaration

See " Declaration ".

Cargo F.P.A. Clauses

The Institute Cargo Clauses (F.P.A.). The standard cargo clauses used in the marine market on cargo policies covering total loss, etc. (See also " Institute Cargo Clauses F.P.A.") The clauses are identical with those enumerated in " Cargo W.A. Clauses " with the exception of Clause number 5. This clause is called the " F.P.A. clause " and provides the same cover as the " Average clause " in the W.A. clauses (as detailed under " Institute Cargo Clauses W.A."), except that where the franchise is applicable under the " Average clause " no partial loss is payable at all under the " F.P.A. clause ". The effect is that partial loss proximately caused by heavy weather is not recoverable under these clauses, except where the vessel etc. has stranded, sunk or burnt.

Cargo Interest
An insurable interest connected with cargo. The term is used when referring to any allied interest other than the cargo owner's, which is obviously a cargo interest, to differentiate from hull interest. The discounts underwriters allow on cargo interest are different from those allowed on hull interest.

Cargo Passage
The passage of a vessel carrying cargo between two ports.

Cargo Port
An opening, in a ship's side, designed for loading and unloading cargo.

Cargo Syndicate
A group of Underwriters in Lloyd's who underwrite cargo business.

Cargo Value
See " Valued Policies ".

Cargo W.A. Clauses
The Institute Cargo Clauses (W.A.). This is the standard set of cargo clauses used in the marine insurance market on cargo policies covering both total and partial loss, subject to an agreed franchise in respect of particular average losses due to heavy weather. The franchise does not apply, however, when the vessel has been stranded, sunk or burnt.

The clauses were revised and reissued from 1st January 1963 and the set now contains the following clauses:- (1) The transit clause (incorporating the warehouse to warehouse clause) (2) The termination of adventure clause (3) The craft etc. clause (4) The change of voyage clause (5) The average clause (6) The constructive total loss clause (7) The G.A. clause (8) The Seaworthiness admitted clause (9) The Bailee clause (10) The not to inure clause (11) The Both to Blame collision clause (12) The F.C. & S. Clause (13) The F.S.R. & C.C. Clause (14) The Reasonable Despatch clause. (All these clauses are defined separately herein). There is also a " note " which requires that for any " held covered " provision to be effective prompt notice of the event giving rise to the invoking of the provision must be given to the insurer and the right to such cover is dependent upon compliance with this obligation.

Cargo War Cancellation
See " War cancellation clause ".

Cargo Worthy
The vessel is reasonably suitable and fit to carry the cargo insured.

This is an implied warranty in the policy at the commencement of the voyage, (Sect. 40 Marine Insurance Act 1906) but there is no implied warranty that the cargo insured must be seaworthy.

Carling

A longitudinal steel section connecting two beams in a ship.

Carpenter Plan

American Reinsurance system to spread losses by way of treaties. Called the Carpenter plan in U.S.A. because it was introduced by a broker named Carpenter.

Carriage of Goods by Sea Act 1924

An Act for the purpose of laying down the responsibilities, liabilities, rights and immunities of the carrier and cargo owner in respect of the carriage of goods by sea. The Act only applies to shipments from ports in Great Britain or Northern Ireland under a bill of lading or similar document and attaches from time of loading onto the vessel. It was proposed in 1970 to amend the 1924 Act but the newly proposed Act had not become law at the time of revision (1974).

Carrier

Shipowner or other person who carries goods by vessel.

Carrier's Liability Clause

A clause attached to a cargo policy advising the assured of his obligation if the consignee receives damaged cargo from the carrier. If the damage is apparent an immediate joint survey should be carried out and a claim lodged with the carrier. If the damage is not apparent a claim should be lodged within three days of delivery and steps taken promptly for a survey. Sometimes the clause also provides that a " clean " receipt should not be given for damaged goods except under written protest.

Carrier's Liability to Cargo

By the Carriage of Goods by Sea Act 1924 the carrier must exercise due diligence to make the ship seaworthy, properly man, equip and supply her and generally make the ship fit to carry the cargo. The carrier must issue to the shipper a bill of lading showing identification marks and details of the quantity and apparent condition of the goods. This bill of lading is prima facie evidence of receipt of the goods. A " shipped " bill of lading is issued when the goods are loaded. The carrier is not permitted to contract out of his liability for damage to the cargo resulting from negligence. Nevertheless, the carrier is not liable for unseaworthiness except where it is for want of due diligence on his part. The Act allows, in article 4, rights and immunities to the carrier which absolve him from liability in specified circumstances, all of which are deemed to be beyond his control. Should the carrier be legally liable for loss of or damage to the goods the limit of his liability is the value stated in the bill of lading or any alternative limit agreed between the parties. If no value is in the bill of lading the minimum limit the Act allows is £100 (or equivalent in other currencies) any one package. This minimum may be increased by agreement but cannot be reduced. By the Gold clause agreement the limit is raised to £200. During 1970 it was proposed to introduce new limits and, in the light of problems regarding carriage of goods in containers, to clearly establish the limit per unit or package. However, these proposals had not become law at the time of revision (1974).

Carrier's Lien
When freight is payable at destination on delivery of the cargo, the carrier has a lien in respect of the unpaid freight whereby he may retain the goods, or cause them to be held in a warehouse, against payment of the freight.

The warehouse rent is chargeable as part of freight.

Since the lien is on the value of the goods, if the freight is not paid for some time so that the freight due plus the warehouse rent is approaching the value of the goods, the warehouseman may sell the goods to obtain the freight and rent. If there is any balance from the proceeds after settling the debts due and sale charges, this is payable to the owner of the goods.

Carrying Vessel
See " Non-Carrying Vessel ".

Case Slip
A strong protective binding consisting of a pair of double covers and 20 narrow stubs of paper ($\frac{3}{4}''$ wide) stitched therein. The placing slip is attached to the first stub and folded concertinawise. Subsequent attachments (wordings, endorsements etc.) are attached to the other stubs, so that the most recent appears uppermost. Case slips are used by brokers in the London market.

Cash in Transit
The insurance of cash and/or bank notes in transit. It is usual to exclude claims which are recoverable under other existing policies on the cash. War risks are excluded. In some cases a deductible is incorporated into the policy.

Cash Loss
This is one of the usual provisions of a Treaty and enables the

reassured to collect immediately, on production of the necessary documents, a large claim without waiting to include it in the usual periodic adjustment. The minimum amount for which such losses can be collected is by agreement with Reinsurers. Such a condition is sometimes included in direct Contracts and open covers.

A cash loss may also occur in direct insurance or reinsurance other than treaty when a large loss arises and the broker wishes to obtain payment for the assured without waiting the periodic settlement of accounts. A special arrangement must be made with the insurer to obtain this service and all due premiums must have been paid to the insurer.

Casualty
An accident or fortuity.

Casualty Report Service
Subscribers to the service, which is operated by Lloyd's, receive slips giving details of casualties as the information is received at Lloyd's. A publication by Lloyd's " Weekly Casualty Reports " reproduces these details.

Catastrophe Excess of Loss
This is a normal Excess of Loss Treaty but only applies to claims for recognised catastrophes such as conflagration, flood, storm, tempest, windstorm, earthquake or riots. In marine reinsurance it is generally limited to land risks incidental to a marine adventure and covers accumulations of cargo on quay or in warehouse.

Catch etc. Exclusion Clause
A clause in the I.F.V.C. which provides that claims under the R.D.C. and P. & I. Sections shall not extend to apply in respect of goods, catch, merchandise, freight or other things or interests on board the insured vessel or in respect of its engagements.

Category Codes
Alphabetical codes used in data processing at Lloyd's to indicate the category of risk applicable to each entry. There are two categories punched into an advice card; being the main category (e.g. PM = premium, CM = claim) and the qualifying category. (See also " Qualifying Category ".)

Category 3
A term used in Lloyd's Central Accounting system to indicate the procedure for closing insurances in convertible currency and exchange to sterling for settlement between underwriters and brokers. The Category 3 procedure was abolished in 1972; being

replaced by a procedure whereby all convertible currency insurances must be converted to sterling before being closed to L.P.S.O.

Causa Causans
The cause of a cause. A legal doctrine used in determining "Proximate Cause" (which see).

Causa Proxima
Proximate cause. Full term is "Causa Proxima non Remota Spectatur".

Causa Remota
The cause, in a series of causes resulting in a loss, which is furthest removed from the proximate cause. It is often the first cause of the series.

Caution Money
A colloquial expression meaning "Reserve Account".

Caveat Emptor
"Let the buyer beware". A legal term relating to the purchase of goods and placing the onus on the buyer to satisfy himself that the goods which he is purchasing are suitable and of sufficient standard of quality for the purpose intended. If the goods are sold by warranty or sample, they must conform with the warranty or sample and the onus lies on the seller to ensure this.

C.B. & H.
Same as "Cont. B.H." Continent between Bordeaux and Hamburg.

C.C. *or* **c.c.**
Civil commotions. The same abbreviation is used in slips to denote "Cancellation Clause" *or* "Collecting Commission".

C.C.R. Clause
A clause, no longer applicable, which at one time attached to reinsurance policies covering French business.

CCY
Convertible currency.

C.D.
Country damage.

C/D
Commercial dock. Also used for "Consular Declaration".

C.D.V.
Current Domestic Value. Refers to local values on goods in the

country of origin. It is often the practice to apply C.D.V. when charging import duty.

Cedant

The original insurer who cedes a line to his reinsurers under a treaty.

Cede

To cede a line. The original underwriter, or reinsured, under a reinsurance contract, such as a treaty, writes a line on an insurance. By the terms of his reinsurance contract he is obliged to " cede " part of this line to his reinsurer. That is, he retains his retained line, the part which he keeps at his own risk, and advises his reinsurer of the ceded line, the amount on which a claim on the reinsurance will be based in the event of loss. A ceded line is called a " cession " and is the same as a " declaration ".

Ceding Company

The reassured under a reinsurance contract who cedes business to the reinsurer.

Cell

A system of perpendicular steel " slides " into which a container is slotted when being carried on a container ship.

Central Accounting

A centralised accounting system operated with the use of an electronic computer for the purpose of co-ordinating underwriters' accounts under one organisation. To this end all brokers submit premium details to the signing bureau following which the central accounting system allocates the proportions to the various under-writers. This system was introduced in January 1961 by Lloyd's. The same procedure is adopted for settlement of claims etc.

Cert.

Certificate.

Certificate of Damage

A standard form used by port Authorities in respect of goods landed damaged.

Certificate of Entry

A form of policy issued by a Protection and Indemnity Club to a member of the club, in respect of a vessel which is the subject of mutual insurance with the club.

Certificate of Insurance

A document issued to the assured certifying that an insurance has been effected and that a policy has been issued. In marine insurance practice, certificates are used where an open cover is effected with underwriters. Such certificates are printed bearing details of the open cover and are issued by Lloyd's, on behalf of Lloyd's Underwriters, or the Institute of London Underwriters, on behalf of member companies. It is customary for certificates to be issued to the assured in triplicate or quadruplicate, in book form, in order that the assured may complete each certificate by inserting details of the relevant shipment. A copy of the certificate is then sent to the broker who makes the necessary declaration against the open cover, whilst the assured uses the remaining copies as evidence of the existence of insurance. Sometimes brokers issue their own certificates against open covers. These certificates give details of the cover but cannot be used in any action against the insurer. (See "Lloyd's Certificates" and "Institute Certificate".)

Certificate of Origin

Gives full details of the country of origin in respect of goods. Is used as evidence of origin.

Certificate of Ownership

A certificate of Registry.

Certificate of Registry

Held by the shipowner it evidences registration of the vessel and gives details of the ship. It is not a document of title to the ship.

Certificate of Seaworthiness

When a classed vessel suffers damage the Classification Society carries out a seaworthiness survey when repairs have been completed. When the surveyors are satisfied as to the vessel's seaworthiness a certificate of seaworthiness is issued by the Classification Society.

Certificate of Survey

See "Survey Report".

Cesser Clause

A clause in a charter party relieving the charterer from certain payments, such as demurrage or freight, and stating that another party shall make such payments. An example would be a clause whereby a shipowner is granted a lien on the cargo for the freight due, for the hire of the ship, from the charterer.

Cession

See "Cede".

Cf.
A legal abbreviation meaning "compare".

C.F.I.
Cost, Freight and Insurance. Meaning the same as C.I.F.

C.F.O.
Calling for orders.

c.f.o.
Calling for orders.

C.F.R.
Code of Federal Regulations—U.S.A.

c.g.a.
Cargo's proportion of general average.

Cge.
Carriage.

C.G.M.E.
Slip abbreviation for "China, glass, marble, earthenware". May be in respect of a limitation in value or an exclusion.

C.g.f. proceeds
Credit given for proceeds. Appears in claim adjustments when showing allowances.

C.g.f.rec.
Credit given for recovery. Claim adjustment abbreviation.

Cgo.
Cargo.

C.H.
Customs House.

Chaf.
Chafage.

Chafage
Damage caused to rolls of newsprint or similar, by chafing or rubbing against each other, other cargo, the sides of the vessel etc., or by chafing from loading slings and the like. The term may be applied to other interests subject to this peril. This is an extraneous risk.

Change of Management
When the Management of a ship changes it has the same effect on the policy as change of Ownership.

Change of Ownership
When a vessel changes Ownership or Management the policy on the ship is cancelled automatically in practice unless the insurer agrees to continue cover. A pro rata daily return of premium is allowed for the unexpired portion of the policy.

Change of Voyage
There is said to be a change of voyage where the destination is voluntarily changed after commencement of the risk. Unless the insurer agrees to the change he is discharged from liability as from the time the decision is made to change the voyage. (See " Change of Voyage Clause " for cargo owner's position.)

Change of Voyage Clause
Appears in cargo clauses and holds the interest covered at an additional premium in the event of change of voyage or error in description of voyage.

Charges of Insurance
The Premium. The payment made to the insurer in return for the indemnity guaranteed. The person paying the charges has an insurable interest in them.

Chartered Freight
The sum paid to the owner of a vessel by the charterer in respect of the hire of the vessel.

Charterer
A hirer of a vessel from the owner either for a period of time or a voyage.

Charter Hire
The hiring out of a ship on charter, either voyage or time.

Charterparty
Conditions under which a charterer hires a vessel.

Charterer's Freight
Payable by a charterer to a shipowner for the hire of his vessel. The charterer has an insurable interest in the freight if it is paid in advance; otherwise it is the shipowner's interest.

Chilled Beef Clauses
Institute clauses for attachment to a cargo policy covering chilled beef from Australia and New Zealand.

These clauses were withdrawn when the Frozen Meat Clauses (1971) were introduced.

Chipping

Peril mainly affecting enamelware and porcelain or china ware. It is usual to exclude this peril unless the premium is loaded to cover the risk.

Ch. ppd.

Shipping abbreviation. Charges prepaid.

C.I.B.

Corporation of Insurance Brokers.

C.I.F. *or* **c.i.f.**

Cost, insurance, freight. A term of sale for goods in transit. The seller pays all costs of transit to the final destination and arranges insurance protection on the terms specified by the buyer. The insurance premium and shipping charges are included in the price paid by the buyer. Whilst the seller is responsible for the goods until they are handed over to the buyer he assigns the policy or certificate to the buyer on receipt of payment for the goods, leaving the buyer to claim on the insurance in the event of an insured loss occurring. It is customary for the insured value to include, in addition to C.I.F., a percentage to cover the seller's profit.

c.i.f. & c.

Cost, Insurance, Freight and Commission.

c.i.f. & i.

Cost, Insurance, Freight and Interest.

C.I.F.C.I.

Sale term which includes, in addition to C.I.F., commission and interest.

C.I.I.

Chartered Insurance Institute.

Circumstance

See " Material Circumstance ". The term includes any information received by, or known to, the assured.

Civil Commotions

Internal national disorders. Loss of or damage to the insured interest is not covered against this peril without the incorporation of the Strikes clauses. The standard Strikes clauses always include this peril.

C.K.D.

Completely knocked down. Motor vehicle shipments where the vehicle is completely dismantled and shipped in boxes.

c.l.
Craft loss.

Cl.
Clause.

Claim
A demand by the assured upon the insurer to fulfil his guarantee of indemnity by reason of an accident in respect of the insured property proximately caused by a peril insured against whereby the assured has suffered a loss.

Claim against Carrier
See " Notification of Claim against Carrier " and " Recovery from a Carrier ".

Claim Agent
Term used mainly in U.S.A. to denote an agent appointed by a marine insurance Company to settle claims on that Company's behalf.

Claimant
The person suffering the loss who presents the claim.

Claimright Insurance
Some sale contracts on goods incorporate a clause which permits the consignee to withhold part of the purchase price pending arrival of the goods. Claimright insurance protects the consignor in the event of failure by the consignee to pay the amount withheld, or any part thereof. This may occur where the goods are not of the quality or type expected. It is usual for the insurer to insist that the consignor retains part of the amount at risk uninsured. There is a limited market for claimright insurance.

Claims Adjuster
An official employed by a Company to be responsible on behalf of the Company for claims settlement.

Claims Bureau
See " Lloyd's Underwriters' Claims Office ".

Claims Control Clause
A clause sometimes insisted upon by a reinsurer in order that he may not be held liable for claims which he feels should not have been paid under the original policy. The clause provides that all claims on the original insurance are submitted to the reinsurer for his approval before they are paid.

Claims Co-operation Clause

A reinsurance clause by which the reinsured agrees to give to the reinsurer immediate advice of any claim notified to him (the reinsured) in which the reinsurer might be interested. The reinsured agrees, also, to co-operate with the reinsurer in defending the claim and settlement thereof. The reinsured agrees not to admit a claim, in which the reinsurer might be interested, on the original insurance without the written consent of the reinsurer. The clause may be used also in connection with underlying reinsurance.

Claims Documents

The documents required for presentation to the insurer when the assured wishes to make a claim under his policy. The main documents required are as follows:—

Hulls—Policy, Surveyors' reports, Repair specifications, Details of tenders submitted, Account receipts in respect of disbursements and repairs carried out, Extracts from engine room and deck log books, Average adjustment.

Cargo—It is customary to attach a clause, called the "Red Line Clause", to cargo policies and certificates which, amongst other things, lists the claims documents required. These are:—

(1) Original policy or certificate of insurance.
(2) Original or copy shipping invoices, together with shipping specification and/or weight notes.
(3) Original Bill of Lading and/or other contract of carriage.
(4) Survey report or other documentary evidence to show the extent of the loss or damage.
(5) Landing account and weight notes at final destination.
(6) Correspondence exchanged with the carriers and other parties regarding their liability for the loss or damage.

Claims Payable Abroad

A provision which may be expressed in a policy and certificate, at the request of the assured, which permits the collection of claims abroad from an authorised person whose name is stated in the policy and certificate. (See "Settling Agent".)

Claims Reserve

Under a reinsurance contract an amount is retained by the reassured against payment of claims which will be collectible under the contract in due course. This is called a "Claims Reserve". (See also "O.C.A." and "Premium Reserve".)

Classification

Refers to the classing of a vessel with one of the recognised Societies. (See "Classification Clause".)

Classification Clause

The "Institute Classification Clause" has been the subject of various alterations in recent years. The current clause was published on 1st January, 1972. The clause is used in Open Covers and Open Policies. Since such insurances are effected subject to subsequent declaration of shipments and carrying vessels it is necessary to incorporate a clause which specifies the minimum standard required for carrying vessels if the premium is to remain as stated in the schedule attached to the insurance. The clause details such minimum standard but if the carrying vessel is not within this minimum the shipment is not excluded from the cover, being held covered at an additional premium to be arranged. It is customary to use the expression "overage" in respect of the additional premium.

The clause embraces vessels of iron or steel construction that are fully classed in any of a list of 10 Classification Societies, being

(1) Lloyd's Register of Shipping.
(2) British Corporation.
(3) American Bureau of Shipping.
(4) Bureau Veritas.
(5) Germanischer Lloyd.
(6) Nippon Kaiji Kyokai (Japanese Marine Corporation).
(7) Norske Veritas.
(8) Registro Italiano.
(9) Register of Shipping of the U.S.S.R.
(10) Polish Register of Shipping.

Generally, a vessel must be not over 15 years old; otherwise the cargo attracts an additional premium. However cargo carried on "liners" (that is vessels regularly and habitually employed on advertised schedules, loading and unloading at specified ports) does not attract an additional premium unless the carrying vessel is over 30 years old. This exception does not apply to cargo carried on : —

(a) Chartered vessels.
(b) Liberty, Fort, Park and Ocean type vessels.
(c) Empire type vessels of 7,000–8,000 g.r.t. built prior to 1946.
(d) Vessels under 450 g.r.t.

Thus, cargo carried on liners in the categories (a) to (d) above, attracts an additional premium if the vessel is over 15 years old.

Cld.

Cleared through Customs.

Clean

An expression used to denote that the conditions of a shipping document are without any detrimental qualifications. A detrimentally qualified document may be referred to as "unclean", "foul" or "dirty". The word "clean" may also be used in insurance when referring to an open cover or a treaty or any other form of insurance or reinsurance for a period of time. In this case it means that the insurance has suffered no claims.

Cleaning of Tanks

In event of a tanker requiring repairs following the carriage of inflammable material it is necessary that the tanks be cleaned and that a "gas free" certificate is obtained. The expense of cleaning tanks is part of the reasonable cost of repairs.

Clean Total Loss Only

An obsolete term once used in ship insurance and reinsurance. It indicated that the T.L.O. policy did not incorporate sue and labour or salvage charges.

C L Form

A form used in the procedures for settling U.S. dollar transactions in the Lloyd's insurance market. (See "Lloyd's American Trust Fund".)

Climatic Conditions Clause

A cargo clause in respect of musical instruments providing that insurers shall not be liable for claims due to climatic conditions unless they would be recoverable under an ordinary fire policy. Breakage of drumheads, reeds or strings is excluded from the policy.

Clms.

Claims.

Closed Bevel

A bevel (angle on a member of ship construction) with an angle less than 90 degrees.

Closed Line

It is the accepted practice for a broker to obtain written lines which in total exceed the value or amount which it is required should be insured. Further, it frequently occurs that the value on cargo advised to the insurer in advance of the shipment is provisional and is not necessarily the same as the actual value shipped. When the actual value is known the broker reduces the written lines in proportion so that they total the true value. The line is then called the "closed line". A broker may not close a line in excess of the written line. (See also "Signed Line".)

Closing

When an insurance has been placed and the voyage or period has commenced the broker " closes " the insurance to the insurer by presenting a premium advice note, together with the slip, to the insurer for signing. In the case of Lloyd's underwriters the closing is made to the L.P.S.O. In the case of Companies the closing is either made to the I.L.U. (Policy Department), if the Company is a member, or direct to the Company. In closing the risk to a Non-Institute Company the broker prepares a closing slip for submission to the Company; retaining his placing (or signing) slip. The policy may be submitted for signing at the same time that the risk is " closed " or it may be signed later.

Closing Slip

This is a form of advice to a Company giving details of the insurance to enable the company to issue a policy. Its use dropped off considerably when the Institute of London Underwriters formed a policy signing department to sign Combined Company Policies but it is still used for non-Institute signings.

Closing Instructions

Instructions given by a principal to his broker to close the Insurance to the insurer.

Close Out

American expression which means the same as " close ". To close out an insurance is to issue a policy against a binder.

Club

Protection and Indemnity Club.

Club Calls

Payments by members of a Protection and Indemnity Club to the Club. When the tonnage of a member's vessel is entered in the Club the member pays only a nominal entry fee. Periodically the Club aggregates the total claims upon the Club together with running expenses and sends a "call" to each member to pay his proportion of the total outgoings of the Club.

Cmd.

Commissioned.

C.M.I.

Comite Maritime International.

Cmpl.

Completed.

C.M.R.

Convention on the Contract for the International Carriage of Goods by Road (Cmd. 3455).

C.M.R. Form

Lloyd's Goods in Transit (C.M.R.) Policy. This form is designed to cover the insured's legal liability as a carrier under the provisions of the C.M.R. Marine insurers are interested in this only insofar as they are prepared to cover liabilities of road carriers, such as container operators in connection with a sea voyage.

C.M.S.

Combined Marine Surcharge. (obsolete)

C/N

Cover note *or* Credit note.

Coal Clauses

Non-Institute Clauses in respect of coal and similar cargoes. They are used generally for overseas shipments only and do not include coastwise coal traffic.

Coaming

See " Hatch Coaming ".

Coastal Liner

Small liners up to 4,500 tons approx. engaged in coastal and local voyages.

Coastal Trade (U.K.)

The coastal trade (U.K.) limitations proposed for the M.S.A. 1970 embrace voyages that begin and end in the U.K., Channel Islands, Isle of Man and the Republic of Ireland without intermediate calls outside these areas and provided the ship is not at any time during the voyage more than 30 miles from a point in the U.K. or Irish Republic.

Coasters

Vessels employed only between home ports on coastal trade. Their carriage contracts are not subject to the Carriage of Goods by Sea Act, 1924.

Coefficient

Coefficient of fineness or block coefficient is the ratio (expressed as a decimal) between the actual volume of the under-water shape of a ship and the volume of a rectangular block having the same extreme depth, breadth and length.

Cofferdam

Cofferdams are transverse double bulkheads, fitted in a ship, at least 3 feet apart. Each bulkhead extends right across the ship and from the keel to the upper deck; thereby making a complete seal between two parts of the ship. The bulkheads are watertight and where a cofferdam separates the engine room space from the remainder of the ship the bulkheads are oil-tight. Cofferdams form part of the collision bulkhead between the bow of the ship and the forward cargo hold.

C.O.B.

Cargo on board (see " W.C.B. ").

Co-Insurance

When two or more insurers each have part of the risk under a single insurance. In practice it is usual for the insurer with the smaller line to follow the decision of the insurer with the larger line, but he need not do this and is not obliged to accept a claim because the other insurer has accepted it. Further, where an assured is under-insured he is regarded as his own insurer for the amount of the under-insurance and is therefore referred to as a co-insurer. It is sometimes required by the insurers that the assured shall run part of the risk as a co-insurer.

C. of G. Act *or* **C. of G.S. Act**

Carriage of Goods by Sea Act, 1924.

Collecting Commission

The broker as agent of the assured is responsible for placing the insurance and for payment of the premium. He has no responsibility for collection of claims for the assured although he usually takes this duty upon himself. If he collects a claim on behalf of the assured the broker is entitled to retain 1% ($\frac{1}{2}\%$ on a total loss) of the claim to reimburse him for the expense and as payment for the service involved in collecting the claim. The broker sometimes waives his right to the settling fee as a special favour to the assured. It is not unusual for the assured to increase the insured value to include the collecting commission.

Collecting Note

A document giving Authority to a broker to collect claims on behalf of his principal.

Coll. *or* **Colln.**

Collision.

Coll. dge.

Collision damage.

Collision

Means collision or actual contact with another ship or vessel. When a liability may arise following contact of the ship with property or due to excessive wash, these are not embraced by the term collision as covered by the " Collision Clause ". (See also " Degree of Blame " and " Collision Liability ".)

Collision is a peril of the seas, thus damage to an insured vessel, or cargo therein, proximately caused by collision is recoverable under the plain S.G. policy form. In the case of cargo it is, frequently, difficult to be certain that damage was proximately caused by the collision so the standard cargo clauses (W.A. and F.P.A.) ignore the principle of proximate cause and make damage *attributable* to collision recoverable under the policy.

In determining collision liability, where the insured ship collides with another vessel it is necessary to be more specific in determining what, in fact, constitutes *collision*; this requires actual physical contact between two vessels and does not embrace excessive wash; nor liability incurred by the assured by reason of contact of the vessel with anything other than a vessel. (See also " Collision Clause ", " Degree of Blame " and " Collision Liability ".)

Collision Clause

Clause number one in the Institute Time Clauses (Hulls). This is a familiar clause in all sets of hull clauses. It forms a separate contract so that under it the insurer is liable in full up to its limits without reference to any other loss paid under the policy; nevertheless claims thereunder are subject to the policy deductible and to the paramount (F.C. & S. Clause etc.) clauses. It covers losses paid by the assured in respect of his legal liability to another for loss of or damage to the other vessel, or property thereon; delay or loss of use of the other vessel or property thereon; general average, salvage, or salvage services attaching to such other vessel or property thereon, consequent on collision. It also pays costs of the assured in defending the claim. English clauses limit the insurer's liability to three fourths of the assured's liability with a further limit of three fourths of the insured value for both the liability and the costs. American and other foreign clauses allow a four fourths limit. Where the insured vessel is damaged in a collision and there is a recovery due from the owners, or managers of the other vessel involved in the collision the insurer is liable for the costs of recovery in full as part of the claim for damage to the insured vessel. The clause specifies that it shall not extend to cover liability for removal of wreck, or of any property whatever, except the other vessel or property thereon; cargo or property on the insured vessel; engagement of the insured vessel; loss of life; personal injury or illness. It is also known as the "Running Down Clause". (See, also, "Amended Running Down Clause".)

Collision Clause Amendment A

An American Institute Hull Clause issued 4th June 1970 for attachment to the American Hull Form (18th January 1970). This amendment was incorporated in the revised American Hull Form (1st July 1971).

Collision Costs

Legal costs incurred in defending an action by the other vessel's owners against the insured vessel or in pressing a claim against the other vessel to recover in respect of damage to the insured vessel. Such costs are, in practice, borne by the insurer but are subject to the limit of three fourths of the costs with a further limit of three fourths of the insured value, when subject to Institute Time Clauses.

Collision Liability

The plain form of policy does not cover the assured's liability in respect of collision. This risk is covered, in practice, by incorporating the collision clause into the policy. (See "Collision Clause", "Omnibus Clause" and "Third Ship in a Collision".)

Combined Company Policy

See "Combined Policy".

Combined Marine Surcharge

A surcharge or additional premium which was at one time charged on cargo policies in respect of the incorporation of the Wartime Extension Clause. The Wartime Extension Clause is no longer in use, being superseded by the Extended Cover Clause. The Extended Cover Clause in the Institute Cargo Clauses has now been incorporated into the Transit Clause.

Combined Policy

To avoid cumbersome unnecessary work it is the practice to confine policy signings to a limited number of policies by signing a combined policy on behalf of each group of insurers. There are three types of combined policy: —

(1) A Lloyd's policy signed by Lloyd's Policy Signing Office on behalf of members of Lloyd's.

(2) An Institute of London Underwriter's policy signed by the Institute of London Underwriters on behalf of its members.

(3) A non-Institute Company Combined policy, prepared by the broker and signed by each non-Institute Company on the

same policy or by the leading non-Institute Company on behalf of the following non-Institute Companies on the same risk, with their written authority.

Combing Clause

Used in wool cargo insurance. The insurer pays the cost of combing wool arriving damaged, thereby reducing the risk of further damage.

Combi Ship

A ship designed to carry both conventionally and by container.

COM *or* Com

Commission.

Commencement of Adventure

The adventure commences when the insured interest is exposed to the possibility of peril. In a time insurance it is the time and date stated in the insurance contract. In a voyage insurance on a ship it is the time and date the vessel sails on the insured voyage. (See also " At and From " and " From ".) In a voyage insurance on goods in transit it is when the goods leave the place named in the insurance contract for the commencement of transit. (See " Commencement of Voyage ".)

Commencement of Risk

See " Attachment of Risk ".

Commencement of Voyage

When an insurer is offered an insurance to write on a voyage he seldom specifies a date for commencement of risk, but he bases his acceptance on circumstances pertaining at the time he considers the risk. It would be unreasonable to expect the insurer to honour an acceptance that does not attach within a reasonable time after he writes the insurance and, to protect him, there is an implied condition in the M.I.A. 1906 (Sect. 42) whereby the insurer can avoid the contract from inception if the adventure does not commence within a reasonable time after conclusion of the contract. The implied condition is negatived if it can be shown that the insurer was aware of the circumstances leading to the delay when he concluded the contract or that he waived the condition.

Commission

Remuneration for services rendered. A person whose commission is dependent on the safe arrival of the insurable property in a marine adventure has an insurable interest in that commission.

Committee of Lloyd's

A body elected from the members of Lloyd's to manage the affairs of the Corporation.

The Committee is composed of sixteen Members who serve for four year terms after which they must retire for one year before being eligible for re-election. Thus four Members retire by rotation each year and four new Members are elected in their place. The Committee elect from their own number a Chairman and two Deputy Chairmen to serve from the first of January each year.

Other than in a few instances, the Committee does not dictate the type of business accepted at Lloyd's or interfere with the day to day conduct of Underwriters' business. The Committee is responsible for new Members and is initially concerned with the financial stability of those doing daily business at Lloyd's. It administers the affairs of the Corporation, including the provision of a number of departments, providing services to Lloyd's underwriters.

The Committee of Lloyd's is also responsible for posting vessels "missing" which, as well as supporting insurance claims, assists the Ministry of Social Security, Probate Officers and other official bodies concerned with loss of life and loss of vessels.

Commixture

The mixing of two cargoes of a similar nature so that they are not sufficiently identifiable to enable them to be separated. The various owners are considered to be joint owners of the mass and if no damage, other than the commixture, has occurred, there is no claim under the policy. If there is damage the total damage is apportioned over the various assureds in proportion to their separate values of the total value.

Common Carrier

A carrier who agrees to carry any goods. A carrier who refuses to carry certain types of goods, mainly for safety of the vessel and other cargo, is not a common carrier.

Common Notoriety

Generally known.

Comp.

Composite.

Companion

The permanent covering to a stairway or ladderway.

Company

A Company engaged in the business of underwriting marine

insurance the liability of which is limited to its assets as declared to the Department of Trade and Industry, which Department keeps a watching brief on the Company's assets in relation to risks accepted by the Company to ensure a solvent insurance market for the benefit of the public. The liability of the Company is undertaken by a Company underwriter who is a salaried official of the Company and has no personal liability. The public may deal direct with the Company and need not use the intermediary of a broker, although it is deemed advisable to do so to obtain the benefit of his advice and experience.

Company Agent
See " Underwriting Agent ".

Company Signing
The issue of a policy by a Company. The broker either uses the original slip or prepares a signing slip and at the same time prepares a premium advice note, sometimes accompanied by a prepared policy form. The whole is presented to the Institute of London Underwriters (Policy Dept.) who check the details and, where it accompanies the premium advice note, sign the policy on behalf of the members who subscribe to the policy. Where the policy is not submitted with the premium advice note it is submitted at a later stage for signing. So far as non-Institute Companies are concerned the broker retains the original slip and merely submits a closing slip to the Company. If a number of non-Institute Companies are concerned in one insurance the broker may obtain authority from the other Companies to allow the leading company to sign a Combined Company Policy on their behalf.

Company Underwriter
A salaried official appointed by a marine insurance Company to write business on their behalf. He has no personal liability in respect of the risks he undertakes.

Compd.
Compromised.

Compen.
Compensation.

Complement
A full crew.

Complex Markets and Signings
A category established by Lloyd's to provide individual account-ing entries where it is necessary to segregate certain parts of a

single closing. Such segregation may be necessary because there is a variation in syndicate participation between certain sections of the risk or statistical codes may be different for two or more sections of the risk.

Compliance with a Warranty

A warranty must be strictly complied with, whether or not it is material to the risk. or the insurer is discharged from liability as from the date of the breach.

Compounding of Engines

Applicable to steam powered engines. The act of cutting out a cylinder in a ship's engines in order to put more pressure into the remaining cylinders. This mis-use of engines is frowned on since damage is almost inevitable and the increase in power is for only a limited period.

Compromised Total Loss

Where an assured wishes to claim a total loss but neither an actual nor a constructive total loss has in fact occurred the insurer may agree to pay a compromised total loss. This may also be called an arranged total loss.

Concealment

Non-disclosure of a material circumstance probably amounting to fraud.

Conclusion of Contract

The contract of marine insurance is concluded between the insurer and assured when the insurer initials the slip.

Concurrent with Discharge

Refers to payment of freight as the cargo is discharged. The shipowner may suspend delivery if freight is not paid as it is due.

Condensation

See " Sweat Damage ".

Condition

A condition is imposed in the contract by the insurer and must be literally complied with unless it is waived by the insurer. A condition goes to the root of the contract and non-compliance by the assured enables the insurer to avoid the policy from inception.

Conds.

Conditions.

Conference Lines

A liner conference is a group of shipping lines regularly serving a particular trade route and aimed at reaching agreement on the stabilisation of freight rates and on organisation and working conditions in that trade. The overall object is to foster trade in the area served by the Conference by providing regular services and stable rates of freight with ships designed for the trade and maintaining a common high standard. Conferences vary from very informal associations to well developed organisations with permanent secretariates depending on the character and importance of the trade.

Conference Ship

A ship belonging to a line which is a signatory to a shipping conference. (See " Conference Lines ".)

Conference System

A system employed by shipping lines to establish regular services and economic running of their lines. (See " Conference Lines ".)

Confirmed Irrevocable Credit

Exists when both an overseas and a British bank have given an undertaking to give credit to the seller against the tender of the documents of title and the marine policy. The undertaking is irrevocable by both banks. An irrevocable credit is one which is not confirmed by the British bank and is therefore only irrevocable by the foreign bank. A revocable or unconfirmed credit may be revoked by either bank.

Confiscation

Confiscation of a ship is usually a political act and, provided it is not a direct act of war, the risk is excluded by the standard war clauses. Under the same principle confiscation of cargo, other than as a direct act of war, is not covered under a cargo policy with the war clauses attached. Confiscation of cargo may, however, arise from various causes which include contravention of import regulations as well as political acts. In certain circumstances there is a market for cargo confiscation risks as a separate insurance but generally insurers do not readily accept the risk.

Consequences of Hostilities

War losses recoverable under a policy which is subject to the standard war clauses. The term is not intended to embrace collisions between vessels navigating without lights in wartime or similar losses. It is intended to embrace only actual hostile acts or loss of or damage to or by vessels engaged in warlike acts.

Consequential Loss

A loss following and consequent on a loss proximately caused by a peril insured against. The insurer is not liable for consequential loss. Neither is consequential loss allowed in general average except where it is directly consequential on the general average act. Loss of market is an example of consequential loss.

Consgt.
Consignment.

Consideration
The insurer in the S.G. Form "confesses himself paid the consideration due—". The consideration being the premium due under the policy and the above words being the operative part of the consideration clause which, in effect, is the receipt for the premium, and is conclusive between the insurer and assured (Sect. 54 M.I.A. 1906). The Company form usually reads "in consideration of the assured promising to pay" which wording is not a form of receipt. The broker is responsible for the premium to the insurer whether or not he has received it from the assured. (Sect. 53 M.I.A. 1906.)

Consign
To despatch goods. To send forward.

Consignee
Person to whom the goods are consigned.

Consignee's Interest
See "Buyer's interest".

Consignment
The goods involved in one sending. The act of consigning.

Consignment Note
A document giving details of a consignment of goods. It is used in inland and coastal trade but is replaced by the Bill of Lading for overseas trade.

Consignor
The person who consigns the goods.

Consortium
Is a group who share a common financial interest. In insurance it applies to a group of Companies who agree to share with each other any risk written by any individual member of the Consortium and applies particularly to Hull insurance. In practice the accepting member issues the policy on behalf of all other members, each for a prearranged proportion. In some cases a "fronting" Company would be registered on behalf of all the members for the purpose of issuing policies. Where a risk is too large for the Con-

sortium the arrangement of reinsurance for the surplus would be the prerogative of the member who first accepted the risk.

Construction of Policy

A policy must be construed with ordinary sense. Ambiguity is to be construed to the benefit of the assured except where it can be shown that the intention or usage was clear despite the ambiguity. In construing the intention of the policy, precedence must be given first to handwritten wording, then to typewritten wording, then to superimposed or stamped wording before applying the printed wording. So far as attachment of clauses or wordings is concerned precedence must be given first to attached clauses or wordings, then to marginal clauses or wording before applying the wording in the body of the policy. (See also " Contra Preferentum ".)

Construction Policy

A policy insuring loss and/or damage to a vessel whilst under construction. (See also " Builders' Risks ".)

Constructive Total Loss

Occurs where the subject matter insured is reasonably abandoned because either (a) its actual total loss appears to be unavoidable or (b) to prevent it from total loss would incur an expenditure greater than its value when preserved. In the case of hull (b) is arrived at in practice by a comparison between the insured value and the cost of recovery and repair, without taking into account the proceeds of wreck. In the case of cargo (b) is arrived at by a comparison between the arrived value at the destination named in the policy and the cost of recovery, reconditioning and forwarding to destination.

Constructive total loss on a freight policy is payable, in practice, if the policy on hull and machinery pays a constructive total loss.

Constructive Total Loss Clause

Appears in most sets of standard cargo clauses. It draws the attention of the assured to the requirements to constitute a claim for constructive total loss. For hulls see " Valuation Clause ". Notice of abandonment is a pre-requisite of any claim for constructive total loss, except where it can be of no benefit to the insurer or where he waives the notice.

Consular Invoice

Invoices signed by the Consulate of exporting countries in the country of import to show that the goods have fulfilled regulations. These are required before the Customs Authorities will permit the import of certain goods.

Cont.

Continent of Europe.

Contact

The striking of the vessel, craft or conveyance against some external substance. Where the ship comes into contact with another ship or vessel this is not contact, but collision. (See " Collision ".)

Contact Clause—Liners

An Institute clause for attachment to a policy where it is required that damage caused by contact of the subject matter insured with any substance shall be excluded from the policy. The clause does not exclude damage from contact with ice or cargo (not being loaded, discharged or handled) nor damage from contact of the subject matter insured with itself or part of itself, nor the extraordinary action of wind or waves.

Contact Damage

Damage caused to the insured interest by contact of the ship, craft or conveyance with some external substance. This does not include damage from contact with water, of course, but does include damage from contact with ice. Where a ship is in contact with another ship or vessel the resultant damage is not contact damage but collision damage. (See " Collision ", " Other Cargo ", " Damaged by Other Cargo " and " Taint ".)

Contact dge.

Contact Damage, (which see.)

Contact with Aircraft

In the event of the ship coming into contact with an aircraft whereby damage is caused to the ship, such damage is covered by the policy. This is provided by the " Inchmaree " clause in the standard hull clauses, which clause is subject to the policy deductible. This does not include bombs, shells and other engines of war since the F.C. & S. clause applies, but if a war plane accidentally damaged a ship by contact, outside a hostile act, the damage would be covered.

Container

A large metal box in which many packages can be stowed in advance of loading on the ship so that the container can be loaded, stowed and discharged as a complete unit. Containers vary in length and size being up to some 40 ft. long and 8 ft. wide. They are of light, but strong, metal construction with opening doors at either end. Some containers, generally of only 20 ft. in length, have been designed with side opening doors as well. Special loading and unloading facilities are generally necessary at the ports of loading and discharge. Uniformity in size and design of the containers and specialisation by the carrying vessels are essential for the efficiency of carriage by containers.

Containerisation poses special problems for insurers mainly because of the difficulty in establishing responsibility for damage caused during transit. A proposal to combine the bill of lading with insurance to provide a solution was suggested some time ago but failed to obtain sufficient support. There is a standard set of clauses to cover the insurance of the containers themselves. (See " Container Clauses ".)

Container Clauses

Sets of marine insurance clauses, introduced to the market in 1969, designed to cover loss of or damage to containers insured for a period of time (usually 12 months). These are intended for insurances effected by container operators and, although there are two sets of clauses covering loss proximately caused by marine perils (a separate set of clauses exists for war and strikes risks) many of the clauses are common to both sets. One set covers " all risks " whilst the other set gives cover only against T.L.O., G.A., Salvage, Salvage Charges and Sue and Labour expenses. A schedule in each set of clauses allows the insertion of identifying detail (clear identification marks on the container are essential), territorial limits and restriction in carrying vessels. For details of the individual clauses, reference should be made to Cl. 9 (All Risks) or Cl. 23 (T.L., G.A., Salvage, Salvage Charges, Sue and Labour). A cancellation clause provides for 30 days' notice. (See also " Container Clauses—All Risks ", " Container Clauses—Total Loss etc. " and " Container Clauses—War & Strikes Risks ".)

Container Clauses—All Risks

A set of Institute Clauses published in 1969 to cover containers for a period of time (usually 12 months) against all risks, but excluding the perils wear and tear, gradual deterioration, inherent vice and delay. Also excluded are war risks, strikes risks, nuclear perils (e.g. radioactivity from any nuclear source), confiscation, pre-emption, requisition and nationalisation. Underwriters pay the reasonable cost of repairs to a damaged container, subject to an agreed deductible on any one accident or series of accidents arising out of one occurrence. For details of clauses refer to Cl. 9. (See also " Container Clauses ".)

Container Clauses—Total Loss etc.

A set of Institute Clauses published in 1969 to cover containers for a period of time (usually 12 months) against total loss, general average, salvage, salvage charges and sue and labour expenses. The perils excluded are wear and tear, gradual deterioration, inherent vice, delay, war risks, strikes, nuclear perils (e.g. radio-activity from any nuclear source). For details of clauses refer to Cl. 23. (See also " Container Clauses ".)

Container Clauses—War & Strikes Risks
A set of Institute Clauses designed for attachment to a policy covering containers for a period of time (usually 12 months) against the war and strikes risks excluded from the Container Clauses— All Risks. The policy is subject to the waterborne agreement and contains an automatic termination clause which becomes effective in event of the outbreak of a major war. For details of clauses see Cl. 15. (See also " Container Clauses ", " Container Clauses—All Risks ", " Waterborne Agreement " and " War Cancellation Clause ".)

Containerisation
The practice of using containers for the carriage of goods.

Container Ship
A ship specially designed or re-designed for the carriage of containers.

Contamination
Losses proximately caused by contamination are not covered by the policy. Losses due to contamination but proximately caused by a peril insured against (i.e. seawater damage) are recoverable. The policy may be extended to cover the risk of contamination if the insurer agrees to accept this peril. (See also " Pollution ".)

Cont. B/H
Continent of Europe, but only in respect of ports and places be-tween Bordeaux and Hamburg.

Cont. H/H
Continent of Europe but limited to ports and places between Havre and Hamburg.

Continent
Continent of Europe. See limits used in practice under " Cont. B/H " and " Cont. H/H ".

Continental United States Limits
A warranty appearing in insurances on small craft navigating from the shores of U.S.A. There has been much controversial opinion regarding the extent of these limits but in the case of Winter

v Employer's Fire Ins. Co. (Florida) 1962 it was understood that the term "within the limits of the Continental United States of America" includes the land surface within the boundaries of the several States of the United States and the District of Columbia, also the rivers, canals and lakes which water the land. In the case of a State with a sea coast the limits shall include the gulfs, bays and straits of the sea and the soil forming the Continental shelf extending under the sea to the seaward edge thereof, including the waters above that shelf. But, nevertheless, the limits shall not extend beyond any boundary determined or confirmed by International agreement.

In locations where the Continental shelf extends for a distance under sea only to rise again above water to form an island or body of land and where that island or body of land is a sovereign nation or a possession of a sovereign nation, then instead of the boundary being the edge of the Continental shelf it is deemed to be the half way point between the closest coast of the United States and the closest coast of the sovereign nation or possession of a sovereign nation.

Contingency

The happening of a foreseen occurrence or event, but which is not an inevitability. For example, "Back Freight".

Contingency Risk

An insurance where the insurer holds himself liable to pay a fixed amount in the event of a specified contingency occurring.

Contingent Expenses

Expenses paid in earning freight after the operation of a general average act. So called because their payment is contingent on the success of the general average act.

Contingent Interest

An insurable interest which may attach during the currency of the adventure by the happening of a contingency. Buyer's interest may be a contingent interest if he acquires title to the goods after the commencement of transit.

Continuation Clause

A clause contained in most sets of hull clauses which came into being because prior to August 1959 no marine policy could be issued for a period exceeding 12 months. If a vessel is at sea, in distress, in a port of refuge or of call when the policy expires it continues to be covered, subject to prior notice to the insurer and payment of a pro rata monthly additional premium, until arrival at its destination.

Because a policy could not be issued for a period exceeding 12 months the clause was considered a separate contract and attracted an additional stamp duty of 6d. Stamp duty is no longer applicable to marine insurance policies but since it is customary to issue hull time policies on a 12 month basis, the clause remains necessary so that the insurance can be continued if the policy expires whilst the insured vessel is short of its destination. It should be noted that the clause does not operate automatically but requires notice to the insurer *prior* to expiry of the policy.

Continuation Sheet

An extension attaching to a synopsis sheet; listing the underwriters' lines, syndicate numbers and references.

Contraband

Goods which enter a country illicitly or the entry of which is prohibited. Smuggled goods.

Contract of Affreightment

The bill of lading or other form of contract in respect of the carriage of goods. It is one of the documents of title required as collateral by a bank when advancing credit against goods in transit.

Contract of Marine Insurance

An agreement whereby the insurer undertakes to indemnify the assured to the extent agreed in the event of a marine loss. The contract is concluded when the insurer initials the slip. The contract is not valid in law unless it is embodied in a properly executed policy.

Contractual Liability

Liability incurred by a party to a contract to the benefit of the other party. Legal liability is in the absence of contract.

Contra Preferentum

Under the principle "contra preferentum" any ambiguity in a marine insurance policy must be construed against the party drafting the contract. If the insurer drafts the policy ambiguity is construed to the benefit of the assured. If the assured employs a broker who drafts the policy this has the same effect as though the assured drafted his own policy and any ambiguity will then be construed to the benefit of the insurer. In all cases of ambiguity the question of "intention" of the parties at the time the insurance was effected must be considered as any court ruling will undoubtedly take this into account, together with usage and custom.

Contribution

There are two meanings for this term in marine insurance.

The first is used when at the time of loss there are in existence two or more insurances covering the same interest. This is termed double insurance and, provided there is no fraud, the Marine Insurance Act 1906 in Section 80 provides that each insurer is bound to contribute, with the other insurers, rateably toward the loss in proportion to the amount for which he is liable under the policy. An insurer who, in such circumstances, has paid more than his rateable proportion may claim a contribution for the amount over-paid from the other insurers. In any case, the insured may not recover more than a proper indemnity, that is the amount of his loss plus any profit included under a valued policy, over all.

The second use of the term " contribution " concerns the insured's contribution to general average or salvage charges and the insurer's liability in respect thereof. (See " General Average Contribution " and " Salvage Charges ".)

Contributory Negligent Navigation

It was once held that contributory negligence could be used by a negligent defendant in a collision case as defence against the claim. Under the Merchant Shipping Act 1894 contributory negligence ranks automatically as proportionate blame when the degree of blame is assessed.

Contributory Reinsurance

Mostly used in non-marine reinsurance, it is a form of quota share reinsurance. (See " Quota Share Reinsurance ".)

Contributory Value

The value on which general average contributions are based. It is the nett arrived value of the interest plus any amount to be made good in general average. To arrive at the contributory value the following should be taken into account: —

Ship—The assessed sound value on arrival at destination after discharging all cargo, less the estimated cost of repair of any damage, plus any amount to be made good in general average.

Cargo—The actual nett arrived value (i.e. gross value less all charges at destination) plus any amount to be made good in general average.

Freight—The actual gross freight at risk at the time of the general average act less any amounts paid by the assured after the general average act for the purpose of earning the freight (Contingent Expenses) plus any amount to be made good in general average.

The contributory value for apportioning salvage charges is calcu-lated in the same manner as for general average, except that the value is assessed at the place where the salvage services end; this maintains equity regarding the benefit derived from the salvage services and ensures that a contribution is levied against any interest, liable for contribution, which becomes lost or damaged between the place where the services are completed and the destination of that interest.

Control a Line

To act as broker or agent on behalf of an assured in U.S.A. in placing insurance.

Conventional Carriage

The carriage of goods packaged or in small units, other than by container.

Convertible Currency

A term used in the London Insurance market to embrace any currency other than, so called, " hard " currencies. Hard currencies are those where payments between countries are made in that currency without conversion to the currency of the country in which payment is made. In the United Kingdom Sterling, U.S. Dollars and Canadian Dollars are considered to be hard currencies and where insurances are effected in such currencies all premiums and claims must be paid in that currency without conversion. Various market practices have arisen, from time to time, to smooth the difficulties incurred regarding rates of exchange used for convertible currencies, but since fluctuating rates of exchange invariably cause a loss to one of the parties to the agreement most practices are no more than compromises to reduce expense and thereby offset the probable loss resulting from the application of the agreement. (See " Reinsurance Waiver Clause ".)

Conveyance

Craft, lighter, rivercraft, barge, road transport, rail or similar. The overseas vessel is not intended to be embraced by the term. Aircraft where no sea transit is involved are not embraced, nor where the use of aircraft is not a customary method of moving the goods inland to or from the port.

CONV. *or* conv.

Conveyance. Also used as abbreviation for " converted from ".

Copy Policy

An exact copy of the original policy but it is not sealed (at Lloyd's) and does not substitute for the original. It is issued for information purposes only. A copy policy should not be marked " Duplicate ". (See also " Duplicate Policy ".)

Copy Seal

An adhesive seal, attached to the foot of a Lloyd's copy policy, in place of the impressed seal that appears on the original policy.

Cord and Seal

A clause used in insurance covering meat in transit to inland U.S.A. destinations. It is a form of "rejection risk" insurance and applies when the goods are forwarded under cord and seal for inspection by the U.S.A. Authorities but without prior inspection at the port of entry. Normally, a rejection risk insurance cover terminates at the port of entry but if the inspection is deferred until the goods arrive at an inland destination, the clause continues the rejection risk insurance (subject to a 7 day limit) until the inspection takes place; with the proviso that the inspection must be carried out immediately the meat arrives at the destination.

Corn Trade Clauses

Standard clauses used in respect of grain. The conditions are basically F.P.A. and a provision is made to allow for increased value insurance to be incorporated in the policy. The clauses may be used for either bulk or bagged grain and for other similar cargoes.

Corn Trade F.P.A. North Atl.

Institute Corn Trade Clauses. These are F.P.A. clauses in respect of North Atlantic shipments.

Corn Trade Liverpool Craft

Institute Corn Trade clauses. Liverpool Craft Risks.

Corn Trade Strikes

Institute Strikes Clauses incorporating strikes risks into a policy containing the Institute Corn Trade F.P.A. clauses.

Corn Trade War Clauses

Institute Clauses reinstating into a policy containing the Institute Corn Trade Clauses the risks excluded by the F.C. & S. clause and incorporating war perils.

Corporate Seal

The impressed seal in a document representing agreement to the document by the Corporation concerned. Where a Corporation or other authorised body signs a policy on behalf of its members it is usual for the policy to be impressed with the Corporate seal. The seal is acceptable by the Marine Insurance Act 1906 (Sect. 24) as being sufficient, but it is not compulsory that the subscription of a Corporation be under seal.

Corporation of Lloyd's
See " Lloyd's ".

Corps
Hull. (French term).

Cost, Insurance, Freight
See " C.I.F. "

Cost of Removal
If it is necessary for the vessel to be removed to another place for repairs, with the insurer's approval, the costs of removal and return if necessary are part of the reasonable cost of repairs.

Cost of Repairs Clause
A clause in a policy insuring a ship against particular average losses whilst on a break up voyage; that is, a voyage to a yard where the vessel is to be broken up for scrap. The clause provides that the insurer's liability shall be limited to the cost of repairing only that damage caused by an insured peril, the repair of which is essential for seaworthiness of the vessel to enable it to complete the voyage.

Cost of Repairs
Where a ship is damaged by an insured peril the insurer has the right to select the repairing firm and port of repair, any additional costs in this respect being borne by the insurer and an allowance being made to the insured in respect of time lost in awaiting tenders invited by the assured at the underwriters request. Such additional costs and allowances are subject to reduction in the event of any amounts being received by the assured from other parties in consequence of such removal etc. or loss of time. Any savings to the insured must also be taken into account. The insurer is liable for the reasonable cost of repairs without regard to a comparison between the insurable value and the insured value, but limited to the sum insured by the policy in respect of any one accident. No deduction is made, in practice, in respect of new material replacing old material. (See also " Depreciation " and " Unrepaired Damage ").

Costs
Legal costs incurred by the assured in defending a claim for which the insurer would be liable. These are customarily borne by the insurer. May also refer to expenses incurred in connection with a general average act.

Costs allowed in General Average
When a vessel enters a port of refuge following accidental damage

all costs are allowed under York-Antwerp Rules from the time of the accident until the vessel returns to its original course. These costs include (1) Bearing up to the port of refuge (2) Port entry dues and pilotage (3) Port charges (4) Discharging cargo (5) Warehousing cargo (6) Reloading cargo (7) Outward port charges.

Under English Law and Practice only the costs of attaining the port of refuge and discharging the cargo are allowed.

When a vessel enters a port of refuge following a general average act all costs are allowed under both York-Antwerp Rules and English Law and Practice until the vessel returns to its original course.

Counter

The part of a ship's stern that overhangs the water.

Counter Guarantee

When the insurer guarantees a general average contribution on behalf of the assured he usually wishes to qualify the guarantee to limit his liability to the proper amount due under the policy. (See " General Average Guarantee ".) Such a qualified guarantee is not satisfactory to the shipowner or adjuster and the assured will, therefore, ask for an unqualified guarantee, in return for which he gives a counter guarantee to the insurer agreeing to reimburse the insurer in the event of his having to pay more under his guarantee than that for which he is liable. (See also " G.A. in Full Clause ".)

Country Damage

Damage or deterioration occuring to baled or bagged goods (such as cotton or coffee), prior to loading on the overseas vessel, caused by the absorption of excessive moisture from damp ground or exposure to weather, or damage or deterioration from grit, dust or sand forced into the subject matter of the insurance by windstorm or inclement weather.

Country of Origin

The Country from which the goods concerned have been exported. In the case of agricultural products this would be the Country where they were grown. In the case of manufactured goods it would be the Country where they were manufactured.

Cover

To cover. To guarantee indemnity as an insurer in event of loss.

Cover Note

A document issued by a broker to the assured evidencing the terms and rate on which an insurance has been placed. The insurer has no legal obligation under a broker's cover note, but in the event of negligence of the broker whereby the assured is prejudiced the cover note may be used by the assured in evidence against the broker.

Cowl
Top of a ventilator.

C/P.
Charterparty.

C.P.A.
Claims Payable Abroad. (See also " S.C.A. ".)

C.P.A. Agent
A " payable abroad " agent. See " Settling Agents " and " Settling Fee ".

Cradle
A structure to support a ship whilst she is out of the water—e.g. in drydock, or awaiting launching. (See also " Keel Block ".)

Craft
Any small vessel such as a lighter or barge used for conveying the insured goods to or from the ship.

Craft etc. Clause
Appears in all sets of standard cargo clauses and extends the period covered by the plain form of policy to include whilst the goods are in craft, lighters or similar to or from the vessel. For franchise and total loss purposes it is considered that each craft etc. is a separate insurance. Further, the clause provides that the assured shall not be prejudiced by any agreement he may have signed exempting lightermen etc. from liability.

Craft Port
See " Overside Port ".

Craft Risks
The risks to which cargo is exposed when being conveyed by craft or lighter between ship and shore, or during transhipment. The Institute Cargo Clauses include the risk of loss or damage to the cargo, proximately caused by an insured peril, whilst the cargo is carried in a craft or lighter as part of the normal course of transit. (See " Craft etc. Clause ".)

Cranage
Dues payable in respect of the use of cranes.

Cratering

Peril encountered in off shore drilling rig insurance. Occurs when the sea bed caves in following release of gases, water or oil from below ground.

Credit System

When goods are sold to an overseas buyer arrangements are made for payment of the goods. A system has evolved whereby the sending of cash or even cheques in payment is no longer necessary. Instead, an arrangement is made whereby one bank, in the seller's area, pays the seller on instructions from another bank, nominated by the buyer. The buyer draws an irrevocable letter of credit on his bank to pay the seller, on presentation of the documents named in the letter of credit and on a certain date, or on delivery of the goods to the buyer, the sum of money stated in the letter of credit. The documents (usually the bill of lading, export invoice and, in some cases, the certificate or policy of insurance) are forwarded by the seller's bank to the buyer's bank where they are released to the buyer against payment for the goods. The buyer cannot obtain delivery of the goods from the carrier until he can show the bill of lading as evidence of title. When the seller's bank receives the letter of credit the seller is notified and he drafts a bill of exchange requesting payment. Where the terms of sale (e.g. C.I.F.) require that the seller arranges insurance on the goods whilst they are in transit, he will have to deposit the insurance certificate, or policy, with the other documents, at the bank. If the seller wants payment in advance of the stated date or prior to delivery of the goods the seller's bank may be prepared to arrange this subject to a charge and subject to production of an insurance policy (sometimes a certificate is acceptable) covering perils specified by the bank.

Crewboat

A term used in the insurance of offshore drilling rigs. A crewboat is used for carrying the crew of the rig between the shore and the rig.

Cristal

Contract Regarding an Interim Supplement to Tanker Liability for Oil Pollution. A cargo owners' scheme intended to supplement Tovalop. It applies solely to cargoes carried in vessels in the Tovalop scheme. Cristal provides compensation in respect of oil pollution additional to that provided by Tovalop. Whereas the intention of Tovalop is to reimburse Governments, Cristal will pay additional compensation to individuals (e.g. hoteliers, fishermen etc.). The scheme envisages a top limit of $30,000,000 any one incident, including compensation from other sources, the scheme paying the difference up to the limit. The oil company members agree to contribute towards the amount paid under the scheme.

Cr. L.
Craft loss.

C.R.O.
Cancelling Returns Only

Cross Liabilities
When two vessels are both at fault in a collision, the degree of fault is assessed. Under Admiralty rule the settlement should then be made on a single liability basis whereby one liability is set against the other so that only the balance is due from the party with the greater liability. Insurers, realising the difficulty in which the Assured could find himself by this principle, agree to settle claims on a cross liability basis so that it is deemed each vessel has paid the full liability due to the other vessel. The Collision Clause in the I.T.C. makes provision for claims to be settled on a cross liability basis.

c/s.
Cases.

CSD
Lloyd's Register indication that the ship has a closed shelter deck.

Csk
Cask.

C.S.T.
Central Standard Time. U.S.A. Central Continental. (i.e. between P.S.T. and E.S.T.)

C.T.C.
Corn Trade Clauses.

Ctge.
Cartage.

C.T.L.
Constructive total loss.

Ctr.
Cutter.

Cts.
Crates.

"C" Type Ships, and others

Amongst the tonnage from American wartime yards were the standard C (cargo) types. There were four basic designs, these being numbered from 1 to 4 (example: C.2) and each had its many variations. In all, about 1,000 of these vessels were built. The first vessels from the earlier types had been designed, built and placed in service "before the war". These ranged from vessels of approximately 3,000 g.r.t. to the smallest (5,000 g.r.t.) of the larger types with only average speed; to the design which was intended to replace the older vessels of the American merchant fleet and which had a good balance of size, speed and capacity (approximately 6,200 g.r.t.); and to those which meet the need for even faster vessels with greater capacity (approximately 8,200 g.r.t.).

The remaining type (C.4, machinery placed aft) was originally intended to be even larger and faster than its predecessors, but was re-designed to a troopship (approximately 12,000 g.r.t.). Many of these latter vessels have, in recent times, been converted by commercial interests into modern container ships.

Other standard types of ship not so numerous as the above, included "P" (passenger) troopships of nearly 20,000 g.r.t., various coaster designs, refrigerated vessels and numbers of special designs —naval, military and commercial. Into the latter category are a number of standard ships built to the order and design of some leading American shipping companies (Waterman, American Export, etc.).

All the above ships were turbine or diesel propelled.

(Further details may be obtained from "Wartime Standard Ships" by W. H. Mitchell & L. A. Sawyer, the forthcoming volume 6, published by The Journal of Commerce and Shipping Telegraph Limited.)

Cubic Ton

For the purpose of calculating displacement tonnage 33 cubic feet of water is deemed to be equivalent to one cubic ton. For the purpose of calculating gross and net registered tonnages 100 cubic feet of space is deemed to be the equivalent to one ton.

Cumulative

This applies to an accumulation of interests which might be subject to claims caused by one occurrence. The insurer may receive many declarations, both on open covers and obligatory reinsurances, on one vessel and if the cumulative amount exceeds the insurer's normal retention for such a vessel he will have to arrange reinsurance for the surplus amount.

C Underwriter

A marine underwriter at Lloyd's who has not given authority to L.U.C.O. to settle claims on his behalf without his initials on the claim form.

Custom and Usage

Where there is no existing contradictory statute "custom and usage" may be upheld as a plea in the Courts. In circumstances where a duty, right or obligation arises by implication of the law such implication may be made negative by "usage" provided the usage is so understood by both parties as to bind them to the contract.

Customary

In accordance with recognised custom or usage of trade.

Customary Average

Not common today, but at one time many commodities were subject to a grouping into series for average purposes. An example is tea, where the franchise was customarily applied to each group of 10 chests or 20 half chests or 40 boxes. The practice has generally fallen out of use, although franchise by series may still be specified in the policy if required. It is more common for the franchise to be applied to each package or on the whole shipment at the option of the assured.

Customary Deductions

In accordance with the Rules of Practice of the Association of Average Adjusters the insurer is entitled to make customary deductions from hull claims, as laid down in the rules, in the event that new material replaces old material in respect of repairs to hull or machinery. In practice, the insurer waives this right and makes no such deductions.

Customary Groundings

See "Customary Strandings".

Customary Groundings Clause

See "Customary Strandings".

Customary Strandings

A Clause in the Institute Time Clauses (Hulls) provides that underwriters will pay the cost of sighting the bottom of the vessel following stranding, even if no damage is found. Nevertheless, the underwriters are not prepared to bear such costs when the vessel grounds in certain areas. These areas are termed areas of customary strandings or groundings and are specified in the "Suez Canal Clause" in the I.T.C.

Custom of Lloyd's

Where a practice has been acceptable for a reasonable period of time at Lloyd's it may be accepted and upheld as a plea by the Courts.

Customs Entry

Details supplied by the shipper or importer of goods to the Customs Authorities in respect of description, weights and values of the goods.

Cutting Away Wreck

Concerned with general average. Parts of a vessel which are cut away and sacrificed under this heading are not general average as the " wreck " is already deemed lost, so there is no sacrifice.

Cutting Clause

A cargo clause in respect of pipes or similar cargoes of length which provides that damaged cargo should be cut off leaving the good pieces for the account of the assured. Insurer's liability being limited to the insured value of the damaged parts and cost of cutting.

The cutting clause used on the Continent provides that unless a minimum agreed length is sound the whole length shall be deemed lost.

CY

Currency.

D

D/A
Deductible average.

D.A.A.
Documents against acceptance.

Daily Index
The shipping index published daily by Lloyd's giving information regarding the movements of ships. Sometimes called the " blue list " because it has a blue cover. The publication is obtainable only by subscription and most subscribers are content to have one copy only per week.

Damage by other Cargo
Taint damage or contact damage to the insured cargo caused by other cargo. Without the operation of an insured peril damage by other cargo is not covered by the policy.

Damage Claim
A claim for partial loss. Such claims are based on the percentage of depreciation on cargo or the reasonable cost of repairs on hull.

Damaged Cargo
See " Partial Loss of Cargo " and " Partial Loss of Freight ".

Damage Done
A term relating to third party liability, usually in connection with ship insurance. The term is used when referring to collision liability or liability for damage to harbours, wharves, piers, buoys and other property.

Damaged Value
The actual value on arrival at destination. On hulls this is the value without any repairs being taken into account. On cargo the value may be net or gross. Gross damaged value is the value of the damaged cargo after all landing charges and duty have been paid. Net damaged value is the value of the damaged cargo before all landing charges and duty are paid. Claims are calculated on cargo by comparing sound and damaged gross values.

Damage Received
A term used in ship insurance. It relates to damage received by the insured ship, usually in collision with another vessel. It can

be used, also, in connection with damage to the insured ship which comes into contact with a wharf, pier or other object or where the ship grounds, strikes rocks, etc.

Damage to Ship
See " Partial Loss of Ship ".

Dangerous Drugs Clause
A clause appearing in a cargo policy excluding claims on dangerous drugs which are shipped without authorisation by the Government of the country importing or exporting the drugs, or which are not shipped by the customary route. The purpose of the clause is to avoid the benefit of insurance being given to assist illicit drug trafficking.

Dangerous Goods
If goods of a dangerous, explosive or inflammable nature are shipped, without consent of the master or his knowledge of their nature, the master may land or destroy or render innocuous the goods without any compensation being payable to the owner. The shipper may be held liable for damages and expenses in respect of such goods. The master may treat equally any goods of such dangerous nature loaded with his knowledge and consent, if they become a danger to the ship or cargo, without incurring any liability except to general average, if any. (See also " T.E.C.H. Cargo ".)

Davit
A support that carries a lifeboat, so constructed that it can be used for lowering the lifeboat into the waters.

Days of Grace
In non-marine insurance a number of days, usually 15, is allowed after the expiry date of the insurance during which the renewal premium may be paid and renewal effected. These days are called " days of grace ". Marine insurance makes no provision for days of grace and for renewal to be effected application must be made to the insurer prior to the expiry date of the insurance, otherwise cover will lapse on such expiry date.

DB
Lloyd's Register notation meaning " double bottom ".

D.B.B.
Deals, battens and boards. Concerns timber shipments.

Dbk.
Drawback.

D/C
Deviation clause.

D.C.O.P.
During currency of policy.

D.D. *or* **D/D** *or* **d/d**
Damage done.

Dd.
Delivered.

D/d.
Days after date.

D-E
Diesel-electric.

Deadfreight
When space is booked on a vessel but is not used the freight is still payable and is called "deadfreight". The right to such deadfreight is usually exercised only under charterparties.

Deadlight
A hinged metal flap that covers the inside of a port hole (port light).

Deadweight
The weight in tons of the cargo, stores, freshwater, fuel and crew which a ship can carry when loaded down to her loadline level. This has nothing to do with the gross or net tonnage of the ship; the latter being calculated on cubic capacity not weight. (See also "Gross Registered Tonnage".)

Deals
Lengths of timber of not less than 5 ft and not more than 30 ft in length, and not less than 9 by 2 inches thick.

Dec.
Declaration.

Deck Cargo
Cargo carried on deck. Such cargo is not embraced by the terms of the Carriage of Goods by Sea Act 1924. Insurance on cargo is deemed to apply only to cargo under deck unless the insurance specifically states the cargo is carried on or over deck. Jettison of deck cargo is only allowable in general average if the cargo is so carried by custom of trade.

Deck Gear

Machinery installed on the deck of a ship for the purpose of operating hoisting tackle and/or winches and/or windlasses and/or steering gear.

Deck Load

See " Deck Cargo ".

Deck Log

Entry book on a ship containing general details of the running of the ship. Entries relating to accidents to ship or cargo may be made therein.

Deck Plating

Steel plates forming the deck of a ship.

Decl.

Declared.

Declaration

A statement. An advice on an open cover declaring a shipment to the insurer. A declaration may be provisional or definite. In practice declarations are advised to the insurer on a special declaration sheet and are embodied in the policy, if any, at a later date. Declarations must be made in the order of shipment unless the open cover contains a provision to the contrary. If no basis of valuation is incorporated in the open cover a declaration made after loss or arrival will be treated as unvalued and will be deemed to be insured for the prime cost of the goods plus the charges of shipping and insurance. All shipments must be declared unless the open cover provides otherwise.

Declaration of Ownership

Made by a person when applying for British Registration of a vessel. Contents include details of nationality of the owner, build and year of the vessel, proportion and the number of shares in the vessel and a signed statement that no unauthorised person is interested in the vessel.

Declivity

Angle of launching ways.

Ded.

Deduction *or* deductible.

Deductible

An amount or percentage specified in the policy which must be exceeded before a claim is payable. When the deductible is exceeded only the amount which is in excess of the deductible is recoverable under the policy. The word "deductible" is common in America and means the same as an "excess". It is called a deductible because it is considered that the specified amount or percentage is deducted from any claim. (See also "Hull Policy Deductible".)

Deductible Franchise *or* Deductible Average
A deductible (which see).

Deductions
See "Customary Deductions". The term may also be used to denote discounts which the broker is permitted to deduct from premiums. Such discounts include brokerage.

Deductions New for Old
See "New for Old".

Deemed Attachment Date
In the "terms of credit" rules at Lloyd's the broker is required to pay the premium to underwriters within a specified period of time. The time allowed for credit commences from the month specified on the slip, by the leading underwriter, for this purpose. It is called the attachment date. When, for some reason the underwriter wishes to vary the period of credit allowed he enters on the slip a month, other than the actual month the risk attaches. This is called a "deemed" attachment date.

Deep Tank
A ship's tank extending between the lowest deck and the double bottom; usually for cargo carriage, ballast or fresh water.

Def.
Deferred.

Def. a/c
Deferred account.

Defeasible Interest
A defeasible interest is an insurable interest which ceases during the currency of the voyage. Such an interest would be the interest of a seller who loses title to goods whilst they are en route. (See also "Contingent Interest".)

Deferred Instalment
See "Deferred Account".

Defence and Demurrage Association
An Association working in conjunction with a Protection and

Indemnity Club, the duties of which are to advise and assist the members of the Club in respect of defence of claims against members following damage to cargo or other property for which the member concerned has been held liable. The Association also advises in demurrage disputes.

Defence Costs

Legal expenses incurred by the assured in defence of a claim for which the insurer would be liable. It is the practice for the insurer to agree to reimburse the assured for such costs where properly incurred with the insurer's consent.

Deferred Account

An agreement whereby the assured is allowed to pay premium by instalments. In marine insurance this system is generally only to be found in hull insurance and treaty reinsurance. The arrangement is not bound by any rules, but insurers do not readily grant such facilities. It is usual in direct insurance to reduce any discount allowed by the insurer in cases where the premium is paid by deferred account.

Deferred Premiums

See "Deferred Account".

Deferred Freight Rebates

See "Deferred Rebate System".

Deferred Rebate System

A system, used within some Conference systems, whereby a shipper is granted a rebate of freight paid over a specified period subject to his having used Conference line vessels exclusively during the period. The practice is dying out, being discouraged by many Conferences. (See "Conference Lines" and "Freight Rebate".)

Deferred Repairs

If the owner of a vessel requests that repairs be deferred the insurer is liable only for the reasonable cost of repairs at the time they should have been carried out. Any excess by reason of enhanced costs due to rise in prices is for the account of the assured. (See also "Unrepaired Damage".)

Deficit Clause

A clause appearing in a reinsurance contract which contains a profit commission clause. The effect of the clause is to transfer a loss in one underwriting year to be set against the profit for the next underwriting year. The transfer continues each year until a profit is shown to wipe out the deficit. This is an important clause because without it the reinsurer may suffer a loss on one year, yet pay a profit commission on the next year even though overall he is making no profit at all. It is customary for a deficit clause to operate on a three year basis, whereby a single large loss (sometimes more than one) is carried forward for three years only then is dropped from the profit commission statement.

Definite
The actual amount insured or reinsured. (See " Definite Advice ".)

Definite Advice
A definite closing or advice follows a provisional closing or advice. This applies particularly to cargo reinsurance on an open cover or treaty basis, when provisional declarations are made or bordereaux issued. The original insurer having written a line advises this provisionally to his reinsurer. When the shipment has taken place the insurance is closed for its actual amount which is then considered " definite " and the reinsurer advised accordingly. It is customary for premiums and claims to be settled only against definite advices although a claim advance may be made against a provisional advice.

Definite Bordereaux
Bordereaux advising the actual amounts closed. (See " Definite Advice ".)

Definite Closing
The actual amount closed. (See " Definite Advice ".)

Definite Order
A firm order given to a broker to place an insurance for a fixed amount which will not be reduced at a later date.

Degree of Blame
When two vessels are in collision the degree of blame is assessed to discover the proportion of liability of one to the other. If the collision is deemed an inevitable accident, where no one is at fault, there is no degree of blame on either side. (See also " Inscrutable Fault ".)

Degree of Fault
See " Degree of Blame ".

Dehydration
The drying out of moisture from solid cargo. Natural dehydration is natural loss. (See " Natural Loss ".)

D.E.I.
Dutch East Indies.

Delay

Losses proximately caused by or consequential on delay are not recoverable under a policy of marine insurance. By special clauses the insurance on cargo may be continued *during* delay, (Transit Clause) but in the absence of such a clause the insurer is discharged from liability in the event of unreasonable delay in prosecution of the voyage, from the time such delay becomes unreasonable. The insurer may avoid the policy in the event of unreasonable delay in commencement of the voyage. Delay in prosecution of the voyage is excused in the same circumstances as deviation is excused. (See " Deviation ".)

Delay in Commencement of a Voyage
See " Commencement of Voyage ".

Delay Exclusion

A clause in the Institute War Clauses and the Institute Strikes Clauses making it quite clear that although the cover of strikes, riots and civil commotions continues during delay, loss proximately caused by delay itself is specifically excluded from the policy. The same type of clause appears in the cargo clauses. Should, however, any expense be the subject of general average but arising from delay, such expense may be recoverable under the policy as a contribution to general average. Loss proximately caused by delay, such as loss of market or deterioration, cannot be recovered under general average. Loss, damage or expense proximately caused by delay is excluded in the standard cargo clauses.

Del Credere

A guarantee by which an agent selling goods on credit guarantees as to the solvency of the buyer.

Deliberate Damage Clause
Another name for the Pollution Hazard Clause.

Deliberate Destruction Endorsement
Another name for the Pollution Hazard Clause.

Delivery Trip

The voyage undertaken by a newly built vessel from the place of construction to the proposed home port. If the owner takes delivery of the vessel at the place of construction the vessel is at his risk and he has an insurable interest.

Delta Ship
See " Delta System ".

Delta System
A ship construction system used for the carriage of bulk oil or similar cargoes. Large detachable caissons are locked into bays in the side of a mother ship. The cargo is contained in the caissons, the mother ship carrying only fuel and ballast. When the ship arrives and anchors at her destination port the ballast is adjusted so that the mother ship rises. The caissons, on which she actually rides, can be detached and towed into berths for unloading or loading. Subsequently the caissons are re-positioned in the bays at the side of the mother ship, which adjusts her ballast to re-engage on the caissons.

Demise Charterparty
Occurs when the charterer agrees to take over the vessel completely for a period of time, whereby he supplies his own master, engineers and crew.

Demurrage
Money paid to the shipowner in compensation for delay of a vessel beyond the period allowed in a charterparty when loading or discharging. In marine insurance the term is used to denote any loss of hire period incurred by the shipowner. (See " Collision Clause ".)

Denting
Peril mainly affecting hollowware metal products. It is usual to exclude this peril unless the premium is loaded to cover the risk.

Deposit
See " Deposit Premium " and " General Average Deposit ".

Deposit Premium
A premium paid in advance as a deposit when it is not practicable at the time of placing to assess the final premium. It is usual for a provision to be made at the time of placing to allow for adjustment on expiry of the policy. In some cases the deposit is specified as a minimum premium, in which case the adjustment is made only if the final premium exceeds the deposit premium.

Deposit Receipt
A receipt given for payment of a general average deposit. Any refund of general average deposit will be paid only to the person holding the receipt. Details of the sacrifice are shown on the receipt, with the steamer's name and identifying marks of the goods. The

provisional contributory value and estimated amount of contribution are also shown.

Depreciation

Loss in value. A percentage of depreciation is assessed in respect of cargo damage to apply to the insured value to ascertain a claim. When a vessel is unrepaired at the expiry of the hull policy a reasonable allowance is given under the policy for depreciation by reason of the unrepaired damage, but not exceeding the reasonable cost of repairs had they been carried out at the proper time.

Derrick

A steel tube (or a wooden spar), hinged to a kingpost (or " samson ") and operated by ropes, used for loading and unloading.

Description of Goods

Goods must be described in the policy with reasonable certainty in order that they may be readily identifiable as being the subject matter covered by the policy. It is usual to show the " marks " on the policy for this purpose.

Designation of Subject Matter

According to the Marine Insurance Act, 1906 (Section 26) the subject matter of the insurance must be designated in the policy with reasonable certainty. Details of the insurable interest need not be designated in a marine policy. General terms may be used but they must be construed to apply to the interest which the assured intended should be covered by the insurance. The designation of the subject matter is acceptable if in accordance with custom and usage.

Destination

The place where the adventure ends.

Destination Port

Applies when no inland destination is designated in the policy. The destination port is the port where the adventure ends. Insurer's liability ceases when the cargo is free of the landing tackle at the destination port unless the policy states otherwise. It is usual, in practice, to continue the insurance to cease when the goods enter the warehouse at the port.

Det.

Detention *or* detained *or* detained at.

Detainment

Detention.

Detention

The detaining of a vessel by the operation of a political or executive act is an insurable interest. Detention under ordinary legal process is not covered by the ordinary marine policy. When another vessel suffers detention of any sort whereby loss of hire is involved and such detention is the result of collision where the insured vessel is wholly or partly to blame, the detention or loss of hire is part of the collision liability claim against the insured vessel and as such is recoverable under the collision clause, if any, in the insured vessel's policy.

Deterioration

Loss in quality without the help of an outside agency. Since this is not a fortuity it is not embraced by the term " risk ", so deterioration is not covered by an " all risks " policy unless it is specifically included. Deterioration cover is generally sought by the owner of perishable goods, the proximate cause of loss being delay. Delay is an excluded peril unless the policy states otherwise, hence it is usual in deterioration insurance to state " including deterioration from any cause whatsoever ".

Deviation

Deviation is the departure of the vessel from the laid down course, or in the event of no stipulated course, the customary direct course, with the intention of returning to that course. The insurer is discharged from liability as from the time the vessel leaves its proper course, unless the policy contains a deviation clause. If the vessel does not intend to return to its original course there is a change of voyage, not a deviation. Deviation is excused when reasonably necessary for the safety of the ship and cargo or for humanitarian purpose or to go to the aid of a vessel where human life may be in danger or to obtain medical or surgical aid for a person on board or to comply with a warranty or where specially authorised by the insurer or where beyond the control of the master and his employer or where due to barratry. The vessel must return to her course immediately the excuse for deviation has ceased to exist. The same excuses permit delay in the prosecution of the voyage.

Deviation Clause

A clause in an insurance policy providing that the assured shall not be prejudiced in the event that the vessel deviates, provided the deviation is beyond the control of the assured. A bill of lading or charterparty usually contains a deviation clause allowing the vessel to deviate without liability of the carrier to the cargo owner in respect of such deviation. (See also " Held Covered Clause ".)

D.f.
Deadfreight.

DF
Lloyd's Register indication that a ship is fitted for a direction finder.

Dft.
Draft *or* draught.

D.I.C.
Difference in conditions.

Different Species
When the insured property may be divided into different species the Marine Insurance Act, 1906 provides that the total value may be apportioned over each species separately in order to assess whether the franchise has been attained for that species, even if the damage does not attain the franchise over the whole value. The assured has, of course, the option of applying the franchise to the whole value.

Different Voyage
When the place of departure and the destination are stated in the policy, but the vessel sails either from a different place or for a different destination there is said to be a different voyage and the risk does not attach.

Digests of Lloyd's Law Reports
Each digest, published by Lloyd's, is a casebook of commercial, maritime and insurance legal decisions. The summary of each case incorporates the facts and contentions of the parties followed by the reasons for the decision.

Diligence
See " Due Diligence ".

Diminution in Value
See " Average Disbursements Clauses ".

Dipper Dredger
See " Dredger ".

Direct Action
When an insurer covers liability risks (e.g. collision liability) the policy usually provides that the insurer does not pay directly to the person who is pursuing an action against the assured. The assured is required to pay the amount for which he is liable, following which he is reimbursed by his insurers. Thus, in the absence of

any law to the contrary, the person claiming from the assured cannot bring an action directly against the insurers. It may be that a country or state will introduce a statement allowing direct action. Such a statute exists in Louisiana.

Direct Insurance
Insurance other than reinsurance.

Direct *or* Direct or Held Covered
A term used in cargo insurance when the insurer's risk may be seriously prejudiced by delay due to the vessel entering several ports of call en route to its destination. It may happen that an insurer agrees to accept the risk of delay in an insurance, such as a deterioration risk on a perishable cargo. It would be essential in such an adventure that the vessel proceeds directly to its destination and to ensure this the insurer will insert a warranty in the insurance requiring the vessel to proceed directly to its destination without calling at any other ports en route. The insurer may be prepared to allow a breach of the warranty to be held covered, subject to prior notice to the insurer and to a reasonable additional premium.

Directly Caused By
Used to emphasise that an indirect cause of loss is not to be considered. This particularly applies to hull insurance where additional perils are incorporated in the policy by the attachment thereto of the " Inchmaree " clause.

Dirty Bill
Dirty bill of lading.

Dirty Bill of Lading
See " Bill of Lading ". A bill of lading is labelled " dirty " when it is qualified by the carrier stating that the goods were not sound or were improperly packed when received by the carrier for carriage.

Disbts.
Disbursements.

Disbursements
Payments made " out of pocket " by the master or shipowner in connection with running the vessel. General average disbursements are expenses in connection with a general average act. The shipowner has an insurable interest in both disbursements and general average disbursements. The maximum amount which the shipowner can insure in respect of disbursements is limited by warranty in the Institute Time Clauses (Hulls) to 10% of the insured value of the vessel. (See also " Disbursements Warranty ".)

Disbursements Clause

See " Disbursements Warranty ".

Disbursements Warranty

A warranty appearing in the Institute Time Clauses (Hulls) providing that no P.P.I. F.I.A. policies shall be effected by the shipowner, or other interested party, in excess of the permitted limits specified in the disbursements clause.

The purpose of the warranty is to ensure that a proper value of the ship is declared on the hull policy in order that the insurer receives an adequate premium to cover partial losses. Without the warranty the assured might be tempted to declare a relatively low value on the hull policy, in an effort to reduce the premium, and to effect a P.P.I. policy on a T.L.O. basis, under the guise of a disbursements insurance, for the balance up to the proper value. The effect being that in the event of total loss the assured could claim in full under both policies, thus gaining full cover, while obtaining the cost of repairs in full under the hull policy up to the agreed value.

The disbursement warranty prevents this undesirable practice by limiting any amount insured on disbursements, managers' commissions, profits or excess or increased value of hull or machinery to 10% of the value stated in the hull policy. As a further protection anticipated, chartered or other freight on a time basis may only be insured up to 25% of the value stated in the policy, less any amount already insured on disbursements etc. The remainder of the clause permits reasonable insurances on actual freight at risk, premiums, returns of premium and war and strikes risks, to ensure that the assured is not prejudiced by the warranty.

Disbursements Warranty—Interchangeable

Whereas the disbursements warranty in a hull policy prohibits the assured from effecting insurances in excess of the limits laid down in the clause for each type of interest, the " Disbursements Warranty—Interchangeable Interest " clause allows the total limit to be applicable to all the specified types of interest, provided the overall limit in the clause is not exceeded.

Discharge

To discharge. To unload cargo from a ship or craft.

Discharged from Liability

Means the insurer is not liable for any claim as from a particular time or date or from inception, depending on the circumstances. The insurer may be discharged from liability due to some breach of warranty by the assured.

Discharge of Cargo at P.O.R.
See "Costs Allowed in General Average".

Disclosure
Before the contract is concluded, that is before the insurer accepts the risk, the assured must disclose every material fact or circumstance to the insurer. This includes everything which would influence the insurer in accepting, declining or rating the insurance and includes all that the assured actually knows and everything which the assured ought to know in the ordinary course of his business.

If the assured fails in this in any respect there is non-disclosure and the insurer may avoid the contract. (See "Material Circumstance" and "Representation".)

Provided the insurer does not enquire, the assured need not disclose anything which diminishes the risk, anything which may be presumed to be known by the insurer such as matters of common notoriety or which the insurer ought to know in the ordinary course of his business, anything concerning which the insurer has waived the information or anything superfluous because of the existence of a warranty.

The broker as agent of the assured is obliged to make the same disclosures and, in addition, he must disclose any material fact or circumstance which he himself knows or ought to know in the ordinary course of his business. (See "Utmost Good Faith".)

Discolouration
Applicable to metal products. Synonymous with "rust".

Discounts
Amounts which the broker is allowed to deduct from the premium before paying it to the assurer, which amounts include brokerage. These may be called deductions. The term also applies to allowances off premiums, if any, given to the assured.

DISPL. *or* **Displ.**
Displacement (tonnage).

Displacement Tonnage
See "Load Displacement" and "Light Displacement".

Division of Loss
Under English law when two vessels which are both to blame are in collision the degree of blame is assessed and the loss divided according to that degree. In the event of one vessel receiving damage from two other negligent vessels, the damaged vessel can claim from either of the other vessels, leaving that vessel to claim from the other negligent vessel for its division of the loss.

Dk.

Deck.

Dk. L

Deck load *or* Deck loss.

d.l.o.

Shipping abbreviation, reference chartering. Dispatch loading only.

Dmge.

Damage.

D.N.O.

Broker's internal reference. Debit note only. Shows that no policy is being issued for the time being.

D/O

Delivery order.

Dock

A place where ships may anchor or berth, which is enclosed from the sea. If permanently open to the sea, it is called a " harbour ".

Dock Dues

Payments by shipowners for the use of dock facilities. They are based on the net registered tonnage of the vessel plus any cargo carried on deck.

Dock Work

The term " dock work " refers to cargo handling by dock workers. Such work is " dock work " if the workers are handling " cargo ". In the Docks Acts (1946 and 1967) the term " cargo " is defined as including " anything carried or to be carried in a ship or other vessel ".

Documents against Acceptance

Used in the credit system. When a bill of exchange is accepted the documents are transferred.

Documents of Title

The documents proving title to the goods which must pass, with the passing of title, to another person acquiring proprietary interest in the goods. The documents of title may be required by a bank as collateral security in respect of a loan advanced on the goods. The documents are (a) Bill of lading (b) Export invoice. The documents of title must be shown to the carrier by the consignee as authority to take delivery of the goods.

Dog
A securing clip on a door or hatch covering.

Dog Shapes
Wedges on launching ways that prevent the ship from sliding down the ways.

D.O.L.
Dock Owner's Liability.

Domestic Value
The value of goods at the selling price in the country of origin.

D.O.T.
Department of Overseas Trade.

Double Insurance
Double insurance occurs when two or more policies are effected on the same interest and adventure so that the total sum insured exceeds the properly insurable amount. The assured may claim on either policy but he may not retain more than the properly allowable indemnity. The maximum amount which the assured may retain is the insured value under a valued policy or the insurable value under an unvalued policy. Any amount recovered by the assured in excess of that properly allowable is deemed held in trust by the assured for the insurers. It is usual for the insurers to decide between themselves how recovery of the excess amount shall be apportioned between them. So far as the insurers are concerned each insurer is bound to bear the loss in proportion to the amount for which he is liable under his policy. Should he pay more than his due proportion he may claim the balance from the other insurer or insurers. Any premium paid by the assured in excess of the proper premium due by reason of double insurance is returnable to the assured, provided the double insurance was not effected knowingly. If the assured did effect double insurance knowingly the insurers may take action against the assured.

Doubling
An extra, strengthening, plate on a ship.

D/P
Documents against payment.

d.p.
Direct port.

d.p.r.
Daily pro rata.

D.P.S.
Data Processing Services. (See " L.D.P.S. ".)

D/R
Deposit Receipt.

Dracone
A long flexible bag which may be filled with any liquid cargo of less density than seawater, whereby it will remain afloat on seawater, or only partly submerged, when filled with cargo. This method is sometimes used for the transportation of fresh water or oil, the dracone being towed by a tug to its destination. When not carrying cargo the dracone can be maintained afloat by the introduction of air.

Draft
See " Draught ".

Draught
The depth of water required to maintain a vessel afloat. (See " Light Draught " and " Loaded Draught ".) May also be spelled " draft ".

Draught Marks
Marks cut in the stem and sternpost of a ship. A mark is cut every 12 inches and the depth from the lowest point of the keel is indicated by 6 inch figures.

Drawback
When goods have been the subject of duty payment on importation they may be re-exported, in which case the Customs authorities give an allowance, called a drawback, equal to the duty paid.

Drawing
An amount drawn against a letter of credit in respect of a claim in U.S. dollars.

D.R.C. *or* **d.r.c.**
Damage received in collision.

Dredge Clauses
Clauses in respect of insurance of dredging equipment being used in rivers, estuaries, harbours and the like.

Dredger
A vessel fitted specially for the purpose of lifting silt from the sea or river bed to clear navigation channels and harbours. Some dredgers are self-propelled, while others are without propelling

power and have to be towed into position. The silt is called "spoil" and may be dumped from the dredger into dumb barges, called "hopper" barges, which are towed out to deep water to dump the spoil. The dredger itself may be a "hopper" dredger, in which case it has hinged doors in the bottom so that it may carry the spoil out to sea itself. A "bucket" dredger is one having an endless chain of buckets which scoop up the silt and dump it into a hopper. A "dipper" dredger is one having only one bucket attached to an arm. A "grab" dredger has grabs fitted to cranes. "Suction" dredgers are used for mud or sand and may be fitted with cutters.

Drilling Rigs
See "Off Shore Oil-Drilling Rigs".

Drill Ship
A ship designed for drilling holes in the sea bed. This is one of the three main classes of drilling rig; the others being "submersible" and "jackup". Drill ships are used for deep water operations. The ship may be held in position by computer linked bow and stern thrusters.

Dry Dock
A dock specially constructed for the purpose of surveying and repairing ships. Permanent dry docks are constructed with lock gates or a caisson at one end. The vessel is floated into the dock, usually at slack water high tide and is moored carefully over keel blocks. The lock gate is closed and the water is pumped out of the dry dock. As the ship settles her stern rests on the keel blocks first and shores are wedged in (working from stern to stem) either side until the whole vessel settles down onto a cradle formed by the keel blocks and shores. A floating dry dock is fitted with immersion tanks and is towed from its home port, usually with a low tidal variance, out to deep water. There the dock is immersed to a sufficient depth to allow the ship to be floated between the immersion tanks. Once the ship is moored, the tanks are pumped out so that the dock rises once more, carrying the ship clear of the water. The dock can then be towed back into port, carrying the ship with it. A reverse process is carried out once the ship has been surveyed and/or repaired.

Dry Docking Expenses
When the ship is dry docked for repairs the cost of which is payable by the insurer the costs of entering and leaving the dock, together with the daily dock dues, are all payable by the insurer as part of the reasonable cost of repairs. The shipowner may take the opportunity to carry out repairs or alterations for his own account

without bearing part of these costs, provided the repairs are not necessary for the seaworthiness of the ship. If the repairs are necessary for the seaworthiness of the ship the shipowner must pay half of the costs of entering and leaving the dock. For each day the seaworthiness repairs are being carried out concurrently with the insurer's repairs the shipowner must pay half the daily dock dues. If the seaworthiness repairs are still in progress after the insurer's repairs have been completed the shipowner must pay the whole of the daily dock dues from then until the ship leaves the dry dock.

D/S
Days after sight. Shipping term.

Dt.
Lloyd's Register notation meaning Deep tank.

D.T.B.A. *or* **d.t.b.a.**
Date to be advised.

D.T.I.
Department of Trade and Industry.

D.T.I. Code
A code entered in documents submitted to a signing office to enable the data processing services to prepare statistics for submission to the Department of Trade and Industry. (See also " B.O.T. Code ".)

D.T.I. Returns
See " B.O.T. Coding Card ".

Dual Valuation Clause
In times of fluctuating or dropping of hull values it often occurs that repair costs are rising. The assured may wish to reduce his value in the insurance to keep pace with the lowering value. The insurers, on the other hand, may wish to maintain the higher value to avoid loss of premium income to cover partial losses. A compromise is then effected by the use of the Dual Valuation Clause which shows two values. One for total and constructive total loss purposes and a higher one for all other purposes. The premium is a compromise between the full rate and the T.L.O. rate.

Due Arrival
Arrival on time.

Due Diligence
The duty of the shipowner or cargo owner to take all reasonable and proper steps or measures to ensure the safety of his own pro-

perty and/or the property in his care and also to avoid damage to the property of others. In English, American and other laws many shipowners' protective clauses in contracts of affreightment are only upheld in court provided the shipowner exercised due diligence to prevent the happening of the damage to the cargo for which he would be liable but for the protective clause.

The interpretation of the term "due diligence" has been severely criticised from time to time. English law requires that a shipowner must ensure that every part of his ship is satisfactory and seaworthy for the carriage of the cargo and that he is responsible when one of his servants, or servants of contractors appointed by him, fails in his duty to carry out a proper inspection, but many shipowners dispute this stringent interpretation and contend that the requirement of English law is unreasonable, stating that the Brussels Convention 1924 was never intended to be interpreted so strictly when the English Carriage of Goods by Sea Act 1924 was drafted. Many countries interpret the expression " due diligence " in different ways but where there is a Statute in force the interpretation given must be in accordance with the Statute.

Dumb Barge

A barge which has no means of propulsion.

Dunnage

Timber or other means of packing used to separate cargo in stowage, thereby preventing damage during the voyage.

Duplicate Policy

An exact copy of the policy of which it is a duplicate. It is signed and sealed in the normal manner and may be used in place of the original policy for all purposes. Because it could lead to complications where there are two legally valid policies in existence underwriters usually insist on holding a letter of indemnity against the issue of a duplicate policy. (See also " Copy Policy ".)

Dutch Hull Form

The Institute set of hull clauses used in respect of Dutch vessels. Basically the clauses are the same as the Institute Time Clauses but with a four fourths collision liability clause. There is a limit to the amount that can be deducted under the machinery damage co-insurance clause.

Duty Paid Value

The gross value of cargo after all landing charges and duty have been paid.

D/V

Dual Valuation.

D/w *or* **d.w.**
Deadweight.

d.w.c.
Deadweight capacity.

D.W.T.
Deadweight tonnage. (See " Deadweight ".)

E

E

Lloyd's Register abbreviation for engine.

Each or Line

A reinsurance term used in covernotes or reinsurance orders for a fleet of vessels. A single reinsured amount is shown followed by the term "each or line". Where the ultimate signed line on any vessel is more than this amount the order becomes a flat line reinsurance of the stated amount in respect of that vessel. Where the signed line on any vessel is less than the amount stated the reinsurance is for the full signed line in respect of that vessel. (See "Full Signed Line".)

Early Signing Account

A procedure whereby a policy may be signed before the premium entry is taken down. This requires the agreement of the underwriter/s concerned. It may be used in cases where the broker has difficulty in obtaining funds from a particular country but it does not relieve the broker from his obligation to pay the premium in due course. (Ref: M.I.A. 1906 Sect. 53, Subsection 1.) In such cases a provisional advice on a non-cash basis is made to the underwriter/s in "notional" sterling. (See "Notional Sterling" and "True Sterling".)

e. & e.a.

Each and every accident.

e. & e.l.

Each and every loss.

e. & e.o.

Each and every occurrence.

E. & O.E.

Errors and omissions excepted.

Earned Premium

Premium in respect of that part of the insurance where the adventure has attached and terminated and during which the insurer was on risk. If the policy pays a total loss the whole premium is deemed earned.

E.C.

East coast.

E.C.C.P.
Maritime abbreviation for United Kingdom east coast coal ports.

E.C.G.B.
Maritime abbreviation for east coast of Great Britain.

E.C.S.A.
East Coast of South America.

E.C.U.K.
Maritime abbreviation for east coast of United Kingdom.

E.E. *or* **e.e.**
Errors excepted.

E.E.C.
European Economic Community. (Common Market.)

Effecting an Insurance
To be a party to a contract of insurance. A broker may effect an insurance on behalf of his principal. To do this the broker prepares the original slip which contains brief details of the insurance to be placed. He selects a " lead ", an insurer whose knowledge of the type of risk offered and whose standing in the market is such that other insurers will follow his lead without question, who is prepared to accept part of the insurance at a rate acceptable to the broker's principal. The " lead " writes the amount he is prepared to accept, which is called his " line ", on the slip and initials against the entry. At this stage the contract is concluded between the leading underwriter and the assured. The broker proceeds to obtain acceptances from other underwriters until he has completed the placing of the full amount required. He then notifies the assured that he has effected the insurance on his behalf.

From the time the contract is concluded with each underwriter the broker is responsible for the premium to that underwriter.

Effecting a Policy
Agreeing to be a party to a contract of insurance whereby a policy is issued. Any person who effects or helps to effect a policy where the assured has no insurable interest nor expectation of acquiring such interest is guilty of an offence under the Gambling Policies Act and is liable to a term of imprisonment not exceeding 6 months or a fine not exceeding £100, and to forfeit to the Crown any monies received under the contract.

Effective Date
Date of attachment.

e.g.
Ejusdem generis (of a like kind) *or* exempli gratia (for example).

Ejusdem Generis
" Of a like kind ". The legal doctrine which applies to the perils specified in the policy form. These perils end with " and all other perils ", which expression is subject to " ejusdem generis " and means only other perils similar in kind to those already specified.

E.L.
Employer's Liability, (which see.)

E.L.S.B.M.
Exposed location single buoy mooring (See S.B.M.). These buoys are used in exposed areas (e.g. off North Sea drilling rigs).

Embargo
A prohibition instituted by a Government regarding shipping movement, cargoes or trade.

Embodied in the Policy
To form part of the policy. To be valid at law a contract of marine insurance must, by statute, be embodied in a marine policy of insurance. Any term or condition specified in the policy is embodied, as are also the implied warranties mentioned in the Marine Insurance Act, 1906.

Empire Type Ships
Use of the word " type " in this context is really a misnomer, for during World War II ships which came under British Ministry of Transport control, other than some very small vessels, were given the prefix " Empire " to their names. These include ships built in the British Isles during the war, a number of old ships acquired from U.S.A. in 1940/41, a number of liners lent to Britain in 1941/42 and ships seized from the enemy. Therefore " Empires " were a mixture of miscellaneous ships, ranging from small to large in size. Vessels of 7,000 to 8,000 g.r.t. built 1940-1945 inclusive (which did generally conform to specific types) are excluded from the scope of the liner definition in the Institute Classification Clause. (Further details can be obtained from " Empire Ships of World War II " by W. H. Mitchell and L. A. Sawyer, published by The Journal of Commerce & Shipping Telegraph Limited.)

E.M.P.L.
Estimated Maximum Probable Loss. A reinsurance term.

Employer's Liability
Any person who pays money to another person to carry out a

service or task for him is an employer in respect of that service or task. Generally, although not in every case, where the employee suffers injury in direct connection with the work involved in the service or task the employer has a liability to recompense the employee. Insofar as such liability exists in law the employer has an insurable interest in such liability. Primarily, "employer's liability" is a non-marine insurance term but it is used in yacht and small craft insurance, also in hull insurance, although in many cases the term takes the form of an exclusion of cover in respect of employer's liability. (See "Workmen's Compensation Act", "Jones Act" and "Maintenance and Cure".) The insurance of employer's liability is compulsory in the United Kingdom and employers must display a current insurance certificate.

Endorsement

Any amendment or addition to an existing document such as a policy, certificate or cover note is made by endorsement. The endorsement giving effect to the amendment or addition is affixed to the document.

Endorsement of Bill

When a named consignee takes delivery of goods he is required to endorse the bill of lading. A "shipper's order" bill of lading requires endorsement by the shipper.

Enemies

The opposing forces in a war between nations.

Enforcement of Return

The right of the assured to a return of premium. If the assured is so entitled he may recover such return if the premium has been paid. If the premium has not been paid, the assured may deduct the return from the premium before paying. The assured has a direct right of return against the insurer whether or not the insurer has received the premium from the broker, if any.

Engagements of the Vessel

Hire or use of the vessel. The ordinary marine policy does not cover loss of hire or loss of use of the insured vessel. This risk is generally undertaken by a Protection and Indemnity Club.

If the owner of the insured vessel makes any payment for a legal liability to another vessel for loss of hire consequent on collision, such payment is recoverable under the collision clause attached to the policy, subject to any special limits imposed by the clause.

Engine Room Log

Ship's log giving details of use of engines and fuel consumption.

Engines

Ship's engines are normally referred to in marine insurance as "machinery" or, more particularly, "propelling machinery".

English Law and Practice

The rules of general average based on principles of law and set down in "The Rules of Practice of the Association of Average Adjusters".

Enhanced Ordinary Charges

These are ordinary charges enhanced by reason of damage to the cargo. For example, freight on wool is charged on the loaded weight. If the wool is landed short of destination with water damage the forwarding freight charges would be enhanced because the water has increased the weight of the wool. These charges may be minimised by substituted extra charges such as drying out the wool before reshipment. Enhanced ordinary charges are recoverable from the insurer in the same way as extra charges. The insurer is not liable for enhanced charges where they are not so enhanced as a result of an insured peril.

Entd.

Entered.

Entered Inwards

See "Entry".

Entered Outwards

See "Entry".

Entering P.O.R.

See "Costs Allowed in General Average".

Entrepot

A port, place or warehouse where transhipment takes place or where goods are held pending re-shipment.

Entry

Procedure for declaring goods to Customs for record and duty purposes. Imported goods are "entered inwards" and exported goods are "entered outwards".

Entry for Free Goods

A form required by the Customs to be completed giving details of goods which are entered free of Customs duty.

Entry for Warehousing

When dutiable goods are imported, with the intention of holding them in a bonded or Government warehouse until they are taken out for use, a Customs House form is issued and is known as an entry for warehousing.

e.o.h.p.
Except as otherwise herein provided.

E.P.A.
Environmental Protection Administration. A U.S. Governmental Authority concerned with pollution.

E.P.I.
Earned premium income *or* estimated premium income.

Erroneous Declaration
Any declaration or omission made erroneously under an open cover or floating policy may be rectified even after loss or arrival provided the error was made in good faith. (See also "Wrongful Declaration of Cargo".)

E.R.V.
Each round voyage. This term is no longer applicable to marine insurance conditions.

E.S.A.
Early Signings Account.

Escalation Clause
A clause in a shipbuilding contract that allows the agreed contract price to increase with inflation and rising costs. A similar clause, "Escalator Clause", is used in Builders' Risk insurance to allow the insured value to increase.

Escalator Clause
A clause used in builders' risk policies whereby the insured value is adjustable. (See also "Escalation Clause".)

E.S.D.
Notation in Lloyd's Register that a ship is fitted for Echo Sounding Device.

Essentials of General Average
See "General Average".

E.S.T.
Eastern Standard Time. Eastern coast of the U.S.A.

Estimated Cost of Repairs
In ascertaining a constructive total loss of ship it is necessary to estimate the cost of repairs for comparison with the arrived sound

value of the ship. In estimating it is essential that the cost of repairs is reasonable and if any of the damage is the subject of general average the contributions from other interests are not to be deducted from the estimate. Salvage operation expenses must be added and any general average contributions due from the ship. In assessing the estimated cost of repairs for general average purposes deduction must be allowed (thirds) new for old in accordance with the rules applicable to the adjustment. (See also " Tender Clause ".)

European/Mediterranean Trade

The European/Mediterranean trade limits proposed for the Merchant Shipping Act (1970) embrace any ports or places on the Scandinavian and European coastlines between Cape Kanin (Barents Sea) and the whole of the Mediterranean Sea; including, also, the North African west coast down to Cape Juby and including the Black Sea and the Sea of Azov.

Even Keel

When the water depth measured at stem and stern of a ship is level with the same numbered draught marks.

EW

Lloyd's Register indication that the ship is electrically welded.

Ex.

From or out of: e.g. Ex ship or ex warehouse. Usually applies to attachment of risk. May also be used as an abbreviation for " excluding ".

Excise

Government duty imposed on home produced goods before sale.

Excess

A deductible. An amount or percentage specified in the policy which must be exceeded before claims are payable. When the amount or percentage is exceeded only the excess of that amount or percentage is payable.

Excess Insurance

An insurance in respect of the difference between the amount acceptable to the insurer and the amount required to be covered. This may occur when a market has refused to take any more of the risk but a balance still remains to be placed. This balance is called " the excess " and is usually placed in another market but subject to the same terms as the other policy, which is called the " underlying " policy.

Excess Liabilities

See " Excess Value ".

Excess Liabilities Clause

A standard Institute set of clauses for use on policies covering General Average Contributions, Salvage Charges, Sue and Labour Charges and Collision Liability in so far as these are not recoverable under the ordinary hull policy because the contributory value is greater than the insured value. The clauses provide for a return of premium in the event of cancellation of the policy by agreement.

Excess of Line Reinsurance

A reinsurance effected when the original insurer finds himself persistently offered larger lines than he is prepared to retain. Many companies, particularly in foreign markets, find that they must accept these larger lines or lose the business altogether. In such cases the original insurer will effect a reinsurance treaty or contract on an excess of line basis. By this method he may write any line up to the aggregate of the maximum retained line and the limit of his reinsurance treaty. He retains the agreed line and declares the remainder to his reinsurer. The reinsurance premium is usually at the same net rate as the original policy, less an agreed discount to the reassured. The original insurer and reinsurer each pay claims in proportion to the part of the original line each bears.

Excess of Loss Reinsurance

A reinsurance very popular with an original insurer who wishes to retain the bulk of the premium on large written lines but wants to protect himself against losses over a fixed amount each line. The reinsurer reimburses the reassured for any loss in excess of the agreed maximum retained loss, up to the maximum amount of the reinsurance. If the total of the two limits is less than the maximum line which the reassured may wish to write, the reassured will attempt to effect a second excess of loss reinsurance to reimburse him for the excess, if any, of a 100% loss paid by his first excess reinsurer. The reinsurer under an excess of loss reinsurance does not share in small losses and is called upon to pay a proportion only of large claims. For this reason it is difficult to assess a reasonable premium to apply to the reinsurance. The premium is paid in advance as a lump sum annually.

Excess Value

This occurs in those rare cases where the vessel is insured on a value which is less than its true or contributory value. In such cases any liability of the insurer in respect of sue and labour, collision liability, salvage or general average contribution is payable taking into account the under valuation, so that a proportion of such amount remains for the account of the assured. Should the assured wish to protect himself he may effect an Excess Value (or " Increased Value and Excess Liabilities ") policy for a value which he considers by estimate to be the difference between the true value and the insured value. The premium rate is low because there is no coverage for physical damage to the vessel. In practice the shipowner sometimes combines his excess liabilities interest with a T.L.O. insurance on the vessel on a P.P.I. basis which gives him an additional amount in the event of the vessel becoming a total loss. Such P.P.I. insurances are subject to the disbursements warranty in the main hull policy.

Excluded Losses

Losses that are not recoverable under the policy. Certain losses are excluded by Statute (e.g. wilful misconduct of the assured—See M.I.A. 1906 Sect. 55). Other losses are specifically excluded in the policy wording, such as war perils, frustration, nuclear weapons, dangerous drugs, earthquakes, loss of life, personal injury.

Excuses for Delay

Delay in the prosecution of the voyage is excused in the same circumstances as for deviation. (See " Excuses for Deviation ".)

Excuses for Deviation

These excuses are specified in section 49 of the Marine Insurance Act 1906 which provides that deviation or delay in prosecuting the voyage contemplated by the policy is excused in the following circumstances.

(1) Where authorised by the policy.

(2) Where caused by circumstances beyond the control of the shipowner and master.

(3) Where reasonably necessary to comply with a warranty.

(4) Where reasonably necessary for the safety of the ship or subject matter insured.

(5) To save human life or to aid a distressed vessel where human life may be in danger.

(6) Where reasonably necessary to obtain medical or surgical aid for a person on board the ship.

(7) Where caused by barratry if this is an insured peril.

The ship must resume her course immediately the excuse ceases to operate.

Exd.
Examined.

Ex dock
A term used in the sale of goods in transit. In general, the term relates to the dock where the goods are discharged from the overseas carrier. The seller is responsible for the goods, all shipping and transit charges and his own insurance protection until the goods leave the dock area. The buyer's responsibility attaches as the seller's interest ceases.

Execution of Policy
The policy is executed when it is signed and/or sealed. Once it is executed it is a legal document. The policy may be executed at the time the contract is concluded (i.e. when the insurance is placed) or at any later date.

Ex facie
In accordance with the documents.

Ex gratia
Act of grace.

Ex Gratia Payment
A payment made by the insurer in respect of a claim for which he is not legally liable. The insurer may make such a payment as a sign of goodwill or to accommodate a valued assured. It is important to note that a reinsurer is not obliged to follow an ex gratia payment made by the original insurer.

Exoneration from Liability
An American shipping term. More often seen as "Exoneration from or limitation of liability". Basically, this means the same as "Limitation of liability" (which see). The effect is that the shipowner involved in a collision dispute denies liability whilst jointly claiming limitation in event of the Court refusing to accept his plea of exoneration.

Expectation
Any representation made in good faith as an expectation is deemed to be true and the insurer cannot avoid the policy if the expectation later proves to be untrue.

Expenses at Port of Refuge
Necessary to define for the purpose of general average. The expenses allowed in general average vary dependent on whether the adjustment is in accordance with English Law or the York-Antwerp Rules and whether the reason for entering the Port of Refuge is

following accidental damage or general average sacrifice. Whether under English Law or the York-Antwerp Rules, if the vessel enters the Port of Refuge following general average sacrifice, all expenses of bearing up to port, entering, port dues, discharge of cargo, cargo warehouse expenses, reloading of cargo, outward port charges and returning to point of the general average act are allowed as general average. The expenses allowed are the same under the York-Antwerp Rules if the vessel enters the Port of Refuge following accidental damage but not all these expenses are allowed under English Law in the same circumstances. English Law allows expenses only up to the attainment of safety and unloading the cargo when the vessel enters the Port of Refuge following accidental damage.

Expenses Form

A form detailing insurance clauses applicable to additional expenses insurance in connection with strikes, riots and civil commotions.

Expenses Incurred for Preservation of Property

If insured property is in danger whereby a claim might arise under the policy the insurer agrees to reimburse the assured for any reasonable expense incurred for the preservation of the property. The assured must always act as a prudent uninsured person would act and any expenditure must be such as he would pay for the preservation of his own property were it not insured. If the expenses are incurred short of destination by the assured or his servants for his own property alone they are sue and labour charges. If they are incurred at destination in a like manner they are particular charges. If they are incurred for the common benefit they are general average expenses. If they are incurred as a liability to a third party for an act of salvage, they are salvage charges. Expenses in defending a legal claim for which the insurer would be liable are also recoverable from the insurer provided the action is with his consent.

Expenses of Removal

Where a vessel is removed to another port for repairs on the underwriter's instructions the expenses of removal and return to the original port are for the underwriter's account. Any expense saved by the earning of freight or other means must be credited to the underwriter's account. Bunkers, crew's wages and provisions during the removal are included in the expenses. If any stores or fuel are used in carrying out underwriter's repairs, these are payable by the underwriter as part of the cost of repairs.

Experience

The past claims experience of the assured. When a broker

approaches an insurer he must be prepared to disclose the experience of the assured to the insurer. Failure to advise the insurer correctly on this material fact, on enquiry, amounts to non-disclosure and the insurer may avoid the policy from inception unless the difference between what was stated and what was true merely diminished the risk.

Explosion

Basically explosion may be considered as synonymous with fire, so that explosion on board a vessel would be an insured peril. On the other hand, explosion emanating from outside the vessel could be argued as not being an insured peril. So far as hull insurance is concerned the question does not arise since the " Inchmaree Clause " in the standard hull clauses provides that damage to the ship directly caused by explosion, whether on the ship or elsewhere, is covered by the policy subject to the policy deductible. The Institute Cargo Clauses (W.A. and F.P.A.) provide that loss or damage reasonably attributable to explosion is recoverable; ignoring the principle of proximate cause and any franchise or F.P.A. warranty.

Export

To export. To send goods overseas either sold or for sale. An export is a particular piece of merchandise so sent.

Export Credits Guarantee

A special type of insurance, designed solely for the protection of U.K. exporters, which provides cover against insolvency of the buyer, revolution or civil disturbance in the buyer's country as well as many other causes of non-payment for goods. These policies are issued by a separate Department of the Government but under the auspices of the Department of Trade and Industry. The Department also assists in financing projects, providing specific groups of insurance for large individual export contracts, such as shipbuilding for export. Details can be obtained from the Export Section of the Department of Trade and Industry.

Export Factoring

A service whereby the factor buys his client's (exporter's) invoiced debts and takes responsibility for all credit control, sales accounting and debt collection. The effect is that the factor takes over the debt at a discount and in return bears the possible non-payment or any loss resulting from market fluctuations in exchange rates. This is a growing ancillary service in the export field.

Export Invoice

A document of title. This is the document which shows the quality, type, quantity and price of the goods.

Express
Specify in writing.

Express Authority
Authority given in writing.

Express Warranty
A warranty is a promise by the assured that a thing shall or shall not be done or that a state of affairs will or will not exist. A warranty may be express or implied. An express warranty is one that is specified in the policy. Frequently, express warranties are incorporated in the insurance to maintain the risk as contemplated by the premium charged and breach of such warranties is held covered subject to notice to the insurer and adjustment of the policy conditions and premium.

Ex. quay
Expression in a sale contract whereby all charges are the responsibility of the buyer once the goods are delivered to the quay.

Exs.
Expenses. Sometimes used as an abbreviation for " Excesses ".

Ex. ship
In a sale contract the obligation of the seller is to pay freight to destination if agreed " ex ship ". The insurable interest is generally a seller's interest on the sea voyage in such cases, the buyer's interest attaching " ex ship ".

Extended Coverage
An American non-marine expression which has no connection with the marine extended cover.

Extended Cover Clause
This cargo clause is now obsolete; its terms being incorporated in the Transit Clause.

Extended Protest
The master makes a " protest " when an accident has occurred. If a court action results a more detailed protest is required and is called an " extended protest ".

Extent of Insurer's Liability
The maximum amount recoverable for a loss under a policy is the insured value on a valued policy or the insurable value, limited to the sum insured, on an unvalued policy. The extent of the insurer's liability is called the " Measure of Indemnity ". If more than

one insurer is liable under the policy, each insurer is individually liable for his specified proportion of the measure of indemnity. (For specific details see " Total Loss ", " Partial Loss " and " Constructive Total Loss ".)

Extent of Interest

The maximum amount financially which the person having an insurable interest may lose in respect of such interest.

Extra Charges

Charges incurred in proving a claim. These are not recoverable under a policy unless the claim is payable. These charges cannot be added to damage to reach the policy franchise, if any, but once the franchise is attained without the charges they may be added to the claim. Certain extra charges may be paid by agreement even without a claim as in the case of the expense of sighting the bottom after stranding. But the assured cannot claim extra charges without this agreement in the policy if there is no claim.

Extraneous Risks

Cargo risks which are not embraced by the perils specified in the policy. Extraneous risks are not covered by a cargo " W.A." or " F.P.A." policy. An " All Risks " policy includes extraneous risks. Extraneous risks need not be only maritime perils, nor need they be incidental to navigation. Examples:—Negligence, hooks, oil, rain, bilgewater, freshwater, theft, pilferage, short delivery, non delivery, sweat, contact with other cargo, leakage or breakage. Claims from extraneous risks, when insured, are always payable without reference to the franchise, if any.

Extraordinary Expenditure

See " Extraordinary Sacrifice ".

Extraordinary Sacrifice

Term used in determining general average. Ordinary sacrifice or expenditure is such as a master or shipowner is liable to carry out or incur under his obligations to carry the goods and deliver them in accordance with the contract of affreightment. The use of spare fuel carried for an auxiliary engine comes in this category. Extraordinary sacrifice or expenditure is any other sort of sacrifice or expenditure such as cargo or part of the ship burned as fuel or the use of tugs to draw the vessel off a strand. If all the other essentials for general average are present extraordinary sacrifice or expenditure is allowed in general average.

Ex warehouse

A term for the sale of goods. The term usually relates to the seller's warehouse. The buyer is responsible for the goods and all charges from the time they leave the seller's warehouse. The title to the goods usually passes to the buyer at this point, subject to agreement to the conditions for payment for the goods, and insurable interest during the whole period of transit is vested in the buyer who normally arranges his own insurance. Where the term relates to a port warehouse or to a warehouse other than that of the seller the seller remains responsible for the goods until they leave such port or other warehouse, arranging his own insurance up to the time his interest passes.

F

F.

Abbreviation used in Lloyd's Register to denote "forecastle". When seen on the side of a vessel next to the loadline marking the letter indicates the freshwater loadline.

f

Lloyd's Register abbreviation for "forward".

F.A. *or* **f.a.**

Free alongside.

F.A.A.

Free of all average. Excluding all partial loss. Generally only applied to cargo insurance.

f.a.c.

A shipping term providing that the vessel must be loaded or unloaded as fast as possible. Stands for "fast as can".

Fac.

Facultative.

Face Amount

An American expression denoting the amount for which the insurer is liable under the policy.

Face of Cargo

A shipping term used in respect of stowage. Where cargo is stowed in such a manner that any side of it is exposed and unsupported by either the side of the ship or by other cargo the exposed side is called the "face of the cargo". This face should be properly braced to prevent the cargo shifting. Particular attention should be given to the strength of the bracing where the face overlooks other cargo which may be damaged by contact in event of movement of the facing cargo.

Fac./Oblig.

Facultative/Obligatory. A reinsurance term whereby the reinsurer is obliged within the terms of a cover or treaty to accept reinsurances of facultative acceptances by the reinsured.

Factoring

See "Export Factoring".

Facultative
The term derives from the word "faculty". Facultative means the "right of option", that is, the right of an underwriter to decide (in insurance or reinsurance) whether or not to accept a risk. Single named risks (e.g. single voyages) are effected on a facultative basis whereby the underwriter assesses the risk. Most hull insurance is effected facultatively but the majority of cargo insurance is effected on an "open cover" basis, whereby the underwriter agrees in advance to accept all shipments coming within the period and scope of the cover (See "Open Cover"). The acceptance by the underwriter of declarations under an open cover is obligatory, rather than facultative.

Facultative Reinsurance
An insurer may protect himself from excessive liability by a permanent reinsurance open cover or he may commit a great part of his business to a Treaty reinsurance. Occasionally, however, he may not be protected by either of these methods but requires reinsurance of a particular acceptance. He effects this through a broker and it is called a facultative reinsurance.

Faggot
A steel measurement of weight, being 120 lb.

Failure of Consideration
Occurs when the risk, in respect of which the insurer has accepted the premiums, fails to attach. The premium paid is returnable in full to the assured, except where there is fraud.

Failure to Complete
When the broker has placed with insurers the full amount to be insured he is said to have completed the placing. The broker is not obliged to complete but he must use all his skill and knowledge in endeavouring to do so. If, despite his efforts, he fails to complete the placing he must immediately notify his principal of his failure. Provided the broker receives the order within a reasonable time before attachment of the risk he must notify his principal of failure to complete before the risk attaches or he may be held liable for negligence.

Failure to Disclose
See "Non-Disclosure".

Falling Market
When the value of goods is falling. The insurer is not affected by falling or rising markets because claims are calculated on "gross" values. He would be affected if "net" values were used.

F & A.P.

Fire and Allied Perils are non-marine risks which are sometimes applied to accumulations of cargo on land and covered in the Marine market.

f & d.

Freight and demurrage.

F.A.P.

French abbreviation which means the same as F.P.A. or Free of particular average. Franc d'Avarie Particulière.

f.a.q.

Fair average quality. Sale contract term.

F.A.R.

Same as F.C.A.R.

F.A.S. *or* **f.a.s.**

Free alongside steamer (or ship). A term of sale for goods in transit. The seller is responsible for the goods and all charges until the goods are delivered alongside the overseas vessel to await loading. The buyer's responsibility attaches as the seller's interest ceases. Whether or not the seller arranges insurance for himself beyond F.A.S. depends on the terms of payment for the goods, for the seller's insurable interest continues until title to the goods passes to the buyer. (See also " f.o.q. ".)

Fathom

Measure of depth of water being 6 feet. May also apply to 6 ft. lengths of timber stacked in a 6 ft. × 6 ft. pile.

Faulty Design—Builders' Risk

A clause providing that the insurer shall not be liable for loss resulting purely from faulty design. The clause usually incorporates a further clause limiting the P & I cover in the policy to the sum insured by the policy.

fbd.

Freeboard.

F.B.I.

Federation of British Industries.

F.C. & S. Clause

See " Free of Capture and Seizure ".

F.C.A.R.

Warranted free of claim for accident reported. A warranty required by an insurer when accepting an insurance where the vessel has been reported as suffering an accident. The insurer accepts the risk but not any loss arising out of the reported accident.

Fch.
Franchise.

F. chgs.
Forwarding charges.

F.C.I.I.
Fellow of the Chartered Insurance Institute.

F.C.S.S.R.C.C.
Warranted Free of Capture and Seizure etc. and of Strikes, Riots and Civil Commotions.

F.C.V.
Full contract value *or* Full completed value. A term relating to a Builders' Risk insurance.

f.d.
Free delivery. Sale contract term that the goods will be delivered by the seller free of charge.

F.D.O.
For declaration purposes only. A form of policy, used a great deal in treaty and contract reinsurance, where a nominal premium only is paid in advance. Since the premium is nominal it is very small and no actual payment is made. As bordereaux are declared subsequently the proper premium is paid, but the policy itself is signed on the "F.D.O." basis without any actual payment of premium.

Fear of a Peril
Insurers are liable for losses proximately caused by an insured peril. Fear of a peril does not constitute a peril so that insurers are not liable for a loss proximately caused by an uninsured peril, even though the loss would not have arisen but for fear of an insured peril. This principle does not absolve insurers from their liability for sue and labour charges, salvage charges or general average contribution when properly incurred to prevent loss from a factual or imminent peril.

Federal Longshoremen's etc. Clause
Federal longshoremen's and harbour workers' Compensation Clause. This is an American clause covering legal liability of shipowners in respect of compensation to harbour workers.

ferm.
Fermentation.

Fender
Material (e.g. rope or rubber) suspended along the side of a ship or along a wharf to minimise contact damage to the ship.

F.f.a.
Free from alongside.

F.F.O.
Fixed and floating objects.

F.G.A.
Foreign General Average.

F.I.A.
Full interest admitted.

f.i.b.
Free into barge *or* free into bunkers.

F.I.C.S.
Fellow of the Institute of Chartered Shipbrokers.

Fidley
Top of a boiler casing.

Fighting Ship
A " fighting ship " is a vessel sponsored by a conference line agreement to discourage competition from non-conference vessels. The ship is made available to shippers for loading at the same place and time as the non-conference ship. Reduced freight rates are offered to encourage shippers to use the conference ship instead of the other ship. If the conference shipowner loses freight by his ship being used in this way the conference reimburses him for his loss. Many conferences disagree with this type of action and some strictly prohibit the practice which is gradually dying out.

F.I.L.
Foreign Insurance Legislation.

F.I.L. Codes
Alphabetical codes used in data processing to prepare statistical information for the Committee of Lloyd's and others. The system enables statistics for overseas business to be maintained; so that returns can be prepared, where required, for foreign Governmental Authorities and for the Comptroller of Finance at Lloyd's.

Finance Act 1959

So far as marine insurance is concerned this Act abolished marine stamp duty on policies and replaced it with a head charge of 6d each policy. It also repealed Article 23 Sub. Sects. 2 to 5 and Article 25 Sub. Sect. 2 of the Marine Insurance Act 1906 whereby (1) It removed the necessity to specify in the policy (a) The subject matter insured and risk insured against. (b) The voyage and/or period of time. (c) The sum or sums insured. (d) The name or names of the insurers; and (2) It abolished the restriction limiting a marine policy for a period of time, to 12 months. Subsequently, stamp duty on marine policies was abolished altogether in 1970.

Financial Guarantee

An insurance to reimburse an unpaid seller for the price of the goods. In effect it is a guarantee of payment and is generally unacceptable in the insurance market.

Fine Arts Insurance

An insurance on art treasures such as paintings etc.

F. Inst. F.F.

Fellow of the Institute of Freight Forwarders. (Formerly, F.S.F. —Fellow of the Institute of Shipping and Forwarding Agents.)

f.i.o

Free in and out. Shipping term. (See " Free in and Out ".)

Fir.

Firkin.

Fire

A peril of the sea, including fire from lightning and including smoke damage. In cargo insurance fire losses are not subject to the franchise but are subject to the policy deductible in hull insurance. (See also " Heating " and " Spontaneous Combustion ".)

First Interest Reinsurance

The same as a flat line reinsurance.

First Loss Reinsurance

A reinsurance whereby the reinsurer agrees to reimburse the original insurer in respect of all claims paid on the original policy up to an agreed fixed amount on a faculative reinsurance, or up to an agreed amount in respect of any one loss on an open cover or treaty first loss reinsurance.

First Surplus Reinsurance

The same as a first excess reinsurance. The original insurer reinsures on this basis when he accepts lines larger than the liability he wishes to retain. This form of reinsurance is usually effected by way of a Treaty reinsurance contract. The original insurer cedes all amounts in excess of the agreed retention to the reinsurer, who accepts them up to the limit of the reinsurance any one line.

Claims are paid directly to the assured by the original insurer, who is reimbursed by the reinsurer in the proportion the ceded line bears to the whole acceptance on the original.

First Three

Means the first three leading underwriters on a broker's slip. It does not necessarily mean the first three syndicates or, where applicable, companies. Where one underwriter writes for more than one syndicate or company the group is considered as one leader only. The term is used in connection with slip agreements.

Fishing Gear Clause

A clause in the Institute Fishing Vessel Clauses (I.F.V.C. No. 12) which excludes loss of or damage to fishing gear during or as a result of fishing operations. The gear is covered for accidental loss or damage from perils expressed in the policy form (e.g. heavy weather) but not for loss or damage from perils such as are covered by the Inchmaree Clause (e.g. negligence).

Fishing Vessel Clauses

A set of 30 clauses published by the Institute of London Underwriters in 1971 for attachment to time policies insuring fishing vessels against partial and total loss. The main clauses in the I.T.C. are incorporated in the I.F.V.C., with special clauses relating to the particular trade of the vessel (e.g. Fishing Gear Clause, Catch, etc. Exclusion). Incorporated are a 4/4ths R.D.C., a P & I clause and a Removal of Wreck Clause. The policy deductible is applied to all partial loss claims and to claims under the R.D.C., S & L, GA, Salvage and P & I sections of the policy. There is a Strikes, etc. Exclusion Clause in addition to the customary war, etc. exclusion clauses, the latter being paramount clauses as in the I.T.C. It should be noted that an amendment (Cl. 38) exists for use in conjunction with the I.F.V.C.; this amendment emphasises the exclusion of liability in respect of pollution in the case of R.D.C. and P & I claims.

f.i.w.

Free into wagons.

Fixed Objects

Term used in respect of liability insurance on hulls to differentiate between "collision", which is contact between two or more vessels, and ordinary contact by the ship with anything other than a vessel. In this way anything other than a vessel is embraced by the term "objects". "Fixed objects" are those which do not move, such as piers and wharves, including fastened buoys. Liability to objects is not covered by the collision clause in a hull policy.

Flag of Convenience

For the purpose of registration under a National flag a vessel must comply with and maintain certain standards regarding equipment, fire and life saving appliances, crew's quarters, victualling and safety regulations.

These standards are less stringent under some flags. The flag being the National flag of the Country with which the vessel is registered. Where a vessel registers with a Country which applies relaxed regulations purely for the purpose of attracting registration, such flag is called a "Flag of Convenience". (See also "F.O.M.".)

Flash Point

The temperature at which a substance or the vapour therefrom will ignite. The lower the flash point the higher the fire risk. The minimum flash point allowed for fuel in a passenger ship is 140 deg. F. (Until recently this was 150 deg. F.) Fuel with a flash point higher than the permitted limit must not be used in a passenger ship.

Flat Cancellation

Cancellation of an insurance outright from inception.

Flat Line Reinsurance

A reinsurance whereby the reinsured agrees to reimburse the original insurer for any claim paid on the original policy up to the fixed amount of the reinsurance. This may be the whole of the original insurer's acceptance or a part of it. If the reinsurance is for only part of the original acceptance the original insurer must himself bear the excess part of any claim which is more than the amount of the reinsurance. It is, in effect, the same as a first line reinsurance. It frequently occurs that the original insurer reinsures only part of his acceptance on a flat line basis but due to short closing the amount closed is less than the reinsurance amount. In such cases the whole of the closed line is deemed reinsured, the reassured retaining none of the premium and being reimbursed for the whole of any claim. The original insurer and the reinsurer each bears his respective proportion of a claim if the shortclosing of the original insurance is for more than the reinsured amount.

F.L.E.

Fire, Lightning and Explosion.

Fleet Policy
A single hull policy covering all the vessels owned by one assured.

Floating Dock
See " Dry Dock ".

Floating Policy
This type of cargo policy is gradually falling into disuse, its function in practice being replaced by the open cover procedure. The policy is for a fixed amount sufficient to cover several shipments the details of which are declared at a later date. It has no time limit but is usually subject to a cancellation clause. The majority of floating policies are issued in conjunction with open covers. Such open covers are customarily effected as " always open " but where the open cover has a time limit the floating policy is, of course, subject to the same time limit. Declarations are made as shipments go forward and the amount insured reduced by the value of each declaration. The policy remains in force until the amount insured is exhausted unless it is cancelled by either party giving the requisite notice of cancellation in accordance with the cancellation clause. To protect the insurer from accumulation of risk in one place at any one time, the policy is subject to a limit in any one vessel and, usually, in addition a limit in any one location prior to shipment. All declarations coming within the scope of the policy must be accepted by the insurer. Equally the assured must declare *all* shipments as they go forward. He cannot elect to insure any shipment elsewhere nor send it uninsured. A valuation clause stipulates the value to be used for shipments lost or damaged before declaration. A classification clause limits cover to goods carried by approved vessels. This type of policy is advantageous to the assured who wishes to know his goods are covered in advance at fixed rates provided he is prepared to pay a lump sum premium in advance. The premium paid is on a deposit basis and is adjusted to the correct premium when the policy expires. (See also " Open Policy ".)

Floors
Vertical plates fitted transversely in a ship's double bottom.

Flotsam
Goods lost from a vessel which remain afloat.

Flour All Risks Clauses
Trade clauses used for the insurance of flour. The clauses cover all claims whatsoever arising from all dangers and hazards of transportation, including loss from short weight through bags being broken or torn in transit. The clauses specifically exclude inherent

vice or nature of the subject matter insured; they also exclude the perils weevils, insects, worms and grubs. The average warranty provides for a franchise of £2 on any one brand arising on any one vessel, otherwise claims are payable irrespective of percentage.

Fm
Fathom.

F.O.
Firm offer.

F.O.B. *or* **f.o.b.**
Free on board. This term of sale for goods in transit can be applied to various points in the period of transit—
e.g. (1) F.O.B.—motor or other overland transport at the seller's warehouse.
    (2) F.O.B.—lighter at port of shipment.
    (3) F.O.B.—overseas carrying vessel.
    (4) F.O.B.—discharge lighter at destination.
    (5) F.O.B.—destination warehouse.

Responsibility for the goods and charges attaching thereto changes from seller to buyer at the time the goods are loaded " on board " at the particular point named and, subject to the terms of payment for the goods, the insurable interest in the goods is transferred at the same time. Thus in (3) above the seller's responsibility and interest passes to the buyer as the goods are loaded onto the overseas carrier. Each party in the sale contract arranges his own insurance for the period of transit during which he has an interest; except where the insurance is arranged outside the terms of the sale contract; in which case the seller might arrange insurance for the whole period of transit and assign the policy to the buyer to collect the claim for any insured loss occurring during the whole period of transit. Where payment for the goods takes place after the goods have passed the F.O.B. point the seller may prefer to arrange the whole insurance in case the interest reverts to him due to non-payment for the goods.

F.O.C.
Flag of Convenience (which see).

F.O.C. *or* **f.o.c.**
Free of claims (see also F.C.A.R.) *or* free of charge, *or* free of cost, (which see).

F.O.D. abs.
Free of damage absolutely.

Follow the Fortunes Clause

A clause in a reinsurance policy or agreement whereby the reinsurer agrees to follow the fortunes of the reinsured, leaving the original insurer free to negotiate and settle claims without reference to his reinsurer, thus an ex gratia settlement by the reinsured could be claimed from the reinsurer since the agreement relieves the original insurer from the need to show that he has a legal liability for a loss before he can recover from his reinsurer.

Follow the Lead

When a broker places an insurance he first obtains a "lead" on the slip. This is an insurer who is sufficiently well known as being versed in the particular type of risk involved, that other insurers will be prepared to "follow his lead" and accept part of the insurance.

F.O.M. *or* f.o.m.

Flag, ownership or management. Refers to vessels and is of concern to cargo insurers who wish not to cover cargo which is in control of vessels of a certain flag, ownership or management. Hull insurers are also interested in the F.O.M. of the insured vessel. (See " Sale of Vessel Clause ".)

f.o.q.

Free on quay. Sale term meaning same as f.a.s.

f.o.r.

Free on rail. Sale term providing that interest of seller ceases as soon as goods have been loaded into the railway wagon or truck. Same as f.i.w. or f.o.t.

Force Majeure

An act of God. Any occurrence completely beyond human control and which could not have been avoided by foresight. An earthquake for example.

Forebody

The part of a ship that is forward of midships.

Forecastle

The raised forward part of a ship. Derived from the days when the upper forward part of the ship was built as a sort of battlemented fort for the purpose of defence and/or attack.

Forefoot

The lower part of a ship's stern. The forefoot is the part that curves to meet the keel.

Foreign General Average
General average to be adjusted in accordance with the law of the Country where the adjustment is drawn up. It is usual in contracts of affreightment and policies to provide for both foreign general average and York-Antwerp Rules. Most adjustments are settled on York-Antwerp Rules in practice.

Foreign Jurisdiction
When it is agreed that claims under a policy shall be settled under the jurisdiction of another Country it is usual to attach to the policy the foreign jurisdiction clause. The title of the clause varies according to the country where jurisdiction is required. e.g. " Belgian Jurisdiction Clause ". (See also " Forum Conveniens ".)

Foreign Legislation
Insurance laws and regulations existing in countries outside the United Kingdom, compliance with which is necessary. (See " F.I.L. Codes ".)

Fore Peak
A watertight compartment at the extreme forward end of a ship.

Forepeak Tank
See " Peak Tanks ".

Forestay
A wire stay fitted as a support to the fore side of a mast. (See also " Backstay " and " Triatic Stay ".)

Forklift
A motorised vehicle with forklike lifting apparatus, used for cargo handling.

Form of policy
The form of policy used in practice for marine insurance is called the S.G. form, so called because the basic form which appears in the schedule to the Marine Insurance Act 1906 was designed to cover both Ship and Goods. The form used in practice is exactly the same as the S.G. form in the Act except that it is separated into hull and cargo.

Form of Subrogation
An authority signed by the assured which enables the insurer to pursue his subrogation rights without the necessity of proving his entitlement to the rights.

Fort Type Ships

Vessels built during World War II in Canadian shipyards for Canadian and British account, also vessels purchased from Canada by U.S.A. There are various types of "Forts" (all basically similar) but they may be recognised by the "Fort" prefix to the ship's original name. "Forts" are excluded from the scope of the "liner" definition in the Classification Clause. (Further details may be obtained from "Wartime Standard Ships—Vol. 2." by W. H. Mitchell and L. A. Sawyer, published by The Journal of Commerce & Shipping Telegraph Limited.)

Fortuitous Accident

See "Fortuity".

Fortuity

Accident or any loss or damage which is not an inevitability.

Forum Conveniens

The country in which circumstances demand that a legal action should be founded. In some countries, notably America and Scotland, there is a legal doctrine of "forum non-conveniens" which allows a plaintiff to insist on the case being founded in that country despite facts that show it would be more suitable for it to be founded elsewhere (e.g. the collision occurred in foreign waters). The legal doctrine of "forum non-conveniens" does not apply in English law where the plaintiff must show that there would be a "solid advantage" in bringing the action in England before an English Court will listen to arguments on the matter. (See "Jurisdiction".)

Forum Non-Conveniens

See "Forum Conveniens".

Forwarding Charges

Expenses of carriage of cargo from a port of refuge, or place of forced discharge, to destination. Such charges are recoverable under the Institute Cargo Clauses, "All Risks", "W.A." and "F.P.A."

f.o.s.

Free on steamer *or* free on ship.

f.o.t.

Free on truck.

Foul Bill of Lading

A bill of lading which has been qualified by the carrier to show that the goods were not sound when loaded. Usually termed a "dirty" bill of lading.

F.P.
Floating policy.

F.P.A.
Free of particular average. Underwriters are not liable for partial loss, other than general average loss. Usually understood to mean the same as Institute F.P.A. Conditions. (See "Institute Cargo Clauses F.P.A.".)

F.P.A. abs
Free of particular average absolutely. Underwriters are not liable for partial loss, other than general average loss. The term "absolutely" is used to make it clear that the insurance does not contain any terms which break the F.P.A. warranty as it does in the Institute F.P.A. clauses. There is a standard set of Institute Hull Clauses on F.P.A. abs. conditions for both time and voyage insurances. (See also "Free of Particular Average Absolutely".)

F.P.A. & Breakdown
Free of particular average but covering breakdown of refrigerating machinery of not less than 24 hours. Applies to insurance on frozen products, mainly meat. (See "Frozen Meat Clauses".) When applied to other interests it is understood to mean the same cover as the Institute F.P.A. clauses plus loss or damage due to breakdown of refrigerating machinery for not less than 24 consecutive hours.

F.P.A. & loss
A slip expression meaning F.P.A.u.c.b. (which see).

F.P.A. Clause
A clause in a policy defining the extent of cover provided on "total loss only" terms. The term is customarily used for cargo insurances, but in certain instances is used in hull insurance. (See "F.P.A.", "Institute Cargo Clauses F.P.A." and "F.P.A. abs".)

F.P.A. Cover
Institute Cargo Clauses F.P.A.

F.P.A.u.c.b.
Free of Particular Average unless caused by. (See "F.P.A. unless caused by".)

F.P.A. unl.
Free of particular average unless.

F.P.A. unless

Free of particular average unless. Means the insurance is on the same terms as provided by the average clause in the Institute F.P.A. clauses.

F.P.A. unless caused by

Free of particular average " unless caused by ". Means the insurance is on the same conditions as provided by the average clause in the Institute F.P.A. clauses, but whereas the franchise in these clauses is broken if the vessel *is* stranded, sunk or burnt, under the F.P.A. u.c.b. conditions only damage *caused by* the vessel being stranded, sunk or burnt breaks the franchise. The remainder of the clause applies equally to both conditions whether " unless " or " u.c.b.".

F.P.I.L.

Full premium if lost (which see).

F.P.I.L. I.P.

Full premium if lost from an insured peril. Means the same as F.P.I.L. P.I.A.

F.P.I.L. P.I.A.

Full premium if lost from a peril insured against (see " Full Premium if Lost ".)

FPT

Fore peak tank. FPT is the abbreviation used in Lloyd's Register.

F/R

Shipping term. Freight Release.

Franchise

An amount or percentage specified in the policy which must be reached before a claim is payable. Once the amount or percentage is attained the claim is payable in full. In some foreign insurances the term may be used to denote a deductible franchise which is not the same as a " franchise ". (See " Deductible "). In the absence of any specified franchise elsewhere in the policy the " memorandum " franchise applies. When the insurer is prepared to dispense with the franchise it is customary to insert into the policy the words " irrespective of percentage ". In modern English practice the franchise is no longer used in hull insurance, being replaced with a deductible.

Franchise Endorsement Clause

A hull clause introduced in 1969, as an interim measure, where underwriters agreed to apply a franchise in place of a policy deductible (the use of a deductible in place of a franchise in hull policies became standard in 1969—See " Hull Policy Deductibles "). This clause has been withdrawn.

Franco
Sale term meaning all charges paid up to delivery of the goods to the buyer.

Fraud
Fraud by the assured vitiates a contract of marine insurance and the insurer is not liable to return any premium paid.

F.R.C.
Free of reported casualty.

F.R.C.C.
Free of riots and civil commotions.

Free Alongside Ship
A sale term for goods in transit which means that the seller's interest in the goods ceases when the goods are delivered alongside the vessel. Loading risk being the interest of the buyer.

Free Alongside Steamer
See " F.A.S. ".

Freeboard
The depth from the underside of the main deck to the waterline.

Freeboard Deck
Deck from which the freeboard is measured.

Free in and out
Chartering term whereby the charterer of a vessel under voyage charter agrees to pay the costs of loading and discharging the cargo.

Freeing Port
An opening in the bulwark which allows water taken on deck to flow off the ship.

Free of
Underwriters have no liability in respect of claims.

Free of Average Warranty
A clause appearing in the policy warranting that the policy shall be free of claim under a fixed percentage or amount. (See " Franchise ".)

Free of Capture and Seizure
The marine insurance term for " excluding war perils ". The

abbreviation is F.C. & S. and the standard clause used is generally referred to as the F.C. & S. clause. At an Extraordinary General Meeting of the members of Lloyd's in June 1898 a resolution was passed to incorporate the F.C. & S. clause in all Lloyd's marine cargo policies and this became effective on July 1st 1898. At a similar meeting on 25th January 1899 it was agreed that thenceforth all agreements (which include slips, of course) shall be deemed to be subject to the F.C. & S. clause unless the contrary has been specified in the slip or agreement and agreed by the insurer.

The F.C. & S. clause is now incorporated in all marine policies and all sets of marine clauses and is a paramount clause in a hull policy. Its purpose is to make it clear that the policy excludes losses proximately cause by war, hostile acts or warlike attempts, whether or not there has been a declaration of war. The wording of the clause makes it clear that if the loss is proximately caused by a marine peril such loss is not excluded by the clause even if the vessel, or any other vessel involved in the accident, is engaged in a warlike operation.

In cargo insurance the perils excluded by the clause may be reinstated in the policy by agreement with the insurer and payment of a scale additional premium. In addition to the reinstatement other war perils are incorporated into the policy and it is customary to incorporate strikes risks at the same time. Hull war risks are customarily insured under a separate policy. There are standard sets of war clauses and strikes clauses for both hull and cargo risks.

Free of Cost

The abbreviation F.O.C. (or f.o.c.) meaning " Free of Cost " or " Free of Charge " is to be seen occasionally in facultative reinsurance orders. It means that the reinsured is not to be charged with brokerage and stems from the days when such charges were made against the reinsured. The practice has almost died out since most brokers now obtain brokerage from the reinsurer, thus having no need to charge the reinsured. Occasionally the abbreviation may be seen on original slips denoting that the insurer is not prepared to allow a discount on the premium indicated. Where no discount is mentioned on the slip and in the absence of " F.O.C." or, in the case of a reinsurance slip " O.N.R." (which see), the standard market discount is chargeable to the insurer.

Free of Damage Absolutely

The insurer is not liable for partial loss whether particular or general average. Used mainly in hull insurance. There is a standard set of Institute clauses on these terms which extend the cover to provide for contributions to general average.

Free of Particular Average

The insurer is not liable for partial loss other than general average loss. Customarily the term is applied to a much wider cover which follows the lines of the Institute Cargo Clauses F.P.A., (which see.)

Free of Particular Average Absolutely

The insurer is not liable for partial loss, other than general average loss. The term is used to make it clear that the policy conditions are more limited than ordinary " free of particular average " conditions. It is unusual to use this form of cover for cargo insurance, but there is a standard set of Institute clauses on these conditions for hulls. These standard clauses also exclude general average damage to the hull of the ship, except damage caused in extinguishing a fire or by contact during salvage operations.

Free of S.R.C.C.

Free of strikes, riots and civil commotions. This clause is contained in cargo policies and in cargo, freight, port risk and builder's risk clauses. It does not in fact exclude strike etc. risks from the policy because the basic policy form does not contain these perils in the first place. The clause is merely there to make it clear to the assured that the policy does not cover these risks. If the F.S.R.C.C. Clause is deleted this does not mean that the risks of strikes etc. are implied into the policy. It is necessary to specify the risks in the policy. This is done, in practice, by attaching the relevant strikes clauses. The scale war premium for cargo includes the additional premium due for strikes etc. so that both war and strikes risks are attached to the policy at the same time. A slightly lower scale is applied if the strikes etc. risks alone are required. It is also customary to cover war and strikes risks in one policy on hulls and other interests. (See also " F.S.R. & C.C. Clause ".)

Free on Board

See F.O.B.

Free Overside

Sale contract term providing that the seller's interest ceases when goods are discharged from the vessel.

Freight

The remuneration due to a carrier for the carriage of cargo. In insurance it also includes profit derivable by a shipowner in carrying his own goods. It does not include money earned on deck cargo nor for carriage of live animals unless specifically mentioned in the policy, nor does it include passage money. If the freight is paid in advance, non-returnable, the insurable interest rests with the cargo owner and the freight is merged in the value of the goods. If freight is payable at destination the insurable interest rests with the shipowner. The shipowner may insure anticipated freight on the actual freight at risk or on a P.P.I. basis but to prevent abuse under P.P.I. policies the Institute Time Clauses (Hulls) warrant that the maximum amount which can be insured on anticipated freight is 25% of the insured value of the ship, less any amount insured under the 10% disbursements warranty. "Freight" may also be applied to money for hire of a vessel in which case it is usually called "Chartered Freight. The term "freight" is used in the U.S.A. and in Canada to indicate "cargo". (See "Back Freight", "Freight Collision Clause", "Time Penalty Clause", "Freight Contingency".)

Freight Abandonment Clause

On payment of a total loss on hull the insurers are entitled to take over the property and are also entitled to any freight being earned by the vessel. In practice, by a clause in the Institute Time Clauses (Hulls), the insurers abandon their right to such freight.

Freight Account

Statement showing freight earned during a voyage. Necessary to establish amount of freight earned in order to discover loss of freight on goods where freight is payable as earned.

Freight at Risk

The amount of freight which the shipowner stands to lose if he fails to deliver the goods at destination.

Freight Clauses

These are sets of Institute Clauses which are designed for policies in respect of shipowner's interest in freight. There is a set for voyage and a set for time risks. Since freight is allied to cargo and loss of freight is based on loss of cargo, as well as loss of ship, many cargo clauses are included together with hull clauses. There is no collision clause this being a separate clause (see "Freight Collision Clause"). The 3% franchise in the freight clauses is based on the cargo average warranty. If the vessel is a total loss the freight clauses pay in full, equally if the cargo is totally lost resulting in a total loss of freight the policy pays in full. Partial loss payments follow freight lost through loss of or damage to cargo. (See also "Time Penalty Clause" and "Disbursements Warranty".)

Freight Collect

Freight payable at destination on delivery of the goods.

Freight Collision Clause

Under American Law when a vessel is held liable in a collision case the freight may also be called upon to contribute to the liability to the other vessel. The freight collision clause is designed to cover this liability and is worded with the same limitations as the ordinary collision clause in the Institute Time Clauses (Hulls). The freight collision clause is not included in the Institute Freight Clauses and is a separate Institute Clause. The clause excludes claims that attach to other policies and claims that would be recoverable under the I.T.C. R.D.C. if the ship were insured on such terms for a value of not less than £32 per g.r.t. (This amount may be increased when the limitation of liability equivalents are increased from time to time.)

Freight—Constructive Total Loss

Many difficulties arise in ascertaining constructive total loss of freight, since it would be necessary to compare the freight which would be earned with the extra cost of forwarding cargo which has been discharged short of destination. In practice, the freight clauses contain a clause which provides that the policy amount shall be payable in full if the *vessel* is an actual or constructive total loss, whether or not the vessel has cargo on board.

Freight Contingency

The insurable interest of the consignee who, paying freight at destination, takes delivery of his goods on the overseas vessel so that during discharge and conveyance to the shore or to some other place the goods are at his risk. Since the consignee has paid the freight on delivery by the overseas vessel he could not have included such freight in the value of the goods because he had no insurable interest in the freight during the overseas voyage. He, therefore, has an insurable interest in the freight which he has paid, while the goods are still in transit, after delivery, until they arrive at their destination. The reason being that if the goods were lost after delivery the consignee would have lost the freight. " Back freight " may be considered a form of freight contingency risk.

Freighter

A vessel primarily engaged in carrying cargo for freight. The term may also be applied to the charterer hiring a vessel.

Freight Forward

Freight payable at destination on delivery of the goods.

Freight Forwarder

One who represents an exporter in arranging overseas shipments. At one time termed " Shipping and Forwarding Agent ".

Freight Negligence Clause

This clause is incorporated in the Institute Freight Clauses and has the same effect as the negligence clause in the Institute Time Clauses. The clause was not reworded to conform with the I.T.C. amendment when the Freight Clauses were reissued in 1970 because there is no machinery damage co-insurance clause in the Freight Clauses. The clause is also printed separately in case it should be needed for a policy on freight which is not subject to the freight clauses.

Freight Rebate

Under the conference system rate tariffs are agreed whereby all vessels in the same conference charge the same freight rates. While these rates may turn out to be the most economic in the long run there is a probability that a shipper may be offered a more attractive rate on a particular shipment by a competitor of the conference line with which the shipper normally ships his goods. The conference system depends on regular support and, to discourage the shipper from sending certain individual consignments by other vessels some conference lines will allow a freight rebate, sometimes called a "loyalty rebate", to a regular shipper using conference vessels exclusively. In many cases the rebate is deferred and is allowed at the end of a specified period provided the shipper uses only conference vessels during that period. Many conferences discourage this system which is a dying practice.

Freight Release

A document authorising the ship's officer or warehouseman in charge of goods to release the goods because the freight has been paid.

Freight Ton

A system of charging freight. A freight ton can be calculated either by weight of 2,240 lbs. of cargo or by area occupied by the cargo at 40 cu. ft. per freight ton. The former method is used when the cargo is heavy but occupies a small space. The latter method is used when the cargo is light but occupies a large space.

Freight War & Strikes Clauses

Institute clauses reinstating the risks excluded from the Institute Freight clauses by the F.C. & S. clause and incorporating into the policy war perils and strikes etc. risks.

fresh

Fresh water damage.

Freshwater

Water other than seawater. Freshwater includes rain, drinking or sweet water, condensation and bilgewater. It is an extraneous risk and without the operation of a maritime peril it is not covered by the ordinary policy. The risk may be incorporated into the policy by specific inclusion or by the term " all risks ".

F.R.O.
Fire risk only.

From
When a contract of marine insurance is effected on a voyage " from " a particular place it is an implied condition that the voyage must commence within a reasonable time or the insurer may avoid the contract, except where the insurer has waived the delay or knew of it when he accepted the insurance. The risk does not attach until the vessel starts from the specified port or the goods start from the specified place for the destination named in the policy.

From the Loading Thereof
Risk on goods insured under this term does not attach until they are loaded on board the overseas vessel. The risk by lighter and/or craft from shore to ship is not covered, nor is the loading risk.

Front
Fronting underwriter, (which see.)

Fronting Company
An insurance Company which acts for other insurers by issuing a policy in its own name thereby holding itself directly liable for claims to the assured, although the liability of the Company is reinsured 100% with the other insurers.

Fronting Underwriter
An insurer who acts for other insurers by accepting an insurance in his own name, making himself directly liable to the assured, while he is reinsured 100% with the other insurers.

Frost Damage
Frost is not a peril of the sea, therefore damage to the insured interest proximately caused by frost would not be covered under the plain form of policy. It may be argued that frost damage is embraced in the term " all risks " but this is unlikely to be supported in law because the circumstances giving rise to the damage would probably show it to be an inevitability and not a risk. A policy covering " all loss or damage whatsoever, howsoever arising " would, on the other hand, probably be held to cover frost damage. Where the frost damage forms part of a loss proximately caused by a marine peril, such as a heavy weather, the damage would be, in practice, merged

with the claim for damage by the marine peril. (See "Risk" and "Inevitable Loss".)

Frozen Food Clauses

There are three sets of these clauses which were first introduced on 1st April, 1968. All three sets exclude frozen meat. The clauses cover (a) Full conditions (1/4/68) (b) All Risks and deterioration attributable to breakdown of refrigerating machinery for not less than 24 hours (1/4/68) (c) F.P.A. and deterioration attributable to breakdown of refrigerating machinery for not less than 24 hours (1/2/69). The transit clause provides cover from the time the goods are loaded into the conveyance at the cold store or freezing works, at the place named in the policy, for the commencement of transit until, following the normal course of transit, the goods are delivered to the cold store or place of storage at destination. Only five days after discharge, from the overseas vessel, is allowed for this or cover expires. The usual conditions of the ordinary cargo transit clauses regarding allocation or distribution are applicable.

The clauses are designed to permit an alternative voyage commencing from the time the goods are loaded on board the vessel. Claims are payable irrespective of percentage and the usual cargo clauses are applicable.

There are precautionary warranties that the goods are in sound condition, properly packed and frozen and that the goods are shipped within sixty days of their entry into the freezing chamber. Claims on the policy must be made within thirty days of expiry of the insurance.

Frozen Food War Clauses

This set of clauses (Cl. 49) was introduced on 1st January 1971 to be used in connection with insurance of frozen food, other than frozen meat. At first glance these conditions seem to be identical to those in the standard cargo war risks clauses for frozen products, used for frozen meat insurances but the former set does not incorporate a clause excluding claims caused by stoppage of refrigerating machinery. (See "Frozen Products War Clauses".)

Frozen Meat Clauses

These are designed for frozen meat voyages from Australia or New Zealand but are frequently adopted in practice to cover other voyages. There are four sets of clauses lettered A to D, covering "all risks" or "F.P.A. and breakdown". Basically the clauses provide cover from time of entering freezing plant to arrival in approved refrigerated warehouses in the U.K. and a specified period after arrival. Undesirable risks such as improper dressing and bone taint are excluded. The clauses are designed not only for frozen beef and mutton, but also for small animals such as rabbits.

Frozen Mutton Clauses
Institute Frozen Meat Clauses. " A " for full conditions and " C " for F.P.A. and Breakdown. Cover also frozen beef, lamb, veal and pork.

Frozen Products
See " Frozen Meat Clauses ".

Frozen Products Strike Clauses
Institute Clauses incorporating strikes etc. risks into a policy containing one of the sets of Institute Frozen Meat clauses.

Frozen Products War Clauses
A set of Institute clauses designed to cover the war risks excluded by the Institute Frozen Meat Clauses; and incorporating war risks into the policy. The current clauses are dated 1/1/71 and bear the reference Cl. 77. They exclude loss or damage due to stoppage of the refrigerating machinery caused by shortage of fuel or labour during strikes, lockouts or labour disturbances.

A similar set of clauses, without the refrigerating machinery stoppage exclusion, is available for use on policies covering frozen food, other than frozen meat (See Frozen Food War Clauses).

Frozen Rabbits Clauses
Institute Frozen Meat Clauses. " B " for full conditions and " D " for F.P.A. and Breakdown. Cover also hares, poultry and sundries.

Frt.
Freight.

Frustration Clause
See " Frustration of Adventure ".

Frustration of Adventure
When by reason of a war peril insured property is prevented from completing the adventure, although the property has suffered no physical loss, there is " frustration of the adventure ". Insurers do not contemplate this as a loss recoverable under the policy, hence it is usual for policies on war risks to contain the " frustration clause " to the effect that no claim which is based on frustration shall be recoverable.

F.S.F.
Formerly a Fellow of the Institute of Shipping and Forwarding Agents. The Institute has changed its title to The Institute of

Freight Forwarders and the qualifying title is accordingly changed to " Fellow of the Institute of Freight Forwarders ". Abbreviation F. Inst. F.F.

f.s.l.
Full signed line, (which see.)

F.S.R. & C.C. Clause
Clause 13 in all three sets of the standard Institute Cargo Clauses. This clause warrants that the insurance is free of loss or damage to the insured interest caused by strikers, locked out workmen, or persons taking part in labour disturbances, riots or civil commotions. The clause also excludes loss or damage to the insured interest resulting from strikes, lock outs, labour disturbances, riots or civil commotions.

The perils enumerated in the exclusion are not covered by the plain form of policy, in any case, so that the clause merely makes it clear to the assured that these risks are not covered. If the clause is deleted the perils would not be instated into the policy, unless some specific provision were made to this effect. The standard cargo clauses, however, provide that if clause 13 is deleted the standard Institute Strikes Clauses are deemed to form part of the insurance. It is customary for a similar exclusion clause to appear in all trade cargo clauses. It is also to be found in the standard S.G. Cargo form in use today and in clauses insuring builder's risks, P & I risks, port risks and yachts.

Fth.
Fathom.

Fuel and Engine Stores Account
A statement drawn up by the chief engineer regarding fuel and engine stores used in connection with repairs to the vessel, or removal of the vessel for repairs.

Full
Abbreviation concerning conditions. Means Institute Time Clauses or similar on hulls, or " All Risks " on a cargo policy.

Full Conditions
When a hull policy is said to be on "full conditions " or "full terms " it means it is subject to the Institute Time Clauses or Institute Voyage Clauses or Time Clauses Excess PA (or some other excess) or similar. Any conditions less wide than these are called " Limited terms ". On a cargo policy " Full Conditions " means " All Risks ".

Full Interest

Having a complete insurable interest in the whole of the subject matter insured.

Full Interest Admitted

See " Policy Proof of Interest ".

Full Outturn

A Full Outturn of cargo is one which arrives without any shortage. It is applied to bulk shipments where shipped and landed weights are compared to discover if there is any shortage. It sometimes happens in certain cargoes that the physical material of the cargo arrives complete but there is a shortage in weight due to drying out on the voyage or for some other reason. The risk of shortage in the case of such cargoes is practically uninsurable.

Full Premium if Lost

A term used in hull insurance when the policy is effected for a period of less than 12 months. The insurer charges a premium at a rate which is pro rata of the annual rate, but inserts a warranty that in the event of the vessel being a total loss before expiry of the policy the full annual premium shall be payable under the policy. The abbreviation used to refer to this term is F.P.I.L., but sometimes this is followed with P.I.A. (Peril insured against) which means that the total loss must be proximately caused by an insured peril for the full annual premium to become payable.

Full Returns

Provision in a slip on hull or hull interest allowing for both cancelling and lay-up returns of premium in specified circumstances.

Full Signed Line

When an insurer accepts a line on a slip this is called his written line. It frequently occurs that the broker over-places the insurance, whereby the total of the lines he receives exceeds the amount of insurance required. This is accepted market practice but it means that when the insurance is finally closed (or signed) each insurer's written line must be reduced in proportion so that the total of the lines agrees exactly the amount of insurance required. The line so arrived at is called the " full signed line ". An insurer may use the expression " full signed line ". (abbreviation f.s.l.) in a reinsurance order in place of the term " full written line ". Where used in this manner both terms mean the same because ultimately the full written line will be reduced to the full signed line when the reinsurance is closed. In cargo insurance, a further reason for reducing the written line to a lower amount when signing occurs when the value which is subsequently shipped is less than the value contemplated by the insurance.

Full Terms
See " Full Conditions ".

Full Written Line
The amount which an insurer writes on a slip when he accepts an insurance. The term, or abbreviation f.w.l. is often to be seen in a facultative reinsurance order where the insurer wishes to reinsure the whole of the line which he has written. The broker, when closing the reinsurance must take care to ensure that in the event of short closing on the original, the reinsured line is reduced in the same proportion as the reinsured's line on the original insurance. (See " Full Signed Line ".)

Fur.
Furlong.

Further Agreed
Used in policy clauses to denote a supplementary contract. (For example:—The Collision Clause in a Hull Policy or the P & I risks in a Port Risks policy). The effect of the words " It is further agreed " is to apply the sum insured by the policy individually to that section of the policy so that the insurer could find himself liable for up to the full insured value under the body of the policy and, *in addition*, up to the full sum insured under the section commencing with " It is further agreed ".

f.v.
Fishing vessel.

F.V.C.
Fishing Vessel Clauses. (See " I.F.V.C. ".)

f.w.d.
Freshwater damage.

Fwd.
Forward.

f.w.l.
Full written line. (Reinsurance term.)

F.W.P.C.A.
Federal Water Pollution Control Act (U.S.A.).

F.W.T. & G.D.
Fair wear, tear and gradual deterioration. A policy exclusion.

G

G/A *or* **G.A.**
General Average.

G.A. Act
General Average act.

G.A. Clause
The Marine Insurance Act 1906 in section 66 provides that the insurer is directly liable to indemnify the assured in respect of a general average loss. The insurer is also liable for his proportion of general average contributions. The G.A. Clause is, therefore, not necessary in the policy to provide this cover but the clause nevertheless, appears in all sets of cargo clauses. The Act, however, does not stipulate the basis on which G.A. shall be calculated, but the G.A. clause states that the adjustment shall be in accordance with Foreign Statement or York/Antwerp Rules if the contract of affreightment so provides. (See "Foreign General Average" and "York-Antwerp Rules".)

G/A con.
General Average Contribution.

G.A.D.
General Average Deposit.

G/A dep.
General Average Deposit.

G.A.D.V.
Gross arrived damaged value.

G.A. in Full Clause
Except where there is an agreement to the contrary in the policy, in all cases where the insured value is less than the contributory value, the insurer's liability for general average contribution is such proportion of the contribution payable by the assured as the insured value bears to the contributory value (M.I.A. Act 1906—Section 73—Sub. 1). It is probable that the insured value is more than adequate but in long term contracts, such as open covers, the broker will probably recommend to the assured that the "G.A. in Full Clause" forms part of the cover. This clause provides that the insurer will pay G.A. contributions in full even when the contributory value is greater than the insured value. The clause may

be extended to embrace salvage charges which are subject to the same principle (M.I.R. 1906—Sect. 73—Sub. 2).

G.A.L.
General Average Loss.

Galliot
Dutch cargo boat or fishing vessel.

Gambling Policies Act
The Marine Insurance (Gambling Policies) Act 1909.

Gaming
Gaming or gambling in marine insurance is prohibited by the Marine Insurance (Gambling Policies) Act 1909, more commonly called "The Gambling Policies Act". By this Act anyone who effects or assists in effecting a marine insurance policy where the assured has no insurable interest or expectation of acquiring one is guilty of an offence under the Act.

Garbling
The removal of damaged tobacco from a bale which contains a quantity of sound tobacco. This prevents further loss and provided the damage is from an insured peril insurers pay the cost of garbling.

Garboard Strake
The shell plating on a ship, adjacent to the keelplate.

Gas Free Certificate
See "Cleaning of Tanks".

G.A.S.V.
Gross arrived sound value.

g.b.o.
Goods in bad order. Shipping term.

GC
Abbreviation appearing in Lloyd's Register denoting that the vessel is fitted for a gyro compass.

Gear (Fishing)
See "Fishing Gear Clause".

Gencon
General charterparty for no particular trade.

General Average
Average is a partial loss. General average is a deliberate partial loss to save all the interests in the adventure from total loss. General

average can, of course, be a total loss of one interest but this is only
a partial loss of the whole. Example:—A small vessel valued at
£1,000 is carrying 10 boxes valued £100 each across a calm bay. A
storm causes rough water threatening to swamp the vessel, which is
prevented by casting overside one of the boxes. This is a general
average act and all the saved interests must contribute toward the
loss of £100. Hence the total of the vessel's value and the remaining
boxes (£1,900 in all) must contribute towards the loss. Since the
owner of the sacrificed box receives contributions from the others
(called " made good ") the £100 so made good must also contribute.
Therefore, the total value contributing is £2,000 and, accordingly,
the vessel contributes £50 and the owners of each of the boxes
contribute £5 per box. General average is an accepted rule of the
sea and applies only to maritime adventures. It has been in existence since the days when vessels first traded on the seas. Rules
have been agreed from time to time, the most common of these in
use being the York-Antwerp Rules 1974. Insurers always pay both
general average loss and contribution, where the peril involved is
an insured peril. Any property, other than the sacrificed property,
which does not arrive at its destination does not contribute toward
the general average loss, by which it has not benefited.

General Average Account
Account opened by the shipowner to receive deposits from con-
tributors to general average.

General Average Adjustment
When a general average act has taken place it is the duty of the
shipowner to arrange for the adjustment to be drawn up. He selects
an Average Adjuster and jointly they set up a Trust Fund of the
deposits secured from the interested parties. The adjuster draws up
the adjustment, which due to complexities may, in some cases, take
a year or more.

General Average Bond
See " Average Bond ".

General Average Contribution
A payment by one of the parties involved in a general average
adjustment toward the general average fund. The contribution is
based on the contributory value of the interest and is such proportion of the fund as the contributory value of the individual interest
bears to the total of the contributory values of all the interests which
benefited by the general average act. Insurers are liable for general
average contributions in full if the act preserved the insured interest

from an insured peril and the policy value is not less than the contributory value. If the policy value is less than the contributory value, the insurer is liable only for his proportion of the contribution, taking into account the underinsurance. For comparison with the contributory value the insured value must be reduced by any particular average claim paid by the insurer.

In practice, the insurer may accept a clause in the policy providing that general average contributions shall be payable in full irrespective of the insured value. (See " General Average in Full " Clause.)

General Average Contributory Value
See " Contributory Value ".

General Average—Definition
General average is defined in the Marine Insurance Act, 1906 under Section 66 (2). It is also defined in Rule A of the York-Antwerp Rules 1974 as follows: —

" There is a general average act when, and only when, any extraordinary sacrifice or expenditure is intentionally and reasonably made or incurred for the common safety for the purpose of preserving from peril the property involved in a common maritime adventure."

General Average Deposit
When a general average act has occurred the onus is upon the shipowner to collect the contributions from the parties concerned. To enforce this he has a lien on the goods so that he may prevent their release to the consignee until the consignee has paid a deposit in respect of the eventual contribution. The deposit is based on the estimated contribution and a deposit receipt is given in exchange. (See also " General Average Guarantee ", " General Average Deposit Receipt " and " Counter Guarantee ".) The Insurer is not compelled to refund a deposit to the assured and he may await the final adjustment if he so desires before paying anything in respect of the contribution.

General Average Deposit Receipt
When a general average deposit is paid to a shipowner a deposit receipt is issued giving details of the interest and contribution due. Any refund of deposit is payable only to the holder of the deposit receipt.

General Average Disbursements
Expenditure, incurred by the shipowner, which is the subject of general average. Since he cannot recover general average disbursements if the property saved by the expenditure becomes a total loss

before arrival at destination, the shipowner has an insurable interest in such disbursements. The general average bond permits the shipowner to draw on the general average fund for such disbursements without awaiting the final adjustment. (See "Average Disbursements Clauses".)

General Average Essentials

(1) The whole adventure must be in peril.
(2) The peril must be factual and imminent.
(3) The act must be intentional and voluntary.
(4) The act must be reasonable and prudent.
(5) The act must be for the purpose of preserving the whole of the interests in the adventure from total loss.
(6) The sacrifice or expenditure must be extraordinary in nature.
(7) Only losses directly consequential on the act are general average.

General Average Expenditure

Expenditure by the shipowner in connection with a general average act such as hire of tugs to pull the vessel off a strand or to tow it into port, or the hire of craft to take off cargo to lighten a vessel to pull her off a strand. Such expenditure is also a general average sacrifice and may be made part of the adjustment. The hull policy does not cover general average expenditure as a direct liability so the shipowner who incurs such expenditure cannot claim it directly from his insurers as he can with a general average sacrifice. He must claim the expenditure from the general average fund and the adjusters may arrange a payment on account prior to the final adjustment. The underwriter's liability for G.A. expenditure is only for that part of the expenditure which is contained in the assured's liability for a contribution to the general average fund. (See "General Average Contribution". See also "General Average Disbursements".)

General Average Fund

A fund created by the shipowner and Average Adjuster jointly from the deposits collected in respect of a general average adjustment. Interest accrues in the fund on the deposits and is credited to the depositors. The shipowner has a right to draw direct on the fund for general average expenditure without awaiting the final adjustment.

General Average Guarantee

In the American market the term "average bond" is used to describe a general average guarantee. When a consignee is required to furnish a general average deposit he may call upon the insurer of the goods to pay the deposit for him. The insurer is not obliged to do this. Alternatively, the consignee may request an underwriter's guarantee. The insurer may agree but he may wish to qualify the guarantee to ensure that he is not held liable for more than the proper amount due under the policy (see " General Average Contribution "). The shipowner is seldom prepared to accept a qualified guarantee. As a compromise the insurer may grant an unqualified guarantee, but only if the assured agrees to sign a counter guarantee to indemnify the insurer against overpayment.

Due to variations in values it is not uncommon today for cargo insurers to accept a clause in the insurance agreeing to pay general average contributions in full irrespective of the insured value. (See " General Average in Full Clause ".) The carrier may be prepared to accept a guarantee from a bank or other party that is prepared to give the guarantee.

General Average in Full Clause

When a general average act occurs as a result of the operation of an insured peril the insurer is liable for the contribution toward the loss sustained by the general average act which is awarded against the insured interest. Where, however, the contributory value of the insured interest is greater than the insured value of that interest, after deducting any particular average claim, the insurer's liability for the contribution is reduced in the same proportion so that it bears the same relation to the contribution as the net insured value bears to the contributory value. Some cargo owners feel that they would prefer to have general average contributions paid in full by the insurer, even if it means paying a higher premium. Hence, in such cases the insurer may agree to incorporate the " General Average in Full Clause " into the policy which clause provides for the insurer's liability for general contribution to be in full irrespective of the contributory value.

General Average—Insurer's Liability

The insurer has a direct liability for general average damage to the subject matter insured whether or not the assured presses his claim for contributions from other parties. The insurer is subrogated to the rights of the assured after paying the claim and may press the right to contributions himself. The insurer is also liable for any general average contribution falling on the interest insured subject to the contributory value not exceeding the insured value less any particular average claim. If the contributory value does so exceed the insured value the insurer is only liable for his proper proportion of the contribution taking into account the underinsurance. Whether the claim is for general average loss or for contribution the insurer is not liable if the sacrifice was made to preserve the property from an uninsured peril.

General Average—Mutual Ownership

Where two or more interests are involved in a general average act but are owned by the same person they cannot be called upon to contribute to the loss of one of them, but in practice they are treated as if separately owned and insurance respects this principle by treating insurers' liability for the contribution as though the interests were separate.

General Average Refund

Since the general average deposit is customarily estimated on the high side it is probable that there will be a refund of deposit. Such refund is payable only to the person holding the deposit receipt.

General Average Sacrifice

The sacrifice of one of the interests in a marine adventure in time of peril for the purpose of preserving the remainder of the interests from a total loss.

General Average Loss

A loss of or damage to the insured interest directly consequential on a general average act. It includes both expenditure and sacrifice.

General Lien

Shipowner's lien on cargo giving him the right to hold the cargo pending payments due from the cargo owner. A general lien is one which applies to any goods belonging to the same cargo owner.

Germanischer Lloyd

This is a German Classification Society. Steel vessels up to 15 years old and fully classed with this Society are acceptable to insurers as carriers. Vessels registered with Germanischer Lloyd may appear in Lloyd's Register with the notation GL. The cypher to denote full class in the Germanischer Lloyd Register is ✠ 100 A4.

g.f.a.

Good fair average. Refers to quality of goods.

Gig

A small boat.

Gimbals

A set of brackets designed to hold a compass in a level position at all times, irrespective of the movement of the ship.

Gin

Factory where cotton is ginned before export.

Ginning

Combing cotton staples to remove the cotton seed. A process carried out in a " Gin " which, due to friction, increases the fire hazard.

GL

Entry in Lloyd's Register denoting that a vessel is registered with the Germanischer Lloyd.

Glass Clause

A clause incorporated in a cargo policy which excludes claims for breakage of glass, but covers damage to the insured interest caused by such breakage.

g.m.b.

Good merchantable brand. Sale contract term.

G.M.T.

Greenwich Mean Time.

g.m.q.

Good merchantable quality. Sale contract term.

g.o.b.

Good ordinary brand. Sale contract term.

Gold Clause Agreement

An agreement entered into by British insurers', shipowners' and merchants' associations who are members of the British Maritime Law Association and commonly called the " Gold Clause Agreement " because it refers to the provisions of the " Gold Clause ". The gold clause appears in the Hague Rules and the Carriage of Goods by Sea Act, 1924 and states that monetary value therein shall be gold value. The term " Gold Clause Agreement " is referred to when dealing with the limit of carrier's liability in respect of goods in the carrier's care. The effect of the agreement is to increase the statutory minimum limit in the Act from £100 to £200 per package or unit. Further the Agreement extends the period allowed for bringing an action from 12 months to 24 months, provided prompt notice of loss or damage has been given and no unnecessary delay has occurred in submitting the claim. The agreement binds the signatories to bring action in the United Kingdom even though the bill of lading may provide for jurisdiction elsewhere.

The agreement came into force on 1st August 1950 for five years as it stood and provision to continue thereafter subject to cancellation by 6 months notice. The Signatories to the agreement include Insurance Companies, Lloyd's Underwriters and British and Dominion Shipowners. It is usual to attach a red clause to all cargo policies drawing to the attention of the assured the need for prompt notice of claim against the carrier.

Good Faith
See " Utmost Good Faith ".

Goods
Refers to merchandise. Does not include personal effects nor provisions nor stores for use on the vessel. Neither deck cargo nor live animals are embraced by the term. These must be mentioned specifically as such in the policy.

Good Safety
A vessel is in good safety when she has arrived at her destination or at the loading port and is safe and seaworthy for the port or place in which she has arrived.

Good Ship
Ancient term for a seaworthy vessel, e.g. the " good " ship *Mayflower*. " Good " means the vessel is seaworthy.

Goods in Transit (C.M.R.)
See " C.M.R. Form ".

G.O.R.
Gross original rate. The same as O.G.R.

Gr.
Gross *or* grain.

Grab Dredger
See " Dredger ".

Grain Cargo Certificate
Issued by Customs at loading port to show grain was loaded in accordance with Board of Trade Regulations.

Graving Dock
Another term for dry dock.

Gross Arrived Damaged Value
The actual damaged value of the goods at destination including all landing charges, duties etc.

Gross Arrived Sound Value
The actual or estimated sound value of the goods at destination including all landing charges, duties etc.

Gross for Nett

A shipping term used where the "tare" or additional weight over the nett weight of cargo is so small that it can be ignored and the gross weight may be taken as the nett weight.

Gross Freight at Risk

When freight is payable at destination on delivery of the cargo the gross freight at risk at any time is the freight payable at destination on the cargo being carried at that time, including all expenses to earn the freight to destination.

Gross Line

When an insurer writes a line on a risk he enters this in his records. If he reinsures part of the risk, the line he originally wrote is called his "gross line".

Gross Net Premium

Gross premium, before deduction of brokerage and discounts, but less gross returns of premium.

Gross Premium

Total premium before deduction of brokerage or discounts.

Gross Proceeds

The actual price obtained at a sale when the seller has paid all the sale charges.

Gross Registered Tonnage

The tonnage of a ship as registered before deduction of light and air spaces, machinery and navigating spaces and other parts of the vessel to arrive at the net registered tonnage. Port charges, canal dues and other charges are based on the net registered tonnage. This form of tonnage is not calculated on weight but on 100 cubic feet per registered ton. The net tonnage of a vessel is approximately two-thirds of her gross tonnage. The gross tonnage of a warship is her displacement tonnage, calculated by the cubic area occupied by the vessel below the water line at 33 cubic feet per ton.

Gross Value

The wholesale price of goods or the estimated value after all freight, landing charges and duty have been paid. If goods are by custom sold in bond the bonded price is deemed to be the gross value.

Groundage

Anchorage charge made by an Authority when a vessel anchors within the Authority's jurisdiction.

Groundage
Fixed ways providing a sliding path for the sliding ways (or cradle) when a ship is launched.

Grounding
Although synonymous with stranding the term grounding is used when a vessel runs aground in an area where groundings are so common that the insurer of the ship considers it should not be deemed stranding. In most hull policies there appears the " Customary Groundings Clause " (see " Customary Strandings ") whereby it is stipulated that grounding in the Suez Canal, Panama Canal, River Danube and other specified places shall not be deemed a stranding so that underwriters do not pay the cost of sighting the bottom for damage.

Groupage
A system whereby relatively small units of cargo are grouped together to be stuffed into a container.

G.R.T.
Gross Registered Tonnage.

Gr. wt.
Gross weight.

Gr. T. *or* **gro. t.**
Gross ton.

G.S.
Good Safety.

g.s.m.
Good sound merchantable. Sale contract term referring to quality of goods.

Guarantee (Salvage)
See " Salvage Guarantee ".

Gulf
Gulf of Mexico.

Gulf Ports
Ports in the Gulf of Mexico.

Gunwale
The part of a ship where the shell plating joins the upper deck,

Gussett Plate
A steel bracket, inside a ship, connecting a side frame to the bottom plating.

Gy. C.
Gyro compass.

Gypsy
A small metal drum on a winch.

H

H.A.D.
Havre, Antwerp, Dunkirk.

Hague Rules
Following an International Maritime Law Conference in Brussels in 1922 a set of rules was agreed to establish the rights and immunities of carriers in respect of the carriage of goods by sea. Many of the countries agreeing to the rules later incorporated them in statutory Acts, such as the "Carriage of Goods by Sea Act 1924".

H & M
Hull and Materials. Refers basically to sailing vessels, H.M. etc. being the abbreviation for steamers. In modern practice it is not unusual for the abbreviation H & M to be used for "Hull and Machinery".

h & o
Hook and oil damage.

H/A or D
Havre, Antwerp or Dunkirk.

Halyard
A light rope used for hoisting flags.

Harbour
A place either natural or artificial where ships may anchor or lay and be protected from the open sea. A harbour has a permanent opening to the sea. If the same sort of place has lock-gates or is sometimes closed to the sea it is called a "dock".

Harbour Dues
Dues or charges levied on a ship by the Harbour Authorities for use of the harbour.

Hard
Instead of being moored against a quay small craft are often hauled up onto a sloping piece of land which may be merely hard mud or may be surfaced. At times this area is wholly or partly covered with water where the area is tidal, but a small craft can, usually, be hauled up sufficiently to make it safe from the normal rise or fall of the tide. Such a piece of land is called "the hard" and,

171

in modern insurance, the expression is to be found in policies effected on yachts and small craft.

Hardening Market

When an insurance market develops a more selective attitude towards insurance contracts offered to it, it is said to be a " hardening " market.

Harter Act

U.S.A. law passed in 1893 to protect shipowners from liability for damage to cargo due to faults or errors in navigation provided the shipowner has exercised due diligence to ensure the vessel is properly manned, equipped and seaworthy. Partly superseded by the introduction of the U.S. Carriage of Goods by Sea Act 1936, the Harter Act now applies only to coastwise shipping not embraced by the U.S. Carriage of Goods by Sea Act.

Hatch Coaming

A raised wall around a hatchway opening. The purpose is to prevent water which washes the decks from entering the hold through the hatchway.

Hatch Cover

Cover over a hatchway. This was, at one time, made of boards covered with tarpaulins which were cleated to the hatch coaming. Shipping regulations lay down specified minimum standards for hatch covers, non-compliance with which renders the ship unseaworthy. Today, hatch covers are usually made of steel, are fitted with steel fasteners to maintain a weathertight fit and, where necessary, are fitted with ventilators.

Hatch *or* Hatchway

Opening in a ship's deck through which cargo is lowered to or brought up from the holds.

Haulage

A charge made by the Rail, Canal or Dock Authorities for the use or haulage of trucks, carriages or wagons whether loaded or not, also for the use of lines. A separate charge is made if the Authorities provide loading and unloading services.

Hawsepipe

An opening in the bow of a ship through which the anchor chain passes.

Hazardous Cargoes

See " Dangerous Goods " and " T.E.C.H. Cargo ".

H.B.
Houseboat, (which see.)

Hbr.
Harbour.

H/C *or* **h/c**
Held covered at a premium to be agreed. As a slip agreement this has no legal effect.

H/C L/U *or* **h/c l/u**
Held covered at a premium which needs to be agreed only by the leading underwriter.

Heating
An appreciable increase in temperature which does not result in ignition. Heating, as an insured peril, is considered as synonymous with fire, but in many cases it is due to cargo being shipped in wet condition. When this occurs the proximate cause of any loss due to the heating is usually inherent vice. Closing of ventilators in heavy weather may cause heating to the cargo, any consequent damage being deemed to be a loss by heavy weather. (See also "Inherent Vice" and "Spontaneous combustion".)

Heavy Grain
Wheat, corn, maize or rye.

Heavy Lift
A single unit of cargo that is too heavy to be handled by the average ship's cargo handling gear. Specialised vessels, termed "heavy lift" ships are fitted with derricks capable of lifting single items, weighing anything between 25 and 1,000 tons. Where a heavy lift is carried by a vessel not so equipped it must be handled by suitable dockside equipment and care must be exercised to ensure that suitable equipment is available at the discharge port for unloading the cargo. Underwriters should bear in mind that a heavy lift cannot be jettisoned or offloaded in time of peril if the ship is not suitably equipped.

Heavy Lift Ship
A vessel fitted with derricks capable of handling single units of over 25 tons; usually up to about 1,000 tons.

Held Covered
This term is used where an assured wishes to be certain, in advance, that his interest will continue to be insured in the event of a circumstance arising whereby the insurance would not continue in the absence of any prior agreement. It may be that a cargo

assured anticipates a storage risk at destination or destination port which would not be within the ordinary course of transit. In such a case the insurance would cease to have effect upon delivery to such place of storage, but the cargo assured, still having an insurable interest, would wish cover to continue. Since he is not certain the storage risk will occur, in fact, he pays his premium on the basis of no storage risk arising but asks his broker to arrange for the possible storage period to be "held covered". It is understood that where a risk is "held covered" an additional premium is payable, in the event of the circumstances detailed by the "held covered" provision arising, and the Marine Insurance Act 1906 in section 31 provides that where no actual amount has been agreed for the additional premium, such premium shall be a reasonable one. What is reasonable being a question of fact. It is customary for periods of storage to be held covered at an agreed rate for each 30 days or part thereof. In hull insurance deviations, variations of the adventure, or extensions of the period of insurance are often held covered subject to a pro rata monthly premium. It is further understood that prior notice of the circumstance giving rise to the application of the held covered period of insurance shall be given to the insurer.

It may happen that a broker has insufficient time before attachment of the risk to effect full cover or the insurer may not wish to cover it himself fully before receipt of special requested information. In such circumstances the insurer may agree to "hold covered" the insurance, say, over the weekend or until the information is obtained. This form of "held covered" is only temporary and the insurer is entitled to withdraw cover in the event of unreasonable delay. In any case, this would be by slip agreement only, using the abbreviation h/c, and therefore would be binding in honour only.

Held Covered Clause

A clause in the Institute Cargo Clauses that provides for immediate notice to be given to the insurers in the event of any "held covered" circumstances arising. (See also "Breach of Warranty Clause".)

Hellenic Register of Shipping

A Greek Classification Society wherein Greek registered vessels are classed. The highest class in this register is shown by the cypher A100E. Vessels classed with the Hellenic Register may appear in Lloyd's Register with the notation HR.

H/H (Europe)

Havre to Hamburg.

Hhd.

Hogshead.

High Seas
Parts of oceans and/or seas which are not within any territorial waters and are therefore beyond the jurisdiction of any State.

Hijacked Ship
See " Malicious Acts Clause ".

hk.
Hook damage.

H.M. etc.
Hull and Machinery etc. (i.e. ship, machinery, fittings etc. of steamers and similar).

Hogged
A ship is said to be hogged when both ends are lower than the midships. This may occur when a ship rests on a sand bar or rocks for a time but with both ends clear. If this goes on for an appreciable time there is a probability that the ship will " break her back ".

Hogshead
Usually a container, although the term really applies to the capacity of the container, which is 54 gallons.

Hold
Part of a ship below deck where cargo is stowed. Ships are divided by bulkheads into several holds which are numbered consecutively.

Hold Covered
See " Held covered ".

Hold Harmless
An American expression used when a claim has been paid but there is a possibility of the claim being put forward a second time legitimately by another party. By the term the assured agrees to " hold harmless " the insurer in such an eventuality. That is, the assured agrees to refund to the insurer the claim paid. Also used when an assured is required to give to a third party a " hold harmless " agreement in which case the insurers are asked to accept the assured's liability arising from such agreement.

Home Foreign Dept.
Mainly a non-marine term for the department in a brokerage office handling insurances from overseas which are placed in the home market, principally concentrating on reinsurances.

Home Port
The Port of Registry of a ship.

Home Trade
Shipping trade within U.K. limits. Usually deemed to include Continental ports between Brest and Elbe.

Home Use Entry
Document used in respect of dutiable goods which are taken out of a warehouse for consumption in the Country where the warehouse is situated. Usually applicable to goods held in bond with the intention of re-exportation, but which are released instead for home use.

Honeycomb Slip
A single slip printed with a " honeycomb " of boxes in which the insurers' syndicate numbers can be inserted in the same order as they appear on the original slip. The slip is used for special agreements which are added to the original slip after the contract has been concluded and the original placing completed. The purpose of the system is to ensure that no syndicate is left off the agreement by making it easier to ascertain that every underwriter who appears on the original slip has initialled the agreement. A standard format for the honeycomb slip is now used in the London Market for all agreements requiring the initials of six or more underwriters.

Honour Policy
A policy which has no legal value and which is binding in honour only. (See " Policy Proof of Interest ".)

Hook Damage
Holes torn in baled goods or made in sacks, causing leakage, by the handling hooks used by stevedores. This is an extraneous risk.

Hopper
See " Dredger ".

Hopper Dredger
See " Dredger ".

Houseboat
When a vessel is used by the owner or others as a place of abode, whilst at her moorings or berth, that is not navigating, she is deemed to be a houseboat. The risk of fire is greatly enhanced when a vessel is used in this manner and it is customary in yacht and small craft insurance to warrant that the vessel shall not be used as a house-

boat. Where the insurance is specifically in respect of a houseboat it is customary for the insurance to warrant that she be used only for this purpose and not for navigating.

Household Effects
See " Household Goods ".

Household Goods
Normal household contents such as furniture. Clothing is not generally embraced by the term, coming within the description " Personal Effects ", but bed linen and soft furnishings are included in " Household Goods ".

Hovercraft
An air cushioned vehicle (abbreviation—A.C.V.). By injecting air pressure into a confined space below the hull the vehicle is lifted onto a cushion of air where it remains until the pressure is relieved. Whilst resting on the cushion of air, the vehicle can be moved easily in any direction, over both land and water, by the operation of propellers situated on the upper part of the hull.

The air pressure is confined below the hull by a flexible skirt, of heavy material, attached to sidewalls. The hull is waterproofed to enable the vehicle to settle and float on the water if the air pressure is relieved over water, when the skirt and sidewalls become submerged. Being relieved from the resistance offered by the water, the vehicle can move much faster over the sea than can a conventional craft and has the added advantage of being able to move with equal ease over land. Its height above the ground when hovering is restricted to the limitations of the skirt which confines the air pressure space.

There is a special policy form designed for the insurance of air cushioned vehicles.

Hoy
Small coastal vessel.

H.P.N.
Horse power nominal.

H.S.S.C.
Heating, Sweating, Spontaneous Combustion.

Hulk
An old vessel used for storage only. Often used for coal storage.

Hull
For insurance purposes this is the ship itself. In cases where a franchise is applicable to the insurance (this is uncommon today)

and separate values are stated, in applying the franchise to separate values the term " hull " includes electrical plant not connected with the main engines, donkey and auxiliary boilers with their condensers, winches, cranes, windlasses and steering gear. Unless separately valued in the policy refrigerating machinery and installation are also deemed to be part of the " hull ". The propelling machinery is deemed to be separate from the hull.

Hull Clauses

The hull clauses most widely used are the Institute Time Clauses, Hulls. The majority of hull clauses, including American and Dutch, are based on these. As the title indicates the clauses are for use on hull policies for a period of time. A similar set of clauses is used for voyage policies. The I.T.C. cover physical damage to and total loss of, the vessel proximately caused by specified perils. The policy is extended to cover 3/4ths of amounts paid by the assured for certain legal liabilities incurred consequent upon collision. The clauses also cover general average sacrifice, general average contributions, salvage contributions and sue and labour expenses. Nevertheless, all partial losses are subject to a specified deductible which is applied to the aggregate loss each accident or occurrence. An additional deductible is applied to machinery damage attributable to negligence of the master, officers or crew. For policies on limited terms there are various forms of T.L.O. clauses.

Hull Franchise

Prior to 1969 the Institute Time Clauses (Hulls) incorporated a franchise provision that extended the provisions of the memorandum in the S.G. policy form. Today, the franchise provision does not, normally, apply to hull policies which are subject to a deductible that is applicable to *all* partial losses. (See " Hull Policy Deductibles ".)

Hull Insurance

Insurance on the ship, its machinery and equipment.

Hull Interest

An insurable interest which is connected with a ship exposed to maritime perils (example: — " Mortgagee's Interest "). The ship-owner, of course, has a hull interest but the expression is customarily used to differentiate from cargo interests or other interests.

Hull Paramount Clauses

When the Institute Hull Clauses were revised in 1969 the war exclusion clause (F.C. & S. Clause) and other clauses relating to war risk exclusion were transferred to the foot of the clauses and made "paramount"; that is, unless the insurer deletes the clauses they override anything in the policy with which they are inconsistent. There are three paramount clauses in the I.T.C., being numbers 23 (F.C. & S. Clause), 24 (Malicious Acts Clause) and 25 (Nuclear Exclusion Clause). A further paramount clause introduced in 1970 for use in the I.T.C. and the American Hull Form provides that the limits set down in the Disbursements Clause ("Additional Increases Clause" in the A.H.F.) shall apply notwithstanding any other provision in the policy.

Hull Policy Deductibles

Prior to 1969 it was customary for the English hull policy to be subject to a franchise which was applied to particular average only. Today, the Institute Time Clauses (Hulls) contain a provision whereby an agreed deductible is applied to *all* claims other than total loss. The deductible, when introduced, was recommended to be not less than £500 but, in practice, is considerably more than this, being based on the tonnage of the insured vessel. All partial loss claims (including R.D.C. claims, GA, S & L and Salvage awards) are aggregated for each accident or occurrence and the deductible applied. Heavy weather damage between two successive ports is deemed to be caused by one accident for the purpose of the deductible. In addition to the agreed policy deductible an additional deductible (10% of the ascertained claim after applying the policy deductible) is applied to claims for partial loss to machinery that are attributable to negligence of the master, officers or crew. (See "Machinery Damage Co-insurance Clause".)

Hull Returns

Returns of premium allowed under a hull policy. (See "Sale of vessel", "Cancelling Returns" and "Lay Up Return".)

Hull Syndicates

Groups of insurers in Lloyd's engaged exclusively in underwriting marine hull business.

H.W.

Heavy weather damage *or* High Water.

H.W.D.

Heavy weather damage.

H.W.M.

High Water Mark.

H.W.O.S.T.

High water ordinary spring tides.

Hydrocraft

A small vessel combining the advantages of the hovercraft, hydrofoil and catamaran to provide a fast light craft. The catamaran configuration has a false bottom under the main hull in which an airduct is situated. Air is directed into the duct through slots, from two axial fans set in the forward end of the craft.

Hypothetical Salvage

When goods have been lost by a general average act, to preserve the principle of equity the " made good " amount must also contribute toward the loss. If a salvage act also occurs during the voyage the saved interests must all contribute toward the salvage award.

Because of this the values contributing toward the general average loss are reduced by the amount of the salvage award, whereas the " made good ", not having paid any salvage award, would pay on a higher value. At one time this apparent inequality caused average adjusters to reduce the amount made good. This reduction was called " hypothetical salvage " and the contributory value of the " made good " was the reduced amount. However, the practice of applying hypothetical salvage to average adjustments has been discontinued.

I

i &/or o
In &/or overdeck.

I.B.
In bond.

I.B.C.
Institute Builder's Risk Clauses.

I.C. *or* **I/C** *or* **i/c**
In commission, (which see.)

I.C.C.
Institute Cargo Clauses.

Icebreaker
A vessel with specially strengthened bows so shaped as to allow the vessel to ride up on the ice and to break the ice by its weight.

Ice Deviation Clause
A clause in a cargo policy permitting the vessel to deviate to discharge cargo at the nearest accessible port to the destination port because the vessel cannot reach the destination port by reason of ice. The cover under the policy continues during forwarding from the unloading port to destination, but the expense incurred is not payable by the insurers.

Ice Deviation Risk
Usually applicable to vessels sailing from Europe for the St. Lawrence ports during October-November. The insurance is to pay £X per ton of cargo which is discharged short of destination because of icing at the destination port or the closing of the river by the Authorities, due to icing. Insurers generally insist on a warranty that the vessel sails not later than a specified date direct for the destination port.

Ice Exclusion Clause
A clause which excludes liability from the policy in the event of damage caused by contact with ice during the winter months. If the damage is incurred in an effort to avoid loss from an insured peril, such damage is not excluded.

Ice Hazards
Certain areas are notorious for ice damage to vessels. It is usual

181

for policies on vessels which are likely to enter these areas to be subject to the Institute Warranties. The greatest damage to vessels is when the ice season commences, at which time there is a possibility of the vessel being trapped in the area. It is almost as hazardous when the ice is breaking up because large floes, being nearly submerged, can be as dangerous as rocks.

I.C.H.C.A.
International Cargo Handling Co-ordination Association.

I.C.S.
Institute of Chartered Shipbrokers.

id.
Idem *or* ditto.

i.f.
In full.

I.F.C.
Institute Freight Clauses.

I.F.V.C.
Institute Fishing Vessel Clauses (See " Fishing Vessel Clauses ".)

I.H.P.
Indicated Horse Power.

I.I.L.
Insurance Institute of London.

I.L.A.
International Longshoremen's Association. An Association for the protection of the rights of longshoremen in the U.S.A.

I.L.U.
Institute of London Underwriters.

I.M.C.O.
Inter-Governmental Maritime Consultative Organisation. (October–1973.)

Imperilled
The insured property is imperilled when it is exposed to an insured peril, even though the peril may not actually be operating. Once a ship puts to sea she is imperilled by perils of the seas. If the insured property has never been imperilled the assured is entitled to a return of the premium paid.

Implied Condition
A condition which does not appear in the policy but which is understood to be incorporated therein and is equally binding as though it were expressed in the policy. There is an implied condition in a voyage policy that the voyage be commenced within a reasonable time after the underwriter accepts the risk. Breach of an implied condition by the assured entitles the underwriter to avoid the contract from inception (M.I.A. 1906, Sect. 42).

Implied Obligation
Occurs where a right, duty or liability arises under a marine insurance contract by implication of law. Such an implied obligation may be varied or negatived by agreement expressed in the policy or by usage. The Marine Insurance Act provides that for usage to override the implied obligation it must be such usage as would bind both parties to the contract (M.I.A. 1906, Sect. 87).

Implied Warranty
A warranty that is not expressed in the policy specifically but which is understood by both parties to be incorporated in the contract. An implied warranty must be strictly complied with and in the event of a breach of the warranty the insurer is discharged from liability as from the date of the breach, but the insurer may waive the breach or the breach may be excused by Statute (See " Breach of Warranty "). The insurer is still liable for claims in respect of losses, by insured perils, occurring before the breach. The two main implied warranties are seaworthiness of the vessel and legality of the adventure.

Implied Warranty of Legality
See " Legality of Adventure ".

Implied Warranty of Neutrality
See " Neutrality ".

Implied Warranty of Seaworthiness
See " Seaworthiness ".

Import
To import: — To acquire goods overseas and to bring them into the Country of import.
An import: — A particular piece of merchandise imported into the Country of import.

" Important " Clause
A coloquial term used in the London market to indicate the

"Red Line Clause" (which see). The term derives from the word IMPORTANT at the head of the clause.

Impossible to Perform
Shipping term whereby a contract may be cancelled due to the impossibility to perform the terms of the contract by reason of a law coming into force prohibiting the action of the contract or for some similar reason.

Inadequate Packing
Not an insured peril. It is always understood that goods when insured are satisfactorily packed, in accordance with custom and trade, to withstand the perils of the voyage. It is not always possible to separate losses by insured perils from those by inadequacy of packing, so that claims are frequently paid, even though inadequate packing is involved. (See "Packing" and "Professional Packing".)

In and/or over
An abbreviation referring to goods being carried on deck or under-deck. When this appears in the slip it means that the goods are covered, even if on deck, at the same rate; except where a separate rate for over-deck shipments is stated. In the absence of this provision all goods are deemed shipped under-deck unless it is the custom of trade to ship them over-deck.

In Ballast
A vessel is in ballast when she is carrying no cargo. No vessel can remain stable at sea without some weight in her, so that when she is not carrying cargo she loads sand, water or some other substance to give her stability. A ballast cargo is a small, but heavy, cargo loaded purely for stability. Low freight rates are possible on a ballast cargo because it saves the shipowner carrying ballast, so it is customary to carry low value cargo in this way.

Inboard
The opposite to outboard (which see).

In Bond
Goods on which duty has not been paid are held "in bond".

inc.
Including *or* inclusive.

Inception of the policy
The time when the insurance comes into force.

Inchmaree Clause
Another name for the "Negligence Clause" (which see) in the Insti-

tute Time Clauses Hulls. So named because the clause was adopted following the decision of the case of Thames & Mersey Marine Ins. Co. Ltd. *v*. Hamilton, Fraser & Co., 1887, commonly known as the "*Inchmaree*" case, after the name of the vessel involved.

Incidental Non-marine
Risks which do not directly fall in the category of non-marine, but which are not strictly in the marine category. Some of the inland marine borderline risks fall in this category. Such insurances are generally placed in the marine market but the insurers in many instances have separate references for these risks so that they may keep them in a separate account.

incl.
Including *or* inclusive.

Included and Excluded Losses
These are specified in Section 55 of the Marine Insurance Act 1906. The included losses are, of course, those proximately caused by an insured peril. The excluded losses are detailed herein under "Excluded Losses".

In Commission
When a vessel is fitted out for navigating, that is capable of being used for the purpose for which she was intended, she is said to be "in commission". The term is used in yacht and small craft insurance, where the policy customarily contains a warranty that the vessel is laid up, out of commission, for part of the year. Where pleasure craft are concerned the warranty is usually for six months, including the winter period. (See "Out of Commission".)

Increased Value (Cargo)
The value expressed in a policy of marine insurance is conclusive between the insurer and assured whether it is correct or not. It is the duty of the assured to advise an insured value which is as near as it is possible to estimate that the actual gross arrived sound value will be. When goods are sold after the insurance has attached they are generally insured for the price the seller expected to get at destination. The buyer, naturally, expects to obtain more for the goods than he paid for them and so the insured value based on the seller's price is probably lower than the arrived value is estimated by the buyer to be. In such cases the buyer will wish to insure for the excess over the existing value to the increased value of the cargo. It is customary for the buyer to insure for an additional amount on the same terms as the existing policy and it is generally more convenient to arrange for an increase in the insured value on that policy. In

fact, some sets of trade clauses actually incorporate an increased value provision in the clauses. If an increased value insurance is effected the value of such insurance must be added to the existing value so that the whole total value is used in the claim calculation. This is important if the increased value is with separate insurers. Sometimes the buyer requests an insurance in his own name for the full increased insured value, and he may offer the existing policy to his new proposed insurers, suggesting that they pay him in full any claim under the new policy and exercise their rights of subrogation in claiming under the first policy. Insurers do not normally accept this proposition. (See also " Policy Proof of Interest ".)

Increased Value (Hull)
See " Excess Value ".

Increase of Weight by Water
In some cases where claims are assessed by the difference between the sound arrived weight and the damaged arrived weight, the commodity may suffer a natural increase in weight by absorption of water. If it is possible bales which have increased in weight and which have no damage should be compared with the shipped weights to determine the percentage of increase per bale. If this is not possible the Rules of Practice for the Association of Average Adjusters lay down principles to be applied to assess the claim in Rules E4 to E6.

Indemnify
To make a payment to an assured to make good a loss which he has suffered. (See " Indemnity ".)

Indemnity
The making good of a loss to the assured by financial payment. It does not include any profit to the assured in its pure sense but may, in practice, embrace some profit by agreement as in the case of cargo " Valued Policies ". (See also " Pure Indemnity ", " Measure of Indemnity " and " Valued Policies ".)

Indemnity (Salvage)
A form of insurance, subscribed by Lloyd's Underwriters, used in connection with a Corporation of Lloyd's salvage guarantee. (See " Salvage Guarantee ".)

Indent
An order for the supply of goods.

Indian Coal Warranty
One of the Institute Warranties. This warrants that the ship must

not carry Indian coal as cargo during the hot humid summer months. During early and late summer the carriage of Indian coal as cargo is limited to voyages not west of Aden and neither east nor south of Singapore.

Indicate

To indicate a rate the broker advises his client that he has obtained a " lead " who is willing to accept a line on the insurance at the rate indicated. When a broker indicates a rate he implies that, in his opinion, he will be able to complete the placing at that rate. He is not negligent if he later finds he cannot complete, but for the sake of his reputation he will usually state that the rate indicated applies only to the " lead " if he thinks he may have difficulty in completing the placing at that rate.

Indication

The rate which a broker indicates. (See " Indicate ".)

Indirect Damage

Damage caused indirectly by a peril insured against but not proximately caused by such peril.

Inevitable Accident

Where an accident occurs and no fault can be attributed to any of the parties involved. No liability therefore attaches to the assured concerned, nor has he any claim on the other party.

Inevitable Loss

A loss which must happen and which is not dependent on a fortuity. This is not an insured peril, nor can it be a general average loss.

INF or Inf

Information.

Infestation

Infested with vermin. Unless the policy specifically includes this risk it is excluded from the policy by the Marine Insurance Act 1906.

In Force

A policy or contract is " in force " from the time it has been accepted by the insurer to the time it expires or is cancelled.

Infra

A legal term meaning " later in the book or document ".

In Full

A premium provision. It is usual for the rate of premium to be specified in the slip or policy as a percentage of the insured value.

Sometimes the premium itself is expressed in currency, in which case it is usual to follow this with the expression " in full ' to denote that this is the whole premium payable under the policy. This is necessary since it is impossible for anyone to check that the premium is correct by comparison with the insured value if no percentage rate is shown. The term may be applied also to claim settlement when it means that no part of the claim remains outstanding.

Ingestion Clause

Because hovercraft are used, frequently, in areas where beaches of sand and grit are to be found, there is always a chance of damage to the power unit by ingestion of sand, water, etc. The clause provides that claims for damage of this type are recoverable only if attributable to a single recorded incident. Progressive damage is not covered, being regarded as wear and tear or depreciation. For multi-engined hovercraft each power unit is considered separately and the deductible is applied to the damage to each unit separately.

In Good Safety

Refers to the warranty which may appear in the policy providing that the vessel be in good safety at the commencement of the risk. If the policy specifies a particular day the vessel need not be in good safety for the whole of that day, provided it is safe at any time during that day.

Inherent Nature

Quality in the insured property which causes damage without the assistance of an outside agency. This has the same effect under the policy as inherent vice.

Inherent Vice

A quality inherent in a cargo which produces damage to the cargo without the assistance of an outside agency and by its own action. The perishable nature of fruit is inherent vice, as also is spontaneous combustion. The Marine Insurance Act, 1906, in Section 55, excludes losses proximately caused by the inherent vice or nature of the insured property, unless the policy specifically includes the peril. Inherent vice is not a " risk ", it is an inevitability, and as such is not covered by a policy covering " all risks '. To emphasise this the standard cargo " all risks " clauses specify that losses proximately caused by inherent vice or delay are excluded. In disputes the onus rests on the claimant to prove that the cargo was in good condition when the insurance commenced and it is improbable that the production of a clean bill of lading would be accepted as sufficient proof.

Initialling

An insurer initials the slip when he accepts a line. His initial is conclusive of his acceptance of the risk. His initial has the same binding effect on any agreement, attachment or amendment on or to the slip. It is usual for the broker to obtain the agreement of the underwriters on an open cover that any endorsement, amendment or agreement subsequently attached to the cover is valid when initialled by the leading underwriter only. This avoids the necessity for all agreements to be initialled by every underwriter on the insurance. Declarations are usually initialled by the leading underwriter on behalf of the others. The "leader only" agreement allows signing slips to be issued with the list of underwriters typed in but only the leader's line physically initialled.

Initial Premium

A deposit premium. A premium paid at inception of the insurance with the intention of adjustment to the correct premium later.

Injury to Harbours, Wharves, Piers etc.

Commonly known as "contact with objects" this refers to the liability of the shipowner in respect of damage caused by the vessel. Although the policy with the standard hull clauses attached covers liability of the assured to another ship, her cargo or loss of hire consequent upon collision, it does not cover liability for contact with objects. In fact liability for injury to harbours, wharves, piers, or similar, and property thereon is specifically excluded by the standard clauses. (See "Protection and Indemnity Risks".)

Inland Marine

Categorisation of insurance into specific channels to facilitate ease of operation results in risks being placed in their allotted category. Inland marine is one of these categories and embraces river, canal and inland water risks of small craft, barges, piers, wharves, bridges and similar items incidental thereto. In the American market the inland marine risks extend to such insurances as "horse and wagon" and others which have no connection with marine business at all. The marine market usually writes inland marine risks, some of which come under incidental non-marine business.

Inland transit risks are usually considered as inland marine. Jewellery and other high value insurances are often deemed to be inland marine risks because the marine market can usually accept higher lines than the non-marine market.

Inland Marine Insurance Bureau

An American organisation based in New York as a rating bureau in respect of inland marine risks.

Inland Marine Underwriters Association
An association of American inland marine insurers, based in New York, formed for the furtherance of the interests of inland marine insurers generally, by means of research and information.

I.N.M.
Incidental non-marine.

Inner Bottom
Another term for " Tank Top ".

In Personam
A legal term referring to legal action against an individual.

In Rem
A legal term referring to an action against an object or thing (e.g. against the ship). If the action is successful the claimant may obtain the arrest of the object as security against payment.

Ins.
Insurance.

Inscrutable Fault
When two ships are in collision but the fault cannot be attributed to either ship. In such cases neither is held to blame.

Insolvency
The broker does not guarantee the solvency of the insurer but he is obliged to use all his knowledge and skill to avoid placing the insurance with an insurer who may become insolvent. If the insurer becomes insolvent the assured who has a claim becomes a creditor of the insurer. Merchants shipping goods against payment on delivery may wish to protect themselves from loss due to the insolvency of the buyer. Since this risk falls in the category of financial guarantee insurers do not readily accept the insurance.

Insolvency Clause
A clause in a reinsurance policy or contract providing that payment for claims is to be made direct to the reassured in the event of the reassured's insolvency irrespective of any diminution of the reassured's liability to the original assured by reason of such insolvency.

Inspection Clause
A clause in a treaty entitling the reinsuring underwriters to inspect the books of the reinsured underwriter to ensure that the ceding underwriter has not failed in his obligation to fulfil the terms of the treaty. The reinsurer seldom exercises his right under this clause.

Inst.
Institute of London Underwriters.

Installation Floater
This is an American policy which covers machinery and equipment in transit to a site, for erection &/or installation, whilst there, and during erection &/or installation. In some cases it includes a period after the installation has been completed.

Instant Certificates
When insurance certificates are printed for specific insurance contracts (e.g. open covers) there is an unavoidable delay between the time the order is given and the time the sets of certificates are available. If this delay is unacceptable to a Lloyd's broker he can obtain a set of " instant certificates " from Lloyd's to help him out until the printed certificates are ready. Lloyd's Certificate Office (part of the S.C.A. Section of the Agency Department) enters the details of the insurance contract on a standard form which is then multigraphed to produce the required number of copies; these being numbered in consecutive sets, before being made available to the broker.

Inst. cls.
Institute Clauses.

Institute Agent
An agent appointed by the Institute of London Underwriters who is authorised to settle claims on Institute policies or certificates where provision is made for claims to be payable abroad.

Institute Amended Running Down Clause
See " Amended Running Down Clause ".

Institute Builders' Risk Clauses
See " Institute Clauses for Builders' Risks ".

Institute Cargo Clauses
There are three standard sets of clauses " WA ", " FPA " and " All Risks ". Apart from Clause 5 (see separate entry for details), each set of clauses has the same effect. In addition to the clause which varies, each set contains the following clauses: — Transit, Termination of adventure, Craft etc., Change of voyage, Constructive total loss, G.A., Seaworthiness admitted, Bailee, Not to Inure, Both to blame collision, F.C. & S., F.S.R. & C.C., Reasonable despatch. Each set of clauses ends with a reminder to the assured that he must give prompt notice to the insurer if any

of the " held covered " provisions in the clauses arise, the provisions being dependent on the giving of such prompt notice.

Institute Cargo Clauses—All Risks

A standard set of clauses, which (apart from a small variation in the transit clause) is identical to the other sets of Institute Cargo Clauses; but with the exception of the " all risks " clause (number 5. The " all risks " clause provides that the policy covers all loss or damage to the insured goods caused by a fortuity. To emphasise this it specifically excludes loss or damage caused by delay or inherent vice or nature in the insured property. Claims under the clause are payable in full without any franchise.

Institute Cargo Clauses—FPA

A standard set of clauses, identical to the W.A. set of Institute Cargo Clauses with the exception of the FPA clause. The FPA clause is also identical to the " Average clause " in the Institute Cargo Clauses WA so far as the vessel being stranded, sunk or burnt is concerned, and also so far as collision, contact of vessel or craft, fire, explosion, packages damaged at port of refuge or totally lost in loading or discharge are concerned. Landing and forwarding charges are recoverable as they would be under the WA clauses. The only difference in cover between the WA and FPA clauses occurs when partial loss is caused by heavy weather and the vessel has not been stranded, sunk or burnt during the voyage. Under the WA clauses the loss would be recoverable subject to the franchise, but under the FPA clauses it is not recoverable at all.

Institute Cargo Clauses W.A.

A standard set of clauses, which have the same effect as the other sets of Institute Cargo clauses with the exception of the " average clause ". The clause provides that a franchise shall apply to partial loss claims, other than general average, under the policy but its practical effect is that the franchise applies only to heavy weather damage. The clause does not specify any percentage for the franchise but relies on the percentage specified in the Policy (i.e. the memorandum). If the vessel is stranded, sunk or burnt the franchise is broken for the whole voyage, even though some of the damage may be heavy weather damage. Damage reasonably attributable to fire, explosion, collision or contact of the vessel and/or craft and/or conveyance with ice or any object or substance, not including water of course, is recoverable under the clause; thus so far as such loss is concerned the principle of proximate cause is ignored. Damage occurring during discharge at a port of refuge is covered. The total loss of an entire package in loading or discharge is treated as a "total loss of part" and the insured value of that package is payable in full. The average clause provisions apply during the whole period of the insurance, that is, from warehouse to warehouse, subject to termination in accordance with the transit clause.

Institute Certificate

A Combined Company certificate of marine insurance printed on behalf of the Institute of London Underwriters to be issued off an Institute policy. It incorporates all the clauses, conditions and details of the policy but is only valid when backed by a properly executed policy. It is usual for such certificates to be issued in respect of individual shipments declared off an open cover and/or open policy and provide documentary evidence for the consignee that insurance has been effected. Such certificates may provide for claims to be payable abroad, in which case the presentation of the certificate to the Institute Settling Agent is sufficient proof of the existence of a policy for him to settle the claim.

Institute Claims Payable Abroad

The Institute of London Underwriters administers a Department to deal exclusively with claims paid abroad by Institute Agents who are authorised to do so by an Institute policy or certificate. Institute Settling Agents are appointed by the Institute Committee and are paid a fee for their services in settling claims. Claims may only be settled in this manner when specially authorised in the policy or certificate.

Institute Classification Clause

See "Classification Clause".

Institute Clauses

Clauses approved by a Committee appointed by marine insurers in London and published by The Institute of London Underwriters. These clauses are the standard clauses used in the marine insurance market. There are sets of Institute clauses covering every major form of marine interest whether hull or cargo.

Institute Clauses for Air Sendings

The Institute Air Cargo Clauses (All Risks). See "Air Cargo Clauses".

Institute Clauses for Builders' Risks

This set of clauses, revised and reissued at 1st December 1972, is designed for attachment to policies covering loss of or damage to vessels whilst at the builders' risk under construction. Nevertheless provision is made to cover the pre keel risk of materials intended for use in the construction of the vessel from the time such materials are delivered to the place of construction. Otherwise, the cover on the hull and machinery, on provisional values (to be adjusted by an escalator clause), commences from the date of laying the keel and continues for the full contract period. The clauses contain a section for entering the proposed period of the contract and should completion of the contract be delayed the subject matter insured is held covered.

The clauses cover all risks of loss or damage including repairing or replacing defective parts condemned solely due to the discovery of a latent defect during the period of insurance. The same basic hull conditions apply to these clauses as in the Institute Time Clauses (Hulls), but average is payable irrespective of percentage. Loss due to faulty design is not covered. The insurance continues during movement within the area of the place of construction and also during trials up to 250 nautical miles by water from such place of construction. Collision liability is covered up to four-fourths of the insured value of the vessel, otherwise the cover provided by this collision clause is identical to that in the Institute Time Clauses (Hulls), except that the specified exclusions thereunder are not so excluded under the Builders' clauses. A protection and indemnity clause, as a supplementary contract, provides cover against P & I risks, but both under this clause and the main clauses forming this set liability is excluded in respect of workmen and employees as covered elsewhere by various protective Acts or Statutes.

Institute Company
An insurance company which is a member of The Institute of London Underwriters.

Institute Container Clauses
See " Container Clauses ".

Institute Fishing Vessel Clauses
See " Fishing Vessel Clauses ".

Institute Freight Clauses
See " Freight Clauses ".

Institute Frozen Food Clauses
See " Frozen Food Clauses ".

Institute of London Underwriters
An association of Company Underwriters representing the Companies which are members of the Institute. The Institute is controlled

by a Committee elected from its members. The purpose of the Institute is to further the interests of insurance by co-ordinating facilities regarding wordings, clauses and conditions and to find grounds for common agreement on problems affecting the insurance market. Principally the Institute concentrates on marine business.

Committees are formed which include Lloyd's Underwriters as well as members of the Institute to decide on matters affecting the whole market and to make recommendations to the market based on their findings. The Institute provides facilities for these Committees to meet. The Technical and Clauses Committee and The Joint Hull Committee are two such Committees. The "Returns Bureau" (The Joint Hull Returns Bureau) operates under the auspices of the Joint Hull Committee for the benefit of the whole market and authorises "lay up" returns for both Lloyd's and Company Underwriters. In addition to its services to insurance, the Institute administers a Policy Signing Office and a "Claims Payable Abroad" service on behalf of its member Companies.

Institute Policy

A combined Company policy issued by The Institute of London Underwriters on behalf of its members who are subscribers to the insurance.

Institute Policy Department

A policy signing office administered by the Institute of London Underwriters for the purpose of signing combined company policies on behalf of member companies. The department also "takes down" additional and returns of premium and signs the endorsements to attach to the policies.

Institute Port Risk Clauses

A set of standard hull clauses for use on policies issued to cover vessels on port risks only.

In addition to the ordinary cover a four-fourths collision clause is incorporated, in which liability to harbours etc. (i.e. all the express exclusions from the Time Clauses collision clause) are specifically included. There is a Protection and Indemnity clause incorporated covering those risks normally covered by a P & I club, including liability for loss of life and personal injury.

All claims are paid irrespective of percentage.

Institute Running Down and Sistership Clauses

In 1971 the I.L.U. issued an amended version of Cl. 24 to replace the clause issued on 1st January 1969. The new clause incorporates the 1971 amendment to the R.D.C. (See "Amended Running Down Clause".)

Institute Speedboat Clauses

A set of clauses designed for attachment to policies covering speedboats to express the special conditions and exclusions. It is required that the assured or other competent person be on board and in control of the craft if under way. The clauses exclude loss occurring whilst the craft is moored or anchored unattended off an exposed beach or shore or if it is taking part in any official race or speed test. Various other exclusions are specified, details of which may be found by examining Clause No. 131. The current clause is dated 1 January 1972.

Institute Strikes Clauses

A set of cargo clauses covering the risks of loss or damage to the insured property caused by strikers, locked out workmen or persons involved in labour disturbances, riots or civil commotions, also persons acting maliciously. Excluding loss or damage proximately caused by delay, inherent vice or nature of the insured property, shortage of labour or similar, expenses following delay or war perils. The provisions of the transit clause are incorporated in the clauses. Claims are payable irrespective of percentage. Separate clauses are printed to apply to policies subject to Trade clauses. There is also an Institute Strikes Clause in respect of builder's risks. Hull strikes cover is incorporated in the hull war clauses.

Institute Time Clauses

A standard set of hull clauses for use on policies covering vessels for a period of time. A space is left in Clause 12 (deductible average clause) in which is inserted an amount to be deducted from the aggregate of all partial loss claims occurring in any one accident or occurrence. The claims to be aggregated include particular average, general average, salvage charges, sue and labour expenses and claims under the R.D.C. Underwriters pay the cost of sighting the bottom following stranding whether or not damage is found but not when the costs are incurred by the vessel grounding in certain specified areas, such as the Manchester Ship Canal. The clauses cover all risks of total and constructive total loss and pay partial loss, subject to the deductible average provisions, without reference to the insured value. An additional deductible amounting to 10% of the net claim is applied to damage to machinery attributable to negligence of master, officers or crew. No deductions are made in respect of new material replacing old. Whilst a depreciation allowance is given on a policy that expires with unrepaired damage such is not paid if the vessel becomes a total loss under the policy. A "tender clause" protects the insurer's right to ensure reasonable cost of repairs. The clauses provide for sue and labour charges, salvage charges and general average contributions to be paid by insurers, subject to the policy deductible. A collision clause gives a limited form of liability cover in respect of collision with another vessel, in addition to any claims under the remainder of the policy. War perils are excluded. The policy is automatically cancelled in event of change of ownership or management without insurer's approval, a pro rata daily return of premium usually being paid for the unexpired portion. Returns of premium are also allowed on a monthly basis in event of mutual cancellation or on a 30 days' basis if the vessel be laid up.

Institute Voyage Clauses

A set of hull clauses for attachment to policies covering vessels for specific voyages. The clauses are based on the Time Clauses and have the same deductible average provisions.

Institute War Clauses

Cargo: — The war cover provided by these clauses is limited by the waterborne clause, to apply only to the period from the time the goods are loaded on the overseas vessel to the time they are discharged from the overseas vessel. If the vessel arrives at the discharge port but the goods are not unloaded, cover ceases 15 days after midnight on the day of arrival. A limit of 15 days is allowed at a transhipping port, but only whilst the goods remain within the port area. If the cover lapses during transhipment it re-attaches as the goods are loaded onto the on-carrying vessel. Craft risk is not covered, except in respect of derelict mines or torpedoes. The clauses reinstate into the policy the risks which were excluded by the F.C. & S. clause and, in addition incorporate warlike operations, hostilities, civil war, rebellion, revolution, insurrection or consequent civil strife, mines, torpedoes, bombs or other war weapons. Losses proximately caused by delay, inherent vice or loss of market or claims arising out of delay are all excluded. The clauses also exclude loss, damage or expenses arising from any hostile use of a nuclear or atomic or similar weapon of war and incorporate a frustration clause (which see).

Hulls: — These clauses reinstate into the policy the perils excluded therefrom by the F.C. & S. clause and in addition incorporate warlike operations, hostilities, civil war, rebellion, revolution, insurrection or consequent civil strife, mines, torpedoes or other war weapons. The clauses extend to embrace a strikes cover, similar to that afforded by the cargo strikes clause.

An automatic termination of cover clause is incorporated so that the policy is cancelled on the outbreak of war between any of the great powers and excludes loss covered by any hostile act resulting in such a war.

Apart from automatic termination or the outbreak of a major war, underwriters can terminate the insurance by giving 14 days' notice to the assured. Loss, damage or expense arising from the hostile detonation of a nuclear, or similar, weapon of war are excluded and the insurance terminates automatically in the event of such detonation, even if the insured vessel is not involved.

A pro rata net return is payable if the policy is cancelled either under the clause or by sale of the vessel.

Freight: — These clauses contain the same provisions as the Hull clauses. There is a separate set of war clauses for attachment to policies insuring containers. (See "Container Clauses".)

Institute Warranties

A set of standard warranties for incorporation in hull policies. They are mainly navigational warranties prohibiting the vessel from entering specified hazardous waters. Basically the vessel is kept between 70° N lat. and 50° S lat. She is also prevented from being in the St. Lawrence approaches or the Baltic (in stages) during the icing and thawing seasons. East Continental ports north of the St. Lawrence on the American Continent and north of Nahodka and Vladivostock on the Asian Continent are prohibited, as are West Coast American ports north of 54° 30′ N lat. or west of 130° 50′ W long.

The final warranty prohibits the carriage of Indian coal as cargo during the hot wet season and its carriage for long voyages (i.e. not West of Aden, not East nor beyond Singapore) during the warm, not so wet, season. (See also "Breach of Warranty Clause".)

Institute Yacht Clauses

A set of hull time clauses designed for attachment to policies covering vessels with a designed speed not exceeding 17 knots and which are used for private pleasure purposes only. The clauses are used for vessels of all sizes, subject to the speed limit above, but there is a warranty that no additional (P.P.I.) insurances be effected unless the insured value is £30,000 or more when 10% of such value, only, can be insured on ancillary interests. It is expected that the vessel will be limited to a specified navigational area and that she will be laid up out of commission for part of the year; the clauses leaving space for entry of the details. Chartering is excluded. The clauses can be extended to embrace vessels with a designed speed exceeding 17 knots but subject to the Institute Speedboat Clauses (which see). A four fourths collision clause and a P. & I. Clause are incorporated. Further details can be obtained by reference to Cl. 97 (1/1/72).

Inst. strikes

Strikes, riots and civil commotions clauses issued by the Institute of London Underwriters.

Inst. T.

Institute of Transport.

Inst. War etc.

War and Strikes clauses issued by the Institute of London Underwriters.

Inst. Wties.

Institute Warranties.

Insufficiency of Packing

See " Packing " and " Professional Packing ".

Insurable Interest

By law no person is allowed to insure unless he has an insurable interest in the adventure, that is, he must stand to lose something if the property at risk is lost, damaged or detained or he may incur a liability in respect of the property or suffer because it fails to arrive on time. (Separate details are shown elsewhere herein regarding individual interests). If any person effects or helps to effect an insurance where the assured has no insurable interest he is guilty of an offence under the Gambling Policies Act. To claim under a policy the assured must have an insurable interest at the time of loss, even though he need not have an interest at the time he effects the insurance.

The insurable interest of an insured is limited to the amount which he stands to lose. Where this can be ascertained, in the absence of a special agreement with the insurer, it must not be more than the insurable value of the interest as provided by the Marine Insurance Act 1906. Where the amount cannot be ascertained with any certainty the amount must be reasonable. In the latter case where hull interests are concerned the insurer on the policy covering the ship limits the amount insurable on ancillary interests by the disbursements warranty. The " special agreement " referred to previously relates to the insured's right to effect a valued policy (see " Valued Policies ", " New for Old ", " Second hand Machinery " and " Machinery Damage ".)

Insurable Property

So far as marine insurance is concerned, insurable property is any ship, goods or other movables exposed to maritime perils.

Insurable Value

In practice the insured value is agreed and is conclusive. If the policy is unvalued it is necessary to know how to calculate the insurable value; that is, the maximum amount which may be insured where a policy has no agreed value. Basically, the insurable value of a ship is the actual value of the ship at commencement of the risk including machinery, fittings etc., fuel stores, outfit, wages, disbursements and insurance premiums. On cargo the insurable value is the cost of the cargo plus freight and insurance charges. On freight or any other interest the insurable value is the amount at risk of the assured, plus insurance charges. In practice all hull and cargo policies are valued so that the above is seldom needed.

Insurance Broker

See " Broker ".

Insurance Charges

The premium paid by the assured. The assured has an insurable interest in the insurance charges he has paid and may insure them.

Insurance Company

See " Company ".

Insurance is Uberrimae Fidei

Insurance is based on the principle of the utmost good faith.

Insurance Premiums

See " Premiums ".

Insurance Society of New York

An educational body, engaged in educating those whose business is insurance.

Insured

The same as Assured, (which see.)

Insured Against

When the property is "insured against" a specified peril, the insurer is liable for loss or damage proximately caused by that peril.

Insured Peril

A peril specified in the policy. Losses proximately caused by such a peril are recoverable under the policy, provided they reach the franchise, if any, or, where applicable, exceed the deductible.

Insured Value
The value, for insurance purposes, of the property insured. (See " Valued Policies ".)

Insured Vessel
When this expression appears in a hull policy it means the vessel which is insured by that policy.

Insurer
The Underwriter. May also be called the " Assurer ".

Insurer's Interest
The insurer undertakes a liability when he accepts an insurance. He therefore has an insurable interest in that liability, so that he may reinsure his liability with other insurers. He may not reinsure on wider terms than the original insurance.

Int.
Interest.

Inter Alia
Amongst other things.

Intercostal
A girder, in a ship, that is fitted longitudinally but does not run the full length of the ship.

Interest
The property which is the subject of the insurance or the rights in or obligation to that property whereby the assured may suffer a loss or incur a liability.

Interest on Deposits
The depositor in respect of a general average deposit is entitled to interest on the money whilst on deposit in the general average fund. This interest is at a fixed rate and added to form part of the fund. When the adjustment is finally agreed and the claims for general average are satisfied the balance of the fund is apportioned in accordance with contributory values, as a refund to the interests which contributed to the fund. Since the interest accrued forms part of the fund it is automatically paid in the refund.

Interest on Recoveries
When a claim is paid to the assured the insurer is subrogated to the rights of the assured in respect of the property. He may recover from third parties, responsible for the damage, amounts by way of damages up to the amount of claim paid to the assured. If the period of time which elapses between the payment of the claim and

the recovery to the insurer is considerable it may be agreed that interest is payable and may be added to the amount of the recovery. It may be provided in the policy that interest is shared between the underwriter and the assured when there is a period of delay between the time the accident occurred and the time the claim is paid to the assured.

Interest or No Interest

Any policy containing this term is invalid in law. The term is seldom used because it implies that the assured has no insurable interest at all. It is more normal to use the expressions " Policy Proof of Interest " and " Full Interest Admitted ".

Interest on Reserve

It is customary for a provision to be made in long term re-insurance contracts (e.g. treaties) for the reinsured to retain part of the premium in reserve to meet claims which will attach, subsequently, to the reinsurance contract. Because the reinsured holds money that should be in the reinsurer's account he is expected to pay interest on each amount for the period (usually 12 months) the money is held in the reinsured's account. The amount of interest to be paid is agreed in the contract and is paid on the amount released in the same account as the release of reserve. Where the amount released has been held for less than 12 months the interest is calculated at pro rata of the annual rate.

Interinsurance Exchange

American term for reciprocal insurance. Reciprocal insurance is the exchange of insurance liability between two or more insurers by which each bears a proportion of the other's risk, by way of reinsurance. The purpose is to spread the risk. The English non-marine market has a similar system, but reciprocity is uncommon in the marine market.

Interruption of Voyage

If goods are discharged at an intermediate port by reason of an insured peril, the insurance continues during any transhipment, reloading or onward carriage until the goods arrive at destination.

In Tort

A legal action outside a contract. A third party legal liability action is an example.

in trans

In transit *or* in transitu.

In transitu

In transit, applies to goods during the voyage. (See " Stoppage in Transitu ".)

Inure

To come into use or effect, or to serve for one's use or benefit. (See " Not to Inure Clause ".)

Invalid Policy

A policy which is inadmissible as evidence in a court of law. The policy need not necessarily be illegal but it is illegal if no insurable interest exists. The only types of policies that are used in practice, but which are invalid, are P.P.I. or F.I.A. policies.

To be valid a policy must be properly executed, further it must not contain the terms " Policy Proof of Interest " or " Full Interest Admitted ", or any like term and, finally, the assured must have an insurable interest.

Invisible Export

A service which brings money into a Country, benefiting the Country's economy. Marine insurance is a very important invisible export.

Invitation to Tender

When a vessel is damaged the insurer is entitled, by the standard clauses, to request that the assured invites tenders. That is, the assured must send details of the damage survey reports to repairing firms inviting them to tender (i.e. submit estimates) for the job. (See " Tender Clause ".)

Invoice

Documentary evidence of the sale contract and price of goods. (See " Export Invoice ".)

Inward Charges

The charges payable by a shipowner in respect of his vessel entering port.

i/o

In and/or over-deck.

i.o.p.

Irrespective of percentage.

I.P.R.C.

Institute Port Risk Clauses.

Irrespective of Percentage

A term in a policy which provides that the memorandum franchise shall not apply and, in fact, that claims are payable without the application of a franchise.

Irretrievably Deprived

Where the assured is deprived of the insured property and it appears unlikely that he will retrieve it, there is an *actual* total loss.

Irrevocable Credit

See " Confirmed Irrevocable Credit ".

I.T.A.

Institute of Traffic Administration.

I.T.C.

Institute Time Clause (Hulls).

I.V. *or* **I/V**

Increased value. Sometimes used for " Insured Value " or " Invoice Value ".

I.V.C.

Institute Voyage Clauses.

I.Y.C.

Institute Yacht Clauses

J

Jack Up

A form of off shore drilling rig that comprises, basically, a barge with legs at each corner. The barge is towed into position and the legs are lowered until they " spud " into the seabed. The barge " climbs " the legs until it is situated a safe height above the surface of the sea. The " jack up " is used, mainly, where the drilling operations involve a water depth of no more than 300 ft. approximately. It may have facilities for self propulsion but it is impracticable to move the rig by this method except in very shallow water without a risk of leg damage.

J (A) Form

A plain form of policy which specifies no perils. It differs from the " J " form in that it does not contain the war and civil war exclusion clause.

j. and/or l.o.

Jettison and/or loss overboard.

j. and/or w.o.

Jettison and/or washing overboard.

Janson Clause

A clause applying an excess to the policy.

Japanese Ice Clause

A clause, seldom used today, on a hull policy covering a vessel which it is anticipated may enter and/or navigate Japanese waters. The clause excludes damage caused by contact with ice whilst the vessel is in Japanese waters during the period from 15th November to 30th April, or some other specified dates showing the winter period. The clause usually provides that such damage caused in an attempt to avert or minimise a loss from an insured peril shall not be excluded by the clause.

Japanese Marine Corporation

See " Nippon Kaiji Kyokai ". The Institute Classification clause shows " Japanese Marine Corporation ".

Jason Clause

A clause appearing in contracts of affreightment where disputes may be subject to American Law. By the Harter Act 1893 the ship-owner is not liable for faults in navigation or management provided he has exercised due diligence to make the vessel seaworthy. Nevertheless he could not claim any contribution from the cargo owner for general average expenditure or sacrifice which resulted from faulty navigation or mismanagement. Carriers, therefore, introduced a clause into contracts of affreightment whereby the cargo owners agreed to pay such contributions. The case of the vessel "Jason" in 1912 tested the validity of the clause, and the present clause, the "New Jason Clause", provides that the expenditure or sacrifice must not result from lack of due diligence by the shipowner for the cargo owner to be liable for general average contributions.

Java Tobacco Survey Clause
A clause warranting that tobacco from the area of the Java Seas has been examined before shipment by Lloyd's Agent or other authorised person to ensure it is suitable for shipment. This clause is not used generally today.

Jerque Note
When a vessel has discharged her cargo a Customs Official carries out an inspection and issues a jerque note confirming no cargo remains on board for delivery at the port.

Jerquer
Customs Official concerned with examination of ship's cargo and inspecting the vessel to see no cargo remains undelivered.

Jetsam
Goods jettisoned from a vessel.

Jett.
Jettison.

Jettison
The sacrificing of cargo by throwing it overboard. A circumstance which may arise in time of common peril, when jettison is necessary to save the rest of the property involved in the adventure. It is the primary example of a general average act and, as such, the loss is shared proportionately by the parties to the adventure who benefit from the jettison. Jettison of deck cargo not customarily carried on deck is not allowed in general average under the York-Antwerp Rules. If jettisoned property is recovered it is still the property of the original owner and may be reclaimed by him, or his insurers, on payment of any salvage due on the salved property. Jettison is an insured peril.

Jetty Clause
A clause used in policies covering flour, grain and similar cargoes,

where the interest will be placed in landing sheds, following discharge, to await onward transit to the final destination. The insurance continues under the Transit Clause but the Jetty Clause provides that a survey be carried out in the landing sheds and that the insurer shall not be liable for any loss by theft, pilferage or shortage occurring after the survey. It may also contain a provision limiting cover to Fire Risk Only following removal from the landing sheds. Notice must be given to the Lloyd's Agent at the port of discharge to permit attendance when the goods are discharged from craft and during any subsequent loading.

Jeweller's Block Policy
See " Block Policy ".

J. Form
A plain form of policy which specifies no perils, but contains the war and civil war exclusion clause. It is used for risks where no sea transit is involved.

Joint Cargo Committee
A committee formed of Lloyd's and Company Underwriters to discuss problems on cargo insurance and to make recommendations to the marine market based on its findings.

Joint Cargo Survey
When there is some question of carrier's liability it is often necessary for a surveyor appointed by the cargo owner to co-operate with a surveyor appointed by the carrier in order to carry out a joint survey.

Joint Hull Agreements
See " Joint Hull Understandings ".

Joint Hull Committee
A Committee formed of Lloyd's and Company Underwriters which meets to discuss hull matters and which makes rating and condition recommendations to the hull marine market. The Joint Hull Returns Bureau is operated under the auspices of this Committee.

Joint Hull Returns Bureau
A bureau operating under the auspices of the Joint Hull Committee. Applications for " Lay-up returns " are submitted to this Bureau for approval.

Joint Hull Survey
A survey of a ship carried out jointly by the surveyor representing

the Insurer in co-operation with the surveyor representing the Assured.

Joint Hull Understandings

A set of understandings between the insurers engaged in writing hull business in the London market. The purpose of the understandings is to obtain a uniform approach on broad principles affecting hull business. Experience has shown that successful operating of the market is based on uniformity of practice and the understandings are agreed for this purpose.

An important feature of the understandings is a formula for the guidance of insurers when considering the adjustment of renewal premium rates.

Joint Survey

See " Joint Cargo Survey " and " Joint Hull Survey ".

Joint Tortfeasors

When two or more vessels are negligent in causing damage to an innocent vessel an action may be pursued in tort jointly against the negligent shipowners or managers or separately at the option of the injured party. The persons being sued jointly are called "joint tortfeasors".

Jones Act

An Act passed by the U.S. Congress in 1920 which provided that a seaman injured in the course of his employment as a result of the negligence of the shipowner, master or fellow crew member, could recover damages for his injuries.

Judgements of Oleron

One of the first compilations of the rules of the sea. Decisions of the maritime court of Oleron, an island off the western coast of France. It is said that the rules are very old, going back possibly to Viking times.

Jumbo-ise

A slang expression that refers to ship reconstruction. Where a ship is rebuilt to make it very much larger (sometimes by joining together the hulls of two vessels) it is said to be jumbo-ised.

Jurisdiction

Claims under a British marine insurance policy are subject to British jurisdiction unless the " Foreign Jurisdiction Clause " is attached to the policy. The term " jurisdiction " means that the policy is subject to the ruling of the Court. The Court will base its findings on the terms of the policy or contract, but will not normally override these with the law of the Country unless such terms are directly contrary to the law. (See " Forum Conveniens ".)

Jury Mast

A temporary mast.

Jute Clauses

F.P.A. clauses used on policies insuring jute from Calcutta or Chittagong. Basically they follow the standard cargo clauses, but incorporate an increased value clause.

K

K.D.

Knocked down.

K.D.C.

Knocked down condition. Refers to vehicles being shipped dismantled in boxes.

Kedge

A small anchor. To kedge: to pull a vessel by means of anchor and cable.

Keel Block

When a ship is drydocked she rests on keel blocks that hold her in an upright position. The trim of the vessel is such that the stern settles on the keel blocks first as the water is pumped out of the drydock and, as it does so, shores are wedged in either side (working from stem to stern) so that, finally, the vessel rests in a sort of cradle.

Ketch

A small coastal vessel, having two masts.

Kild

Kilderkin.

Kilderkin

A measure of liquid being 18 gallons.

Kingpost

A vertical mast supporting a derrick. (Also termed " Samson ".)

King/Pres.

Kingston/Prescott Clause (Lakers).

Knocked Down Condition

Applicable to vehicle transit as cargo. Vehicles may be shipped in a dismantled or " Knocked down " condition.

Knock for Knock

The principle of single liability applied between insurers. Where two vessels are in collision the principle could be applied, although in marine insurance practice this is seldom so. The expression is more common to motor insurance where under this principle, each insurer bears the cost of repairing the property which he insures, to the extent that it is covered by the insurance, without seeking to recover the cost from the insurer of the other property involved in the accident.

Knot

A measurement of speed. One nautical mile per hour. A nautical mile measures 6,080 feet.

Known Loss

A loss of which the assured and/or the insurer is aware at the time the insurance is effected.

In most cases, marine insurance is placed on a " lost or not lost " basis, whereby the insurer agrees to cover losses occurring prior to acceptance, if the risk has already commenced, provided the assured was not aware of the loss at that time. If he was aware of it he must have communicated the information to the insurer or there would be non-disclosure of a material fact. In some cases the insurer is aware of a casualty occurring to the vessel carrying the cargo which he is asked to insure. He may then insist on a warranty that there is " no known loss ".

L

Label Clause
There are two types of this clause in use in the marine market, both of which concern canned or similar goods where identification or sale may be affected by damage to the attached labels. In the event of contact with water the labels may be damaged or washed off. The most common form of the clause excludes claims for lost or damaged labels and limits the insurer's liability to the cost of re-labelling and repacking the goods. The little used form of the clause excludes claims for lost or damaged labels unless caused by the vessel being stranded, sunk, burnt, on fire or in collision or contact with any substance other than water.

Labour Costs
When repairs are carried out on a ship for the insurer's account all ordinary labour costs are part of the cost of repairs and are payable under the policy. If, however, overtime enhances the labour costs and the overtime is to release the ship for service at an earlier date, the insurer is only liable for the additional cost of labour up to the amount saved in dock dues and similar expenses. The expense of a shipowner's superintendent to superintend the repairs is allowable under the policy as part of the cost of repairs.

L.A.C.C.
Lloyd's Aviation Claims Centre.

Laden in Bulk
Expression denoting that a vessel is carrying bulk or loose cargo.

Laden Loadline
The loadline marked on the side of a ship indicating the maximum depth the vessel is allowed to sink, when laden, to comply with the loadline regulations. Also termed, " Load Waterline ". (See also " Light Loadline ".)

Lagen
Goods jettisoned or lost overboard which have been buoyed and/or marked for subsequent recovery.

Laid Up
See "Lay up Return", "Lay up Warranty" and "Out of Commission".

212

Lakers
Vessels employed in the American Great Lakes and the North American canal system.

Lake Cls.
Lake Time Clauses (Hulls).

Lake Time Clauses (Hulls)
There are several sets of these clauses, some published by the American (U.S.A.) Institute and others published by the Canadian Board of Marine Underwriters. The clauses are based on the standard hull time clauses suitably amended to cover the special conditions of vessels operating on the Great Lakes and canals of North America.

LANBY
Large automatic navigation buoy. These buoys, sometimes as large as 40 ft. in diameter and weighing about 40 tons, with an equal weight in water ballast for stability, are fitted with diesel generators to supply electric power for a long range light and a fog signal. Up to 1973 two such large buoys had replaced light vessels, one near Portland Bill and the other at Morecambe Bay, representing a considerable saving in running costs to Trinity House.

Landed Weight
The weight of the goods when landed at destination.

Landing Account
Record kept by the dock Authorities showing weights, condition etc. of goods landed.

Landing Book
When goods are landed and received by the wharf Warehouse Keepers or Dock Companies entries are made in the landing book giving details of the goods, their weights and condition.

Landing Charges
Charges payable on cargo at the port of destination. These include expense of unloading, temporary warehousing, duty and freight, if this is payable at destination. Particular average claims are calculated on the " gross " value which is the actual value of the cargo when sold or delivered at destination and therefore includes landing charges. The net value of goods is the gross value less the landing charges. In the case of general average or salvage it should be noted that the landing charges would not be paid if the goods did not arrive at the destination port, hence they have not been saved

by the general average or salvage act. The adjustments for general average or salvage contribution must, therefore, be calculated on net values.

Landing Order

An order giving authority to the wharfinger or dock Company to receive the goods from the vessel.

Landing Weight

Landed weight.

Land Risks

Those perils which may operate when cargo is in transit on land to the port of loading or from the port of discharge. These risks are not maritime in nature and unless embraced by the perils specified in the policy form (i.e. fire), they are not covered by the ordinary policy except when expressly specified therein. They are covered by the term " all risks " when the policy contains a warehouse to warehouse clause.

L.A.S.H.

Lighter aboard ship. A system for carrying loaded barges or lighters on ocean voyages. The " mother " ship is a unique large type carrier. The first to be designed, " Acadia Forest " is a 43,000 ton, 20 knot vessel with an overall length of 860 ft., a beam of 107 ft. and a draft of 37 ft. It is propelled by a diesel engine generating 26,000 h.p. The lighters are raised, laden, and stowed in the mother ship by a moving gantry; each lighter weighing about 400 tons. The mother ship can carry 70 or more lighters and the gantry crane has a lifting capacity of over 500 tons. On arrival at the destination port the lighters are lowered into the water for onward transit and the mother ship takes on a fresh batch of lighters for the return trip. In 1974 a U.S. court held that a L.A.S.H. barge cannot be deemed to be a " vessel " by itself.

Lat.

Latitude.

Latent Defect

A hidden flaw or defect in the construction of the ship which is not readily discoverable by a competent person using reasonable skill in an ordinary inspection. Unless the policy so provides damage caused by a latent defect is not recoverable, nor is the mere discovery of a latent defect. (See " Latent Defect Clause ".)

Latent Defect Clause

A clause attached to a hull policy covering loss or damage to the hull or machinery directly caused by a latent defect in the hull or machinery. The mere discovery of a latent defect is not covered by the policy, but if the effect of the defect becoming apparent directly causes damage to another part of the vessel this damage is covered, subject to the deductible in the policy. In effect, the clause incorporates latent defect as an insured peril.

The " Liner Negligence Clause ", if in the policy, includes, not only the damage caused by the latent defect, but also replacement of the part with the defect therein. It is not customary for the clause to cover the mere discovery of a latent defect. Besides latent defects the clause incorporates the *perils* of negligence, breakage of shafts, bursting of boilers, contact with aircraft, explosion, nuclear reactors or installations and accidents in loading, bunkering or discharging.

L.A.T.F.
Lloyd's American Trust Fund.

Launching Ways
Baulks of heavy timber constructing a path down which a ship slides to enter the water during launching. (See also " Poppet ".)

Lawful Adventure
There is an implied warranty in every marine insurance contract that the adventure must be legal. That is, it must be lawful and within the law of the land.

Lawful Merchandise
Goods which it is not unlawful to carry.

Lay Barge
A large vessel designed to lay sections of pipe on the seabed to form the oil or gas carrying medium to take the products of a well drilled off shore. The lay barge is usually a semi-submersible vessel but with no facility for conveying pipe to the site or for storing pipe. The pipe is carried to the lay barge by a supply vessel. The barge is propelled by laying anchors astern and forward; drawing the vessel on the anchor cables along a pre-determined path. (See " Suitcasing Anchors ".)

Lay Days
Under a voyage charterparty it is essential that the vessel is not delayed longer than necessary when discharging or loading cargo. For this reason a fixed number of " lay days " is allowed for the purpose of loading or discharge. It is usual to specify the number of days allowed separately for either loading or discharge but in

some cases "reversible lay days" are agreed. This agreement allows a fixed number of days in total for both loading and discharge. If the vessel is still "lying" at the wharf on expiry of the specified lay days "demurrage", or loss of hire, is payable by the charterer.

Lay up Refund

An American expression for the return of premium due by reason of the vessel being laid up. (See "Lay Up Return".)

Lay up Return

The premium charged on a hull time policy is based on the vessel navigating and being exposed to full maritime hazards during the whole currency of the policy. If the ship is laid up in protected waters for any reasonable length of time the risk is considerably reduced. The premium for the laid up period should naturally be lower since the only major risk is that of fire. The marine market has agreed a scale of the premiums chargeable for the laid up risk calculated as a percentage of the navigating rate. Since the premium on the policy has been paid at the full navigating rate a return of premium is payable to the assured, by agreement, in respect of the difference between the laid up risk premium and the navigating premium. The laid up risk premium is therefore called a "retention" as it is part of the navigating premium which is retained by the insurer. The amount of return is calculated by deducting the gross annual retention from the gross annual policy premium. From the difference 15% is deducted to arrive at the net annual lay up return, such deduction being necessary to enable the broker to retain his brokerage for the work involved. The net annual lay up return is then divided by 12 to provide the net lay up return allowed per period. To qualify for one period of lay up the vessel must be laid up for a period of not less than 30 consecutive days. A part period does not qualify for a return, except where it forms part of a full period which overlaps two policies. Retentions are varied according to whether or not the vessel is under repair. All returns, under the clause, are subject to "and arrival" which means that they are not payable until expiry of the policy and only then if the vessel has not become a total loss before the date of expiry of the policy. For this reason, the assured has an insurable interest in his lay up returns, whereby he may insure them. At 1st January 1964 the system of lay up retentions was changed from a fixed amount to a percentage basis. Thus, the retention for a vessel under repair is 40% of the annual net premium per annum and the retention for a vessel not under repair is 20% of the annual net premium per annum. By this method the circumstances resulting in a high or low navigating premium rate on a particular vessel are reflected in the lay up retention but, so that neither insurer nor assured shall be unduly affected by any substantially enhanced or reduced rate the retentions are subject to fixed maximums and minimums. The maximum and minimum retentions vary according to whether the insurance is on full terms or limited terms. The above scale of retentions applies only to iron or steel vessels and does not apply where owner's special clauses, or clauses for trawlers or yachts are used. Nor does the scale apply to insurances with discounts other than the standard market discounts.

If the premium has been paid on a deferred basis, whereby the deductions were allowed at 13·1% instead of the customary 15% for cash, the deduction for lay up returns shall, nevertheless, be a rate of 15%, despite the reduced deduction on the premium.

Where a period of thirty days lay up is partly in protected waters and partly in unprotected waters this is allowed by the clause but a pro-rata return is payable only for the period spent in protected waters.

Lay up Warranty

A warranty in a hull policy, particularly on yachts and small craft, providing that the vessel be laid up out of commission during a specified period. It is usual for the insurer of U.K. yachts to insist that they are laid up during the winter months. The vessel may be laid up afloat, or on mud or the " hard ".

Lazarette *or* Lazaret

A term applied to a small compartment, at the aft end of a ship, in which ropes and other equipment are stored.

Lazaretto

A term (now obsolete) applied to a small compartment at the aft end of a ship, which was used for a variety of purposes, such as fumigation of goods in transit and hospitalisation or quarantine of crew or passengers. (Sometimes termed " Lazarette ".)

L/C

Label Clause *or* Letter of Credit.

L.C.T.A.

London Corn Trade Association.

L.C.T.F.

Lloyd's Canadian Trust Fund.

L.d.d.

Loss during discharge.

L/Def.
Latent defect.

Ldg.
Loading.

Ldg. and dely.
Landing and delivery.

L.d.l.
Loss during loading.

L.D.P.S.
Lloyd's Data Processing Services.

Lds.
Loads.

L.d.t.
Loss during transhipment.

Lead
Leading underwriter.

Leadage
Term applied to the charge for the carriage of coal from the pit-head to the loading port.

Leader
Leading underwriter.

Leading Underwriter
The first insurer on a slip. A good " lead " is essential for the completion of the placing. The " lead " a broker must find is the one who is well versed in the particular type of insurance involved, who will give the most reasonable rate to the assured and who is of sufficient standing for other insurers to accept his lead and to follow by writing a line. In some cases the broker obtains agreement from the insurers who follow the leader to accept automatically any agreements or amendments accepted by the leader. The leader cannot amend the written line of a following insurer.

Leading Underwriters' Agreement
An agreement whereby all underwriters subscribing an insurance agree to accept subsequent alterations approved solely by the leading underwriters. Alterations are submitted by the broker to the 2 leading Lloyd's and the 2 leading Institute Company underwriters. Where one market only is involved alterations are submitted to the first 3 underwriters. To implement this the initials

L.U.A.M.H. for hull business, or L.U.A.M.C. for cargo business, will be shown on the broker's slip. The first leader will indicate whether it is necessary for the alteration to be seen and/or approved by the other underwriters (usually 5 days is allowed for the relevant alteration to be shown to the following underwriters). The power of leading underwriters to agree on behalf of the following underwriters is limited to those alterations which do not materially affect the risk.

Leakage

Ordinary leakage is the natural loss expected to occur in liquids by reason of evaporation, soaking into the container or other natural causes. If there is a loss of liquid cargo where the container is intact and where no peril has operated, this is usually due to ordinary leakage. Ordinary leakage is not insurable as a rule. The standard policy form does not in itself cover leakage or shortage where no peril has operated, but the policy may be extended to cover this as an extraneous risk by specific inclusion.

Leave to Tow

See " Tow and Assist ".

Leeboard

A term applied to a board, used in the days of sailing ships, which was hinged or fastened to the left hand (port) side of a vessel and assisted in steering the vessel through shallow waters and prevented the ship from making too much " leeway ". A starboard served the same purpose on the right hand (starboard) side of the ship. The leeboard was hinged, in some cases, to allow it to lie flat against the side of the vessel when she berthed.

Leeside

The side of a ship opposite to that exposed to the weather; generally the leeside on a coastal passage would be the landward side.

Leeway

Unintentional deviation of a ship from a set course.

L.E.F.O.

Lands End for Orders. Abbreviation used to indicate to a vessel sailing on a U.K./Europe voyage that the destination port will be advised after sailing.

Left Out

See " Short Shipment ".

Legal Charges
See " Legal Expenses ".

Legal Costs
See " Legal Expenses ".

Legal Expenses
It is the duty of a cargo owner to claim against the carrier for damage for which the carrier is liable and if, with the insurer's consent, a law suit is pressed the legal expenses so incurred are payable by the insurer. The legal expenses in defending a claim made against the assured are also paid by the insurer if they are for the purpose of minimising a loss recoverable under the policy, such as would arise under the collision clause in a hull policy. A reinsurer is liable for his proportion of legal expenses paid by the original insurer to avert or minimise a claim which would have been recoverable under the reinsurance policy.

Legality of the Adventure
There is an implied warranty of legality in every marine insurance contract whereby the adventure must be lawful at commencement and must be legally prosecuted throughout. A breach of this warranty discharges the insurer from liability as from the date of the breach. This warrant of legality is specified in section 41 of the Marine Insurance Act 1906.

Legal Liability
A liability to a third party incurred by the assured. This is customarily termed " third party liability ". If the liability results under the terms of a contract it is " contractual liability ". The plain policy does not cover third party liability of the assured, but may be extended by the insurer to cover risk.

Leg. Chgs.
Legal charges.

Lender of Money
A person who lends money on the security of property involved in a marine adventure has an insurable interest in that property up to the amount of the loan plus any interest due on the loan, in so far as the loan is not repayable in the event of loss.

Letter of Countermart
An authorisation given by a Government, in time of war, permitting reprisals against persons carrying out acts of aggression under letters of mart authorised by the enemy.

Letter of Credit

In general, the term indicates a document which authorises payment of an agreed sum of money to the person named therein. When such a document is used in the " credit system " for payment of goods it is usually " irrevocable " and authorises the bank named in it to pay for the goods; the document being honoured by the issuing bank when the goods arrive. The term is also used to indicate a document issued to an assured or a reinsured Company by the underwriter, authorising settlement of a claim amount.

Letter of Hypothecation

Under the credit system the buyer's bank must be in a position to dispose of the goods to refund the money paid against a bill of exchange if the consignee fails to meet his commitments. A letter of hypothecation gives the bank the required authority.

Letter of Indemnity

This is a document which is given to a party of whom it is required that an unqualified guarantee be given when the circumstances demand a qualified guarantee. The letter agrees to indemnify the guarantor against any loss he may suffer by reason of not qualifying the guarantee. Such letters are used in respect of bills of lading or in the form of a counter guarantee in general average or in circumstances where an insurer is requested to settle a claim or pay a return of premium where the policy is unobtainable or in other special circumstances. The insurer will probably require a letter of indemnity from the assured if he is asked to issue a duplicate policy.

Letter of Marque

See " Letter of Mart ".

Letter of Mart

Sometimes called a " letter of marque ". No longer used, this is an authorisation given to the owners of a private vessel who, having posted a bond with the Government of the country to which they owe allegiance, are permitted to carry arms. The letter permits the vessel, whilst trading peacefully, to defend itself against attack and if possible to take an attacking vessel as a prize. In many cases the liberties granted were abused and the authorisation used by privateers to attack other vessels, particularly those of an enemy power.

Letter of Subrogation

A document giving authority to the insurer to sue a third party in the name of the assured for damages when that third party is responsible for a loss which has resulted in a claim under the policy. The insurer is entitled to his subrogation rights by the Marine Insurance Act 1906.

Letter of Undertaking

A letter whereby the signatory undertakes to fulfil certain conditions or maintain certain circumstances. In the event of an accident to a vessel involving the shipowner in liability whereby the vessel may be arrested pending payment in respect of such liability the representative of the shipowner may avoid arrest, and consequent delay, by giving a letter of undertaking to provide bail if required and to comply with the terms of any eventual legal liability arising out of the accident.

L.H.A.R.

London, Hull, Antwerp or Rotterdam.

Liab.

Liability.

Liabilities to Third Parties

See " Liability Insurance ".

Liability Insurance

An insurance to reimburse the assured for any amount paid by him by way of damages in respect of a wrong done to another party. The liability may be due to damage to another's property or person, or to infringement of another's rights. Such insurance covers only the *legal* liability of the assured and although the Marine Insurance Act, 1906 states the measure of indemnity to be the amount of the liability, it is usual for the insurer to fix a limit as the maximum amount recoverable under the policy. The most common form of liability insurance in the marine market is that for collision liability under a hull policy. Most other shipowner's liabilities are covered in Protection and Indemnity Clubs.

Liability of the Assured

The plain policy does not cover the liability of the assured to any other person. Nevertheless, since the assured may lose financially by any liability to another person incurred during the marine adventure, he has an insurable interest in the liability. He may, therefore, take the plain form of insurance cover or have his marine policy extended to cover the liability and, unless the policy wording imposes some limitation, the measure of indemnity is the total amount paid by way of the liability. It is usual for the limit recoverable under the policy in respect of the liability to be specified in the policy.

Liability of the Carrier

The carrier, by his contract of affreightment, is obliged to supply a vessel reasonably fit to carry the cargo and properly to stow and care for the cargo. If any damage to or loss of the cargo occurs while it is within the carrier's care the carrier has no liability if he has exercised due diligence to fulfil his obligations and the loss has occurred without his actual fault or privity. Where the carrier is liable for damage to cargo, his liability can be limited to £100 per package (increased by the Gold Clause agreement to £200 per package). In the interests of insurers it is the duty of the cargo assured to press any valid claim against the carrier to obtain a recovery for the insurer. The carrier's liability to his cargo is insured through a P. & I. club and not in the ordinary marine insurance market. At the time of revision (1974) the Carriage of Goods by Sea Act (1970) has been considered but has not yet become law. This Act would amend the limits of liability enjoyed by the carrier.

Liability of the Insurer

The insurer is liable for losses proximately caused by an insured peril. The limit of the insurer's liability is called the " measure of indemnity ". (See " Measure of Indemnity " for details.)

Liability of the Shipowner

The shipowner may incur liabilities in respect of damage to the person or property of another or infringement of rights. Apart from collision liability most shipowner's liabilities are insured in P. & I. clubs and not in the ordinary marine market. Regarding collision liability, it is the practice of the marine insurance market to cover only three-quarters of this liability, the remainder also being covered in a P. & I. club. (See also " Limitation of Liability ".)

Liable or not Liable

A reinsurance term. In the absence of any agreement to the contrary the reinsurer is liable to reimburse the reinsured only for claims for which the reinsured is legally liable under the original policy. The reinsured may wish to be reimbursed for " ex gratia " or " without prejudice " claims and the reinsurer may agree to accept the reinsurance on the basis of reimbursing the reinsured for all claims paid whether or not he is strictly liable. The term " liable or not liable " will then appear in the reinsurance slip and policy giving effect to this agreement.

Liable to Pay

Wording in the collision liability clause in a hull policy. Emphasises that the policy covers only the legal liability of the assured.

L.I.B.A.

Lloyd's Insurance Brokers' Association.

Libel Bond

In the special terminology on the Admiralty side of American Federal District Courts the "complaint" is referred to as "libel" while the plaintiff is called the "libellant". The owner of a vessel libelled "in rem" may arrange the release of the vessel from arrest by the posting of a libel bond with approved surety. (See also "Surety and Bonding Companies" and "Short Form of Indemnity".)

Liberty Type Ships

Liberty Ships, constructed between 1942 and 1945, were the most numerous of all tonnage built in the U.S.A. during the war years. Totalling nearly 3,000 in number, the majority were identical vessels and, generally, were of all-welded construction.

The basic type was of a standard 7,176 g.r.t., and a variation of this produced the Liberty tanker—which nevertheless retained "dry cargo" characteristics. After the war most were converted to the dry-cargo type.

A further variation produced the transport for army tanks and aircraft; here the major differences concerned the hatches and cargo-handling gear. The majority of these vessels were retained after the war as naval or military auxiliaries.

The Liberty collier was a complete re-design of the basic ship. The propelling machinery was placed aft instead of in the customary midship position and these ships were slightly less than 7,000 g.r.t.

The names given to Liberty ships were, generally, the names of individuals—usually American. Ships were named after the historic, the famous and after persons from all walks of life—including shipyard workers, nurses, Indian tribal chiefs and the like. There were some notable exceptions to this form of nomenclature; the two major ones concerned ships which served with the Armed Forces and those transferred on Lease/Lend terms. Of the latter, those which served under the British flag were given the prefix " SAM " when named or renamed. These are often referred to as "SAM " ships.

Another feature common to all Liberty Ships was their identical triple-expansion steam propelling machinery. In post-war years a few have been re-engined with diesel machinery.

Liberty Ships are excluded from the definition "Liner" in the Institute Classification Clause.

(Further details may be obtained from "Wartime Standard Ships Volume 4" by W. H. Mitchell and L. A. Sawyer published by The Journal of Commerce & Shipping Telegraph Limited.)

Lien

A legal right whereby a person may prevent another from taking possession of property until the other person has satisfied a liability due to the person with the lien. A broker has a lien on a policy for unpaid premiums. A carrier has a lien on cargo against which freight is due. A shipowner has a lien on cargo in respect of which a general average deposit is payable. A salvor has a maritime lien on salved property in respect of the salvage award due to him. A warehouseman may have a lien on goods in store for unpaid charges.

Lien for Freight

See "Carrier's Lien".

Lien for Premium

See "Broker's Lien".

Lien for Salvage

See "Salvor's Lien".

Lien of the Seller

See "Stoppage in Transitu".

Life Salvage

When a vessel is in peril and life is saved by a salvor, the salvor has a right to claim life salvage from the shipowner. It is not necessary for property to be salved to entitle the salvor to life salvage. The liability of the shipowner for life salvage is independent of the ship, so there is no recovery under the hull policy for such salvage. Life salvage is usually recovered by the shipowner from his P. & I. club.

Light Displacement

A measurement in cubic tons that is equivalent to the quantity of water displaced by the vessel when she is unladen.

Light Draught

The depth of water required to maintain an unladen vessel afloat.

Light Dues

Payments collected from ships to maintain lightships, lighthouses, marker buoys and similar warning indications.

Lightening a Ship

In some cases when a ship is on a strand it is possible to refloat her at high tide only by removing some of her cargo to lighten her. The expense of removing, warehousing (including fire insurance) and reloading the cargo are all general average. Any consequential damage to the cargo is also general average. Jettison of cargo may be necessary to save the vessel and other cargo by lightening the ship. This is also general average.

Lighter

A small craft used for carrying cargo to or from a ship.

Lighterage

Money paid by the shipowner, shipper or consignee for the use of craft or lighters in carrying cargo.

Light Loadline

The loadline marked on the side of a ship to indicate the maximum depth the ship is allowed to sink, when unladen, to comply with the loadline regulations. Sometimes termed " Light Waterline ". (See also " Laden Loadline ".)

Light Waterline

See " Light Loadline ".

Lightweight

The weight of the fabric of the ship (this is the load displacement tonnage minus the deadweight).

Like Kind

See " Ejusdem Generis ".

Limber Hole

Drainage hole in a ship.

Limit

Insurer's maximum liability under a policy. Several limits for separate sections of the policy may be specified. The term is an abbreviation of " Limit of Liability ".

Limit any one Vessel

When a contract of marine insurance covers goods to be shipped by several vessels, either named or to be advised later, it is usual to limit the insurer's liability on the amount carried by any single vessel. This provision always appears in open covers and open policies. In some cases it may appear in an open slip.

Limitation of Liability

This does not refer to the insurer's limit of liability. It is the statutory limitation of liability of which the shipowner may take advantage in the case of liability of his ship for damage to another's property. Provided there is no actual fault or privity on the part of the shipowner, he may limit his liability to the maximum provided by law if his vessel causes damage to property by reason of faulty navigation or mismanagement. The limitations with regard to property, loss of life and personal injury liability are laid down by the Merchant Shipping Act 1894 and subsequent amendments. Limitation of carrier's liability to cargo is laid down by the Carriage of Goods by Sea Act 1924, amended in practice by the Gold Clause agreement. (See also " Carrier's Liability to Cargo ".)

Limited Conditions
Limited terms.

Limited Market
When the insurance does not find a ready market and there are a limited number of insurers prepared to accept the risk there is said to be a " limited market ".

Limited Terms
An expression in marine insurance embracing " total loss only ", " free of particular average " or similar terms. " Limited terms " are any insurance conditions which do not cover partial loss. Reinsurances are often on " limited terms ", so that the original insurer pays all partial losses but claims on his reinsurance for a total loss.

Limit of Liability
Insurer's maximum liability under a policy.

Limit per Bottom
The limit any one vessel.

Line
The amount of liability accepted by an insurer on the original slip. (See " Written Line ".)

Line Checking
A policy signing and accounting term. It refers to the procedure for checking the underwriter's line, etc.

Liner
Vessel engaged on a regular run and keeping to a time schedule. The liner is considered a better risk than the " tramp " which is a vessel not engaged on a regular run. Liners generally carry parcel or package cargo and usually have some passenger accommodation. The fire risk is greater on a liner than on a tramp. Liners

generally have a higher standard of maintenance and the better class of officers and crew.

In the Classification Clause published 1st October, 1968 a definition of a " liner " was given as follows: —

" A vessel sailing regularly and habitually on a publicised service and loading and unloading at specified ports. " This definition is omitted from the current Classification Clause.

Liner Negligence Clause

The " Liner Negligence and Additional Perils Clause ". A form of negligence clause used in hull policies which are subject to Owner's Clauses. The cover is generally only granted on policies on vessels which keep to a regular schedule and it gives a slightly wider cover than the ordinary negligence clause. The additional cover provided is that the part with the latent defect, the shaft which is broken or the boiler which had burst are all recoverable under the policy in addition to damage caused by the latent defect, breaking shaft or bursting boiler, but it is customary for the policy to exclude claims based on the mere discovery of a latent defect.

Underwriters do not encourage the use of this clause and the view was expressed in 1970 that it is hoped the clause will eventually fall into disuse. In fact it is recommended that if the clause continues to be used the wording of the policy will state that the provisions of the standard Negligence Clause (I.T.C. No. 7) shall apply. Further, the wording " attributable in part or in whole to negligence, error of judgement or incompetence of Master, Officers or Crew " is deemed to be incorporated in place of the similar wording contained in I.T.C. No. 11.

Line Sheet

Used in treaty reinsurance where the limit of liability is expressed in " lines ". In effect, it is a table of limits, each limit representing one line. The reinsurer writes so many lines, thus denoting his maximum liability in respect of any one risk.

Line Stamp

A rubber stamp held at the box of a Lloyd's syndicate and used to impress on a slip written by the underwriter his syndicate's pseudonym and number. The underwriter writes his line in the box and inserts his reference in a space provided for that purpose.

Liquefied Natural Gas Carrier

A ship (tanker) specially designed to carry liquefied natural gas. Natural gas occupies a very much smaller space in a liquefied form than it does in its evaporated form. Accordingly transport of natural gas can be most economically achieved if it is carried in a liquefied form. To maintain the liquefied form the liquid must be kept at a sub-zero temperature (e.g. 162 degrees centigrade below zero). The tanks of a L.N.G. carrier are constructed of metal capable of withstanding very low temperatures.

Liquefied Petroleum Gas Carrier

This is a purpose built vessel designed for the carriage of petroleum gas, such as propane or butane or a combination of both. To reduce the volume of the gas and so assist carriage it is liquefied either by pressure (as in a gas cigarette lighter filler) or refrigerated. The gas remains in its liquid form until the pressure or refrigeration is relieved.

List

Incline of a ship as opposed to upright.

Litre

Measure of liquid. Equal to 1.75980 pints.

Live Animals

These are not included in the general terms " merchandise ", " goods " or " cargo " and are not, therefore, covered on an ordinary cargo policy unless specified therein. There is a limited insurance market for insurance of live animals and they are usually insured under special clauses called " Livestock Clauses ".

Liverpool Market

A marine insurance market of Companies based on Liverpool. A combined Company policy form is also used in the Liverpool market but there is no central signing office so that it is necessary for the broker to present the policy to each office in turn for signing against its relevant line. Otherwise the market runs on much the same lines as the London Company market.

Liverpool Underwriters' Association

This Association was founded in 1802 and its membership embraces not only marine underwriters but also shipowners, marine insurance brokers, average adjusters, and other sections of the commercial world.

The Association provides a comprehensive information and intelligence service to members and provides underwriters with a forum for discussion and consideration of marine insurance matters, as well as facilities for liaison with kindred organisations. The Association acts as Lloyd's shipping correspondents in Liverpool, reporting to Lloyd's Intelligence Department the movements of all ships passing in and out of the Port of Liverpool.

Livestock Clauses

Clauses used in connection with insurance on livestock in transit. They are not standard clauses and there are three sets. The first set is the most widely used and covers death or mortality only, including destruction due to fractured limbs, jettison and washing overboard. Death due to pregnant condition is excluded. The insurance is subject to the F.C. & S.S.R.C.C. Warranty but this may be deleted by agreement. The second and third sets of the clauses also cover periods before and after shipment and in addition cover the fodder.

Livestock Insurance

Insurance on horses, cattle and similar against death or injury. Often restricted to mortality risk only.

Lkge.

Leakage.

Lkge. & Bkge.

Leakage and breakage.

Llds.

Lloyd's.

Ll.L. Rep.

Lloyd's List Law Reports.

Lloyd's

Lloyd's and the London marine insurance companies together form the largest marine insurance market in the world, commonly known as the "London Market". Lloyd's itself is a Corporation and does no underwriting. The Corporation provides facilities for its underwriting members to carry on the business of underwriting in "The Room". Only a Lloyd's broker may transact business in "The Room" at Lloyd's, so that no member of the public can place business directly with a Lloyd's underwriter. Lloyd's underwriters do not restrict their underwriting to marine business, but also write other classes of insurance such as Aviation, Motor, Fire, Compensation, Public Liability, etc. The liability of a Lloyd's underwriter is unlimited and such is the reputation of Lloyd's that no person is permitted to be a Lloyd's underwriter without a strict examination of his financial position and ability to meet his potential liabilities. An annual audit enables the Corporation to maintain up to date knowledge of each underwriter's affairs. The name "Lloyd's" is traditional and dates from the days when underwriting first began in the coffee house of a Mr. Edward Lloyd which was generally known as "Lloyd's Coffee House". (See, also, "Syndicate".)

Lloyd's Advisory and Legislation Department

This Department is *inter alia* responsible for the promulgation of various regulations drawn up by the Committee of Lloyd's from time to time in connection with underwriting and broking practices in the Lloyd's Market and is available to assist Underwriters and Brokers in connection with any queries that may arise in regard to such regulations. The Department, also, keeps a close watch on legislative developments, in foreign countries, relating to insurance etc. and wherever necessary takes appropriate action to safeguard the interests of Lloyd's market.

Lloyd's Agency Department

This Department is responsible to the Committee of Lloyd's for the control and supervision of the work of Lloyd's Agents throughout the world.

Lloyd's Agents

Agents of the Corporation of Lloyd's whose primary duty is to keep Lloyd's informed of shipping movements, casualties and other matters of interest to Insurers and the commercial community generally. They are not insurance Agents, but it has become customary for Underwriters and Insurance Companies to utilise the services of Lloyd's Agents in connection with surveys of damaged vessels and goods, as well as the adjustment and settlement of claims.

Lloyd's Agents also deal with non-marine matters and aviation losses. There is a Lloyd's Agency or Sub-Agency at most of the principal ports in the world.

Lloyd's American Trust Fund

Controls are exercised in regard to U.S. dollar premiums and claims, etc., whereby payment is not made via the ordinary banking arrangements. By arrangement with the relevant Government Departments Lloyd's operates a trust fund for U.S. dollar transactions. Enquiries regarding the procedures should be directed to the L.A.T.F. Office at Lloyd's. (See also " C.L. Form " and " Lloyd's Canadian Trust Fund ".)

Lloyd's—Annual Subscribers

Individuals connected with Underwriting Agents at Lloyd's or Lloyd's Brokers, who are not Underwriting or Non-Underwriting Members of Lloyd's, but who wish to have the right of entrée to the Underwriting Room in connection with insurance business placed with Lloyd's Underwriters.

Lloyd's Arbitration Agreement

Lloyd's standard form of Arbitration Agreement in cases of collision. An agreement between Shipowners whose vessels have been in collision (or Owners of property which has been struck) whereby they agree to refer the decision as to the degree of liability and the amount of damages suffered to an Arbitrator appointed by the Committee of Lloyd's. The findings of the Arbitrator are acceptable to Insurers as an alternative to a decision in the Law Courts.

Lloyd's Associates

Individuals such as assessors, solicitors, accountants, etc., who, although not directly engaged in insurance, wish to obtain entrance to the Underwriting Room to interview Underwriters.

Lloyd's Audit Department

This Department now forms part of " Lloyd's Membership Services Group " (which see).

Lloyd's Average Bond

Standard form of average bond.

Lloyd's Aviation Department

Lloyd's Aviation Department comprises two Branches. The Technical Service has as its prime function the safeguarding of Underwriters' interests in connection with claims for damage to aircraft and air cushion vehicles (hovercraft) and their subsequent repair and disposal. It also provides technical advice. The Intelligence Service is designed to provide general aviation information and incorporates a library of aeronautical publications and aircraft registers covering most of the world. Records of operators' histories including fleets and casualties, particulars and prices of aircraft and other valuable information are published as " Lloyd's Aviation Intelligence Service " for the use of Underwriters, Brokers and Companies dealing in Aviation Insurance throughout the world.

Lloyd's Broker

A Member of or Subscriber to Lloyd's who acts as agent of the assured. Only a Lloyd's broker may effect an insurance at Lloyd's.

Lloyd's Brokers' Association

See " Brokers' Association ".

Lloyd's C.A. Account

The banking account used for Lloyd's Central Accounting.

Lloyd's Calendar

Published by Lloyd's annually, this book gives general information to those engaged in shipping and marine insurance. Its contents include copies of standard Lloyd's Policies and article of maritime interest.

Lloyd's Canadian Trust Fund
The transfer of Canadian dollar payments for premiums and claims, etc. is conducted on similar lines to the American Trust Fund. (See " Lloyd's American Trust Fund " and " R Form ".)

Lloyd's Central Accounting Office
An office for the central settlement of premiums and claims due to and from Underwriters and Brokers.

Lloyd's Certificates
Insurance certificates issued by the Committee of Lloyd's. These certificates are issued for the use of Lloyd's Brokers or, in some cases, for completion by merchants and shippers in their own offices throughout the world. Provision is made in the certificates (see term C.P.A.) for settlement of claims abroad by Lloyd's agents, or settlement may be effected through the brokers in London if required.

Lloyd's Claims Bureau
See " Claims Bureau ".

Lloyd's Common Market Secretariat
This department is responsible for furthering the interests of Lloyd's Underwriters in connection with Common Market developments.

Lloyd's Data Processing Services
In 1973 the data processing services operating within L.P.S.O. became a separate organisation. The organisation, with the use of two large computers, provides data processing services to other Lloyd's Organisations (e.g. Lloyd's Life Assurance) besides L.P.S.O.

Lloyd's Form—General Average Deposit Receipt
The standard form of General Average Deposit Receipt used in practice. (See " General Average Deposit Receipt ".)

Lloyd's Form of Salvage Agreement
This is the standard form of agreement, published by Lloyd's, which is customarily used by the parties interested in salvage operations. The agreement is based on the " No Care—No Pay " principle whereby the salvor must save the property to be entitled to a salvage award. It is customary for the master of the vessel in distress to sign the agreement on behalf of the owners and the cargo and freight interests, thereby binding such parties to the

terms of the agreement. There is a space in the form in which can be inserted an agreed award but where this is left blank an amount is decided by arbitration. The form has been redrafted several times since its inception to conform with modern conditions, the most recent being in 1972. The salvor has a maritime lien on the salvaged property until satisfactory "security" arrangements are made. (See also "Salvage Guarantee".)

Lloyd's Goods in Transit (C.M.R.) Policy
See "C.M.R. Form".

Lloyd's Information Department
This department deals generally with enquiries on Lloyd's from members of the public and outside organisations. These cover, among other matters, telephone enquiries regarding the due dates of vessels in the United Kingdom and their agents and enquiries from the Press and Broadcasting Organisations on matters affecting Lloyd's generally.

Lloyd's Insurance Brokers' Association
Trade Association of Lloyd's Insurance Brokers formed to protect and promote in all ways open to it the interests of its Members.

Lloyd's Intelligence Department
Lloyd's Intelligence Department collects information concerning movements of, and casualties to, merchant vessels for Underwriters and also distributes it to subscribers in the insurance and shipping industries, the press, etc.

Lloyd's Law Reports
A fortnightly publication by Lloyd's giving details of Law cases heard in connection with maritime, insurance and commercial disputes.

Lloyds List
Once entitled "Lloyd's List and Shipping Gazette". A daily newspaper for all who may be interested in world shipping. Besides containing interesting items of shipping and insurance news, it gives up-to-date reports of arrivals and departures of vessels in all parts of the world together with the latest casualties to ships and aircraft.

Lloyd's Log
Published by the Corporation of Lloyd's Information Department, this is the house journal of the Corporation. When it first appeared in 1930 it was published for Lloyd's Committee staff

under the title " Monthly Notes ". Later it was called Lloyd's
Office Gazette but in 1944 the initial letters L.O.G. were used in
a change of title to " Lloyd's Log ". It is now a monthly magazine
containing informative articles and items of social interest to
those connected with Lloyd's both at home and abroad.

Lloyd's Maritime Atlas

An atlas designed for shipping and marine insurance purposes. It
concentrates on ports and shipping places, emphasising repair ports.
Maps of bad weather areas are also included.

Lloyd's Membership Department

This Department now forms part of " Lloyd's Membership Services Group " (which see).

Lloyd's Membership Services Group

This Group was formed in 1973 to co-ordinate the activities of
three separate Departments, viz. the Audit Department, the Membership Department and the Underwriting Agents' and Brokers'
Registration Department.

The Audit Department is responsible for promulgating the
regulations which, subject to the approval of the D.T.I., are laid
down annually by the Committee of Lloyd's in connection with
the audit of Underwriters' Accounts and for ensuring that the
necessary documents in relation to the audit of every Syndicate
operating at Lloyd's are lodged each year with the Committee at
Lloyd's and the D.T.I. The Department deals, also, with the Committee's solvency requirements for Lloyd's Brokers and handles
all applications for release of Members' Lloyd's Funds.

The Membership Department deals with the underwriting
arrangements, premium limits, Special Reserve Funds and the
Lloyd's Deposit Investments of individual Members of Lloyd's. The
Department also deals with the admission of new Members, Annual
Subscribers and with the admission of Associates (e.g. Assessors,
Accountants, Solicitors, etc.), who wish to obtain entrance to the
Room to interview Underwriters.

The Underwriting Agents' and Brokers' Registration Department deals with various matters relating to the admission of Underwriting Agents and Lloyd's Brokers and with changes in the
constitution of such Companies. It also includes a Central Records
Office of Members' Deposit Securities and handles dividends, rights
issues and bonus issues on Lloyd's Deposit securities.

Lloyd's Policy Office

This Department maintains stocks of all the various standard
Lloyd's Policies and wordings, together with many of the support-

ing documents and supplies them, on demand, to the Lloyd's market.

A printing service is also provided enabling Members of Lloyd's and Lloyd's Brokers to have their own private policies and wordings printed on the premises.

Lloyd's Policy Signing Office

Often referred to as " The Bureau ". A central signing office, administered by the Committee of Lloyd's, where policies are checked with slips, signed on behalf of syndicates and sealed with the seal of Lloyd's Policy Signing Office. The L.P.S.O. also " takes down " details of premiums, additional premiums, return premiums, claims and recoveries and advises the debits and credits to Underwriters and Brokers.

In 1963 a system of Central Accounting was introduced to process premiums etc. on behalf of Lloyd's Underwriters and brokers. This service is operated by Lloyd's Data Processing Services (L.D.P.S.). Settlement is made centrally on the agreed figures prepared by L.D.P.S., whereas previously each Underwriter had to agree his account for premiums and claims directly with the Broker.

Lloyd's Publications

Lloyd's List.
„ Weekly Casualty Reports.
„ Calendar.
„ Maritime Atlas.
„ Law Reports.
„ Survey Handbook.
„ Voyage Record.
„ Shipping Index.
Digests of Lloyd's Law Reports.

Lloyd's Recoveries Department

The Recoveries Department at Lloyd's acts for Marine, Non-Marine and Aviation Underwriters and Insurance Companies both at Home and Overseas in connection with the exercise of their subrogation rights against shipowners, air, rail and road carriers, bailees and other third parties. These services include investigations into the liabilities and rights of Insurers in connection with general average, salvage and collision cases on receipt of deposit receipts, and/or other documents of title or details of other security which has been provided.

This Department also deals with the collection and distribution of Non-Marine salvages on behalf of Underwriters.

Lloyd's Register of Shipping

An independent, non-commercial Society whose function is the classification of merchant ships, the establishment of standards for their construction and maintenance and the provision of a world-wide technical service. Lloyd's Register, the oldest and largest classification society, was founded in 1760 by the underwriters who frequented Lloyd's Coffee House, and was reconstituted in essentially its present form in 1834. It has no direct connection with the Corporation of Lloyd's. It is governed by a General Committee representing marine underwriters, shipowners, shipbuilders, engine builders and steelmakers. There are similar national committees in twelve countries outside Britain.

Construction and maintenance standards are expressed as Rules, published annually. Almost all classed ships are built "to class", i.e. according to the Rules and under the supervision of the Society's surveyors. Classification is undertaken at the request of owners and the Society classes nearly half the effective world's tonnage, or more than 55 million tons. An annual Register of Shipping gives details of all known merchant ships in the world of 100 tons gross and above and indicates the survey position of classed ships.

Lloyd's Register of Shipping—Surveys

In order to remain in class, ships must be submitted at prescribed intervals for various surveys, the biggest of these being the special survey held every four years.

Lloyd's Register of Shipping—Surveyors

The Society employs nearly 1,100 exclusive surveyors stationed at ports and industrial centres all over the world. They can be broadly divided into ship surveyors and engineer surveyors, but they include many specialists in such matters as vibration, strain, gauging, electricity, refrigeration and electronics. A number of surveyors are employed in the Engineering Investigation Department, which offers a service for the investigation of engineering failures and breakdowns all over the world. Others are engaged in research; the Society has its own research laboratory.

Lloyd's Register of Shipping—Statistics

The Society's statistical department issues quarterly returns covering the world's shipbuilding, quarterly analyses of ship losses and casualties, and annual statistical tables.

Lloyd's Register of Shipping—Yachts

The Society also undertakes the survey and classification of yachts, through its Yacht Department. The Register of Yachts and the Register of American Yachts are published annually. Survey of yachts is carried out by a staff of special yacht surveyors.

Lloyd's Rep.
Lloyd's Law Reports.

Lloyd's Salvage Agreement
Lloyd's standard form of Salvage Agreement. This is an agreement between the Master of a vessel on behalf of the Owners and a Salvage Contractor, whereby the latter agrees to use his best endeavours to salve the vessel and cargo (if any); the services to be rendered and accepted as salvage services upon the principle of " No Cure—No Pay ".

The Agreement provides for the amount of the Salvor's remuneration, if any, to be decided either by agreement or by arbitration. The Agreement also provides that if the services are only partially successful, the Salvor shall receive reasonable remuneration not exceeding a certain percentage (to be fixed) of the salved values.

The Salvage Contractor has a maritime lien for services rendered as in pure salvage (see " Salvor's Lien "), pending the provision of security for his claim.

Lloyd's Shipping Index
Frequently referred to as the " Blue List ", this Index is published daily from Monday to Friday and contains, in alphabetical order of vessels' names, a list of ships engaged on oversea trading, together with current voyages and latest movements, in addition to details of owners, classification, tonnages, etc.

Lloyd's Standard Slip
See " Standard Slip " and " R/I Treaty Standard Slip ".

Lloyd's—Substitutes
Authorised representatives of Members, Subscribers or Associates who are admitted to the Underwriting Room by authority of the Committee of Lloyd's and on the nomination of their employers.

Lloyd's Survey Handbook
A Lloyd's publication used as a book of reference by those engaged in marine insurance and shipping when commodity losses occur. It is particularly useful to marine superintendents and others concerned with handling of cargo.

Lloyd's Underwriter
An Underwriting Member of Lloyd's. The liability of the Lloyd's Underwriter is unlimited and even though he may be a member of a Syndicate he is still personally liable for his proportion of claims attaching to the Syndicate and he is not subsidised by other

members of his Syndicate if he is unable to meet his liabilities. For this reason, the financial resources of each underwriter are subjected to a strict examination by the Committee of Lloyd's before he can become a member. Since 1970 women have been admitted to membership of Lloyds.

It should be noted that, in practice, the term "Lloyd's Underwriter" is normally used to describe the active underwriter of a Lloyd's Syndicate who accepts risks on behalf of the members of his syndicate in the Underwriting Room at Lloyd's Such active Underwriters need not necessarily be Underwriting members of Lloyd's, but may be employed by the syndicate as Underwriters.

Lloyd's Underwriting Agent

Despite the title the Lloyd's Underwriting Agent does not take any active part in the underwriting of insurance risks. The Corporation of Lloyd's requires its members to conduct their insurance business at Lloyd's through syndicates and through the medium of underwriting agents approved by the Committee. There are two types of agent. The first type is a members' agent who acts in all respects for the "name" other than managing the syndicate; the latter being delegated to the second type of agent, a "managing agent". A managing agent manages the affairs of a syndicate, appointing staff, keeping records, managing the premium trust fund and, generally, seeing that the syndicate operates within the requirements of Lloyd's. The agent does not entertain any underwriting liability, this being vested in the agent's "names".

Lloyd's Underwriters' Association

Lloyd's Underwriters' Association, which was formed in 1909, officially acts for marine underwriters at Lloyd's in all technical matters relating to their business. It neither effects nor underwrites marine insurances. The Association's membership comprises all Lloyd's marine underwriters, and each year fifteen members are elected by ballot to form the Committee. The Chairman and Deputy Chairman of Lloyd's are ex officio members of the Committee in addition to the fifteen underwriters elected by ballot. The Committee meets regularly to discuss the various underwriting and general administrative problems which arise in the Lloyd's marine market, and the results of their deliberations are usually embodied in the form of a recommendation which is submitted to all members of the Association for ratification. In addition, the Association keeps its members advised of all developments and other pertinent information that is likely to have some bearing upon the underwriting of marine business at Lloyd's.

The Association acts in close liason with Lloyd's Insurance

Brokers Association, the Institute of London Underwriters and Liverpool Underwriters' Association, and appoints Lloyd's representatives to serve on various Joint Committees which deliberate upon problems that are common both to the Lloyd's and Company marine markets. It is also directly represented on the International Union of Marine Insurance and the British Maritime Law Association.

Lloyd's Underwriters' Claims Office
An office which is authorised by the majority of Lloyd's Underwriters to deal with claims and advices in respect of loss of, or damage to, ships, cargoes, freight, salvage, legal liabilities and marine reinsurance on a centralised basis. (Abbreviation L.U.C.O.)

Lloyd's Voyage Record
Issued weekly, this gives comprehensive coverage of vessels' past movements.

Lloyd's Weekly Casualty Reports
A publication by Lloyd's giving details of marine and aviation casualties, navigation and weather reports.

L.M.C.
Lloyd's Machinery Certificate.

L.M.C. C.S.
Lloyd's machinery certificate, continuous survey. Entry in Lloyd's Register denoting that the engines of the ship are the subject of a continuous survey.

L.N.G. Carrier
Liquefied natural gas carrier.

L.n.y.d.
Liability not yet determined.

Load Displacement
A measurement in cubic tons that is equivalent to the quantity of water displaced by the vessel when floating at her load draught.

Loaded Draught
The depth of water required to maintain a laden vessel afloat.

Loading
Placing of goods onto a vessel for carriage.

Loading of Rate
Increasing the basic rate of premium.

Loading the Premium
Increasing the premium to charge more than would normally be charged.

Loadline
The marking on the side of a ship below which the ship must not sink when the vessel is loaded and in still water. There are generally two loadlines, one for summer and the other for winter. A vessel may also have a fresh water loadline. The loadline is recognisable on the side of the hull at mid-ships and has the initials of the Authority which calculated the measurement shown either side of the line. Example: " L " on the left and " R " on the right, denoting Lloyd's Register. (See also " Light Loadline " and " Laden Loadline ".)

Load Waterline
See " Laden Loadline ".

L.O.C.
Letter of Credit.

Location
A place on land, usually a warehouse. The expression is used in referring to cargo and any specified limitation of insurers' liability is considered to apply to a location prior to shipment.

Location Clause
A clause contained in any open cover, or similar contract, limiting the insurer's liability in any one location. The limitation applies only to locations prior to shipment, since the assured has no control over the goods once they are shipped. The purpose of the clause is to discourage the cargo assured from sending goods to the docks for shipment when no vessel is available and so building up an accumulated liability for the insurer in one location. The clause usually provides that the insurer's liability shall not exceed the limit per vessel (called " 100% location clause "). In some cases double the limit per vessel may be allowed (called " 200% location clause ").

Loco
Sale contract term referring to the price of goods. It is necessary to specify the place where the contract commences, such as " ex ship ".

Log
Log Book.

Log Book
A record kept by the master of a ship, giving details of position, condition, weather and other matters of interest. It is a sort of

official diary of the vessel's progress and is sometimes called the "Log" or "Ship's Log". Separate log books are kept to record fuel consumption and the use of engines, also for details of the crew's behaviour. (See "Engine Room Log" and "Deck Log".)

Log Extract
Section taken by copy from a Ship's Log for the purpose of claim documentation.

L.O.L.
Loss of life.

London Market
Lloyd's and the London Insurance Companies.

Long.
Longitude.

Longitudinal Metacentre
See "Metacentre Longitudinal".

Longshoremen
Harbour workers. (See "Federal Longshoremen's etc. clause".)

Long Term
Policy issued for a period exceeding 12 months. (See also "Term Policy".)

Long Ton
Weight measurement of 2,240 lbs. (Metric ton is 2204·60 lbs.)

Loss
Amount for which an insurer is liable in respect of a claim under a policy. An occurrence resulting in a claim under a policy.

Losses not covered
See "Excluded Losses".

Losses Occurring Basis
When this basis is not used the reinsurer under a treaty is liable for all losses on risks which attach during the treaty period. This means that he is not liable for losses occurring during the treaty period where the risk attached prior to inception of the treaty, but he is liable for losses occurring after the treaty expires if the risk attaches during the treaty period. This latter is called "run off" of risk. The "Losses Occurring Basis" does away with this complication because the treaty reinsurer is liable for all, and only such, losses as *occur* during the treaty period, irrespective of when the risk

attached. This basis is particularly useful for "Excess of Loss Reinsurance".

Loss of Engagements

The loss of hire or use of a ship. The collision clause in a hull policy covers only loss of engagements of the other vessel and not of the insured ship. An insurance can be effected for loss of engagements following an accident to the vessel, but this is generally covered in a Protection and Indemnity Club.

Loss of Hire

See "Loss of Engagements".

Loss of Labels

See "Label Clause".

Loss of Life and Personal Injury

These risks are not covered by marine insurers under either hull or cargo policies, except where the policy so specifies. A policy which includes P. & I. risks usually covers these perils, with the exception of the builders' risk policy which only covers L.O.L. & P.I. consequent on collision.

Loss of Market

This risk is not insurable in the marine insurance market. Neither is loss of market admitted as general average, since it is not directly consequential upon the act.

Loss of Profits

The only basic form of profit insurance is that on ordinary cargo when the profit anticipated is included in the agreed insured value of the cargo. Provision is made for the inclusion of such profit in the valuation clause in open covers and floating policies. Insurances on loss of profit alone are, in effect, loss of market insurances and are not readily acceptable in the London market.

Loss of Specie

This is an actual total loss. Loss of specie occurs where the insured property is so damaged that it ceases to be a thing of the kind insured, that is, it changes its specie. An example would be cement which when immersed in seawater becomes concrete.

Loss of Time

In the event of delay losses proximately caused by delay are not covered by the policy unless specifically stated as covered therein. It is customary for the insurer not to cover delay and to emphasise this by incorporating a specific delay exclusion in the policy. In a freight policy loss proximately caused by delay is not excluded by the Marine Insurance Act, 1906 as it is for ship and goods. To avoid freight claims based on loss of time the " Time Penalty Clause " appears in all freight policies providing that the insurer shall not be liable for claims consequent on loss of time, whether or not this is caused by an insured peril.

Loss of Use
See " Loss of Engagements ".

Loss Overboard
The loss of deck cargo, or cargo on craft, over the side. Where there is a possibility of this the broker may insert " including jettison and/or washing overboard " in the insurance, although he may often replace this with " including jettison and/or loss overboard " to give a wider cover.

Loss Payee Clause
A provision, in a policy, which states the name of the person or persons to whom claims, if any, are to be paid.

Loss Ratio
The ratio found by applying the total of claims paid in proportion to the net premium income over a given period.

Loss Reserve
A reinsurance Treaty provision entitling the ceding Company to retain an amount of money to cover claims which have been presented to the ceding Company but have not yet been actually settled under the original policy. Usually the reserve is set up at the end of the year. When any of the claims involved are settled by the ceding Company they are paid out of the reserve. The proportion recoverable from the Treaty Reinsurer is then collected in the normal way and the amount set up in the reserve for that particular claim is released to Reinsurer's credit. In some cases interest is charged on the amount held in reserve.

LOSS RES or Loss Res
Loss Reserve.

Lost or Not Lost
This provision appears in most marine policies automatically. The expression means that the risk attaches to the policy even though at the time of acceptance by the insurer the property may have been lost. The acceptance by the insurer on these terms is conditional on the assured advising the insurer of any known loss prior to accep-

tance. The assured cannot acquire an insurable interest after loss if he is aware of the loss, so that he cannot insure a known loss, even by advising the insurer, if he had no interest at the time the loss occurred. The purpose of the provision is to facilitate the continuance of insurance cover on goods as the title changes hands and so that the assured shall not be prejudiced by a loss of which he is unaware at the time of effecting the insurance.

Loyalty Rebate
A freight rebate allowed by some conference line shipowners to shippers who use conference liners exclusively. (See " Freight Rebate ", " Deferred Rebate " and " Conference Lines ".)

L.P.G. Carrier
Liquefied Petroleum Gas Carrier.

L.P.O.
Lloyd's Policy Office.

L.P.S.O.
Lloyd's Policy Signing Office.

L.P.S.O. Signing Number and Date
See " Signing Number and Date ".

L.R.
Lloyd's Register.

L.R.M.C.
Lloyd's refrigerating machinery certificate.

L.S.
Locus sigilli. (Place of seal.)

L.S. Cls.
Livestock clauses.

L.S.H.W. liab.
Longshoremen's and harbour workers' liability.

L.S.R.
An abbreviation used in relation to Lloyd's policies. It indicates "Line, syndicate and Reference " and refers to the syndicate list in the policy. The term " syndicate " in this context is the syndicate pseudonym and number.

L.T.
Law Times Reports. This private series of law reports merged with the All England Law Reports in 1948.

LTGE *or* **ltge**
Lighterage.

Ltr.
Lighter.

L/U
Leading underwriter.

l/u
Laid up or lying up (see "Lay Up Return").

L.U.A.
Lloyd's Underwriters' Association.

L/U agreement
Leading Underwriter agreement.

L.U.A.M.C.
See "Leading Underwriters' Agreements".

L.U.A.M.H.
See "Leading Underwriters' Agreements".

L.U.C.O.
Lloyd's Underwriters' Claims Office.

Lutine Bell
The bell salved in 1859 from the frigate *Lutine*, which was lost at sea in 1799, now hangs in the Underwriting Room at Lloyd's. Traditionally it is rung to command attention for any announcement of importance.

L.W.
Low water.

L.W.O.S.T.
Low water, ordinary spring tide.

Lying Up
See "Lay up Return", "Lay up Warranty" and "Out of Commission".

Lying Up Return
The same as "Lay Up Return".

M

Machinery

The propelling machinery in a ship. The policy does not cover damage to machinery not caused by a marine peril, but it may be extended to cover damage caused by negligence, a bursting boiler, a broken shaft or a latent defect. (See " Negligence Clause ".) Cargo insurance on machinery is divided into " heavy " or " light " machinery. Heavy machinery is particularly subject to breakage. Light machinery insurance is generally subject to the " Replacement Clause " and " excludes mechanical derangement ".

Machinery Breakdown

Breakdown of the propelling machinery in a ship. When deterioration due to breakdown of machinery is covered by a cargo policy it is usual to specify that claims are only recoverable if the breakdown lasts for not less than 24 hours. Cover against breakdown of refrigerating machinery is subject to the same conditions.

Machinery Certificate

A surveyor's certificate of soundness of the ship's propelling machinery.

Machinery Damage

Where damage is caused to a ship's machinery by an insured peril there is a claim under the policy. If the machinery breaks down or is damaged by a mechanical fault, lack of maintenance or any reason, other than an insured peril, there is no claim under the policy.

The general average rules regarding ship's machinery provide that damage is allowed in general average only for the extraordinary use of the engines, such as endeavouring to pull the vessel off a strand. Damage to engines incurred in keeping the vessel off shore or head on to a storm is not allowed in general average, nor is damage from compounding of the engines.

Where machinery is damaged by an insured peril the insured is entitled to recover from the insurer the reasonable cost of repairs, including the damaged part. The insurer is not liable to replace the damaged part with a new part and the insured cannot insist on such part being new. If the insurer elects to use a new part he is entitled to recover the difference in value from the insured but, in practice, he usually waives this right by inserting the " new for old " clause in the policy. (See " New for Old ".)

When damage to machinery arises from negligence of the master, officers or crew a policy covered by the I.T.C. applies an additional deductible of 10% of the net claim after applying the ordinary policy deductible. (See also "Machinery Damage Co-insurance Clause".)

Machinery Damage Co-insurance Clause

A clause, in the Institute Hull Clauses, which relates to the additional perils incorporated in the policy by the Inchmaree Clause (which see). The perils in the Inchmaree Clause are separated into two parts, (a) and (b), and any damage to the ship directly caused by any of these perils is covered by the policy, subject to the deductible expressed in the Deductible Average Clause. The Machinery Co-insurance Clause provides that any loss of or damage to any boiler, shaft, machinery or associated equipment, arising from any peril specified in section (a) of the Inchmaree Clause and attributable, in part or in whole, to negligence of the Master, officers or crew shall be subject to a further deductible. The further deductible is 10% of the balance of the claim *after* applying the policy deductible. The clause does not apply to total loss.

Machy.

Machinery.

Made Good

In the event of a general average act the person whose property has been sacrificed is entitled to claim rateable contributions from the owners of the property or interests saved by the sacrifice. The value of the sacrificed property is declared and since the claimant will benefit by the contributions he has, in effect, benefited by that much from the general average act. It, therefore, follows that the amount so recovered by the claimant must in turn contribute towards the loss. To achieve this the contributory value of the property which suffered the sacrifice is calculated by taking the arrived saved value and adding the value of the part which was sacrificed. The value of the part which was sacrificed is called the "made good". The "made good" on cargo is the net value of the cargo sacrificed. The "made good" on ship is the reasonable cost of repairs of general average damage. The claimant in general average is entitled to interest on the amount to be made good.

Made Merchantable

When damaged goods are reconditioned and made fit for sale.

Maintenance and Cure

Under American maritime law a seaman has the right to

maintenance and cure from the shipowner if he is injured or becomes ill while in the employment of the shipowner. This right is not, in any way, dependent upon the shipowner's negligence. The payment of maintenance and cure continues until the seaman recovers or until he reaches the point of maximum cure.

Malicious Acts Clause
A paramount clause which was introduced to the I.T.C. in 1969. The clause excludes damage to or loss of the insured ship, liabilities incurred by the shipowner and expenses which might, otherwise, be recoverable under the policy, when any of these arises from detonation of an explosive or any weapon of war where such is used by persons acting maliciously or from a political motive.

mal. d.
Malicious damage.

Malicious Damage
A peril covered by the standard Institute Strikes Clauses.

Malicious Damage
See " Malicious Acts Clause ".

Managing Owner
When a vessel is owned jointly by several persons it is the practice for the owners to appoint one of their number to manage the ship. He is called the managing owner.

M. & W.
Marine and War risks.

Manhole
Opening in the top of the double bottom, or a tank top, in a ship.

Manifest
The document which contains all details of the cargo on board the ship. It is more reliable than a bill of lading because bills of lading may be issued when the cargo is delivered for loading, but the manifest is not completed until the cargo is loaded. The manifest must be accurate because it is the official document for Consular and Customs Authorities.

Mar.
Marine.

Margin Fee
A charge by the Inland Revenue Dept. of a Country on the amount remitted from that Country for the purpose of reinsurance placed abroad. In the Philippines this has been as high as 25%.

Marine Adventure

A voyage or period of time during which property is exposed to maritime perils. A more specific definition may be found in Section 3 of the Marine Insurance Act 1906.

Marine Insurance

Where an insurer enters into a contract with the assured agreeing to indemnify the assured, subject to the limits of the contract, for losses incidental to a marine adventure.

Marine Insurance Act 1906

An Act which came into force on the first day of January 1907 to codify laws on marine insurance existing at that time.

Marine Insurance Company

See " Company ".

Marine Insurance (Gambling Policies) Act 1909

See " Gambling Policies Act ".

Marine Market

That section of the body of Underwriters and Companies of the insurance market which specialises in marine risks. In practice the marine market also underwrites incidental non-marine and inland marine risks.

Marine Perils

Maritime perils.

Marine Policy

An insurance policy covering cargo, hull, freight or any insurable interest allied to these, against marine perils or perils incidental to a marine adventure.

The standard form of marine policy is the Lloyd's S.G. form, an example of which appears in the first schedule to the Marine Insurance Act 1906. A marine policy must specify the name of the assured or his agent. The subject matter must be designated with reasonable certainty, although it may be expressed in general terms in which case it is construed as being the subject matter which it was intended should be insured. A policy may be valued or unvalued. Most marine policies are valued (See " Valued Policies "). No contract of marine insurance is admissible as evidence in court unless it is embodied in a correctly executed policy. The policy must be signed or may be sealed by a Corporate Seal. If more than one insurer appears in the policy it is deemed to be a separate contract for each insurer.

Marine Syndicate

A group of Lloyd's underwriters nominating one underwriter to accept business on behalf of the Syndicate and specialising in marine insurance. There is little syndication in this way amongst the English Companies, but some American Companies group themselves into syndicates.

Marine Underwriter

One who accepts liability for marine losses. (See "Lloyd's Underwriter" and "Company Underwriter".)

Maritime Conventions Act 1911

Before this Act came into force collision cases where both vessels were to blame were settled as though each vessel was equally to blame. The effect of the Act was to provide that the degree of blame should be assessed and the degree of liability calculated accordingly. If it is not possible to assess the degree of blame each vessel is deemed equally to blame. The Act does not govern loss of life or personal injury liabilities. The claimant for such liability may proceed against either or both the shipowners responsible or their property.

Maritime Lien

See "Lien".

Maritime Perils

Perils of the seas and incidental thereto.

Market

A group of insurers in a particular area or in a particular branch of insurance (e.g. Lloyd's Market, Company Market, London Market, Marine Market).

Market Capacity

The maximum amount of liability that an insurance market (say, the London Marine Market) can, or is prepared to, accept. Underwriters are very conscious of their capacity limits. (See also "No Market".)

Market Practice

A modern expression meaning custom and usage. It means a practice which is generally acceptable in the insurance market.

Market Values

The insurer is not concerned with fluctuations of market values and does not cover loss of market. For this reason gross values are always used in the settlement of cargo claims. If net values were used fluctuations in market values would be reflected in the percentage of depreciation.

Marks

Identification marks on a crate, box, parcel or similar. The term is used, also, to indicate the loadline markings on the side of a ship.

M.A.S.

Maximum Amount Subject. A reinsurance term.

Master

Captain of a merchant ship. The master is responsible to the owners for his vessel. The title " Captain " is purely a courtesy title.

Master Cover

A form of open cover, usually in the name of a broker or agent, designed to take a wide variety of insurances from a certain source. Open covers are issued, as required, off the master cover and it is usual for the broker to operate the cover. The master cover is sometimes called a " Broker's Cover ".

Master's and Seamen's Wages

See " Wages ".

Master's Declaration Outwards

When a vessel is about to sail the master must complete this declaration that there is no contravention of the Merchant Shipping Act and stating whether the vessel is with cargo or in ballast.

Material Circumstance

Before conclusion of the contract (i.e. before the insurer accepts the risk), the assured and his broker must disclose every material circumstance to the insurer. A circumstance is material if it would affect the decision of the insurer to accept the risk or in the rating of the premium. Non-disclosure of a material circumstance entitles the insurer to avoid the contract. An enquiry by the insurer, before conclusion of the contract, about any circumstance makes that circumstance material. A circumstance which is not material need not be disclosed. The following circumstances need not be disclosed in the absence of enquiry:— Any circumstance which diminishes the risk, or which the insurer is presumed to know or should know in the ordinary course of his business, or which is waived by the insurer, or which is superfluous because of a warranty. Any information known to or received by the assured is a circumstance.

Material Fact
See " Material Circumstance ".

Material Representation
Before the contract is concluded (i.e. the insurer accepts the risk), the assured must, not only disclose but also, truly represent every material circumstance. A representation to the insurer is material if it would affect him in accepting the risk or in rating the premium. Misrepresentation entitles the insurer to avoid the contract. A representation must be true, or, at least, substantially true, that is, the difference between what is represented and fact would not be material. If a representation is made in good faith of an expectation or belief this is considered to be a true representation even if at a later date the expectation or belief proves to be untrue.

Mate's Receipt
Given when goods are loaded from lighters instead of direct from quay. A bill of lading subsequently replaces the mate's receipt.

m.b.
Motor boat.

M.B.D.
Machinery Breakdown.

M.B.S.
Notation in Lloyd's Register that the machinery is classed in accordance with the rules of the British Corporation.

M/c
Machinery certificate.

Mchy.
Machinery of a ship.

Mchy. dge.
Machinery damage.

M.C.M.V.
Mine counter measure vessel.

M.D.
Malicious damage.

Mdse.
Merchandise.

Mean Nautical Mile
The exact distance of a nautical mile being 6076·91 feet. It is usual to use the measurement of 6080 feet to a nautical mile and a knot is so measured.

Measure of Indemnity
The extent of the liability of the insurer for loss; that is, the amount which the assured can recover from the insurer in the event of loss from an insured peril. For a total loss under a valued policy it is the insured value, but under an unvalued policy it is the insurable value. (See "Valued Policies".) For a partial loss of goods it is whatever proportion the loss bears to the insurable value, applied on a percentage to the insured value in a valued policy, or the insurable value in the case of an unvalued policy. For partial loss of ship it is the reasonable cost of repairs or a reasonable depreciation at expiry of the policy if the repairs have not been carried out. For partial loss of freight it is whatever proportion the loss bears to the whole freight at risk applied as a percentage of the sum insured fixed by the policy. (See also "Partial Loss of freight", "Partial Loss of Goods" and "Partial Loss of Ship".)

Meat Clauses
See "Frozen Meat Clauses".

Mechanical Derangement
Certain types of light machinery, electrical equipment and similar are often subject to "not working" after arrival at destination, although they have not suffered from an insured peril. This is due to mechanical derangement and, to prevent misunderstandings, it is usual for the insurer specifically to exclude mechanical derangement from the policy.

Medcon
Coal charterparty applying from U.K. east coast to the Danube and River Plate.

Med. Exps.
Medical Expenses.

Member of Lloyd's
See "Lloyd's Underwriter".

Membership Services Group
See "Lloyd's Membership Services Group".

Memo Dollars
The same as "true sterling" (which see), but in U.S. dollars instead of sterling.

Memorandum

The original franchise provision which is printed at the foot of the standard policy form. It provides that corn, fish, salt, fruit, flour and seed are not covered for particular average; that particular average on sugar, tobacco, hemp, flax, hides and skins is subject to a 5% franchise, and that particular average on any other interest is subject to a 3% franchise. All these special provisions are wiped out if the vessel is stranded, sunk or burnt. In practice, the memorandum is completely overridden by the wording "irrespective of percentage" or an alternative franchise or deductible inserted in the policy. If neither of these amendments is made the memorandum applies. In practice the memorandum is applied, today, only to particular average on goods in transit.

Memorandum Advice

An advance notification to an underwriter of a premium or claim entry. Sometimes termed "non-cash advice".

Men of War

Ships for the purpose of hostilities, acts of aggression or defence

Merchandise

Goods which are sold or to be sold.

Merchant Shipping Act

The Merchant Shipping Act 1894 but when referred to it is meant that the various amendments and supplements should be embraced. This is the primary Act concerned with merchant shipping.

Metacentric Diagram

See "Metacentre, Transverse".

Metacentric, Height

See "Metacentre, Transverse".

Metacentre, Longitudinal

This is the same as a transverse metacentre except that it relates to the trim of the vessel and is calculated by horizontal rather than vertical imaginary lines.

Metacentre, Transverse

The transverse metacentre is the point at which two imaginary lines intersect in a ship. One line is exactly halfway between the sides of a ship (i.e. in line with the stem and stern) and is vertical when the ship is upright but inclines to one side or the other as the ship rolls. The second imaginary line remains vertical all the time so that when the ship is upright it is in exactly the same position as the first line. As the ship rolls one line twists over whilst the other remains upright and the intersecting point, the transverse metacentre, moves up or down indicating the stability of the ship in relation to the centre of gravity. A new ship is inclined to determine its metacentric height and the centre of gravity. Variations in draft and cargo disposition can affect a ship's metacentre, so a metacentric diagram and capacity plan are necessary when assessing cargo loading and fuel and ballast allowances. (See also " Metacentre, Longitudinal ".)

M.F.C.
Maximum Foreseeable Loss; a reinsurance term.

M.H.
Main hatch.

M.H.W.S.
Mean high water spring tide.

M.I.A. *or* **M.I. Act**
Marine Insurance Act 1906.

Min.
Minimum.

MIN/DEP
Minimum and deposit premium.

Minderwert
Loss in value and/or loss of market. An expression used in fruit insurance where it is usual to exclude losses due to minderwert.

Minimising a Loss
It is the duty of the assured to act all the time as though uninsured and to take all reasonable measures to minimise or avert a loss, even though the loss may be recoverable under his policy of marine insurance. If the assured or his servants take any such measures to preserve the property from an insured peril the expense, if any, is recoverable from the insurer under the suing and labouring clause. Any expenses incurred by way of salvage or general average contributions are recoverable in a like manner. All such recoveries are subject to proportionate reduction if the property is not insured for its full value. Except where the policy provides otherwise it is customary for insurers to pay the expense of minimising or preventing an insured loss without applying the policy deductible or franchise, if any. However, in hull practice the policy deductible is applied to *all* partial loss claims including expenses incurred to minimise or prevent an insured loss.

Minimum Premium

Usually specified in conjunction with a deposit premium. When a cargo insurance is effected in respect of many sendings the insurer may only agree to accept the insurance subject to a guaranteed minimum premium. The agreed minimum is customarily paid as a deposit in advance. This system is often used in connection with land transit risks and non-marine construction risks. Most Companies and Lloyd's have a minimum premium understanding whereby an insurance is not acceptable if the premium is for less than the agreed minimum; this being based on the expense of processing the entry.

Min. wt.

Minimum weight.

M.I.P.

Marine insurance policy.

Misconduct

Loss attributable to wilful misconduct of the assured is excluded from the marine policy by the provision of Sect. 55, Marine Insurance Act, 1906. (See " Statutory Exclusions ".)

Misdescribed Cargo

If cargo which has been wilfully misdescribed is sacrificed as part of a general average act, the cargo owner cannot claim contributions from the interests saved. If, on the other hand, the misdescribed cargo benefits by a general average act the cargo owner must contribute towards the sacrifice.

Misrepresentation

The insurer is entitled to avoid the contract if there is misrepresentation of a material fact by the assured or broker. (See " Material Representation " and " Representation ".)

Missing Ship

A missing ship is an actual total loss. When after a reasonable lapse of time no news has been received of a vessel it is considered a " Missing Ship ". It is usual for the vessel's name to be posted at Lloyd's as a missing ship and in peacetime it is considered to be a loss by marine perils. Insured cargo on a " missing " ship is also deemed to be an actual total loss. (See also " Overdue Market ".)

Mixed Sea and Land Risks

The Marine Insurance Act 1906 provides that a marine policy may be extended to cover land risks, or risks on inland waters, which may be incidental to any sea voyage. A marine policy may also be used for ship construction or similar.

Mixed Policies

A mixed policy is one which covers both a voyage and a period of time. Before the stamp laws were changed in August 1959 it was necessary to distinguish between this type of policy and the ordinary marine policy because stamp duty problems arose. Marine policies today no longer attract stamp duty.

M.L.W.S.

Mean low water spring tide.

m/m

Made merchantable.

M.M.A.

Merchant Marine Act (1920)—U.S.A. Law.

M.O.H.

Medical Officer of Health.

Mole

An artificial part of a harbour. A long jetty or pier at the entrance to the harbour, giving protection from the waves of the open sea.

Monthly Codes

To facilitate punching of cards in Lloyd's Data Processing Services the Central Accounting Office utilises alphabetical codes to indicate each month of the year. With the exception of those shown below each month is indicated by its initial letter (i.e. J = January). The exceptions are Y = May, U = June, L = July, G = August, T = October.

Monthly Total of Entries

Items closed in the L.P.S.O. Contract Scheme are advised to the relevant broker once each month on a listing termed Monthly Total of Entries.

Moon Pool

The centre well of a drill ship, over which the derrick is mounted.

Moral Hazard

The risk of a loss occurring by reason of intention or lack of responsibility of the assured.

Mort.

Mortality.

Mortality

Applicable to insurance on live animals. Insurers covering this interest usually limit their liability to death only, including destruction for humane reasons.

Mortgagee

A person who lends money against the security of property. In the case of money loaned against the security of property which is at sea, such as a ship or cargo, the mortgagee may lose his security. The mortgagee, therefore, has an insurable interest in the property and may insure it in so far as the loan is not repayable in the event of loss. In many cases the mortgagee insists on a clause appearing in a hull policy giving him rights under the policy. (See " Mortgagee Clause ".) The mortgagee may effect a " Mortgagee's Interest " policy separately from the hull policy.

Mortgagee Clause

A clause in a hull policy giving beneficial rights under the policy to a mortgagee or other lender of money on the security of the ship.

Moth Damage

Liable to occur in furs and fabrics. Excluded from the policy as vermin.

Movables

Any tangible property which is movable, other than a ship. It includes valuables, money, documents, securities and the like.

m. pack

Missing package.

M.P.L.

Maximum Probable Loss. A reinsurance term.

M/R.

Mate's receipt.

M.S.

Machinery survey. May also mean " motor ship ".

M.S.A.

Merchant Shipping Act 1894.

M.S.C.

Manchester Ship Canal.

mst.

Measurement.

M.T.

Mean time.

mt.

A slang abbreviation in carrying goods, " empty ".

M.T.E.

Monthly Total of Entries.

M.T.L.

Mean tide level.

Mule

A vehicle (often electrically powered) used to tow vessels through canals and/or locks.

Multi Packed

More than one item packed in one case or parcel.

Multiple Values

A term once used in relation to a hull policy where the insured value was expressed separately for each part of the ship. (See " Multiple Values Clause ".)

Multiple Values Clause

When hull policies were subject to a franchise there was a clause in the standard hull clauses which provided that the values of the hull and of the machinery be considered separately in applying the franchise. A further clause clarified which parts of the vessel be deemed part of the hull. Where a vessel had refrigerating machinery it was usual to specify the separate values in the policy. The clause was advantageous to the assured because it enabled him to attain the franchise on a separate value where he was unable to do so on the whole value.

Mutual Agreement

Claim settlements, returns of premium, cancellation of policies and other arrangements may be made by mutual agreement even though the party granting the concession is not strictly obliged to give it. In the case of cancellation of a policy by mutual agreement it is usual for the insurer to agree to return the unearned premium to the assured.

Mutual Cancellation

A policy may be cancelled by mutual agreement even after the risk has attached. Unless agreement to return part of the premium, in the event of mutual cancellation, was made when the insurer accepted the risk the insurer is not obliged to return any part of the premium once the risk has attached. In a hull time policy there is usually a clause providing that in the event of mutual cancellation the insurer will return one-twelfth of the annual net premium for each uncommenced month.

Mutual Insurance

When a group of persons engage to contribute rateably to the losses of one of the members of the group there is mutual insurance. The effect is that each insures the other.

In marine insurance this occurs when shipowners form themselves into a mutual club as in a Protection and Indemnity Club. In marine insurance it is usual to dispense with premium arrangements in respect of mutual insurance and to replace these with a guarantee of payment when called for.

M.V.

Motor vessel.

Mysterious Disappearance

The disappearance of insured property from no known cause. Mainly a non-marine expression. It generally falls in the category of non-delivery of cargo in the marine market. The mysterious disappearance of a ship is an actual total loss under the principle of " missing ship " and in peacetime is usually recoverable under the policy as a loss by marine perils.

N

N.

Noon.

Nail to Nail

A term used in transit insurance on such interests as paintings. The term denotes that the insurance attaches when the painting is removed from the wall fastening for transit and terminates when the painting is fastened to the wall at the destination specified in the policy.

Name

An underwriting member at Lloyd's. Business at Lloyd's is transacted with syndicates. Each syndicate comprises several "names", being the members who subscribe the policies written on their behalf by the syndicate. (See also "Attestation Clause".)

Named Peril

A peril specified in a policy. Same as a "Named Risk".

Named Policy

A term not used very often in the marine insurance market but sometimes referred to in shipping circles. It means a cargo policy where the name of the carrying vessel is shown. In practice, a cargo policy, other than an open policy, is seldom issued until the name of the carrying vessel is known and in that case the name is always inserted in the policy.

Named Risk

A risk specified in a policy.

Named Steamer

The acceptance or rating of cargo insurance is influenced by the carrying vessel. When an insurer accepts an open cover he agrees to accept any approved steamer as a carrier, that is, any reasonable vessel up to 15 years old (liners, other than war built tonnage, are acceptable up to 30 years old.) It is customary for underwriters subscribing an open cover to hold covered overage vessels subject to a suitable additional premium. In some cases, the insurer will only accept the cover provided he is advised of and approves the carrying vessel before attachment of each declaration. The acceptances being by "named steamer" only.

Name of the Assured

The name of the assured must appear in a marine policy. Alter-

262

natively, the name of the agent (the broker) may appear in place of the name of the assured. It is not necessary for the address of the assured to appear in a marine policy.

N.A. *or* **n.a.**
Net absolutely.

National Cargo Bureau
The American National Cargo Bureau is a non-profit membership organisation operating on a nationwide basis and maintaining offices in the principal U.S. ports. Its purpose is to assist shippers, carriers and insurers regarding safe secure stowage and careful loading and unloading of cargo, also the safety of ships' handling gear. The Bureau acts as a source of information on cargoes, their inspections and surveys. It also makes safety recommendations to the U.S. Authorities and issues certificates of inspection.

Nationality of Vessel
There is no implied warranty in a marine policy that a vessel must be of a certain Nationality, nor any warranty prohibiting any change of Nationality during the risk. Nevertheless, the Nationality of the vessel is important to the insurer particularly if the vessel sails under a " Flag of Convenience ". The insurer, may warrant expressly that the carrying vessel in respect of a cargo policy is not of a certain flag. (See " F.O.M.")

Natural Harbour
A harbour built in a natural basin and protected from the open sea by natural rock formations extending out to sea and embracing the harbour. A harbour protected from the sea by man-made moles or piers is called an artificial harbour.

Natural Loss
Natural loss in weight. In the case of liquid cargoes this is synonymous with natural leakage or " trade ullage ". In the case of solid cargoes it is usually due to shrinkage or drying out of moisture from changes in temperature. Potatoes are particularly susceptible to natural loss in weight. Since this is an inevitability and not a fortuity it is not covered under the term " loss in weight " unless this is qualified with " from any cause whatsoever " or a similar term. It is usual specifically to exclude loss in weight from insurances covering deterioration risks.

Nautical Mile
A measurement of distance at sea, used mainly for speed measurement. One knot is one nautical mile per hour. The exact measurement varies dependent on the Latitude but the average may be

applied by using a mean nautical mile of 6076·91 feet.

Nav.

Navigating *or* navigation.

Navigation Risks

Risks or perils incidental to a vessel navigating or at sea as opposed to being in port or laid up.

NB

Notation in Lloyd's Register indicating that a new boiler was fitted on the stated date. Also an abbreviation for " nota bena " (i.e. " note well ") by which the " memorandum " may be recognised at the foot of the standard policy form.

N.C.A.D.

Notice of cancellation at anniversary date. When an insurer writes an insurance on an " always open " basis, he may wish to ensure that he sees the ratio between premium income and claims at the end of each 12 months period. To ensure this he inserts N.C.A.D. next to his initial on the slip. The broker must then make certain that he takes the slip and the statistics to the insurer in good time before the anniversary date in order to have the notice of cancellation withdrawn or carried forward a further 12 months.

N.C.A.R.

No claim for accident reported (which see.)

N.C.B. *or* **N.C.O.B.**

No cargo on board. This abbreviation was used at one time in connection with " lay up " returns on a policy insuring a ship. However, from 1st January 1964 the variation in the lay up retention dependent on whether or not the ship had cargo on board was withdrawn, so that the abbreviation is no longer in use.

N.C.C.

No collecting commission. (See " Collecting Commission ".)

N.C.V.

No commercial value.

N.D. *or* **N/D**

Non delivery *or* no discount.

n.d.

Non delivery.

ndb

New donkey boiler. Lloyd's Register notation giving date when fitted.

N.D.O.
Number and date only.

N.E.
Not entered. A slip abbreviation used by an underwriter as a reference to indicate that he has made no entry in his books of the details of the risk. It is only used for facultative acceptances. The abbreviation is also used in a slip before the name of a location, in which case it means " not east of ". Further, it is shown as a notation in Lloyd's Register indicating that a new engine was fitted on the specified date.

N/E *or* n.e.
Not exceeding.

Near Continental Trade (U.K.)
The near Continental trade (U.K.) limits proposed for the Merchant Shipping Act (1970) embrace any ports or places on the continental coast of Europe and Scandinavia from below 60°N. latitude (on the Norwegian coast), to include the Baltic and the north and north west European coasts, as far as Spain.

Neg.
Negligence.

Negative Films
The original film strips " shot " by a film company in making a film. The value of these is the cost of making the film and, therefore, large values are often involved. The marine market undertakes a large proportion of these insurances, but a great deal of the risk is ceded to other insurers by way of reinsurances.

Negative Film Syndicate
A New York organisation of Companies engaged in insurance of film negatives. Mentioned herein only because negative film insurance is often placed in the marine market.

Negligence
Failure to properly carry out or perform an act, service or duty. The improper performance of an act, service or duty.

Negligence Clause
This clause was introduced to hull policies in 1888 following the decision in the case " Hamilton Fraser & Co *v* Thames & Mersey Marine Insurance Company Limited (1887) ". It is frequently termed " Inchmaree Clause " after the name of the vessel involved in the case. The clause has been amended several times and is incorporated in the standard hull clauses (I.T.C.). It extends the

policy perils by adding further perils in two sections (a) and (b). Section (a) incorporates the perils: Accidents in loading, discharging or shifting cargo or fuel, Explosions on shipboard or elsewhere, Breakdown of or accident to nuclear installations on shipboard or elsewhere, Bursting of boilers, breakage of shafts or any latent defect in the machinery or hull, Negligence of master, officers or crew, Negligence of repairers (other than the assured). Section (b) incorporates the perils: Contact with aircraft, Contact with any land conveyance, dock or harbour equipment or installation, Earthquake, volcanic eruption or lightning. Provided the damage does not result from want of due diligence by the assured, owners or managers, and subject to the policy deductible and paramount exclusion clauses, damage to the ship directly caused by the specified perils is covered. However, where damage to machinery under Section (a) is attributable to negligence of the master, officers or crew an additional deductible of 10% of the net claim (after applying the basic policy deductible) is applied.

Negligence of Broker
The marine insurance broker is the agent of the assured. He is deemed to be an expert in marine insurance and it is his duty to use all his knowledge and skill in obtaining the best terms and cover for the assured. If he is negligent in his duty whereby the assured is prejudiced the broker may be sued for damages by the assured. The broker is not negligent if he places the insurance with an insurer who is unable to meet his liabilities, since the broker does not guarantee the solvency of the insurer. (See also "Failure to Complete".)

Negligence of Master
See "Negligence of Shipowner".

Negligence of Shipowner
The plain policy form does not cover the risk of negligence so that, unless the risk is specifically expressed in the policy, losses proximately caused by negligence are not recoverable. On the other hand, losses proximately caused by an insured peril are recoverable even though they would not have arisen but for the negligence of the master or crew.

In practice, the Negligence Clause is attached to all hull policies incorporating the peril of negligence of the master, officers, crew pilots or repairers. To be recoverable the loss must not be caused by negligence which arises through want of diligence on the part of the owners, assured or managers. In this respect if the master, or any of the officers, crew or pilots hold shares in the ship they are not to be considered as part owners. (See also "Negligence Clause".)

A shipowner may be guilty of negligence in respect of the cargo in his care as well as his own vessel. A negligent act of a servant of the shipowner is in effect the negligence of the shipowner himself, but an act of wilful or criminal negligence of his servant may not become the liability of the shipowner provided he exercised due diligence, as a certain amount of responsibility must remain with the individual. (See also "Collision Clause".)

Negligent Navigation

The master, officers or others responsible for the navigation or management of a ship must be sufficiently skilled to carry out their duties properly. If any of them fails to exercise his skill properly in the navigation or management of the ship, thereby causing damage to property belonging to or an infringement to the rights of a third party, the responsible person is guilty of negligence. Since the responsible person is a servant of the shipowner the shipowner is liable for damages to the third party in respect of such negligence. This is particularly important in connection with collisions at sea. (See also "Collision Clause" and "Limitation of Liability".)

Negotiable Instrument

A document of value which is negotiable. That is, it can be endorsed to give another party beneficial rights. A non-negotiable instrument is one where no rights of assignment exist. A marine policy is negotiable but only a cargo policy is freely assignable in practice, because insurers prohibit the assignment of the hull policy without their consent. (See also "Assignment of Policy".)

Nesting

The packing of cargo which is subject to breakage or denting by reason of its hollow nature. Such as baths, bowls or similar. Each piece is placed or "nested" in another, with some form of soft packing such as paper or straw to prevent actual contact or jamming.

Net Absolutely

To emphasise that all discounts, without exception, have been taken off. The word "absolutely" is added to the word "net" when referring to premiums net of discounts. The expression is frequently used in connection with premium returned to the assured, where it is understood that the broker shall retain his brokerage when making the return of premium.

Net Line

The amount of liability retained by a reinsured after deducting from the total amount of the originally accepted line the proportion which it has been agreed shall be ceded to the reinsurer.

Net Net Weight

Only occurs where goods are wrapped in separate cartons or similar inside the " tare " or outside container. The net net weight is the actual weight of the merchandise excluding both wrapping and " tare ".

Net Premium

The premium after all discounts have been taken off, alternatively the premium following the deduction of a return of premium. The latter, if before deduction of discounts, may be called the " Gross Net Premium ". (See also " Net Absolutely ".)

Net Registered Tonnage

The actual carriage capacity of a ship. The gross tonnage less engine room, navigation, light, air, locker room spaces and similar. It applies only to the enclosed space of the ship and, therefore, does not include open shelter deck spaces. The tonnage is calculated on cubic capacity at 100 cub. ft. per ton.

Net Retained Line

The net retained line is the amount an insurer retains for his own account after having arranged all reinsurances.

Net Retention

See " Net Retained Line " and " Lay Up Return ".

Net Tonnage

Net registered tonnage.

Net Values

The net value of cargo is its actual arrived value or sale value at destination less all charges incidental to landing the goods at destination. Claims for partial loss of cargo are calculated on gross values unless the policy specifically provides for net values to be used.

Contributory values for general average and salvage purposes are always based on net values.

Net Values Clause

A clause in a cargo policy permitting the use of net values when calculating partial loss claims. In the case of some bulk cargoes, such as coal, the landing charges are so heavy that they form a large part of the gross value. Since the landing charges remain constant for both damaged and sound goods, heavy landing charges could affect the claim considerably if gross values are used. For many years the net values clause appeared in many sets of trade clauses but, following abuse, insurers refused to accept the clause from 1942.

Net Weight

The weight without the " tare " or container.

Neutrality

During time of war it is common for the insurers of a vessel registered with a neutral Country, or of goods on such a vessel, to warrant that the vessel and/or goods are neutral. This means that so far as the assured can control the matter the vessel must be properly documented and the documents of neutrality must be proper and not false or simulated. If any loss occurs through a breach of this warranty the insurer is discharged from liability. By the warranty the vessel must have a neutral character at the commencement of the risk and, so far as the assured can control the matter, the neutral character must be preserved throughout the risk.

New F.C. & S. Clause

The current marine war exclusion clause. It was adopted in its present form in 1943 following the decision of the " Coxwold " case. The previous clause did not contain the wording which now states that the exclusion does not apply to marine casualties such as collision, stranding, fire etc. unless the casualty is a direct result of a hostile act, irrespective of whether or not the vessel is on a warlike engagement. (See also " Free of Capture and Seizure ".)

New for Old

When hull repairs are carried out and new materials are used to replace old materials the insurer is entitled, under the Marine Insurance Act, 1906 (Section 69), to make certain specified deductions from the claim. In practice, this right is waived and the insurer agrees to make deductions " new for old ". The fact that the insurer agrees to waive his right to the deductions does not entitle the assured to claim new material, nor to claim the difference in value if the insurer elects to use old material.

The practice of the insurer with regard to waiving "new for old" deductions does not affect the allowances made in a general average adjustment. "New for old" is sometimes referred to as "thirds".

New York Suable Clause

A policy clause which provides that although the policy is issued in London any service of suit shall be brought in the State of New York, U.S.A. The insurer agrees to accept the jurisdiction of the U.S. Court.

270   MARINE INSURANCE TERMS

New Zealand Carriage of Goods Act 1940
An Act to give force of law to the rights, obligations and immunities of carriers of goods in respect of bills of lading on shipments from New Zealand.

Nippon Kaiji Kyokai
This is a Japanese Classification Society. Unchartered steel vessels up to 15 years old (liners other than war built vessels, are acceptable up to 30 years old) and fully classed with this Society are acceptable to insurers as carriers. Vessels registered with the Nippon Kaiji Kyokai may appear in Lloyd's Register with the notation NK shown. The cypher to denote full class in the Nippon Kaiji Kyokai is NS*. This Society is often referred to as the " Japanese Marine Corporation ". (See also " Classification Clause ".)

N.L.U.R.
No lying up returns. Alternatively the abbreviation can be used for " net lying up returns ". Other interpretations replace " lying up " with " lay up " but the effect is the same.

N.M.
Non marine *or* no mark.

N.M.A.
Lloyd's Non Marine Underwriters' Association.

N.M.A. War Exclusion
It is understood in the insurance market that war risks are not covered on goods or property whilst on land. Lloyd's Non Marine Underwriters' Association has drafted a standard war and civil war exclusion clause to this effect. When goods or property in transit on land, not being incidental to a sea voyage, are insured in the marine market, it is usual to use either a " J " form or a " J(A) " form for such risks. These forms have no perils specified in them but the " J " form has the war and civil war exclusion clause incorporated. When goods in transit by sea are issued against war risks the policy is subject to the Waterborne Clause (which see).

N/N *or* N.N.
Not north of. A geographical limitation.

No B.N.A.
Warranted the vessel is not calling at British North American Ports or places. This means Canadian ports and refers particularly to ports in the vicinity of the St. Lawrence, where ice hazards exist during winter. The Warranty is usually applicable to voyage policies during the autumn, winter and spring.

No Claim for Accident Reported

An insurer may be asked to accept an insurance after the risk has attached. If he agrees to accept he will usually do so on a " lost or not lost " basis, whereby he is liable for losses occurring before acceptance. Should an accident to the vessel have been reported in " Lloyd's List " the insurer may warrant that no claim be paid in respect of this accident.

No Claims Return

There is no standard form of " no claims bonus " in marine insurance as is found in motor insurance, but in certain cases it may be agreed to return part of the premium paid in the event of no claim. In such cases it is usual for the insurer to charge an inflated premium at inception, agreeing to return a specified amount in the event of there being no claims under the policy. The return of premium is generally agreed " N.A.", that is, the amount paid to the assured is the amount received from the insurer, the brokerage being deemed earned and retained by the broker.

No Cure, No Pay

A principle of pure salvage. To entitle a salvor to a salvage award property of value must be saved in order that it may pay the award. If it is not saved there is no award. It is not necessary that the property arrives at its final destination, only that the salvor brings it to a place of safety where the owner may take possession of it on payment of the salvage award. Lloyd's Salvage Agreement is on the principle of " No cure, no pay ".

No Interest

Where the person requiring the insurance has no insurable interest.

No Known Loss

An insurer may be asked to accept an insurance after the risk has attached. If he agrees he will usually accept on a " lost or not lost " basis, whereby he is liable for losses which occurred before he accepted this risk. The assured should advise the insurer if he knows of any loss at the time of placing or there is non-disclosure, but many insurers avail themselves of the additional protection of warranting " no known loss ".

No lying up returns

Alternatively " No lay up returns ". A term used in insurance of hulls which limits the return of premiums permitted under the policy. Basically, this is taken to be the same as " cancelling returns only " but, taken in its strict sense, it simply means that the provision for returns in the event of the vessel being laid up is deleted from the policy, no provisions for other returns being affected.

No Market

A term used by a broker to advise his client that a risk is not placeable in the market in which he operates, or to which he is referring when using the term. This might apply in the case of a particularly hazardous risk, or it may be used when the market capacity is insufficient to take the risk.

Nominal Premium

The premium entered in a policy where no actual payment is made. F.D.O. policies are signed on a nominal premium.

Non-Admitted Company

In the U.S.A. this is a Company in a particular State which is not licensed to insure the business in hand. Many Countries permit only certain Companies to write their business, others being called non-admitted Companies.

Non Arrival

For cargo see " Non Delivery ". For hull see " Missing Ship ".

Non Carrying Vessel

Expression used in connection with claims by cargo owners against carriers in respect of collision liability. In disputes the vessel carrying the cargo concerning which the claim is made is called the " Carrying Vessel ". The other vessel is called the " Non Carrying Vessel ".

Non-Cash Entry

An entry that is advised to underwriters on a provisional basis. It is a form of preliminary advice. Such entry may be made in connection with claims and for convertible currencies where the rate of exchange is not available at the time of entry or where a policy is required to be signed before the cash premium entry is taken down.

Non-Compliance with a Warranty

A warranty is a promise by the assured that something shall or shall not be done or that a state of affairs will or will not exist. A warranty must be strictly complied with. Non-compliance discharges the insurer from liability as from the date of the breach. Non-compliance is excused where the reason for the warranty no longer applies by reason of change of circumstances, where it would be illegal to comply with the warranty or where the underwriter waives the breach. (See also " Compliance with a Warranty ".)

Non contrib. cl.
Non contribution clause.

Non-Contribution Clause

A clause in a policy providing that in the event of a loss occurring which would be recoverable under the policy no claim is payable if another policy exists covering the same risk. This may occur where a fire policy and a marine policy overlap on the same goods. In the absence of the clause each policy should pay proportionately toward the loss. Difficulties may arise where both policies contain this clause.

non. d.
Non delivery.

Non-Delivery

The insurance covers losses proximately caused by the perils specified in the policy, extending the specified perils to those " of a like kind " (see " Ejusdem Generis "). If goods fail to arrive without proof of the cause of loss, this is simply non-delivery or shortage. Non-delivery, as a term, is restricted to the non-delivery of a whole package and the loss is not covered by the terms of the policy unless so specified therein. Where non-delivery is a specified peril losses by this peril are always paid irrespective of percentage.

Non-Disclosure

The assured and/or his agent (the broker) must disclose to the insurer, before the risk is accepted, any material fact or circumstance which is known or should be known to either and/or both the assured and/or his agent. If either of them fail in this obligation the insurer may avoid the contract. A fact or circumstance is material if it would influence a prudent insurer in accepting, declining or rating the risk. The Marine Insurance Act 1906 permits non-disclosure, in the absence of enquiry, of any circumstance which diminishes the risk or which is waived by the insurer or which is superfluous by reason of a warranty or which is known or may be presumed to be known to the insurer in the ordinary course of his business, or because it is general knowledge. (See " Utmost Good Faith ".)

Non Institute Clauses

Clauses which are in current use in the marine market but which are not published by the Institute of London Underwriters. Trade clauses and owner's clauses fall in this category, as do various special wordings for individual cargoes or interests.

Non-Payment Risk

The risk of non-payment by the buyer of goods. This is a form of financial guarantee although it does not depend on insolvency of the buyer, since non-payment may be due to non-fulfilment of the sale contract terms. In the main, the insurance market does not like to cover financial guarantee risks but there may be a limited market for non-payment following the terms of sale contracts. It is usual to exclude claims arising from physical damage to the goods or ship.

Non-Separation Agreement

When a ship puts into a port of refuge to effect repairs which are the subject of a general average act the shipowner may discharge the cargo, or part thereof, and arrange for it to be transhipped to another vessel for onward carriage. Once the ship and cargo separate they become separate entities so far as subsequent general average loss and expenditure is concerned so that the cargo could not be called upon to contribute in general average to the additional expenditure incurred by the carrier. To protect himself the carrier will incorporate a clause in his contract of affreightment whereby the cargo owner agrees that such separation shall not affect any rights to general average contribution which the shipowner would have had under Rule X1 of the York/Antwerp rules but for the separation of the interests in the adventure.

Non-Separation Clause

A clause in a contract of affreightment giving effect to a non-separation agreement. (See " Non-Separation Agreement ".)

N.O.R.

Net original rate. The same as O.N.R.

No Risk

Same as " Not on risk ".

Normal Course of Transit

The insurer intends, when he accepts an insurance on cargo for a voyage, that cover will attach when the cargo commences transit for the voyage stated in the insurance, shall continue during the voyage and shall terminate when the cargo is delivered at its destination at the end of the voyage. The rate of premium charged is based on the voyage being prosecuted with reasonable despatch and, in fact, the Marine Insurance Act 1906 in section 48, stipulates that the voyage shall be so prosecuted. Not only does the insurer expect the voyage to be prosecuted with reasonable despatch, he is also entitled to expect that only normal forms of transport, in addition to the named vessel, shall be used. Bearing this in mind, the normal course of transit is transit by normal forms of transport and without unreasonable delay. Storage in a warehouse, at the request of the cargo owner for any reason other than customs inspection or whilst awaiting transit, would not be considered to be part of the normal course of transit. (See " Transit Clause " and " Delay ".)

Norske Veritas

This is a Norwegian Classification Society. Unchartered steel vessels up to 15 years old (liners, other than war built vessels, are acceptable as carriers without additional premium up to 30 years old) and fully classed with this Society are acceptable to insurers as carriers. Vessels registered with the Norske Veritas may appear in Lloyd's Register with the notation NV shown. The cypher to denote full class in the Norske Veritas Register is ✻ 1.Al. (See also " Classification Clause ".)

North American Warranty

One of the Institute warranties. By this warranty the assured promises the vessel will not proceed to or from any port or place on the east coast of North America north of 52° 10′ N. lat. and west of 50° W. long.; nor south of 52° 10′ N. lat. in an area bounded by Battle Harbour/Pistolet Bay/Cape Ray/Cape North/Port Hawkesbury/Port Mulgrave/Baie Comeau/Matane between 21 December and 30 April, both days inclusive; nor west of Baie Comeau/Matane (but not west of Montreal) between 1st December and 30th April, both days inclusive. Also prohibited by the warranty are the Great Lakes and St. Lawrence Seaway west of Montreal, Greenland waters and the North American Pacific coast, its rivers and adjacent islands north of 54° 30′ N. lat. or west of 130° 50′ W. long.

Northern Range Ports

Ports U.S.A. (Atlantic Coast); Newport and north thereof.

North Sea Boat

An oil or gas drilling rig designed with enormous strength, deep freeboard, moderately powerful engines and thrusters to meet the sea and tidal hazards of the North Sea.

No S.I.

No short interest. (See " Short Interest ".)

Not At Risk

Same as " Not on risk ".

Noted

If, after an insurance has been placed, the assured advises his broker of information which is material to the insurance, but which does not require the insurer's agreement, the broker should pass this information to the insurer who " notes " it. The practice is for the broker to prepare an attachment to the original slip commencing with " noted that——". The insurer, or leader if there are several insurers on the same slip, initials the attachment. In some instances the attachment commences with " Noted and agreed ", which has the same effect as any other agreement by the insurer. Sometimes the insurer will write " seen " on the document advising the information, which means that it has been presented to him but he does not wish to " note " it in his records. Provisional claim advices often follow this procedure.

Notice
Notice of cancellation. (See " Cancellation Clause ".)

Notice of Abandonment
If the assured has reason to believe he may have a claim for constructive total loss he must abandon the property to the insurer to substantiate his claim. If it can be of any benefit to the insurer the assured must give notice of his intention to abandon the property. This enables the insurer to take any steps he deems necessary to prevent a total loss or to reduce the loss. The " Waiver Clause " in the policy states that any such steps taken are not an acceptance of abandonment nor a waiver of the right of the insurer to reject abandonment. Notice may be given either in writing or by word of mouth or both, stating the intention to abandon unconditionally the interest to the insurer. Notice must be given with reasonable diligence after receipt of reliable information. If the insurer accepts the notice he conclusively admits liability for the loss. It is usual for the insurer formally to reject the notice of abandonment but this does not prejudice his right to take steps to prevent or reduce the loss and he retains the option to take over whatever may remain of the property after he has paid a total loss. Notice need not be given if it can be of no benefit to the insurer. Notice may be waived by the insurer. Notice of abandonment need not be given to a reinsurer. Failure to give notice of abandonment to the insurer, except as excused above, entitles the insurer to treat the loss as a partial loss.

Notice of Cancellation
See " Cancellation Clause ".

Notice of Liability Clause
A clause in the I.Y.C. that has the same effect as the Tender Clause in the I.T.C.

Notice of Readiness

When a ship has "arrived", notice of readiness is given by the shipowner to the charterer or shipper indicating that the vessel is ready to load the cargo.

Notification of Claim against Carrier

When there is apparent damage to goods on discharge the consignee must give notice of the damage in writing to the carrier or his agent at the port of discharge before or at the time of removal of the goods into the custody of the person entitled to take delivery of them. It is the duty of the consignee to carry out an immediate examination of the goods on discharge or as soon as practicable thereafter, but in any case notification of damage which is not immediately apparent must be given to the carrier within 3 days of discharge. Notice need not be given if the survey is a joint survey. Failure to observe these principles will excuse the carrier from liability.

The Carriage of Goods by Sea Act 1924 allows one year for suit to be brought against a carrier but signatories to the British Maritime Law Association's Agreement (commonly known as the Gold Clause Agreement) have agreed to extend this period by a further 12 months. In the absence of any agreement or law limiting the period, claims could be brought only within six years under the provisions of the Limitation Act 1939. (See Gold Clause Agreement".)

Notional Sterling

Before the abolition of the Category 3 procedure at Lloyd's a broker would close a convertible currency insurance entry to L.P.S.O. in currency; notifying L.P.S.O. of the true sterling equivalent in due course. L.P.S.O. would exchange the entry to "notional" sterling at a notional (provisional) exchange rate and advise it as such to the subscribing syndicates. When the true sterling equivalent was advised to L.P.S.O. a further advice would be sent to the syndicates, notifying them of the difference between the notional sterling entry and the true sterling entry but only if the difference was more than £7.50 per syndicate on average over the insurance. This procedure is used today only in relation to E.S.A. entries.

Not on Risk

The policy has not attached and the insurer has no liability.

Not to Inure Clause

Clause 10 in the Institute Cargo clauses. The Carriage of Goods by Sea Act 1924 provides, in clause 8 of article 3, that any clause in a contract of carriage relieving the carrier from liability, or reducing his liability below the limitations providede by the Act, shall be null and void. The Act goes on to say that a "benefit of insurance" clause comes in this category. Nevertheless, coastal shipments and shipments not under bill of lading are not subject to the Act so that there is nothing to prevent a carrier from inserting a "benefit of insurance" clause in his contract. The insured cargo owner may have no control over this practice but the insurers do not wish the carrier to avoid his liability by claiming benefit under the cargo policy. The insurers, therefore, state in clause 10 of the cargo clauses that the insurance shall not inure to the benefit of the carrier or other bailee. (See "Inure".)

Not Under Repair

This phrase may be found in the returns clause in a hull policy. The retention of premium when calculating a lay up return is affected by the degree of fire hazard and so a higher retention is applicable when the ship is under repair.

N/P

Net proceeds.

N.R.

No risk.

n.r.a.d.

A carriage of goods condition meaning "no risk after discharge" whereby the carrier is free from liability as from the time the goods are discharged.

An insurer may also use this abbreviation on a slip where he does not wish to undertake the risk at a certain unsavoury destination. In the absence of the abbreviation most cargo insurances would continue after discharge until delivery in accordance with the transit clause.

n.r.a.l.

No risk after landing. Same effect as "no risk after discharge" except that the risk ceases when the goods are "landed" which may be some time after discharge if lighters are used.

n.r.a.s.

No risk after shipment. Sale term having same effect as seller's interest in F.O.B. The seller has no risk from time goods are loaded on the vessel.

N.R.T. *or* n.r.t.

Net registered tonnage.

n.r.t.b.
No risk until on board.

n.r.t.o.r.
No risk until on rail.

n.r.t.w.b.
No risk until waterborne.

N.S.
Nuclear Ship.

n.s.p.f.
Not specially provided for.

Nt. wt.
Net weight.

Nuclear Contamination
See " Radioactive Contamination ".

Nuclear Exclusion
Since the invention of the atom bomb insurers have been concerned not to cover the catastrophic risk occasioned by nuclear detonation. It will be found that all marine insurance policies exclude war risks (see " F.C. & S. Clause ") and where a policy is extended or issued to cover war risks it is customary to exclude claims arising from hostile nuclear detonation and in the case of hull policies (whether time or voyage) the policy is, automatically, cancelled immediately there is a hostile detonation of a nuclear weapon anywhere in the world (see " Institute War Clauses ").
It should be noted that in a hull policy the " Inchmaree " Clause incorporates loss of or damage to the insured ship directly caused by " breakdown of or accident to nuclear installations or reactors on shipboard or elsewhere "; such claims being subject to the deductible average clause and the machinery damage co-insurance clause.

Nuclear Reactor
An installation used for the purpose of generating heat from atomic fission which could be coverted into energy for domestic purposes. As practicable, ships are being fitted with nuclear reactors to avoid the need for constant refuelling. The first alteration of insurance policies to meet this new field was the adaption of the negligence clause to cover damage to the ship caused by nuclear reactors or installations.

Numbered Rules

" The Numbered Rules " refers to the rules specified in the York-Antwerp Rules on general average, other than the lettered rules therein. When applying the York-Antwerp Rules the circumstance must first be considered under the numbered rules. If none of these rules applies, then the lettered Rules must be considered to determine whether there is general average.

N.U.R. *or* **n.u.r.**

Not under repair (which see).

NV

Norske Veritas.

O

o.a.

Overall measurement.

O/A

Overage.

O.A.L.

Overall length.

o/b

On or before.

O/B

On board.

O.B.A.

Abbreviation used in relation to insurance certificates issued by Lloyd's for use of brokers overseas, where claims are payable abroad. These certificates are issued via Lloyd's brokers in London.

O.B.C.L.

Abbreviation used in relation to insurance certificates issued by Lloyd's, for use of brokers overseas, but where claims are payable in London. These certificates are issued via Lloyd's brokers in London.

Objects

An embracing expression used in hull insurance to denote harbours, wharves, piers, buoys, jetties, quays, goods thereon or any object other than a ship or vessel. It is used in connection with "Contact" and "Collision". The collision clause in the standard hull clauses excludes liability to objects.

Obligatory

This term relates to the acceptance of a risk by the insurer. "Facultative" (which see) implies no obligation on the part of the insurer but an obligatory insurance allows the insurer no option but to accept the risk. When an insurer agrees to an open cover he is obliged to accept all declarations attaching to the cover. Other forms of long term insurance or reinsurance may contain a similar provision.

Obligatory Reinsurance

Mainly found in treaty reinsurance. By a treaty the reassured agrees to cede a fixed proportion of all, or a certain part, of his

281

business to the reinsurers. It often occurs that foreign Companies are obliged to cede a fixed proportion of business by way of compulsory reinsurance to a Government reinsurance pool. This is respected by the treaty reinsurers who waive their right to the proportion ceded under obligatory reinsurance. Sometimes the obligatory reinsurance is ceded as a reinsurance of the treaty, the treaty underwriters paying the premium for the reinsurance. (See also " Reinsurance of Common Account ").

Oblige Line
A line written by an insurer to accommodate a broker or an assured where the general account is desirable to the insurer but the particular line is written on a risk which the insurer would not normally have accepted. Sometimes referred to as an accommodation line.

Obliteration of Marks
Where goods arrive at their destination in specie (i.e. as shipped) but are identifiable by reason of obliteration of the marks the loss, if any, is a partial loss and must not be construed as a total loss. (M.I.A., 1906, Section 56, Sub. 5).

O.B.O.
Ore/Bulk Oil. Term used in relation to very large carriers that have a dual rule.

O.C.
Open cover.

O/C
Off cover *or* open cover.

O.C.A.
Outstanding claims advance.

Oc.B/L
Ocean bill of lading.

Occurrence
A chain of events which together form one happening. Example:— A ship collides with another, catches fire and sinks. The whole is one occurrence. If there are no contributing factors a single event may be termed an occurrence.

Ocean Marine Insurance
American expression used to define pure marine insurance on ships, cargoes and allied interests as distinct from inland marine insurance.

Ocean Type Ships

Vessels built in U.S.A. during World War II on behalf of the British Government. The vessels were largely of welded construction. The ships were approximately 7,000 g.r.t. and can be recognised by the prefix " Ocean " to the original name. Ocean type vessels are excluded from the scope of the " liner " definition in the " Classification Clause ". (Further details of Ocean Ships can be obtained from " Wartime Standard Ships, Volume 2 " by W. H. Mitchell and L. A. Sawyer, published by The Journal of Commerce and Shipping Telegraph Limited.)

o.cgo.

Damage caused by other cargo to the insured cargo.

O/D or o/d

On deck or over-deck. On demand.

Of a Like Kind

See " Ejusdem Generis ".

Official Log

The main log book in a ship. It contains details of important events and circumstances occurring during the voyage.

Off Risk

When an insurer has been " on risk " in respect of an insurance and his liability has ceased he is said to be " off risk ". The term applies mainly in respect of long term contracts such as open covers or treaties, where an insurer may wish to cancel his acceptance by giving the requisite notice. The broker will usually place the line with another insurer and as soon as the notice period expires the first insurer is " off risk " and the new insurer is " on risk ".

Off Shore Drilling Rigs

Various types of drilling rig used for seabed drilling for oil, gas, etc. (See also " Off Shore Oil Drilling Rigs ", " Drill Ships ", " Submersible Rig ", " Semi-Submersible Rig " and " Jack Up ".)

Off Shore Oil Drilling Rigs

Rigs (usually floating) used for drilling for oil or gas under the sea-bed. Insurance is usually effected under the Standard Drilling Risks Form—All Risks. It is customary for the supporting legs of the rig to be hydraulically powered for support. A floating rig may be fitted with motors to enable it to move under its own power in a small area and to maintain its position without tug assistance. A rig is towed into position and remains there until it is required elsewhere when it is towed to its new position. It is inadvisable to move the rig into or out of position when the wave height exceeds 4 feet.

Off Slip
See " Signing Slip ".

O.G. *or* **o.g.**
On gross.

OG
Notation in Lloyd's Register that oil glands are fitted in a ship's propeller shaft junctions.

O.G.P.
Original gross premium.

O.G.P.I.
Original gross premium income.

O.G.R.
Original gross rate.

Oil Damage
Cargo can become damaged by oil from the ship's machinery if it is badly stowed. Leaking bilge pipes or valves may cause oily bilge water to enter the hold and damage cargo. Where motor ships are constantly berthed there is a likelihood of oil on the quay which may damage cargo awaiting loading or on discharge. Oil damage is not one of the perils in the plain form of policy. It is an extraneous risk and must be specified in the policy for damage so caused to be recoverable. In recent years the release of oil into the sea, usually when an accident occurs to an oil tanker, has become a major threat to the environment. Pollution caused to water, beaches and property may result in a heavy third party liability claim against the shipowner at fault and legislation seems loth to allow limitation of this liability except for very high limits. The collision clause specifically excludes liability in this respect, other than damage to the other ship and/or property on the other ship, and P. & I. clubs have reservations in accepting the liability. (See also " Oil Pollution ".)

Oil Drilling Rigs
See " Off Shore Oil Drilling Rigs ".

Oil Pollution
See " Pollution ".

Oleron
See entry " Judgements of Oleron ".

Omnibus Clause
This clause is not an Institute Clause but may be used in insurance of ships. There are two parties to a contract of marine insurance, the insurer and the insured. Any indemnification under the policy is in respect of the insured interest of the insured. It follows, therefore, that where the terms of the policy are extended to include third party liability it is the legal liability of the insured only which is covered by the policy and liability incurred by any person, other than the insured, is not covered by the policy even though such person may have an interest in the adventure which is the subject of the insurance. In practice, the hull policy is customarily extended to cover collision liability, subject to certain limitations and it is to such policies that the " omnibus clause " may be attached. The clause may also be used in policies covering P & I risks.
The clause provides that any liability covered by the policy terms shall embrace not only the liability of the insured but also the liability of any firm, corporation, person or other concern to whom the insured has given prior permission to operate the vessel. Nevertheless, the clause excludes persons who are paid employees of the insured such as master or crew of the vessel. The clause is also worded to prevent the cover allowing owners or operators of boat repair yards, shipyards, service stations, yacht clubs and similar from using the policy to cover their own liability. In any case, the clause excludes liability of the additional insureds to the named insured in the policy, thus preserving the insurer's subrogation rights. An additional insured is, of course, subject to the same warranties or conditions in the policy as the named insured and right to claim under the clause is dependent on such compliance. (See " Collision Clause ".)

o.n.
On net.

On a Strand
See " Strand ".

On Consignment
When goods are sent overseas with the intention that they are to be put up for sale on arrival at destination, they are said to be sent " on consignment ". In the event of a claim the insurers are not liable for sale charges.

One Occurrence
See " Occurrence ".

On Gross
Term used to indicate the premium figure to which a discount percentage is to be applied. In this case the percentage is applied on the gross premium before any deductions.

On Net
Term used to indicate premium figure to which a discount percentage is to be applied. In this case the percentage is to be applied to the gross premium less previous deductions.

On Passage
Expression in the bulk cargo trade indicating that the carrying vessel has not yet reached her destination.

O.N.P.
Original net premium.

O.N.P.I.
Original net premium income.

O.N.R.
Original net rate.

On Risk
The insurer is " on risk " when an insurance attaches in respect of which he has written a line.

O.N.R.P.I.
Original net retained premium income.

O.N.R. to H.O.
Original net rate to head office. The same abbreviation may be used to apply the expression to " home " office in place of " head " office but, in this context, both mean the same thing. This is a reinsurance term which is used when a company or underwriter obtains reinsurance cover in respect of a risk which has been received from a branch or through an agent. The rate of premium payable to the reinsurer is the rate of the actual premium received by the head/ home office, being net of any deductions from the gross premium rate allowed to the branch or agent. It is not net of any overrider or deduction to the head/home office. The head/home office is, of course, the company or underwriter obtaining the reinsurance cover and thereby becoming the reinsured.

On Signed Lines
Expression used in claims settlement indicating that the propor-

tion of each insurer's liability for the total claim shall be the proportion that his signed line bears to the total of the signed lines on the slip.

On the Berth
Shipping expression indicating that a ship is ready to load or is loading.

Onus of Proof of Claim
The onus always lies with the claimant. The assured must prove his loss. The insurer defending a claim on the grounds of unseaworthiness must prove the unseaworthiness. The effect is that the person making the claim must prove his right to the claim and a person defending a claim must prove his grounds of defence. The onus is on the person whose property has been sacrificed in general average to claim contribution from the general average fund.

O.P.
Open Policy.

Op. cit.
A legal term meaning the book, document or matter to which reference has been made previously.

Open Bevel
A bevel (angle on a member of ship construction) with an angle greater than 90 degrees.

Open Contract
An open cover, open policy or floating policy.

Open Cover
A form of long term cargo contract effected by a broker on an original slip without any limit in the aggregate. It has no more legal value than any other original slip and it is necessary that policies be issued off the cover on declared shipments to give legal effect. The open cover is agreed to cover all shipments commencing transit within a specified period or, if " always open ", from a specified attaching date. All shipments of the assured, coming within the scope of the cover, from the date of attachment must be declared as they go forward. Late or overlooked advices are acceptable if the lateness or error is in good faith. A valuation clause is inserted in the cover so that there can be no disagreement over the value to be declared, in the event of declaration after loss. The insurer undertakes to accept all shipments coming within the scope of the cover without exception, subject only to a specified limit any one vessel. The limit any one vessel is also specified

as the limit of liability in any one location prior to shipment but in some instances this may be increased to more than the limit any one vessel.

To protect the insurer from continuance of an open cover which is proving unprofitable a cancellation clause is included permitting either party to cancel the cover by giving the requisite period of notice (usually 30 days notice, but 7 days notice for war and strikes risks or 48 hours notice for strikes risks on shipments to or from the U.S.A.). An assured who wishes to cancel is equally obliged to give the requisite notice of cancellation and must continue to declare shipments until the notice period expires. The advantage of the open cover to the merchant is that he has permanent forward cover at fixed rates and can carry on his business without worrying about future insurance charges or whether insurance cover is obtainable. The advantage to the insurer is a continuous flow of premium income from a recognised source and the cutting down of detail work. The broker equally benefits from the reduction in work since he only has to place the insurance at the commencement of the cover. Insurance certificates detailing the insurance conditions are issued " in blank " to the assured. As each shipment goes forward the assured completes a certificate by filling in the name of the carrying vessel and details of the shipment. He sends a copy of the certificate to his broker who advises the insurer. Periodically, the broker calculates the premium on all copy certificates to hand, debits the assured for the premium and settles with the insurer. Open covers can be effected, also, directly between the assured and a Company without the intermediary of a broker.

Open Indent

Sale term. An order given by a buyer to the supplier permitting the supplier to send suitable goods at a reasonable price instead of specified goods.

Open Market

A term used in relation to long term contracts. Declarations not covered entirely by the contract and insured partly elsewhere are said to be partly insured in the open market.

Open Policy

An open policy is usually effected for a period of one to twelve months, subject to a cancellation clause. The terms of such a policy are identical to those of a floating policy, which is seldom used today, except that there is no aggregate limit of cover; this obviates the necessity for keeping a check on the outstanding balance. Payment of premium is generally effected monthly, based on the value of the shipments which have gone forward during the preceding month. This form of policy always has a limit per vessel and location and is, generally, issued off an open cover.

Open Roadstead

A relatively safe anchorage area for ships. It is usually protected from the open sea by a large land mass such as an island. Since it is not as safe as a harbour lay up returns are not allowed on a vessel laid up at anchor in an open roadstead.

Open Slip

A form of original slip used when the assured is a merchant contractor with a large contract to fulfil by several shipments. The total amount to be insured is known so the insurance is effected for this amount. As each shipment goes forward the insurer is advised and the total insured value reduced by the value of the declared shipments. Declarations continue until either the contract is fulfilled or the total insured value is exhausted. There is no cancellation clause in an open slip but it is understood that the shipments will commence and terminate within a reasonable time. The insurer may wish to insert a limit any one vessel but this is not always the case. Policies may be issued as each shipment goes forward or on several shipments at once. Premiums are payable as declarations are " closed ".

Option Request Form

A document used in the Lloyd's market which enables an underwriter or broker to apply to L.P.S.O. for certain statistical information.

O.R.

Original rate.

O/R

Overriding commission *or* Overrider.

Or as Original

A reinsurance term by which the reinsurer accepts not only the risk as presented to him but any variation from the presented facts which may exist in the original policy. This is a protective wording in a slip or policy in case an error has occurred in transmitting the information to the broker effecting the reinsurance.

Ordinary Breakage

Occurs to cargoes of brittle nature or which are particularly subject to breakage. This is breakage which arises without the operation of an insured peril and it is not covered by the ordinary standard policy unless specifically expressed therein as being covered.

Ordinary Course of Transit
See "Normal Course of Transit".

Ordinary Leakage
See "Natural Loss".

Ordinary Loss
See "Natural Loss".

Ordinary Wear and Tear
See "Wear and Tear".

Orig.
Original, meaning "Conditions as per original policy". (Reinsurance term.)

Original Assured
The assured in a policy in which the liability has been reinsured. The original assured has no right or interest in the reinsurance, which means that if the original insurer becomes insolvent and is unable to meet his liabilities the original assured cannot press his unsatisfied claim against the reinsurer.

Original Conditions
The conditions in a policy which is the subject of a reinsurance. The reassured cannot effect reinsurance cover on wider terms than the original conditions but may reinsure on more limited conditions.

Original Cover
The original slip used for placing an open cover.

Original Deductions
The deductions or discounts allowed on the original policy by a reassured.

Original Discounts
See "Original Deductions".

Original Gross Premium
The premium charged by the reassured to the original assured before any discounts have been taken into account. The reinsurer usually requires to know the original gross premium to ensure that he is not backing the liability of a reassured who is retaining high commissions and thus encouraging bad underwriting.

Original Gross Premium Income
Referred to in long term reinsurance contracts such as Treaties. When the contract is being placed the reinsurer will wish to know

the gross and the net premium income over the preceding years in order that he may compare the claims ratio and assess the desirability of the reinsurance. The original gross premium income is the total premium charged to the original assured by the reassured, excluding all discounts, over a period of time.

Original Gross Rate
Referred to in reinsurance. The original rate charged to the assured by the reassured before any deductions or discounts.

Original Net Premium Income
Reinsurance treaty term indicating the net premium income over a period of time to the reassured.

Original Net Rate
Referred to in reinsurance. The original gross rate charged to the original assured by the reassured less the original deductions. That is, the net rate of premium received by the reassured.

Original Net Retained Premium Income
Reinsurance Treaty term. The part of the net premium income to the reassured which is retained by the reassured. This is applied over a period of time.

Original Open Cover
The original slip used for placing an open cover.

Original Policy
A policy in which the insurer's liability has been reinsured.

Original Policy or Policies
Reinsurance policy interpretation of the abbreviation "as original".

Original Rate
The rate of premium charged on a policy which is the subject of reinsurance.

Original Slip
The slip used for placing an insurance. Off the original slip there may be issued duplicate slips, off slips or signing slips. The original slip may be recognised by the acceptances thereon being indicated by a line stamp with a handwritten line. It has no legal value in itself but may be used as evidence of the date of conclusion of contract.

Original Terms
Original conditions.

Origin of Goods
The Country of manufacture or production.

Orlop
Lowest deck on a ship.

Ors.
Others. When preceded by the name of the underwriter for a Lloyd's Syndicate it refers to the other members of the Syndicate and indicates that the underwriter represents them.

O/S *or* **o/s**
Outstanding.

OSD
Lloyd's Register abbreviation for " Open shelter deck ship ".

o.s.l.
On signed lines.

Other Cargo
The insurer is not liable for damage caused by the insured cargo to other cargo, unless the policy specifically incorporates this peril. (See also " Damaged by other cargoes ".)

Other Perils
See " All Other Perils ".

Other Ship's Cargo
The collision liability clause in the hull policy does not cover liability to the insured ship's own cargo but it does cover liability to the other ship's cargo.

Other Ship's Engagements
The collision clause in a hull policy does not cover loss of engagements of the insured vessel. Nevertheless, it covers liability for the loss of engagements of the other ship.

Outboard
The outside of a ship's hull (the opposite to " inboard ").

Out of Commission
When a vessel is not required for the purpose for which it is intended it is usual for the owner to have it laid up, out of commission. This means that the vessel is not used for any purpose whatsoever, but repairs, repainting, dismantling and fitting out can be carried on during the period the vessel is out of commission. Provision is made in the policy for a return of premium in event of the vessel being laid up for at least 30 consecutive days. (See

" Returns Clause ".) In yacht and small craft insurance there is usually a warranty requiring that the vessel be laid up, out of commission, for six months, including the winter months. Whilst the yacht or small craft is so laid up she must be dismantled being not fitted out or available for immediate use. It is usually required that the vessel be laid up ashore, on the hard or in a mud berth. Loose gear is usually stored ashore.

Outstanding Claims

Claims which have been provisionally advised by the assured or reassured but which are in the process of investigation and so have not been settled.

Outstanding Claims Advance

A term used in marine claims practice mostly in marine treaties. It is customary for a marine treaty contract to make provision for the reinsured to retain a proportion of the premium in order to build up a fund from which claims can be paid. (See " Reserve Account ".) When the claims outstanding on original policies are greater in the aggregate than the total premium paid under the policy the reassured will undoubtedly find that his reserve account is inadequate to meet such claims.

It is probable that the contract will make provision for the reinsurer to pay his proportion of the total amount of the claims outstanding to the reinsured, as part of the reserve account, without waiting for such claims to appear in the periodic accounts. When the total of the outstanding claim reserve requested exceeds the total premium income such payment then becomes an " advance " and as such is called an " outstanding claims advance ".

Outstanding Claims Reserve

A reinsurance treaty provision which operates in the same way as a claims reserve but in respect of outstanding claims.

Outstanding Liability

See " Outstanding Claims ".

Outstanding Loss Reserve

A reinsurance treaty provision which operates in the same way as a loss reserve but in respect of outstanding losses.

Outturn

In shipping this is the amount or weight of the cargo discharged from the ship. In insurance the expression may also refer to the condition of the cargo on discharge. This is particularly important in respect of bulk cargoes where claims are calculated on a comparison between loaded and unloaded weights.

Outturn Report

Report on the outturn of the ship. The report may be on the daily outturn figure or on the whole outturn.

Outward Port Charges

See " Costs Allowed in General Average ".

Overage

A term used in respect of the additional premium payable on an open cover or policy when insured goods are carried by a vessel which does not come within the scope of the provisions of the Institute Classification Clause. The term derives from the fact that most such additional premiums are payable because the carrying vessel is over 15 years of age. (See also " Classification Clause ".)

The term is used, also, where a liquid cargo is landed at a weight greater than that apparently shipped. The excess amount is called " overage ", the emphasis in pronunciation being on " over ".

Overcarriage

When it is not possible for the carrier to discharge the goods at the destination he may carry them on to another port. This is " overcarriage ". In the absence of a clause in the policy permitting deviation beyond the control of the assured, the cover ceases on the grounds of deviation. Under the standard cargo clauses the goods remain covered until arrival at destination, but this does not have any effect on the carrier's right to claim the expense of overcarriage from the cargo owner. There is no cover under the standard clauses for this additional expense. (See " Back Freight " and " Additional Expenses —Strikes ".)

Overclosing

A broker may short close a placing but he is not allowed to overclose it. That is, he may close to the insurer a line smaller than the written line, but he must not close a line larger than the written line. The broker must not anticipate the insurer's agreement to increase his written line.

Over-deck

Any loaded cargo which is not stowed under-deck is stowed overdeck. The term is synonymous with " on deck ". Cargo carried overdeck attracts a higher rate of premium than under-deck cargo and must be advised to the insurer as being over-deck. If no such advice is given to the insurer cargo is always deemed to be shipped underdeck. The term " Goods " does not embrace deck cargo, which must be insured specifically.

Overdue Market

When a ship is overdue or has suffered a serious casualty which may result in total loss, the insurers may seek reinsurance to "lay off" the risk. In these circumstances, there may be available a speculative market of reinsurers who are prepared to write the risk at very high rates; sometimes as high as £99 per cent. Such a market is termed an "overdue market".

Overdue Ship

See "Missing Ship" and "Overdue Market".

Overinsurance

See "Double Insurance".

Overplacing

When a broker has an insurance to place he obtains a "lead" and continues to other Insurers until he has sufficient lines to total the amount to be insured. It is the practice for the broker not to stop at that point but to obtain a few extra lines. This is called "overplacing" and is an accepted recognised practice as it is part of the principle of spreading the risk.

Of course, when the broker "closes" the insurance he finds he has more cover than he requires, so he "short closes", that is, he reduces each line in proportion so that all total the correct amount.

Overrider

Overriding commission.

Overriding Commission

A discount allowed to an agent or reinsured Company to cover overhead expenses. In some instances Companies, generally outside the United Kingdom, engage in writing insurance business while reinsuring the whole or part of the liability elsewhere. If the reinsurance is on a treaty or open cover basis it is usual for the reinsurers to agree to accept the "original net rate" of premium, which means the net rate received by the reassured. To reimburse the assured for the work involved in obtaining and running the original insurance the reinsurers allow to the reassured an overriding commission which is a percentage of the original net premium. To discourage the reassured from writing business merely for the overriding commission the reinsurers may insist that the reassured must retain a proportion of the risk for his own account. This encourages prudent underwriting and to further this aim the reinsurers often allow a profit commission to the reassured based on the net annual profits to the reinsurer.

Over Ship's Rail

The shipowner's responsibility for the cargo attaches as loading commences and ceases when it is landed and free of tackle.

Overside Port

A port where goods are discharged into lighters or craft instead of being landed direct onto the quay. May also be called a "Craft Port" or "Surf Port".

Overtime

The reasonable cost of repairs to a ship does not include cost of overtime since this is only incurred to complete the repairs rapidly for the convenience of the shipowner. Since, however, the repairs carried out during overtime would normally be paid for at the proper rate by the insurer, the insurer is still liable for that part of the overtime costs which represents the normal rate for the repairs. That is, the insurer is not liable for the *additional* expense of overtime.

Overvaluation

The value in a valued policy is conclusive between the insurer and the assured and cannot be reopened except where there is fraud. Excessive overvaluation may permit the insurer to reopen the value on a cargo policy only, but it must be clearly excessive overvaluation. A hull value cannot be reopened by the insurer, except in the case of fraud.

Owners' Clauses

Usually applicable to hull clauses but the term may be applied to the clauses of big exporters or importers of raw materials such as sugar. Owners' clauses are clauses specially drafted on behalf of specific assureds and for use on their policies only. A separate scale of lay up retentions is applicable to owners' clauses. Insurers will only accept such clauses on very big fleets of vessels where the account is sufficiently large to encourage the insurer to compromise on the conditions.

Owner's Declaration

Completed by a part owner of a vessel declaring his right to own a share in the ship in accordance with Registration Regulations. When completed by the sole owner or by the part owner appointed by the other part owners to act in respect of the vessel, the document contains an undertaking that no unauthorised person has a share in the ship. This has no connection with shareholders in a Shipping Company or Line.

Owner's Interest

The owner of insurable property has an insurable interest not only in the property itself, but also in respect of liabilities incurred by the property and losses incurred by reason of his ownership, such as loss of profit. The standard policy covers only the damage to or loss of the property itself, but the policy may be extended by agreement to cover the other insurable interests. The owner's interest remains for the full value even though a third party may have agreed to indemnify him in the event of loss. This latter not to be taken as a right to effect double insurance.

Owner's Repairs

The shipowner may carry out his own repairs during the period when the ship is in dry dock for insurer's repairs. He incurs no dock dues nor entry or leaving fees provided the repairs are not necessary for the seaworthiness of the vessel. If the repairs are necessary for the seaworthiness of the vessel the owner must share the cost of entering and leaving the dock equally with the insurer and, in addition, pay half the dock dues for each day his repairs are carried out concurrently with the insurer's repairs. Of course, if the owner's repairs continue after the insurer's repairs are completed the owner must pay the whole of the dock dues for each day the vessel remains in dock until the owner's repairs are completed.

Owner's Survey Fees

The onus is on the claimant to prove the claim so it is usual for a shipowner to pay for the survey to be carried out to ascertain whether there is a claim under the policy. Provided there is a claim and the survey fee is reasonable this is recoverable in addition to the claim.

Oxidation

See " Rust ".

Oxter Plate

A steel plate fitted at the top of a rudder post.

P

P.A.
Particular average.

P.A. and/or G.A.L.
Particular average and/or general average loss.

Pac.
Pacific coast ports.

Pacific Warranty
An ice warranty, appearing in the Institute Warranties, which prohibits the vessel from being within the waters or rivers of the Pacific coast of North America or adjacent islands north of 54° 30′ N lat. or west of 130° 50′ W long.

Package Insurance
A form of overall insurance cover, used in the U.S.A. It combines fire, marine and other risks all in one insurance.

Package Policy
A combination in one policy of insurances against diverse perils. (See also " Bumbershoot ".)

Packing
Goods are always deemed to be properly packed to withstand the ordinary perils of the contemplated voyage. Insufficiency of packing entitles the insurer on goods to avoid the policy on the basis of misrepresentation unless he was aware of the type and quality of the packing when he wrote the risk. The carrier should not issue a " clean " bill of lading for insufficiently packed goods. (See " Professional Packing ".)

Paid Freight
See " Prepaid Freight "

Painter
A rope fastened to a small boat or a lifeboat. Used for making fast, mooring or towing.

Painting the Bottom
The painting of the underside of a vessel. Neither the cost of painting or scraping the bottom of the vessel are payable by the insurer whether or not there is a claim for repairs. A clause is inserted in the policy to this effect.

Pair and Set Clause

This is not strictly a marine clause but is mentioned herein because art objects and jewellery are frequently insured in the marine market. Where an article is damaged or lost and the object is part of a pair or set the pair or set is ruined by such loss or damage and the assured may feel entitled to indemnity for the whole pair or set, requiring the insurer to take over whatever may remain. To obviate this the pair and set clause is incorporated into such insurances limiting the insurer's liability to the insured value of the lost or damaged part or object only.

P & I Club

Protection and Indemnity Club.

P & I Risks

Protection and Indemnity risks.

Pallet

A platform on which packaged goods are stacked for the purpose of ease of handling in storage on a vessel. The packages are fastened to the pallet so that the whole can be moved as one unit during loading, transit and discharge.

Palletisation

The use of pallets in the carriage of goods.

P.A.N.

Premium Advice Note.

Paramount Clause

A clause, in a policy, the conditions of which in the event of ambiguity, override all other provisions in the policy. It is customary for hull clauses to incorporate a number of paramount clauses which exclude war risks and similar risks from the policy. (See "F.C. & S. Clause" and "Hull Paramount Clauses".)

Parcel Tanker

A liquid cargo tanker designed to carry, if necessary, several different types of liquid cargo at once. These vessels are used for the carriage of refined oil and chemicals, where the quantity to be carried to any one destination does not justify the use of a whole vessel's cargo carrying capacity.

Parent Company

A Company which controls other subsidiary Companies.

Parity Clause

It may occur that an assured has two covers operating in respect of similar interests, particularly where he has large sendings and has to use two different markets to obtain full cover. In such cases he wants to maintain the same rates on both covers and to ensure this a parity clause may be incorporated into one, or both, covers. The clause provides that where there are differing rates between the covers the lower rate shall prevail and the insurers of the cover with the high rate will reduce their rate to agree. Of course, if an insurer feels that he does not consider the rate to be sufficient he is at liberty to invoke the cover cancellation clause and give notice to cancel his line, so that the parity clause is not the complete answer to the assured's problem.

Park Type Ships

Vessels built in Canadian shipyards and operated by the Park Steamship Company (formed in 1942) on behalf of the Canadian Government. These ships can be recognised by the suffix " Park " to their names, although some were renamed with " Fort " type names in 1944/45. " Parks " included both dry cargo vessels and tankers and are of various types. " Parks " are excluded from the scope of the "liner" definition in the Classification Clause. (Further details may be obtained from " Wartime Standard Ships—Volume 2 " by W. H. Mitchell and L. A. Sawyer, published by The Journal of Commerce and Shipping Telegraph Limited.)

Partial Interest

An insurable interest of part only of a full interest in the property at risk. A person having a partial interest has the same insurance rights in respect of that part as he could have if he had an interest in the whole.

Partial Loss

This is any loss of the subject matter insured not amounting to a total loss. If the assured brings an action for total loss and it later proves only to be a partial loss the assured may still claim a partial loss. Goods arriving at destination with marks obliterated are the subject of a partial loss not a total loss claim. (See " Particular Average ".)

Partial Loss of Freight

In practice such claims seldom arise because freight is usually paid by the cargo owner in advance and is merged in the value of the cargo. Should, however, freight be insured separately then partial loss of freight arises where cargo is lost and the amount recoverable from the insurer is the freight due on the part of the cargo lost. All freight insured on the cargo must be taken into account to ensure that there is no underinsurance.

Partial Loss of Goods

Any loss of goods caused by an insured peril and not resulting in a total loss is a partial loss of goods. It is customary for only valued policies to be used on goods and the amount recoverable from the insurer for partial loss is the percentage of depreciation applied to the insured value.

Partial Loss of Ship

Any damage to a ship caused by an insured peril and not resulting in a total loss is a partial loss of ship. The amount recoverable from the insurer in respect of such loss is the reasonable cost of repairs, less the policy deductible. If the damage is not repaired or is only partially repaired before expiry of the policy the assured is entitled to a reasonable depreciation for the unrepaired damage. Should the ship be totally lost before the expiry of the policy no amount is recoverable from the insurer in respect of unrepaired damage. If the partial loss is the subject of general average it is still recoverable as above, but the insurer is entitled to any recovery from other parties contributing towards the general average. When damage to a ship has been repaired there is no reduction in the insured value so there is no need for reinstatement of the amount of claim, as in non-marine insurance. (See also " Successive Losses ".)

Partial Repairs to Ship and Unrepaired Damage

See " Partial Loss of Ship ".

Participate

An insurer who writes a line in an insurance " participates " therein.

Particular Average

A partial loss of the subject matter insured proximately caused by an insured peril, other than a general average loss. Particular charges are not included in particular average, and, therefore, may not be added to particular average to attain the franchise, if any. The plain form of policy covers particular average as well as total loss, except where it is amended to exclude particular average (e.g. F.P.A.). The plain policy applies the franchise in the memorandum to particular average but this is frequently overridden in cargo practice (see " Irrespective of Percentage ") and in hull practice is replaced by a deductible.

Particular Average Warranty

See " Franchise ".

Particular Charges

An expense incurred by the assured, his agents or assigns to prevent or minimise a loss of the subject matter insured from an insured peril. Neither general average nor salvage charges are included in the term " Particular Charges ". Particular charges are not particular average and cannot be added to attain the franchise, if any. Sue and labour charges are a form of particular charge but are not referred to as such in practice because it is customary to use the term " Particular Charges " to apply only to charges at destination. This is an important difference because charges at destination are merely a means of assessing loss rather than preventing loss, so that there can be no question of the insurer paying particular charges at destination following a total loss as there could be with sue and labour charges. Of the two, only sue and labour charges are recoverable from the insurer if there is no loss, particular charges not being recoverable unless there is a claim under the policy. (See " Sue and Labour Charges ".)

Part of

Reinsurance term used when the original insurer retains a proportion of the risk and reinsures the remainder. Any short closing of the original equally affects both the retention and reinsurance.

The reinsurance premium on original conditions is pro rata of the original net premium and the reinsurer shares claims with the original insurer in the proportion that the part reinsured bears to the original acceptance which has been reinsured. If the reinsurance is on F.P.A. conditions the reinsurer still shares the loss in proportion to the reinsured amount but only in accordance with the F.P.A. clause. A " part of " F.P.A. reinsurance is affected by short closing in exactly the same way as a reinsurance on original conditions.

Parturient

In labour. Applicable to livestock insurance and related to pregnancy.

Passenger

The term " includes any person carried on a ship other than the Master and crew, the owner, his family and servants " (M.S.A. 1894). A further definition appears in the M.S.A. (Safety and Loadline) Conventions Act 1949 and is repeated in the M.S.A. 1949 as " any person carried on a ship except a person employed or connected in any capacity on board the ship with the business of the ship ". From these two legal definitions it would appear that payment or non-payment of passage money does not affect the status of " passenger ".

Passengers' Luggage

Unless it is shipped under a bill of lading, passengers' luggage is

not classed as Goods or Cargo. It is not, therefore, liable to contribute to general average. (See also " Personal Effects ".)

P. & W.S.A.
Ports and Waterways Safety Act (1972)—U.S.A.

Pauschal
A Dutch or German marine cargo insurance term providing for
a provisional annual premium on a contract to be paid in advance
subject to adjustment based on the annual turnover at the end of
the term of insurance.

Pauschal prime (Dutch)	= Lump sum premium
„ tariff („)	= Flat rate premium
„ verz. („)	= Insured at a fixed premium
„ eutschadigung (German)	= Lump sum premium
„ mitabsthreibung („)	= Declaration insurance
„ saltz („)	= Flat rate premium
„ Dekking (Dutch)	= Global

Payable Abroad Agents
Agents authorised by the terms of the policy to settle claims
abroad. (See " Settling Agents " and " Settling Fee ".)

Pay as may be Paid
A reinsurance term providing that the reinsurer will follow the
claims paid on the original policy without question, but under the
term the reinsurer is liable only to reimburse claims which are
properly recoverable under the original policy. This does not include " compromised ", " ex gratia " or " without prejudice " settlements.

Payment of Claims
The insurer is directly liable to the assured for payment of claims
under the policy. It is customary, however, for the assured to request
that the broker who effected the insurance should collect the claim
on his behalf. The broker is entitled to a collecting commission,
deductible from the claim, for this service.

Payment of Premium
See " Premium ".

Payment Order
The insurer is directly liable to the assured for claims but it is
customary for the assured to use the services of a broker for claims
collection. The payment order is the authority given by the assured
to the broker to enable him to collect a claim on behalf of the
assured. The payment order is particularly important to the insurer

where there is the possibility that another party may have a right of claim, as in the case of a mortgaged ship.

P.B.
Permanent bunkers.

P/C
Particular charges *or* profit commission (which see.)

Pc.
Prices.

P.chgs.
Particular charges.

Pcl.
Parcel.

P.D.
Property damage *or* Port dues.

Peak Location
When a schedule of cessions or statistics is presented to insurers giving information on amounts at risk in various locations the highest amount in one location is called the " Peak Location ". The term is generally used only when the amount concerned is exceptionally high. It may often be used in connection with American inland marine translocation policies.

Peak Tanks
Compartments at the extreme ends of a ship, (e.g. " Fore Peak Tank " or " Aft Peak Tank "). Generally, these are used as ballast tanks.

Peak Value Clause
A clause used in insurance on cotton which enables a buyer who buys while the cotton is en route to be certain that he is adequately insured. The clause provides that the amount insured by the policy shall be deemed to be the peak value pertaining in the cotton market at the time of loss.

Percentage of Depreciation
Generally this term applies to claims on goods only, because the measure of indemnity for partial loss of ship is the reasonable cost of repairs regardless of the insured value of the ship. The percentage of depreciation is the percentage which is applied to the insured value on a cargo policy to ascertain the claim for partial loss. It is arrived at by comparing the gross arrived damaged value of the goods with the estimated gross arrived sound value, the difference being applied

to the estimated gross arrived sound value as a percentage. In some cases the surveyor may assess the percentage of depreciation to be applied.

Peril Insured Against
A risk covered by the policy.

Perils
See " Maritime Perils " and " Insured Peril ".

Perils of the Seas
Only fortuitous accidents are embraced by this term. The ordinary action of wind and waves is not a peril of the seas. " Collision " and " stranding " are both perils of the seas, as, also, is " heavy weather ".

Period Policy
See " Time Policy ".

Perfecting the Sight
Shipping term applicable where a bill of sight is lodged without full details. The bill of sight is perfected by adding the omitted details.

Per. inj.
Personal injury.

Permiability
Indicates the proportion of a ship's space that can contain water whilst she still remains afloat.

Pers. Acc.
Personal accident.

Personal Accident
See " Personal Injury ".

Personal Effects
Personal effects are not classed as goods when they are not shipped under a bill of lading. Personal effects are not called on to pay general average contribution.

Personal Injury
So far as marine insurance is concerned this falls in the same category as " Loss of Life ". Personal accident or injury is never covered under a marine policy unless the policy has been extended to cover Protection and Indemnity risks.

Photocopy Slip
In Lloyd's market the broker may use a photocopy of an original

slip for signing and accounting purposes only if it is certified by a Director of his office as being a true copy of the original, including all amendments; or when it has been initialled by the leading underwriter.

P.I.

Personal Injury.

P.I.A.

Peril insured against. (See " Full Premium if Lost ".)

Pickings

Damaged material picked off bales of cotton or similar cargoes to make the balance saleable. The cost of picking is recoverable from the insurer provided the damage was caused by an insured peril. No reference is made to the franchise in respect of picking costs. The insurer is entitled to any recovery from the sale of the pickings.

Pilf.

Pilferage.

Pilferage

Petty theft without breaking open cases or boxes. It is usually difficult to prove that pilferage is the cause of shortage; for which reason it is customary, when adding this peril to a cargo policy, to include, also, theft and non-delivery.

Pilot

A person authorised to navigate a ship in specified waters. This applies mainly to entering or leaving a port or in navigating canals or rivers. The pilot is authorised by the Authority responsible for the navigation in the particular waters and each vessel must employ an authorised pilot while in such waters.

Pilotage

The fee payable to a pilot for his services.

Pilotage Account

Account of expenses for pilotage in connection with repairs to the ship.

Pinnace

A small, mechanically propelled, craft.

Pirates

Persons attacking property whilst outside the jurisdiction of any state, and owing allegiance to no recognised flag, but the term includes passengers who mutiny and rioters attacking a ship from the shore. A pirate acts for his own personal gain and not for political ends. The peril " Pirates " is included in the perils specified in the standard marine policy form, but is excluded therefrom in practice by the attachment of the F.C. & S. clause. Effectively, losses from this peril are covered only by a policy covering war risks.

Pitch
The movement of a ship in rising to the crest of a wave then descending into the trough. The term may be used, also, in relation to the distance the ship advances at one revolution of the propeller.

Pitwoodcon
Code word for the pitwood charterparty from France to Bristol Channel.

Pkg.
Package.

P.L.
Public liability. May also be used to denote " partial loss ".

P/L
Partial loss.

P.L.A.
Port of London Authority.

Placing
The act of effecting an insurance *or* the insurance which has been effected.

Placing Insurance
It is customary for marine insurance contracts to be effected through the medium of a broker. Marine insurance is placed, that is to say effected with insurers, by means of an original slip. The original slip is a piece of stiff card on which are written or typed brief details of the insurance to be effected. The broker prepares the original slip and takes it to an insurer who he considers is a suitable " lead " (see " Lead "). When the " lead " has accepted a " line " (see " Line ") on the insurance he impresses his line stamp on the slip and inserts therein the amount accepted and enters his reference. The contract is then concluded between the assured and that insurer. The broker continues to approach other insurers who enter their acceptances on the slip, following the lead. When the whole amount of the insurance has been so placed the placing is complete. (See also " Original Slip " and " Overplacing " and " Failure to Complete ".)

308   MARINE INSURANCE TERMS

Plain form of Policy
The standard policy S. G. form with no clauses or special conditions attached.

Plank
Timber measurement for softcords. Irrespective of length a plank is a piece of timber between 2″ to 4″ thick by 11″ and wider.

Plimsoll Line
See " Plimsoll Mark ".

Plimsoll Mark
Named after Samuel Plimsoll, its instigator, this means the load-line mark on the side of a vessel. (See " Loadline ".)

Plumber Block
A block, situated in a shaft tunnel, that supports the propeller shaft.

Pm.
Premium.

P.M.L.
Possible maximum loss. May, also, be used for probable maximum loss.

p.o.c.
Port of call.

P.O.D.
Port of distress.

Policy
The instrument of the insurer, the policy is legal evidence of the agreement to insure and may be produced by the assured, in court, to press a claim against the insurer. The broker has a lien on the policy and may retain it until the assured has paid him the premium due or any outstanding premium on other insurances. At one time the Marine Insurance Act, 1906 specified five essentials which should appear in a marine policy, but four of these were repealed by the Finance Act 1959 so that it is now only essential that the policy contains the name of the Assured or his agent. In practice, of course, the policy contains full details of the insurance so that the amendment to the M.I.A. merely prevents invalidity of the policy because of the omission of one of the specified essentials. The standard S. G. form is commonly used for marine policies. In hull insurance the policy must be produced to establish a claim;

but in cargo insurance claims, particularly those settled by agents abroad (See " S.C.A. "), claims are often settled on production of a certificate accompanied by supporting claim documents. Nevertheless, it is unlikely that a Court of Law will accept a suit without production of a policy.

Policy and Stamp

This term was once used in brokers' debit notes as a fee to cover the expense of preparing a policy and to reimburse the broker for paying the stamp duty thereon. Since the abolition of stamp duty on marine policies brokers have either waived the fee or referred to the policy preparation charge only.

Policy Assignment

See " Assignment of Policy ".

Policy Conditions

See " Policy Terms ".

Policy Construction

See " Construction of Policy ".

Policy Exclusions

See " Specific Exclusion ".

Policy Holder

The assured. A term more commonly used in non-marine insurance.

Policy Lien

See " Broker's Lien ".

Policy Proof of Interest

The assured under a policy must have an insurable interest at time of loss and he is obliged, if required, to prove this interest at the time he makes his claim. There are certain insurable interests which, although they exist, are difficult to define or the extent of which is difficult to arrive at. An example of the former would be an insurance on anticipated " Increased Value " of cargo when the goods are lost en route, and it could not be proved that they would have warranted the increase in value on arrival. An example of the latter would be " Anticipated Freight " when the shipowner could prove that his vessel would be operating as a freight earner but the amount of freight is only estimated and he could not prove how much he had lost if the vessel sank. In such cases it is common to use a policy the production of which is in itself sufficient proof of interest. In the eyes of the law there is no difference in the invalidity of a policy which dispenses with actual proof of interest and one where there is no interest, so that a P.P.I. policy could not be enforced in a court of law. It is not, however, an illegal policy, provided there is a bona fide insurable interest, and such policies are scrupulously honoured by insurers. It has been thought that if the P.P.I. clause is only pinned to the policy it may be removed to make the policy legally valid. This is incorrect, for once a policy is invalid at inception no act can make it valid subsequently. It must be remembered that the insurer has no rights of subrogation under a P.P.I. policy and he is, therefore, wary to whom he issues such policies. The amount which can be insured by the shipowner on P.P.I. policies is limited by the terms of the disbursements warranty in the hull policy. It is customary for the slip also to be produced with the policy and for evidence of loss or accident to be required, although in most cases the P.P.I. policy makes provision to pay in full once the loss has been established on the main policy.

Policy Signing Office

A central office for the signing of policies on behalf of a group of insurers. There are two such offices in the London market. Lloyd's Policy Signing Office and the Institute of London Underwriters' Policy Signing Office. The former signs policies on behalf of Lloyd's Underwriters while the latter signs policies on behalf of Companies that are members of the Institute of London Underwriters.

Policy Terms

The conditions of and cover provided by the policy. (See also " Construction of Policy ".)

Polish Register of Shipping

Referred to in the Institute Classification Clause. Unchartered iron or steel vessels, registered with the highest classification of this Society, that are not more than 15 years old are acceptable as carriers of cargo insured under an open cover without payment of an additional premium. Liners, other than warbuilt tonnage, are, generally, accepted without additional premium up to 30 years old. (See " Classification Clause " and " Polski Rejestr ".)

Pollution

Waste material which cannot be absorbed by the surroundings in which it is discharged. Waste can take many forms (e.g. liquid, solid, dust, radiation, odours etc.). If the release of waste cannot be controlled pollution of air, water and soil can create a critical situation for the continuance of life in all forms. As a marine insurance peril underwriters may be asked to insure the risk of heavy liabilities imposed on shipowners following pollution of the seas and shores. Various countries, notably the U.S.A., have intro-duced severe penalties against shipowners and others who infringe laws restricting oil spillage and contamination of all sorts. The legal liabilities that may be incurred are heavy and marine insurers, who normally give cover against certain legal liabilities incurred con-sequent upon collision are not prepared to extend the R.D.C. to embrace pollution and contamination liabilities, other than when these cause damage to the other ship or property thereon. (See " Amended R.D.C. ", " Tovalop ", " Cristal ", " W.Q.I.S. ", " Pollu-tion Hazard Clause " and " Pollution Exclusion Clauses ".)

Pollution Exclusion Clauses

Clauses incorporated in marine hull policies to exclude the perils pollution and contamination. Such a clause excludes, from the insurance, claims for liabilities incurred by the assured; including expenses and measures taken to avert or minimise pollution or con-tamination arising from discharge or escape whether real or appre-hended. The clause may be incorporated in the standard clauses or be attached by a separate clause, (e.g. Pollution Exclusion Clause attaching to the Institute Port Risks Clauses, *or* the Amended R.D.C.).

Pollution Hazard Clause

Sometimes termed " Deliberate Destruction Endorsement " or " Deliberate Damage Clause ", this Clause was introduced in 1973 for attachment to policies covering hull and machinery, with the Institute Clauses attached thereto. There are two forms of this clause. Clause A is for attachment to policies covering full condi-tions and B is for attachment to policies covering limited terms. Both forms of the clause extend the insured perils to embrace deliberate damage to the ship by Governments in an effort to minimise or avert the risk of oil pollution when the ship has been in an accident whereby an oil pollution hazard is present.

Polski Rejestr

A Polish Classification Society.

Pool Schemes

See " AP/RP Pool Scheme " and " Small claims etc. Pool Scheme ".

Poppet

A vertical support to a ship on launching ways.

P.O.R.

Port of Refuge.

Port

The left side of a ship when forward. The term derives from a practice of removing, or dropping on hinges, the leeboard to allow the vessel to berth with the left hand side facing the harbour or wharf; thus " portside " developed, later abbreviated to " port ". (See also " Leeboard ".) It was not practicable for a sailing vessel, fitted with a fixed " starboard ", to berth the other way round.

Portage

Services of crew as watchmen or for other duties in connection with repairs to the ship.

Portage Account

An account of expenses concerning a claim where services of crew have been used in connection with the repairs.

Port Area

The area within the jurisdiction of the port Authority.

Port Charges

The charges payable to the port Authority by a ship for the use of the facilities of the port. These are only recoverable from the policy when incurred by reason of removal of the vessel for repairs for the insurer's account. Indirectly the insurer may pay general average port charges when he contributes toward these with other insurers of the saved interests as general average expenses.

Port Dues

See " Port Charges ".

Portfolio

Defines all the business, or a specified section of the business, written by an insurer. He reinsures his " Portfolio " usually by means of treaty reinsurances.

Portfolio Transfer

A term used in treaty reinsurance. The reinsurer undertakes to accept the whole portfolio of an existing reinsurance from a specified date. He accepts not only the premiums due on risks attaching from that date but also the losses payable after that date in respect of premiums paid to the previous reinsurer. He is, of course, also entitled to recoveries paid after the inception date of the treaty even though these may be in respect of claims paid by the previous reinsurer, but is equally liable for returns of premium payable after the treaty inception date even though the premium was originally paid to the previous reinsurer.

Porthole
See " Portlight ".

Port Light
A circular opening in the side of the ship, or in a deckhouse, allowing light to enter a cabin or compartment. The opening is sealed with a heavy glass screen which keeps it watertight, and is fitted with a hinged metal cover (see " Deadlight "). Also termed " Porthole ".

Port of Call
A port in the itinerary of a voyage where the vessel is entitled to call. A port of refuge is a port into which the vessel enters for safety, but which is not a port of call.

Port of Distress
Same as " Port of Refuge ".

Port of Entry
The port where the ship is " entered " by the Authorities into a Country or where goods pass through Customs.

Port of Refuge
A port, other than a port of call, into which a vessel enters for safety.

Port of Refuge Expenses
See " Expenses at Port of Refuge ".

Port of Registry
Registration port of a ship. The name of the Port of Registry is always shown on the stern of the ship.

Port Risks Insurance
A special set of clauses is published by the Institute of London Underwiters to cover Port Risks. The conditions have no deductible and the collision clause covers four-fourths of any collision liability, limited to the insured value in respect of any one occurrence. The liabilities specifically excluded in the normal collision clause are not excluded in the Port Risks Clauses, but it is customary to attach the Pollution Exclusion Clause to the policy. The clauses further cover protection and Indemnity risks, including liability for loss of life and personal injury but excluding claims coming under any Statutory or Common law liability of the employer to his employee. The clauses are warranted free of war, strikes, frustration of the adventure and earthquakes. There is a 25% disbursements warranty. Claims are payable irrespective of percentage. Otherwise the clauses follow the same terms as the ordinary hull time policy,

though the clauses have not been amended to conform with the 1969/70 amendments to the I.T.C. There is no clause providing for returns of premium, nor any return of premium when the policy is automatically cancelled due to change of ownership or management.

Ports of Discharge
See " Several Ports of Discharge ".

Port to Port
The period of cover effected by a voyage insurance on the plain form of policy. On goods the risk attaches as the cargo is loaded onto the overseas vessel and terminates when the goods are discharged at the destination port onto the quay. If the consignee's own craft is used at destination the cover ceases as soon as the goods have been discharged into the craft. In hull insurance the risk attaches when the vessel sails and ceases when the vessel is moored in good safety at the destination port. It is usual to continue cover for 24 hours after arrival of the vessel.

Possessory Lien
A right in law to retain the property of another pending payment of money due from the owner of the property. The lien is discharged by payment of the due amount. The holder of the lien may pass the property to a third person to be held on his behalf until the payment is made. (See " Carrier's Lien " and " Broker's Lien ".)

Posted
Posted missing.

Posted Missing
See " Missing Ship ".

Post Entry
A Customs entry by an importer in addition to the entry already made.

Power of Attorney
A legal instrument, or document, authorising a person to act on behalf of another. Such a power may be given by a Company to an agent of that Company.

P.P.
Parcel post.

ppd.
Prepaid.

P.P.I.
Policy " proof of interest ".

PR
Polski Rejestr.

P.R. *or* **p.r.**
Port Risks *or* Postal receipt *or* pro rata.

Practice
Term meaning " Custom and Usage ".

Pratique
When a vessel is about to make direct contact with a port it is necessary for a medical officer to ensure that the ship has a clean bill of health and that quarantine regulations have been observed. The " Pratique " is the permit issued after the medical officer has been satisfied, following which the vessel may contact the port.

Pre-emption
A right, usually imposed by a Government, to buy property without the opportunity to purchase being given to others. Since such compulsory sale may be deemed to be a claim under the peril " Seizure " insured by a hull war policy, it is usual for the policy to contain a clause excluding claims arising from pre-emption.

PREM *or* **Prem.**
Premium.

Premium
The consideration, or sum of money, paid by the assured to the insurer in return for which the insurer agrees to indemnify the assured in the event of loss from an insured peril. The insurer is not bound to issue a policy until the premium is paid, particularly as some policies embody a receipt for the premium in the wording.

Where the insurance is effected through a broker the broker is responsible to the insurer for the premium and it is not usual for the insurer to withhold the policy pending premium payment. In view of his responsibility for the premium the broker has a lien on the policy whereby he may withhold the policy from the assured until the premium has been paid. (See " Broker's Lien ".) The payer of the premium has an insurable interest in the premium paid. The cargo premium is merged in the value of the goods but the premium on hulls is insured separately. (See " Premiums Reducing ".) Hull premiums are insured on T.L.O. terms.

Premium Advice Note
A document used in the accounting procedures at Lloyd's and the I.L.U. This document replaced the bureau sheet in the reorganisation of signing and accounting procedures in 1970. A

similar document is used for presenting return premium entries to the signing office but this, by custom, is referred to, also, as a P.A.N.

Premium in Full
See " In Full ".

Premium Reserve
A reinsurance treaty provision whereby the ceding Company may retain a proportion of the reinsurance premium to set up a reserve against the payment of claims or returns of premium. The ceding Company must pay claims and returns of premium on the original insurance before collecting from the reinsurer. Therefore, if for political or other reasons the assets of the reinsurances were frozen or payment withheld, the ceding Company could be in a difficult position. The premium reserve is to protect the ceding Company from such difficulties and it is usual for interest to be paid on the premium reserve by the ceding Company. The reserve is released to the reinsurer after 12 months.

Premiums Reducing
The assured has an insurable interest in the premium which he has paid. In cargo insurance he includes the premium in the value of the policy but in hull insurance it is not possible to do this. There are no restrictions imposed on the assured as regards hull premiums (see " Disbursements Warranty "), but it would be inequitable to permit the full insurance of the hull premium on a time policy for the whole period, because the assured charges this in his freight earned during the course of the period and therefore stands to lose only a small part of the premium in the event of loss near the expiry date of the policy. For this reason the hull premium is insured separately on a " reducing " basis. That is, it is insured for the full premium paid at the beginning of the period, but the sum insured reduces by one-twelfth monthly by agreement as it is earned in the freight. Hull premiums are insured on T.L.O. terms.

Premium to be Arranged
A condition of the insurer's agreement to " hold covered " any particular circumstance is the payment of a " premium to be arranged ". This may alternatively be phrased as a " premium to be agreed ". In either case, if no premium is agreed the amount to be paid must be a *reasonable* premium. What is reasonable is a question of the facts pertaining. (See " Held Covered ".)

Premium Transfer
As Lloyd's by reason of its Charter cannot ordinarily accept a

risk for more than 12 months a method is adopted on long term policies whereby the Syndicate in being at inception of the risk returns, at the end of the first 12 months, a pro rata proportion of the premium for the balance of the period. This premium is then paid as an A.P. to the same Syndicate as it is reconstituted for the ensuing year. Further transfers are made on each subsequent year until the policy has expired.

These transfers are arranged internally between the Lloyd's broker and the L.P.S.O. and do not affect the assured.

Prem. Red *or* Prem. Rdg.
Premiums reducing.

PREM RES *or* Prem. Res.
Premium Reserve.

Pre-paid Freight
Where freight is pre-paid, and it is agreed in the contract of carriage that the freight is not returnable in the event of non-delivery of the cargo, the cargo owner has the insurable interest in such freight. The cargo owner may include the freight paid in the value of the goods. It is not usual for pre-paid freight to be returnable by the carrier to the cargo owner.

Preserving from Loss
The insurer pays any reasonable expenses incurred for the purpose of preserving the property from loss or damage by an insured peril. (See " Sue and Labour Charges ", " General Average ", " Particular Charges " and " Salvage Charges ".)

Press of Sail
A term once used in relation to general average and referring to an allowance when the expanse of sail was increased to drive a vessel further aground for the common safety. In 1974 the provision in the York/Antwerp Rules regarding this was deleted because it was deemed to be obsolete.

Prevention of Loss
It is the duty of the assured to take all reasonable measures to prevent or minimise a loss. Any reasonable expense incurred by so doing is recoverable from the insurer. (See " Sue and Labour ", " Particular Charges ", " General Average " and " Salvage Charges ".)

Primary Reinsurance Clause
A clause, seldom used, in a policy which is intended to make reinsuring Underwriters directly responsible to the original assured in respect of losses under the original policy which have been

reinsured. In the absence of such a clause the reinsurer has no direct liability to the original assured.

Principal
The person or body for whom an agent acts. The Principal of a marine broker is the assured.

Private Carrier
A carrier of specified types of goods, as opposed to a Common Carrier who carries any goods.

Private Pleasure Purposes
A term used in yacht insurance. The I.Y.C. contain a warranty whereby the vessel must be used for private pleasure purposes only and must not be let out on hire or charter, without the underwriter's agreement.

Private Wordings Scheme
See " S.W.S. ".

Privity
Knowledge and consent.

Proceeds
The amount received from the sale of goods. (See " Gross Proceeds ".)

Proceeds t.b.a.f.
Proceeds to be accounted for. Claims abbreviation.

PROF COM *or* **Prof. Com.**
Profit Commission.

Professionally Packed Warranty
A warranty in a cargo policy where the goods are particularly subject to breakage if the packing is not 100% sound. By the warranty the assured agrees that the goods will be packed for shipment by a packing firm specialising in the type of packing required. Breach of the warranty discharges the insurer from liability whether or not a loss was caused by the type of packing.

Professional Packing
Although the insurer is not liable for losses proximately caused by insufficiency or inadequacy of packing, losses for which he is liable, being proximately caused by insured perils, may be enhanced if packing is insufficient or inadequate. Where the insurer anticipates the probability of such a loss occurring to cargo he insists on a warranty in the insurance that the cargo be packed by professional packers. Such a warranty does not imply that the policy covers loss or damage proximately caused by insufficient or inadequate packing.

Breach of this warranty would discharge the underwriter from liability whether or not a claim arose from faulty packing or any other cause.

Profit

An unvalued policy does not cover profit on goods. That is, it covers only the prime cost of the goods plus pre-paid freight plus insurance costs on the whole. The seller has an insurable interest in the profit and may include this in the value under a *valued* policy.

Profit Commission

A system agreed to by a reinsurer to encourage prudent under-writing by the original insurer. Operating on an annual basis the reinsurer allows a commission to the reassured on a percentage of the net profit received by the reinsurer. It is usual to apply a deficit clause to balance the profit of one year against the loss of a succeed-ing year. (See " Deficit Clause ".) Most treaties contain a profit commission clause.

Proof of Loss

The onus to prove loss rests with the assured, who must also prove the loss was caused by an insured peril. If the insurer does not agree the onus to prove that the loss was caused by an uninsured peril rests with the insurer.

A sworn statement by the assured giving details of the loss is also called " Proof of Loss ". This is seldom required in marine insurance because the survey report usually gives sufficient details.

Under an " All Risks " policy the insurer does not generally require to know the cause of loss although he may ask the assured to produce evidence that, in fact, an accident has occurred which results in the loss.

Prop.

Propeller of a ship.

Propeller

The cost of a new propeller is not recoverable from the insurer unless the average adjuster shows in his adjustment what happened to the old propeller. Neither can the assured avail himself of his claim to replace the lost propeller with a better type or to replace an old propeller with a new one at the insurer's expense. The insurer may install a new propeller if he wishes.

Proposed Lead

Used in communications between the broker and the assured when the broker has found a " lead " who is prepared to accept a line in an insurance subject to receipt of further satisfactory information. An insurer who has been approached in anticipation of his becoming the "lead" is termed the "proposed lead".

Proprietary Rights

Rights of ownership. The insurer is only entitled to these rights if he takes over whatever may remain of the insured property following payment of a total loss.

Pro Rata

In proportion. Pro rata cancellation is arrived at by calculating the proportion the unexpired part of the policy period bears to the whole period covered by the policy. This proportion is then applied to the policy premium. A pro rata additional premium is arrived at by a similar calculation.

Prosecution of a Voyage

When an insurer writes a risk on a particular voyage it is understood that the voyage must commence within a reasonable time. Once the voyage has commenced it must be prosecuted throughout with reasonable despatch. If it is not so prosecuted and the delay is not excused by the Marine Insurance Act, 1906 the insurer is discharged from liability from the time when the delay becomes unreasonable. (See "Excuses for Delay".)

Protection and Indemnity Club

A mutual club formed by shipowners to cover Protection and Indemnity risks not insurable in the ordinary marine market. (See Protection and Indemnity Risks".) Each shipowner "enters" his tonnage in the club and receives a "Certificate of Entry" for each vessel entered. He pays a nominal amount for entry and is requested to pay "calls" periodically by the club. (See "Club Calls".) The club is operated by a manager and controlled by a Committee appointed from members of the club. It is usual for the club also to advise members on charter disputes and defence of claims made by cargo owners. The premium provisions of the Marine Insurance Act, 1906 do not apply to mutual clubs. Further, the provisions of the Act may be modified by agreement between both parties in mutual insurance.

Protection and Indemnity Risks

Hull risks not insurable under the ordinary marine policy. These are basically liabilities of the shipowner to others or expenses unintentionally incurred by the shipowner in running his ship. Of the former the one-fourth collision liability (see "Collision Clause") is the most obvious, followed by liabilities to objects, own cargo, own engagements, loss of life and personal injury and other liabilities. The sort of expenses recoverable as Protection and Indemnity risks in a club are quarantine expenses, fines, shipwreck indemnity and the like. The only standard policies to cover Protection and Indemnity risks are " Builder's Policies ", " Port Risk Policies " and " Yacht Policies ". The marine policy may, in some cases, be extended to cover Protection and Indemnity risks, but this is unusual. (See " Shipowner's Liability ".)

Protest

A declaration signed by the master of the carrying vessel in respect of damage to the cargo. It may also apply to damage to the vessel.

Provisional Certificate

A temporary Certificate of Registry issued on a ship which has been purchased abroad and which will be officially registered on arrival in U.K.

Provisional Premium

A deposit premium.

Proximate Cause

The most direct cause of loss or damage to the insured property. It is not necessarily the nearest cause in time but is the nearest cause in effect. The furthest cause is called " Causa Remota ". The legal term for proximate cause is " Causa Proxima Non Remota Spectatur " which means that the nearest cause and not the distant cause must be taken into account when considering the cause of loss.

It is essential that the proximate cause of loss be determined to ensure whether the loss is a result of a peril insured against, for if it is not there is no claim under the policy. In some cases it is necessary to obtain a legal ruling to determine the effective cause of loss and after the second World War there were many test cases before the Courts to determine whether losses were proximately caused by marine or war perils. Where there are two or more causes of loss and one of these is an excepted peril it is necessary to determine the " causa causans " (that is, which was the most effective cause of the loss?) For example, where an excepted peril causes an insured peril, from which a loss occurs, in an uninterrupted sequence of events (e.g. earthquake causing fire) there is no claim in a policy that does not cover earthquake.

Pseudonym

See " Broker's Pseudonym " and " Underwriter's Pseudonym ".

P.T.

Perte totale. French term meaning " total loss ". The abbreviation may be used, also, to indicate Premium Transfer.

P.T.

Premium Transfer.

Pt.

Pint.

P.sett.

Previous settlement.

P.S.T.

Pacific Standard Time. U.S.A. Pacific Coast.

Publications

See " Lloyd's Publications " and " Lloyd's Register of Shipping ".

Pure Indemnity

An expression used to denote indemnity as laid down by the Marine Insurance Act 1906 for unvalued policies. Pure indemnity represents the actual loss suffered by the assured as though the adventure had never taken place. In the case of total loss of hull it is the actual market value of the vessel. In the case of total loss of cargo it is the actual cost of the goods to the assured plus charges of freight and insurance, not including profit. In practice, valued policies are always used in hull and cargo insurances, thus overriding the principles of pure indemnity. This is permissible by the Marine Insurance Act 1906. (See " Valued Policies ".)

Putrefaction

Putrification or deterioration.

Putrification

Deterioration of perishable goods such as fruit. (See " Deterioration ".)

Q

Q

Lloyd's Register notation that a ship is fitted with quadruple engines.

Quadrant

The part of a rudder head that is connected to the steering gear.

Qualifying Category

A code used to categorise a risk in data processing. Code letters indicate the qualifying categories. Letters A to I indicate " premium " categories, letters J to R indicate " claim " categories and letters S to Z indicate reserve categories. (See also " Category Codes ".)

Qualitative

See " Quantitative and Qualitative ".

Quantitative and Qualitative

In some Countries it is the practice for the consignee to withhold payment in respect of part of the goods. This amount is paid if the goods arrive in full quantity and of sound quality in accordance with the sale contract. The practice is called " Quantitative and Qualitative Control ". The consignor has an insurable interest in the amount withheld but it is not an insurance which is normally acceptable to insurers.

Quantum of Interest

A mortgagee's interest jointly with the owner's interest in the insured property. The mortgagee has an insurable interest in the property up to the amount due under the mortgage. This right does not defeat the right of the owner of the property to insure up to the full value of the property.

Quarantine Restrictions

The health Authorities impose these restrictions to prevent the spread of infection or contagion. The ship is isolated, no person on board being permitted to land or make direct contact with other persons outside the ship. When the port medical officer is satisfied that there is no further danger of the spread of infection or contagion the restrictions are lifted. The carrier is exempt from liability to the cargo owner for loss due to complying with quarantine restrictions, by the authority of the Carriage of Goods by Sea Act 1924. (See also " Pratique " and " Protection and Indemnity Risks ".)

Quay Port

Port where goods are discharged direct onto the quay from the overseas vessel. A port where lighters are used for discharge is called an " Overside Port " or " Craft Port ".

Quay to Quay

The period of cover under a cargo policy which attaches as the goods are lifted from the quay at the port of loading and terminates when the goods are freed from the ship's tackle or landed from craft onto the quay at the port of destination. This can be a wider cover than " Port to Port " which does not include craft risk at the port of loading, if any.

Quota Share Reinsurance

A system used in reinsurance treaties whereby the reinsured cedes a fixed proportion of all or a specified part of his business to his reinsurers. Claims are reimbursed by the reinsurer to the reinsured in the same proportion. Premiums are paid in a like proportion to the reinsurer and are based on the original gross premiums to the reassured, less the original discounts. It is usual for the reinsurer to allow the reassured an overriding commission as a percentage of the original net premium. Sometimes this is called " Contributory Reinsurance ".

Quotation

When a merchant is calculating his costs he may wish to know the insurance rate without committing himself to a firm order. The broker then obtains a quotation from the insurer. A shipowner's agent may also wish to obtain a quotation for insurance on a ship. The broker when giving the quotation to the assured implies that he can complete the placing at that rate provided he receives a firm order within a reasonable time. An insurer who quotes a rate does so on existing circumstances but if the circumstances change he is not bound to maintain the quotation, although he will usually do so if the firm order is given within a few days.

R

Racing Risks Extension Clause

A clause for attachment to a hull policy subject to the Institute Yacht Clauses. The clause provides that, subject to an additional premium, the policy covers two-thirds of the costs of replacing or repairing sails, masts, spars, standing or running rigging lost or damaged while the vessel is racing. If the loss or damage is caused by the vessel being stranded, sunk, on fire, in collision or in contact with ice or any external substance, other than water, it is payable in full, except for "new for old" deductions and subject to any deductible contained in the policy. The clause warrants that no other insurance shall be effected on the same risks and it limits the insurer's liability to a fixed amount, any one occurrence, for the replacement cost of sails, masts, spars and rigging.

Radioactive Contamination

The introduction of radioactivity onto, or into, cargoes or hulls by radiation escaping from some radioactive substance which may be carried by the vessel as cargo or fuel. Radio isotopes, radioactive ores, irradiated and non-irradiated nuclear fuel, radioactive waste and by products are all carried by vessels occasionally in present day commerce. The insurer's liability for radioactive contamination is the same as that for any other form of contamination. Shipowner's liability may be involved where the contamination is caused by negligence, faulty stowage or breakdown of nuclear installations. (See "Contamination" and "Negligence Clause".)

R. & C.C. *or* **r. & c.c.**

Riots and civil commotions.

R Form

A form used in the procedures for settling Canadian dollar transaction in the Lloyd's insurance market (see "Lloyd's Canadian Trust Fund").

Rake

The mast of a ship "rakes" when it inclines from the vertical.

Ranging

In its marine insurance context this relates to a situation where two vessels approach and lie alongside each other, usually for the purpose of transferring property from one vessel to the other. Except where this is customary (e.g. transfer between lighter and ship) or the insurer has agreed to the transfer, the insurer exempts himself from liability under the hull policy for damage to the insured ship or third party liability incurred during ranging at sea for the purpose of loading or discharge. (See also " Tow and Assist Clause ".)

Rate

Rate of premium. The percentage which will be applied to the sum insured to assess the premium.

Ratification of Contract

When a broker or agent effects in good faith an insurance on behalf of his Principal the Principal may ratify, that is approve and sanction, the contract even though the Principal may be aware of a loss. (Ref. Marine Insurance Act 1906—Sect. 86.)

Raw Sugar Clauses

Trade clauses used for shipments of raw sugar, other than bulk shipments. The cover is basically " W.A." and the perils in the policy are extended to cover certain extraneous risks. All claims are payable " irrespective of percentage ".

r.d.

Running days.

R.D.C.

Running down clause. (See " Collision Clause ".)

Realised Amounts

See " Proceeds ".

Reasonable

What is " reasonable " is a question of fact. That is, all the circumstances must be taken into account to decide whether a particular act or circumstance is reasonable

Reasonable Cost of Repairs

See " Cost of Repairs ".

Reasonable Despatch Clause

Clause 14 in all three sets of the standard Institute Cargo Clauses. It is the duty of the assured to act at all times as though he were uninsured and the Marine Insurance Act 1906 in section 48 requires that the voyage shall be carried out with reasonable despatch. This clause in the Institute Cargo Clauses reminds the assured of his obligation and makes it a condition of the policy that the assured shall prosecute the voyage with reasonable despatch in all circumstances within his control. The clause also requires that the assured act with reasonable despatch in other matters, such as advice to underwriters in connection with "held covered" provisions and in the prevention of loss.

REASSD. *or* **Reassd.**
Reassured.

Reassurance
Reinsurance.

Reassured
Same as "Reinsured".

Reassurer
Same as "Reinsurer".

Rebate
American term for discount allowed to the assured by the broker out of brokerage. In some U.S. States this is forbidden by law.

Receipt on the Policy
Many marine policies, such as the Lloyd's policy, contain a receipt for the premium in the policy wording. This receipt is conclusive of receipt of the premium between the insurer and the assured. The broker is liable to the insurer for unpaid premiums but has a lien on the policy whereby he may retain the policy until the assured pays him the premium.

Received Bill of Lading
The bill of lading is prima facie evidence of receipt of the goods by the carrier for shipment. A "received" bill of lading does no more than this and does not acknowledge that the goods have been shipped. A "shipped" bill of lading acknowledges shipment.

Received for Shipment
See "Received Bill of Lading".

Receiving Note
A note given to the chief officer of the ship requesting receipt of the goods on board by the carrier.

Reciprocal Exchange
See "Reciprocity".

Reciprocity
The practice of reciprocal exchange. By this system an insurer offers part of his acceptances by way of reinsurance to another insurer, who in exchange agrees to offer part of his own acceptances as reinsurance. The effect is that each shares part of the liability of the

other, so furthering the principle of "spread of risk". Reciprocity was uncommon in marine insurance at one time but competition has encouraged its introduction into the practice of effecting long term reinsurance contracts such as marine treaties.

Reconditioning Cargo

See "Reconditioning Charges".

Reconditioning Charges

Where practicable it is the duty of the assured to recondition cargo damaged by an insured peril, thereby minimising a claim under the policy. Provided the charges for reconditioning are incurred short of destination and are to prevent a loss which would be recoverable from the insurer, the assured is entitled to recover these charges under the policy as "Sue and Labour Charges". Reconditioning charges at destination are not necessarily recoverable under the policy since they are merely a means of assessing the loss. (See "Particular Charges".)

Record

See "Experience".

Recover from Underwriters

To press a successful claim under the policy.

Recovery

Amount of money recovered from a third party by an insurer under his subrogation rights.

Recovery Agent

A person who specialises in obtaining recoveries from third parties and others. Generally, the term is used in connection with recoveries from carriers by cargo owners or cargo underwriters.

Recovery from a Carrier

Most cargo insurances are effected on "All Risks" conditions which include extraneous risks. Many of these perils are the subject of a claim against the carrier, which the assured must pursue despite the fact that the loss is covered under his policy. It is the duty of the assured to take the necessary steps to advise the carrier immediately of an apparent loss on discharge and to advise him within three days of discharge if the damage is not immediately apparent. The insurer is entitled, under his rights of subrogation, to any recovery from the carrier up to the amount of the claim paid. (See "Notification of Claim Against Carrier".)

Recta

A bill of lading which specifies the name of the consignee.

Reefer

Refrigerated vessel *or* refrigerated space.

Red Line Clause

A clause overprinted in red in a cargo policy drawing to the attention of the assured his obligation to preserve his right of recovery against the bailee or carrier, thus protecting the insurer's subrogation rights. (See also " Bailee Clause ".)

The clause is usually printed in red on certificates of cargo insurance or alternatively a separate clause may be attached, also printed in red, to the policy or certificate. There are five types of separate clauses. One set is issued by Lloyd's Policy Office and provides instructions to the consignee regarding the preservation of rights of recovery against the carrier and the port authorities in order that the insurer's subrogation rights are protected. In addition the L.P.O. Clause gives instructions for Lloyd's agent to be advised regarding a survey of damaged goods and lists the documents required to substantiate a claim. The remaining four sets of clauses are issued by the Institute of London Underwriters, being A, A1, B and B1 Sets. The " A " sets are for use on policies and certificates on which claims are payable abroad and, in addition to the instructions given on the " B " set, they also state the name and address of the local settling agent. The " B " sets are for use on policies and certificates on which claims are payable in London, hence no settling agent is inserted, and instructions are given therein regarding protection of rights against carriers etc., survey and claims documentation. " A " and " B " sets are for use where Companies only subscribe the insurance whereas " A1 " and " B1 " sets are for use when both Lloyd's and Companies subscribe the insurance. (See also " Claims Documents ".) This clause is referred to in practice, frequently, as the " Important Clause " because it is headed " Important ".

Reducing Insurer's Liability

See " Reinsurance ".

Ref.

Entry in Lloyd's Register indicating that the vessel is fitted for refrigerating machinery.

Refrigerated Cargoes

Perishable cargoes carried in refrigerated holds. Where the cargo is not in refrigerated containers the temperature is gradually raised from approximately 24 hours prior to discharge to enable handling of the cargo. It is important that the refrigeration temperature is kept even throughout the voyage or deterioration of the goods is expedited. Insurers covering deterioration risk on refrigerated cargoes insist on a certificate of soundness prior to shipment. Provided the goods are sound when shipped and refrigeration is properly maintained the goods should be sound on arrival. Except where the goods are carried in refrigerated containers, Insurers seldom extend the insurance to cover any period after discharge, except for discharge into cold or refrigerated stores. It is usual for a survey to be carried out immediately after discharge.

Refund
See " Refund of Claim ".

Refund of Claim
Refund to the insurer of all or part of a claim which has been paid. This may occur where the claim has been over-paid due to an error or misunderstanding, or, more often, where a recovery has been made on the insurer's behalf; in the latter case it is usually termed a " recovery ".

Registered Tonnage
Charges in respect of the use of canals and similar are based on a ship's net registered tonnage. The tonnage is found by calculating the cargo carrying capacity of the ship in cubic tons at 100 cubic ft. per ton. The gross tonnage of the ship is arrived at by taking into account the whole area inside the hull and the net registered tonnage is calculated by deducting certain specified spaces from the gross tonnage. These spaces include engine room space, crew's quarters, space used in navigating and operating the vessel, light and air spaces, locker rooms and similar. An open shelter deck is not included in the net registered tonnage but a permanently closed shelter deck is.

Register of Shipping of the U.S.S.R.
Referred to in the Institute Classification Clause. Unchartered iron or steel vessels, registered with the highest classification of this Society, that are not more than 15 years old are acceptable as carriers of cargo insured under an open cover without payment of an additional premium. Liners, other than warbuilt tonnage, are, generally, accepted without additional premium up to 30 years old.

Registration of Ships
Every British ship of over 15 tons, other than coastal and river craft, must be registered with the Registrar General of Shipping. Fishing vessels and Newfoundland trading vessels up to 30 tons are exempt.

Registro Italiano
This is an Italian Classification Society. Unchartered steel vessels up to 15 years old and fully classed with this Society are acceptable to insurers as carriers. Liners, other than war built tonnage, are acceptable as carriers up to 30 years old. Vessels registered with the Registro Italiano may appear in Lloyd's Register with the notation RI shown. The cypher to denote full class in the Registro Italiano is ★ 100 A 1.1.Nav.L.

Registry Certificate
See " Certificate of Registry ".

Reg.P.
Registered Post.

REINSD. *or* **Reinsd.**
Reinsured.

REINST. *or* **Reinst.**
Reinstatement.

Reinstatement
A non-marine practice, whereby the amount which has been the subject of a claim is reinstated in the policy on payment of an additional premium; thus reverting the amount of cover which was reduced by the claim to the original sum insured. This practice is, generally unnecessary in the marine market because (a) cargo is seldom insured on a time basis and any loss is calculated at expiry of the policy, and (b) repairs are carried out on hulls, thus reinstating the actual value of the vessel to its sound value. Reinstatement is therefore automatic in the marine market and no additional premium is charged, with the exception of excess loss reinsurance where it is common to apply the principle of reinstatement of losses by payment of an additional premium. Hull policies, nevertheless always contain a clause providing that no claim is recoverable in respect of unrepaired damage if the vessel becomes a total loss before expiry of the policy.

Reinsurance
When an insurer accepts a line on a slip he becomes liable for a loss under the insurance contemplated by the slip. This places him in the positon of being able to lose financially in the event of loss of or damage to the insured property, so that he has an insurable interest in respect of his liability. This liability he may reinsure with another insurer or several insurers who become his reinsurers. No insurer may reinsure for more than his liability nor on wider terms. He may reinsure for less than his liability or on narrower terms. The

reinsurer, subject to the terms of the reinsurance, must reimburse the original insurer for all losses for which he (the original insurer) is legally liable, but, unless the reinsurance so provides the reinsurer is not obliged to follow the original insurer in respect of ex gratia payments, W.P. (without prejudice) payments or compromised settlements. Reinsurance is mostly carried out by treaty reinsurance, but it may be the subject of individual placings or by a form of ordinary open cover. Some insurers devote the whole of their business to reinsurance.

Reinsurance Clause

A clause in common use in the marine market which reads : —

"Being a reinsurance of .... Subject to the same terms and conditions as the original policy or policies and to pay as may be paid thereon."

If the reinsurance is to be on limited terms on cargo the clause continues to read : —

" but only in respect of those risks which would be recoverable under a policy with the Institute Cargo Clauses F.P.A. attached thereto "

or some similar wording. A hull reinsurance clause on limited terms replaces the above extension with " but against total &/or constructive &/or arranged total loss only." (See also " Pay as may be Paid ".)

Reinsurance of Cargo

The main reason for cargo reinsurance is to relieve the insurer's liability in any one vessel. The insurer may be obliged to accept shipments under open covers and through agents so that his maximum liability in one vessel is greater than the amount he wishes to retain. Many insurers protect themselves against such accumulation of liability by effecting a treaty or other reinsurance contract to take all their acceptances over a fixed retention. Facultative reinsurance is less common but may arise where the insurer has no treaty reinsurance.

Reinsurance of Common Account

Abbreviation R.I.C.C. used in practice. A term used in marine treaty reinsurance and sometimes referred to as R.O.J.A. (Reinsurance of joint account.)

When an insurer enters into a long term reinsurance contract he may agree to cede a fixed amount or proportion of all the business he accepts despite an obligation which he already has to cede a proportion elsewhere. In order to fulfil his obligation under both contracts he cedes in full under the second contract but reinsures, on behalf of his reinsurers, such proportion of his cessions as relates to the first contract. Thus cessions of premiums are advised in full on the second contract but subject to a deduction, under the heading R.I.C.C., of the premium payable in respect of the proportion due on the first contract.

Reinsurance of Hulls

There are two basic reasons why an insurer may wish to reinsure a hull risk. The first being because he has been obliged to accept a larger line than he wishes to retain in order to obtain a portion of a good risk. His reinsurance would probably be on original conditions and at the original net rate. The second reason being because he wishes to retain the risk of partial loss and the bulk of the premium but does not wish to bear the risk of total loss, when his reinsurance would be on original conditions but against total loss only.

Reinsurance Treaty

See " Treaty Reinsurance ".

Reinsurance Waiver Clause

In many cases where adjustment of the terms of an insurance take place the additional premium or return of premium due is relatively small. Where a reinsurance of part or the whole of one line on the original insurance is in force the relevant additional premium or return of premium applicable to the reinsurance may be so small that it becomes uneconomical to collect. Nevertheless, in the absence of any agreement to the contrary, if such payment is not made on the reinsurance the reinsurers are not subject to the adjustment in the terms of the original insurance. In anticipation of this situation arising the reinsurance waiver clause has been evolved and is in common use in the London market. This clause provides that, where an additional premium or return of premium, is closed on the original insurance under the Small AP/RP Scheme (i.e. is too small to allocate to subscribing underwriters so is paid into or out of a pool) the amount due to or from the reinsuring underwriters is waived, though they remain bound by the amendment to the original insurance conditions that led to the small AP or RP; thus, the parties to the contract agree to waive such payment without prejudice to the rights of the other party to the contract. In 1963 it was agreed in the London market that the clause should be extended to embrace small differences arising due to rates of exchange where currencies are converted.

Reinsured

An insurer who has reinsured his liability with another insurer, who becomes the reinsurer.

Reinsurer

An insurer who agrees to reimburse another insurer in respect of claims on the latter's liability.

Rejection of Abandonment

See "Notice of Abandonment".

Rejection Risk

Under the U.S. Pure Foods and Drugs laws standards are imposed on the import of foodstuffs, which are rejected if they do not conform with the minimum standard required. Rejected goods must be returned to the country of origin, shipped elsewhere or destroyed. Rejection risk insurance reimburses the assured for his loss in this respect. London market underwriters do not readily accept such insurances. Where a market for the risk can be found, the underwriters charge a high rate of premium and insist on insuring, also, the ordinary marine risk. A broker will arrange an open cover wherever possible with a clause providing that a large part of the premium will be returnable to the assured if there are no rejection claims during the year.

Released Bill

The "Released Bill of Lading Clause" is not uncommon in the American market. It is used to make it clear in the insurance contract that the shipper may ship his goods under a bill of lading which is not "ad valorem" (i.e. is not specified as being for the full declared value of the goods). The effect is that recovery from the Carrier is limited to the amount specified by law in the U.S. Carriage of Goods by Sea Act or, in the case of air shipments, the Warsaw Convention. The term is used, also, in British shipping circles in cases where the bill of lading is stamped on its reverse side with a Delivery Order whereby the consignee can use the released bill as his authorisation to take delivery of the goods.

Release of Reserve

A reinsurance treaty provision. A reserve is retained by the ceding Company either as a premium reserve or as a claim reserve. Periodically, annually as a rule, this reserve is released by transferring the item to the reinsurer's credit. The release of the old reserve and creation of a new reserve are usually concurrent operations. (See also "Interest on Reserve".)

Release to True Sterling
Advising the correct rate of exchange for a convertible currency entry and the sterling equivalent.

Reloading Cargo at P.O.R.
See " Costs Allowed in General Average ".

Remedy Against Third Parties
See " Subrogation ".

Removal of Ship for Repairs
See " Cost of Removal ".

Removal of Wreck
When a vessel is sunk in the fairway, in a harbour or in some other place where it is a danger to shipping the Authorities have the right to mark, light, buoy or even to destroy it, if the owner does not remove the wreck and to charge the owner of the vessel with the cost thereof. The insurer is not liable for the expense of removal of the wreck of the insured vessel unless he has taken over proprietary rights on having paid a total loss. Insurers do not cover the assured's liability for removal of wreck following collision (see " Collision Clause "), this being a P. & I. risk.

Removal of Wreck Extension
A clause in the I.Y.C. that provides for payment of expenses for removal of wreck from the assured's own premises. It is an extension of the R.O.W. provisions in the P & I clause. The maximum amount recoverable under both provisions is the sum insured by the policy applied to any one accident or series of accidents arising out of one event.

Removal of Wreck (I.F.V.C.)
The P & I clause in the I.F.V.C. covers legal liability of the assured incurred consequent upon removal of wreck of the insured vessel, its gear, catch, cargo, etc. A further clause covers the expense incurred by the assured for removal of the wreck, etc. from the assured's own premises. The amount recoverable under both clauses jointly shall not exceed the amount insured by the policy in respect of any one accident or series of accidents arising out of one event.

Removals Ashore Clause
A clause in a hull policy providing that any part of the insured ship, its gear, etc. is covered whilst removed ashore for the purpose of repair, overhaul or refitting, including during transit from and to the insured ship. Such a clause appears in the I.F.V.C. and the I.Y.C., the latter including cover during storage ashore.

Renewal

The practice of renewing an insurance which is due to expire. Renewal depends on the claims experience on the expiring insurance and the insurer may decline the renewal, increase the premium or insert special conditions if the experience is poor. On the other hand, if the experience is exceptionally good he will usually renew and may agree to a relaxation of conditions or a reduction in rate. There is no responsibility on the broker to effect renewal without instructions from the assured, but most brokers maintain a system to remind them when renewals are due so that they may contact the assured to ascertain whether he desires to renew. A broker may provisionally effect renewal or hold it covered pending instructions from the assured. Renewal generally applies in cargo business where open covers are involved and in hull business it applies to time policies.

Renewal Sheet

A standard form of attachment to a broker's slip, used in the Lloyd's market, providing for renewal of an expiring policy.

Repacking

Where goods are damaged by an insured peril it may be possible to minimise the loss by reconditioning and/or repacking the goods. In such cases where the repacking follows damage recoverable from the insurer, the cost of repacking is also paid by the insurer. Repacking short of destination is an expense to prevent loss and is recoverable from the insurer as a sue and labour charge. It may occur that the packing alone is damaged and repacking at destination is necessary to enable the goods to be sold. This repacking is not recoverable from underwriters. (See also " Label Clause ".)

Repair Accounts

Periodic accounts of repair costs presented during the carrying out of repairs, for the approval of the surveyor appointed by the insurer.

Repair Specification

A document necessary to support a claim for cost of repairs to a ship. It contains details of the proposed repairs and usually accompanies a tender.

Repairs to Ship

See " Cost of Repairs ".

Replacement Clause

Used mainly in insurances on machinery as cargo, the clause provides that in respect of damage the insurer's liability shall be limited to replacing and fitting the broken part. This prevents the assured from claiming a total loss on the grounds of " loss of species ". Such a claim being based on the assured's contention that he is unable to use the machine for the purpose for which it was intended. (See also " Secondhand Replacement Clause ".)

Replacement of Machinery

This refers to machinery as cargo. (See " Replacement Clause ".)

Reporting Form Basis

A system of premium calculation used in insurance of hull interests or construction risks. The annual premium rate is agreed when the insurance is effected but the premium is paid in periodic instalments based on the monthly value at risk. The values are advised monthly, on a reporting form, to the insurer, hence the derivation of the term. The system may provide, alternatively, for daily or other periodic reports.

Representation

A statement of fact, belief or expectation made by the assured and/or his broker to the insurer when placing the insurance. A material representation is one which would affect a prudent insurer in deciding whether to accept, decline or how to rate the risk. What is material is a question of fact. A material representation must be substantially true or the insurer may avoid the contract. It need not be actually correct provided the difference between what is stated and what is true would not affect the insurer's decision. The insurer may not avoid the policy if a statement is made in good faith but turns out to be untrue later. The broker or assured may amend or withdraw the representation before the contract is concluded if he so wishes. (See " Utmost Good Faith ".)

Request Form

A document, prepared by a Lloyd's broker and presented to L.P.S.O. to request a search for a policy and/or slip that has been, previously, deposited at L.P.S.O.

Request Note

Normally no cargo can be landed before the ship has cleared at the Custom House. A request note allows perishable cargoes to be landed before clearance.

Requisition

The taking over of property by a Government for its own use. The owner of the property is usually reimbursed by way of compulsory purchase (see " Pre-emption ") or by payment for hire. It is usual for war cover on hull specifically to exclude requisition as a peril.

Reserve Account

Term used in Treaty Reinsurance. It is a condition in a reinsurance contract that the reinsurer is only liable for losses already paid by the reinsured. In many instances the reinsured depends on the payment of the claim by his reinsurer to provide the cash for settlement of the claim on the original policy but the above condition creates a difficulty in this respect. To obviate this difficulty, and to provide a fund from which the original claim can be paid, it is customary to permit the reinsured to retain part of the reinsurance premium and to place this into a special account, called the Reserve Account. Most contracts provide for the amount so held to be released to the reinsurer at the end of twelve months and for interest to be paid thereon. (See " Premium Reserve ", " Claims Reserve " and " Interest on Reserve ".) A reserve account may be created, also, when the Government of the producing country legislates that an amount must be retained in the country to provide a fund against which claims can be met.

Re-shipment
See " Transhipment ".

Re-signing Addendum
An endorsement to a Lloyd's policy giving effect to a change in syndicate participation.

Res Nullius
Nobody's responsibility.

Respondentia
An insurable interest which a lender of money has in respect of a loan to the master of a vessel to enable the vessel to continue the voyage. In respondentia the security lies in the cargo. It is practically only of academic interest today. (See also " Bottomry ".)

Restraints
One of the perils specified in the plain policy form. This does not include arrest of the vessel for contravention of regulations or pending a claim for liability. It is restraint by political acts and similar. Restraints are excluded from the policy form by attachment of the F.C. & S. clause thereto.

Ret.
Return of premium.

Retained Line
The proportion of a line written by a reassured and not ceded to his reinsurer. Sometimes called his " retention ".

Retention
An amount held back or not released. In reinsurance it is the

same as a retained line which is the proportion of the line written by the original insurer that is not ceded to the reinsurer. In hull insurance the retention is also the amount of premium held back by the insurer to cover the lay up risk when a return of premium is allowed in consideration of the vessel being laid up, out of commission.

Retiring from a Line
An American expression used when an insurer either refuses to renew an expiring insurance or cancels his proportion of liability under an existing insurance.

Retroactive
See " Retrospective ".

Retrocedant
One who retrocedes.

Retrocede
To reinsure further what has been accepted by way of reinsurance. The original insurer cedes a line to his reinsurer. If the reinsurer himself effects a further reinsurance with another reinsurer on the same risk he retrocedes part or the whole of the line ceded to him. The term is used also for subsequent reinsurances of the same risk.

Retrocession
A cession which is retroceded. (See " Retrocede ".)

Retrocessionaire
One who accepts a retrocession.

Retrospective
Taking into acount what has gone before. This term is to be found mainly in reinsurance in circumstances where the reinsurer's liability attaches some time after the original insurer's liability. The reinsurance contract may be made retrospective whereby the reinsurer agrees to accept cessions which are concerned with risks which attached before the reinsurance attached. The term retroactive may be used instead of retrospective.

Return by Agreement
See " Return of Premium ".

Return for No Claim
When an insurer is asked to accept an insurance containing a peril which he would not normally write at the rate required, he may only accept at a higher rate but be prepared to grant a return of

part of the premium in the event of no loss occurring proximately caused by the undesirable peril. For example, the insurer may be asked to write an open cover to insure both the ordinary marine perils on goods and the risk of rejection by the importing Authorities. He may be quite agreeable to cover the marine risks but the rejection risk demands a higher rate beyond that acceptable to the assured. In such cases the insurer quotes the higher rate but agrees to insert a provision in the contract that in the event of no claims arising from the rejection risk during (say) one year the assured will receive a return of part of the premium charged for rejection. The final result being that, provided there are no rejection claims, the insurer retains the premium for the marine risks and a small part of the premium for the rejection risk.

Return for Non-attachment

Return for failure of consideration. (See " Return of Premium ".)

Return of Premium

There are two basic types of return of premium, being (a) returns for failure of consideration or non-attachment of risk and (b) returns by agreement.

Under (a) the assured is entitled to the return of any premium he has paid, in full, if the risk has never attached and the insurer has never been liable. If the insurer avoids the policy from inception and the risk has not attached the premium is returnable, provided there has been no fraud. If double insurance is effected in error, each policy bearing a proportion of the risk, a proportionate return of premium is due on each policy.

Under (b) if the circumstance occurs as detailed in the agreement the premium or such part of the premium as has been agreed is returnable. The main returns by agreement are detailed elsewhere herein. (See " Return for No Claim ", " Sale of Vessel ", " Cancelling Returns " and " Lay Up Returns ".)

Returns

Returns of Premium.

Returns Bureau

See " Joint Hull Returns Bureau ".

Returns Clause

A clause in a hull time policy by which the insurer agrees to allow a return of premium to the assured if either of two circumstances arise. (a) The policy is cancelled by mutual agreement or (b) the vessel is laid up out of commission in port for not less than 30 consecutive days. In the case of (a) one-twelfth of the annual net premium is allowed for each uncommenced month. In the case of (b) one-twelfth of the annual net premium, after deducting a percentage retention for the port risk, is allowed for each period of 30 consecutive days the vessel is laid up. The retention, which is at a percentage rate applied to the net monthly premium for each 30 day period of lay up, varies according to whether or not the vessel is under repair. The scale of retentions is lower if the policy is on limited terms.

All returns of premium under the clause are subject to "and arrival", which means no return is paid until expiry of the policy and is then paid only if the vessel has safely "arrived" at that time. The effect being that if the vessel is totally lost before expiry of the policy no returns are payable. A lay up return is allowed only for a period when the vessel is laid up in protected waters but if the underwriters agree that part of a lay up period is in the vicinity of an approved area and the remainder of the period is in the approved area a pro rata return is allowed for that part of the period spent in the approved area. Loading, discharging or the presence of cargo on board does not debar a lay up return but if the vessel is being used for storage no lay up return is allowed. If a lay up period of 30 consecutive days falls on two policies by overlapping the date of expiry of the old policy and inception of the new policy, the old policy pays its proportion of the return immediately and the new policy pays its proportion when the new policy expires, subject to "and arrival".

Returns Clause (A.C.V.)

A clause published by Lloyd's (L.P.O. 77) which is used in conjunction with A.C.V. Form No. 1. The clause allows a percentage of the premium to be returned to the assured for each full period of 30 consecutive days the A.C.V. is laid up ashore, otherwise than as a result of an insured accident or for normal maintenance.

Reversible Lay Days

The days permitted for loading a cargo are termed "lay days". The same applies to discharge of cargo. If a total number of days is allowed which can be used for both without distinction, such lay days are called "reversible".

Revocable Credit

See "Confirmed Irrevocable Credit".

RI

Notation in Lloyd's Register indicating that a ship is classed with "Registro Italiano".

R/I
Reinsurance.

R.I.C.C.
Reinsurance of Common Account. (A reinsurance treaty term.)

R/I Closing Form
A form on which a reinsured sets out closing details. A broker, having placed a reinsurance on the basis of a R/I order form will await the arrival of the R/I closing form before he closes the risk to the reinsurers. Lloyd's publishes a standard R/I closing form for the use of Lloyd's syndicates, under reference L.P.O. 85.

Right of Contribution
If there is double insurance each insurer is liable to contribute rateably to the loss in the proportion that the amount insured under his policy bears to the whole amount insured. (See also "Non-Contribution Clause".)

Right of Insurer Against Carrier
See "Right of Recovery".

Right of Recovery
The insurer has a right to any recovery from a third party in respect of damage which was the subject of a claim under the policy. paid by the claim. Where it is clear that the assured is a co-insurer for part of the risk and, therefore, bears part of all claims he participates in any recovery in the proportion that his part of the claim bears to the whole claim, but if the assured bears the first part of a loss by way of a deductible or an excess the insurer has the *first* right of recovery. Nevertheless, the insurer has no right to recovery until after he has settled the claim. An insurer is not entitled to recover more than the amount paid as a claim.

Rights of Carrier
The rights and immunities of the carrier are detailed in Article 4 of the Carriage of Goods by Sea Act 1924, to which reference should be made.

Rights of Subrogation
See "Subrogation".

Right to Take Tenders
See "Tender Clause".

R/I Order Form
A form on which an insurer sets out details of a risk he wishes to reinsure. In the London market this form is given to the broker

to effect the reinsurance. Lloyd's publishes a standard R/I order form, for use of Lloyd's syndicates, under reference L.P.O. 27

R/I or direct
A term used on a broker's slip when the broker has an order to place a risk but does not know whether the risk will be a direct insurance or by way of reinsurance.

Riots and Civil Commotions
See " Strikes, Riots and Civil Commotions ".

Rising Market
When the value of goods is rising. It is preferable for a merchant to send goods for sale at destination (i.e. " on consignment ") on a rising market. The insurer is not interested in whether the market rises or falls because claims are settled by comparing gross arrived sound values with gross arrived damaged values and applying the percentage of depreciation, so arrived at, to the insured value. (See " Net Values " and " Gross Value ".)

Risk
A fortuity. Something which *may* happen but not something which *must* happen. Does not include an inevitability.

R/I Treaty Standard Slip
A broker's slip format introduced to the London market in 1973 for mandatory use by brokers placing business at Lloyd's and with Institute Companies with effect on and after 1st January 1974.

R.L.N.
Running landing numbers.

R.M.S.
Royal Mail Ship.

R.N.R.
Renewal not required.

R.O.A.
Reinsurance Offices Association.

Roads
Roadstead.

Roadstead
An anchorage for ships which is not within the enclosure of a harbour.

r.o.b.
Remaining on board. Refers to goods.

R.O.D.

Rust, oxidation and discolouration.

R.O.J.A.

Reinsurance of joint account. (See "Reinsurance of common account".)

Roll on Roll off Vessel

A ship designed with side, and/or rear and/or bow entrances each with a "let down" ramp which enables loaded vehicles to drive into and out of the ship.

Ro Ro

Abbreviation for "Roll on, Roll off".

Rotation Clause

Where an open cover provides for a large limit in respect of any one declaration it is customary for the broker to obtain lines from many insurers in order to spread the risk as widely as possible. The result, in the event of a small declaration being made, is that each insurer receives only a very small part of that declaration. The economics of an otherwise profitable cover could be seriously impaired by the expense of closing trifling amounts and to avoid this the rotation clause may be incorporated into the cover. The clause provides that all declarations up to an agreed proportion of the cover limit shall be allocated only to a specified group of the insurers on the cover. To preserve equity the insurers on the cover are split into such groups, each group receiving small declarations in rotation.

Round Voyage

A term that was used in relation to hull time policies when a franchise was applied to particular average. Its purpose was to apply the franchise to all particular average occurring during the round voyage and a clause defining a "round" voyage was incorporated in the policy. Basically, a round voyage was 3 consecutive passages but not exceeding 2 cargo passages. The deductible that appears in hull time policies today is applied to partial losses occurring during any one accident or occurrence; not any one round voyage.

Rovers

Synonymous with "Pirates" so far as insurance is concerned.

R.P.

Return of premium.

R.T.

Rye terms.

R.T.A. Cl.
Rubber Trade Association Clauses.

R.T.B.A.
Rate to be agreed.

Rtng.
Returning premium.

Rubber Clauses
A set of cargo " trade " clauses the use of which is approved by the Rubber Trade Association of London, the Institute of London Underwriters, the Liverpool Underwriters' Association and Lloyd's Underwriters' Association.

Although similar to the standard cargo clauses there are some important variations in the transit clause and the average clause. An " Arbitration Clause " and an " Increased Value Clause " are incorporated. The variations, too detailed to outline here, should be studied by examination of the clauses themselves. (The Clause No. is 163 1/1/71 and copies can be obtained from Messrs. Witherby & Co. Ltd.)

Rubber Trade Association Clauses
See " Rubber Clauses ".

Rudder Clause
A clause, attaching to a hull policy, excluding loss of or damage to the rudder, propeller, shaft or machinery unless caused by the vessel being stranded, sunk, burnt or in collision with another vessel.

Rules for Construction of Policy
These rules are part of the first schedule to the Marine Insurance Act 1906. The rules serve to interpret the meanings of specified perils and words in the policy form. (See the Marine Insurance Act 1906 for details.)

Rules of Practice
The Rules of Practice of the Association of Average Adjusters, known as " English Law and Practice ". These are rules for settling general average disputes in the U.K. where the York-Antwerp Rules are not specified in the contract. Certain of the rules also relate to particular average.

Rummaging a Ship
Search carried out by Customs Officials.

Run Off
Applicable to long term contracts such as treaties. When the contract has been cancelled there are often many risks which attached

before the cancellation became effective, particularly time risks, which still have to be " run off ". That is, the insurance or reinsurance remains in force in respect of those risks until they have " run off ".

Running Days
Connected with loading or unloading cargo. Consecutive days, but excluding Sundays and holidays.

Running Down Clause
Another name for the " Collision Clause ".

Running Landing Numbers
A policy provision, seldom used today, for the purpose of ascertaining whether damage on cargo reaches the franchise. When the franchise is applicable to " series " on a number of packages and the packages are not numbered it is customary to apply the franchise to each series of packages as landed. That is, the consecutive order of packages landed is applied until the first series is reached. Example: Franchise 3% on each series of 10 packages, running landing numbers. The first ten packages landed form the first series and the particular average damage over this series is totalled to see if it reaches 3% of the sound value of the series. Each subsequent series is treated similarly. If the last series is less than 10 packages it is called the " tail series " and is treated separately on the same principle.

Russian Register of Shipping
See " Register of Shipping of the U.S.S.R. ".

Rust
Not covered by the policy unless specified. A policy covering " All Risks " would cover damage to or loss of an article due to rust proximately caused by an insured peril, such as immersion in seawater.

Rye Terms
Appears in contracts for sale of grain. It is a guarantee by the seller of the condition of the grain on arrival whereby the buyer agrees to accept damaged grain subject to a deterioration allowance from the seller. Rye terms are generally required by the buyer when grain is shipped in tankers in bulk. (See also " Tale Quale ".) The seller has an insurable interest in the guarantee, but it is not the sort of risk which would be readily acceptable to the insurer. So far as the *buyer's* interest in the grain is concerned, the clause is of benefit to the insurer.

S

S.

Loadline marking showing the summer loadline level. This abbreviation is also used for "salvage".

S.A.

South America—May also be used for South Africa *or* Salvage Association *or* Société Anônyme.

S/A

Subject to acceptance. Written at the top of the broker's "slip". It is used when a broker has not received a firm order in respect of a risk which has attached and completes the placing "subject to acceptance" by the assured of the terms of the insurance. The abbreviation is also used for "Salvage Association".

S & A

Signing and Accounting. A procedure at Lloyd's whereby the premium accounting entry and the policy signing procedures are carried out as one operation. (See also "Separation Procedure".)

S.A. a/c

Salvage Association account.

Sabotage

A deliberate act of destruction. (See "Malicious Damage".)

Sabotage to Ship

See "Malicious Acts Clause".

Sacrifice

Usually a general average act. When a sacrifice is made of property involved in a maritime adventure for the purpose of preserving the whole adventure from an insured peril, such loss is recoverable under the policy as being a loss by that peril. The assured can recover the claim directly from his insurer without waiting for the general average adjustment to be completed. When the adjustment has been completed the underwriter is subrogated to the rights of the assured to recover the claim from the general average fund. Each party contributes rateably towards the fund in the proportion the saved value of his interest bears to the whole value saved by the general average act.

Safely Landed

Goods are "safely landed" when they have been landed in the

customary manner within a reasonable time after arrival at the discharge port.

Safe Port

This term applies not only to a port where a ship and/or cargo are protected from the hazards of the sea, but also where there is no likelihood of political interference.

Sagging

When a ship is supported at both ends but not in the middle. This can occur when a ship runs aground on rocks and the tide ebbs leaving her " sagging ". (See also " Hogged ".)

Sailed as per List

Note on a slip, using the initials s.a.p.l., to the effect that at the time of acceptance it is understood that the sailing date of the vessel is as published in Lloyd's List. The expression is used when it is thought that the ship may have sailed but at the time information has not been received of the exact sailing date.

Sailing Card

Shipbrokers issue such cards to clients giving details of ships they propose to load, capacity available, place of loading and expected date of sailing.

Sailing Warranty

There is an implied warranty in a voyage policy on a vessel that the vessel sails within a reasonable time after the acceptance by the insurer of the risk. (See " Attachment of Risk ".) The underwriter may require an express warranty in the policy specifying a date by which the vessel must sail. (See also " Breach of Warranty ".)

Sale Account

See " Account Sales ".

Sale Charges

The insurer is not liable for sale charges on damaged goods which were sent to the destination with the intention of offering them for sale. (See " On Consignment ".) When goods are not intended for sale at destination but are sold following damage from an insured peril which results in a policy claim, the insurer is liable for the sale charges.

Sale Fees

See " Sale Charges ".

Sale of Vessel

If a ship is sold with unrepaired damage the insurer usually allows a reasonable depreciation for such damage, although the Marine Insurance Act 1906 provides that the insurer is liable for depreciation only for a policy which expires without the vessel being sold. In practice, the policy is automatically cancelled on sale of the vessel. (See "Sale of Vessel Clause".)

Sale of Vessel Clause

A clause in a hull policy providing that the policy is automatically cancelled in the event of change of ownership or management. The insurer may agree to continue the insurance if he wishes but this must be in writing. A pro rata daily net return of premium is allowed for the unexpired portion of the policy. If the vessel is at sea at the time of cancellation the cover continues until arrival at her destination. Since the insurer takes into account the ownership and management of a ship in the premium charged, the clause prevents the benefit of one owner's or manager's good record being given to another.

Sale Terms

The conditions on which goods are sold. In regard to goods in transit the sale terms usually determine the point at which title to the goods passes from seller to buyer; thereby affecting their individual responsibilities for the goods, carriage charges, etc. and insurance. (See "Ex dock", "F.O.B.", "C.I.F.", "F.A.S.", "C. & F.". "Ex Seller's Warehouse", "Assignment of Interest" and "Assignment of Policy".)

Sales Contract

An agreement between a seller and a buyer. The sales contract also determines the point at which interest in and responsibility for the goods changes from one party to the other; affecting the transfer of title and transfer of insurance interest. This is very important when goods are in transit for it determines responsibility for paying shipping and other charges and for arranging insurance coverage. (See "F.O.B.", "Ex-Warehouse", "F.A.S.", "Ex dock", "C.I.F.", "C. & F.", "Assignment of Interest" and "Assignment of Policy".)

S/A L/U

Subject to acceptance by the assured, to be advised to the leading Underwriter only.

Salvage

An award payable to a third party for services rendered to preserve maritime property from peril at sea. Pure salvage is awarded only to a third party acting independently of contract and is payable only when the property has been saved. The award is based on the value of the property saved, the hazard and degree of skill involved and the expense of the operation. The contributory value for apportionment of salvage is calculated in the same way as for general average but the values are assessed at the place where the salvage operation is completed. The contributory value is compared with the insured value, as with general average, and any resultant undervaluation is reflected in a proportionate reduction in the contribution paid by the insurer. Any guarantee given by the insurer is therefore subject to qualification unless a counter guarantee is given by the assured. A salvor cannot claim an award where the circumstances leading to the salvage act were brought about by the wrongful or negligent act of the salvor.

The insurance term for a salvage award is " salvage charges " and such charges incurred to preserve the insured property from a peril insured against are recoverable under the policy as a loss by that peril. Whereas contribution to general average is not payable by any of the interests involved which do not reach their destination, any salvage contribution is still payable on such property, provided the salvage operation was successful. For this reason, salvage charges are payable by insurers in addition to a total loss resulting from a subsequent casualty. Despite the principle of pure salvage, in practice Lloyd's form of Salvage Agreement is used on a " no cure no pay " basis. The term " Salvage " may also be used to describe the property saved. (See also " Lloyd's Form of Salvage Agreement " and " Guarantee (Salvage) ".)

Salvage Agreement
See " Lloyd's Form of Salvage Agreement ".

Salvage and Recovery Clause
A clause in a reinsurance treaty entitling the reinsurer to press for his share of any recovery obtained on the original insurance.

Salvage Association
The Salvage Association was formed in 1856 by Marine insurance and shipping interests in London. Its cumbersome former title " The Association for the Protection of Commercial Interests as respects Wrecked and Damaged Property " was discontinued when a new Royal Charter (Eliz. II) redefined the objects of the Association in 1971 and granted the title " Salvage Association ". The basic foundation of the Association is the investigation of casualties in which marine underwriters are interested, but since 1971 its activities have been extended to offer services to a much wider field, including non-marine and aviation matters.

When a casualty is reported and a claim seems possible it is common practice for the interested underwriters (Lloyd's or Companies') to instruct the Salvage Association to act on their behalf. the Association initiates an examination of the circumstances of the casualty and ascertains the extent of damage to the property; subsequently providing the owner with information and recommendation for the protection and preservation of the interests of all parties.

The Association is non-profit making and its affairs are managed by a Committee comprised of representatives from Lloyd's and English Insurance Companies. The head office of the Salvage Association is in Lloyd's Building, London, EC3M 7EU.

Salvage Charges

Money properly payable in an award to a third party acting independently of contract to preserve from an insured peril the property insured in a marine adventure. Services in the nature of salvage are not included in the expression " Salvage ". The insurer's liability for salvage charges is reduced in proportion to underinsurance if the insured value of the policy is less than the contributory value. (See also " Average Disbursements Clauses " and " Contributory Value ".)

Salvage Guarantee

An agreement, whereby a guarantor agrees to make good a salvage award if the party responsible fails to pay it to the salvor. The salvor (termed " Contractor " in the form) will discharge the maritime lien which he is entitled to attach to the salved property, in exchange for such an agreement subscribed by an acceptable guarantor or guarantors. Lloyd's may issue such an agreement for use in conjunction with Lloyd's Standard Form of Salvage Agreement. Payment in relation to the Lloyd's form is guaranteed by the Corporation of Lloyd's who require to hold a policy written by acceptable insurers, or an Indemnity subscribed by syndicates at Lloyd's; whereby they will be reimbursed if they have to make good any sum under the guarantee.

Salvage Loss

This occurs when goods are sold short of destination as a result of damage which is the subject of a claim under the policy. Under the principle of salvage loss the assured retains the proceeds after deducting the sale charges and survey fee and the insurer pays the difference between the proceeds and the insured value stated in the policy.

Salvage Services
See " Salvage " and " Services in The Nature of Salvage "

Salvage Tug
A tug, often ocean-going, specially built and equipped for salvage work.

Salved Property
Property which is the subject of a claim by salvors for a salvage award.

Salv. L.
Salvage loss.

Salvor's Lien
When a salvor has salved property he has a lien on that property whereby he may retain the property until the salvage award has been settled. Under Lloyd's Form of salvage agreement the vessel is released on the provision of security to the Committee of Lloyd's.

Sams
See " Liberty Type Ships ".

Samson
See " Kingpost ".

S and/or N.D.
Shortage and / or Non-Delivery.

S.A.N.R.
Subject approval no risk.

s.a.p.l.
Sailed as per list,

Saving Human Life
A ship may deviate to save human life on board or elsewhere without the assured being prejudiced, but the marine insurer has no liability in respect of such human life.

S.B.M.
Single buoy mooring. A large buoy, designed to be anchored permanently at sea, to which large ships can be moored.

s.b.s.
Surveyed before shipment.

SBS
Entry in Lloyd's Register which indicates that the ship is fitted for submarine signalling equipment.

S/C
Salvage charges.

S.C.A.
Settlement of Claims Abroad. (See "Settlement of Claims Abroad" and "C.P.A.".)

Scale of Feet
The stem and stern of a British ship are marked on both sides by a scale in feet upwards from 0 which is level with the lowest point of the keel. This is compulsory to enable the draught taken by the ship to be clearly seen.

Scale of Rates
A schedule attached to an open cover or open policy detailing the rates of premium applicable to each interest and voyage.

Scantling
Thickness of a steel plate on a ship.

Sch.
Schooner.

Schedule
A list containing relevant details for attachment to a slip, policy or other documents.

Schedule to the Act
The first schedule to the Marine Insurance Act 1906. The schedule deals exclusively with the policy form. It gives the form of the S.G. policy and rules for the construction of the policy. (See "Rules for Construction of Policy".)

Schooner
A two-masted sailing vessel. Built with sharp lines for speed.

Scrap
Any scrap resulting from repairs to a ship is sold and the proceeds are used to reduce the cost of repairs. In no case are the insurers liable to pay the cost of repairs in full and left to recover what they can from the scrap.

Scrap metal as cargo is not readily insurable on full conditions including shortage. If the scrap is of valuable metal there is a risk of pilferage. In any case a great deal of scrap metal consists of filings which are easily lost if not contained in sealed drums. Iron scrap is usually shipped in bulk or in metal netting. In many cases scrap metal is shipped in vessels destined for the breaker's yard. (See "Break Up Voyage".)

Scraping the Bottom

Scraping or cleaning the bottom of a ship. It is practice to exclude entirely from the policy all expense incurred in scraping or painting the ship's bottom, whether or not it is in connection with repairs. The ship's " bottom " is the area of the hull below the boot topping. (See "Boot Topping ".)

Scratching

The risk of scratching to painted, enamelled or polished surfaces. This risk is not covered by the policy unless it is proximately caused by an insured peril or is specifically included in the policy. " Scratching, bruising and denting " are risks which follow the same principle and are often found on the same policy as a specific inclusion or exclusion. The term " scratching " may be, also, used as a slang expression for initialling. (See " Initialling ".)

Scuppers

Drains by which water is carried from a ship's deck.

Scuttles

Port lights.

Scuttling

Opening sea cocks or letting in water deliberately to sink a ship. The only time this is condoned is when it is necessary to put out a fire. A ship which is on fire in relatively shallow water may be scuttled to extinguish the fire with the intention of salving the vessel later. Such scuttling is general average. Other forms of scuttling are usually wilful misconduct or barratry. Scuttling is not an insured peril, but "barratry " is one of the perils specified in the marine policy form. (See "Barratry ".)

S.D. *or* s.d.

Steam drifter.

S/D

Steel diesel *or* short delivery.

S.D.H.F.

Standard Dutch Hull Form. (See " Dutch Hull Form ".)

Seaman's Lien

The right of a seaman to exercise a lien on a ship for non-payment of wages. (Ref. Merchant Shipping Act 1894 and subsequent supplements.)

Searcher

A Customs Official responsible for permitting the shipment of dutiable goods or stores.

Sea Risks
Marine perils.

Seaworthiness
There is an implied warranty in every voyage policy that the vessel is seaworthy at the commencement of the voyage. That is, the vessel must be reasonably fit in all respects, including the hull, equipment, stores, bunkers, crew and officers, to encounter the ordinary perils contemplated for the voyage. If the vessel is in port she must be reasonably fit to encounter the perils of the port. If the voyage is in stages (i.e. part river part open sea) she must be reasonably fit at the commencement of each stage to meet the ordinary perils of that stage, but she need not be fit to meet the perils of the subsequent stage until she commences it. A time policy does not contain this absolute warranty that the ship must be seaworthy at any stage, but if the ship is sent to sea in an unseaworthy state with the privity of the assured the insurer can repudiate any loss attributable to unseaworthiness. So far as goods are concerned there is an implied warranty not only that the ship is seaworthy but that she is reasonably fit to carry the goods to their destination. The goods themselves need not be seaworthy. Since the cargo owner has very little control over the seaworthiness of the ship it is usual for the " Seaworthiness Admitted " clause to be incorporated into the cargo policy. It is the duty of the carrier to provide a seaworthy ship but he cannot be held liable for damage to the cargo resulting from unseaworthiness where he has exercised due diligence to provide a seaworthy ship.

Seaworthiness Admitted Clause
A clause in a policy whereby the insurer admits that no claim under the policy will be repudiated as a result of unseaworthiness. This clause does not defeat the right of the insurer to proceed, in the name of the assured, against a carrier who is liable for the loss.
The clause in the Institute Cargo Clauses goes on to ensure that the assured is not prejudiced by reason of the wrongful act or misconduct of the shipowners or their servants, committed without privity of the assured.

Seaworthy Ship
See " Seaworthiness ".

Second Hand Machinery
When machinery is insured as cargo it is deemed to be new machinery unless the policy specifically states that it is second hand.

It is usual to incorporate the " Second Hand Replacement Clause " in a policy covering second hand machinery enabling the insurer to replace damaged parts with second hand material.

Second Hand Replacement Clause

Used on policies covering second hand machinery as cargo. (See " Second Hand Machinery ".)

Second Leaving

Policy signing and accounting term. Queried documents are returned to the broker who, having answered the query, re-submits the documents to the signing office (L.P.S.O. or I.L.U.) as a " second leaving ".

Security

The Insurer is the " security ". The term is used when referring to the Insurer in discussion. A group of Insurers may be embraced collectively by the one expression " security ".

Seen

A term used on slips and other documents presented to the insurer to advise him of information relevant to the insurance. The insurer, having examined the document writes the word " Seen " thereon and follows this with his initial. This action does not bind the insurer to agreement with the statement contained in the document, merely indicating that it has been shown to him for information. If it is a matter for the insurer's agreement, it is customary for the insurer upon agreement to write " agreed " instead of "seen " on the document.

Seizure

See " Capture and Seizure ".

Self Insured

A risk undertaken by the assured himself, not placed with in-surers elsewhere. (Own Insurer.)

Seller's Interest

The insurable interest of the seller. The seller has such an interest only until the title to the goods passes to the buyer. The policy may be assigned by the seller to the buyer but assignment must take place before, or at the time that, the seller's interest ceases. The seller cannot assign the policy *after* he has lost his insurable interest.

Semester

Half of a year.

Semi-Submersible Rig

An off shore drilling rig, comprising a number of pontoons that are towed into position at the drilling site. Whereas the pontoons of the submersible drilling rig sit on the seabed, those of the semi-submersible rig are sunk only to sufficient depth to provide a stable base for the drilling platform (e.g. 50–90 feet below the surface where the water is relatively undisturbed). The rig is secured by anchors. Some such rigs are large enough to incorporate their own propulsion machinery, to give assistance to the towing effort. The rig may, also be equipped with facilities for self positioning.

Sentimental Loss

This is, in effect, loss of market and is not covered by the policy. It occurs when undamaged cargo is discharged from a ship which has damaged cargo on board. Tea is particularly subject to loss in value if stowed in proximity with damaged cargo.

Separate Values

When hull policies were subject to a franchise it was customary to specify separate values for hull, machinery and refrigerating machinery. When the franchise system was replaced with a deductible average condition in 1969 the need for separate values to be specified ceased.

Separation Box

A space on a premium advice note wherein the broker indicates whether the entry is to be processed in Stage 1 of the Separation procedure or in the S & A procedure.

Separation Procedure

A procedure at Lloyd's whereby the premium accounting entry is processed separately from the procedure for signing the policy. Stage 1 is the accounting procedure. Stage 2 is the policy signing procedure. (See also " S & A Procedure ".)

Series

The application of the franchise or deductible to a group, or series, of individual packages instead of to each package or on the whole shipment. This practice is seldom used today. (See also " Running Landing Numbers ".)

Service of Suit

Service of suit for claims against the carrier must be made within twelve months from the date of delivery or date the goods should have been delivered. By the " Gold clause agreement " the period for service of suit is extended to two years.

A service of suit clause in a policy is one whereby the insurer agrees to accept service of suit, in respect of a claim under the policy,

in another country. (See " Notification of Claim against Carrier ",
" New York Suable Clause " and " Gold Clause Agreement ".)

Services in the Nature of Salvage

Salvage services under contract of hire. These are not included in
the term " Salvage Charges " and may not be claimed as such under
the policy. Where properly incurred to prevent or minimise a loss
from an insured peril the costs of services in the nature of salvage
are recoverable under the policy directly as sue and labour charges
or indirectly by way of general average contribution, according to
the circumstances.

Settlement Calendar

A card, issued annually by Lloyd's Central Accounting Office,
that sets out the date each month for settlement, on balance, of
Underwriter's and Brokers' accounts in sterling, U.S. dollars and
Canadian dollars.

Settlement Date

The date each month by which the broker is required to settle
the balance due to Lloyd's Central Accounting Fund. Such dates
are published annually by Lloyd's on a card which is made available
to all Lloyd's brokers. A basis for allocating an entry to the settlement date is established by the L.P.S.O. signing number and date.

Settlement of Claims Abroad

With the insurer's agreement a policy or certificate can provide
for claims to be settled by a settling agent at a named place abroad.
This practice is fairly common in cargo insurance where the consignee prefers to collect any claim payable on the insurance in the
country of destination, rather than submit his claim to London.
The policy or certificate is marked C.P.A. (Claims Payable
Abroad) and the name and address of the settling agent to whom
claims should be presented is shown. Where there is no local
settling agent there may be a provision for the claim to be presented
to the nearest Lloyd's Agent; though not all Lloyd's Agents are
authorised to settle claims. In the absence of this agreement all
claims must be presented to the insurer in London. In the case of
Lloyd's, the claim must be presented through the medium of a
Lloyd's broker, though not necessarily the broker who effected
the insurance. A fee may be charged to the assured for the C.P.A.
service but this is often paid by the insurer. Lloyd's operates a
Settlement of Claims Abroad Office which acts for both Lloyd's
and British Insurance Companies. (See also " Red Line Clause "
and " S.C.A. ".)

Settlement Statement

Once every month Lloyd's Data Processing Services prepare settlement statements listing payments due to and from Lloyd's underwriters and brokers. The settlement statement to each syndicate includes entries in tabulations issued previously and the settlement statement to each broker includes entries in daily statements issued previously. Generally, settlements are in sterling, U.S. dollars or Canadian dollars only. Convertible currencies received by brokers are converted to sterling for payment to underwriters. The final dates for settlement by brokers are set out in a " calendar " issued annually by Lloyd's Central Accounting Office. (See also " Tabulations " and " Broker's Daily Statement ".)

Settling Agent

An agent authorised to pay claims under a policy. It is customary for the name and address of the settling agent to be specified in a marine policy where payment is permitted at any place other than the head office of the insurer. Usually such payment is only authorised where the assured or assignee is domiciled abroad so that the term " settling agent " in marine insurance becomes synonomous with " Claims payable abroad " agent. Cargo C.P.A. certificates make provision for settlements by a settling agent.

Settling Fee

If the assured so desires he may request the insurer to make provision for claims to be paid by settling agents overseas. The fees allowed to agents for these services are in accordance with a scale, laid down by the Committee of Lloyd's or the Institute of London Underwriters, when the settlement is in respect of a Lloyd's or an Institute policy or certificate. In the case of Non-Institute Company policies the Company makes its own arrangements regarding the fees. The settling fees are not, normally, charged to the assured, payment being made by the body laying down the scale.

Settling Tank

A tank used for separating water from fuel oil in a ship.

Several Ports of Discharge

Where the policy specifies several ports of discharge the ship must proceed to them in the customary order or in the order specified in the policy, otherwise there is a deviation. There is also a deviation if she does not proceed to ports, in a given area, in their geographical order unless it is customary to proceed in another order, or the policy otherwise provides.

S/Fee *or* **S/F**

Survey fee.

S.G.

Ship and goods. Refers to the basic policy form. Derives from the days when both ship and goods were insured by the same policy. Although policies are now printed on separate forms for ship and cargo the plain form for either is still termed the " S.G." form.

s.g.

Specific gravity.

Shafts

When a shaft in a ship is to be replaced the insurer is liable only to replace the old shaft with one of a similar age and quality. In practice, the insurer usually replaces with a new shaft, but he is under no obligation to do so. When submitting the claim a report must be made of what happened to the old shaft.

The " Negligence Clause " in a hull policy includes damage to the ship directly caused by the breaking of a shaft but does not extend to the replacement of the shaft itself. Of course, if the breaking of the shaft is proximately caused by an insured peril the replacement is recoverable under the policy, but if the breakage is due to a flaw or latent defect in the shaft the insurer is not liable to replace the shaft.

Shaft Tunnel

An enclosed space extending from the ship's propelling machinery to the stern tube. The propelling shaft is contained within the shaft tunnel.

S/H.E.

Sundays and holidays excepted. (See also " SHEX ".)

Sheathing

Wooden planks covering a ship's deck.

Sheer

The side of a ship from stem to stern down to the bilge keel.

Sheerstrake

A strake (see " Strake ") of shell plating that runs from stem to stern at deck level.

Shell Plating

Steel plates forming the sides of the ship.

Shelter Deck

A superstructure above the main deck. This may be " open " or

" closed ". A true shelter deck is " open ", which means it has a permanent opening in it whereby it is exposed to some extent to wind and waves. A " closed " shelter deck is one which was constructed as an open shelter deck but the opening of which has been fitted with a permanent means of closing. A closed shelter deck is treated as an ordinary deck.

Shelter Deck Steamer
A steamer having a shelter deck.

SHEX
Sundays and holidays excepted.

Shifting boards
Boards forming a partition in a hold for the purpose of separating cargoes which are liable to shift. Loose grain carriage necessitates the fitting of shifting boards. Without the boards the ship would become unstable.

Ship
Any vessel which is propelled other than by oars, but generally excluding very small sailing vessels.

Shipbrokers
Persons acting as agents for shipowners to arrange for charters, cargo carriage or passengers.

Shipbuilding Codes
Codes, comprising letters and figures, that indicate the type and features of a vessel under construction. These codes appear in shipbuilding lists under column headings. The first columns indicate the type of vessel (e.g. A.R.R. = Crane/derrick barge, river). The remaining columns show codes for other detail (e.g. M = motor propulsion, U.S. = U.S.A. flag, C.B. = converted barge).

Shipowner
The owner of a ship, or a person entitled to register as the owner of one or more of the 64 shares of a ship. For the purposes of ownership all ships are divided into 64 shares. To own a share in a British ship a person must be a British subject, either born or naturalised, or a citizen by a letter of denizenship. Alternatively a Company or Corporate body may own a British ship provided its head office is situated in the United Kingdom. Where a ship is owned jointly by several persons, each has his own rights individually although management is subject to a majority decision. If a minority objects to the decision of the majority, the majority must give a guarantee

of recompense to the minority should the ship be lost. If the vessel returns following such a guarantee the minority are not entitled to any profit from the voyage. Every shipowner or part owner has an insurable interest in the ship, but a shareholder in a shipping line has no insurable interest. It is usual for owners to appoint managers to operate the ship and shipbrokers to arrange the freight earning side of the business.

Shipowner's Interest

The shipowner has an insurable interest in the ship, its fittings. equipment and tackle. Further, he has an insurable interest in liabilities to the cargo owner and to third parties for damage to property or person or infringement of rights. He has an insurable interest in freight which he expects to earn and money for hire of the vessel, under charter or otherwise. Further insurable interests of the shipowner are disbursements, profit from use or loan of the ship, commissions payable for ship management, increased value of hull and machinery, premiums paid on time policies, returns of premium subject to " and arrival " and, finally, general average and/or salvage contributions.

Shipowner's Liability

There are two forms of legal liability which a shipowner may incur (a) contractual liability, or (b) liability in " tort ", that is, in the absence of contract; being generally called " third party " liability. The plain form of marine policy does not extend to cover either form of liability, but it is the practice for hull insurers to extend the terms of the policy to embrace third party liability consequent upon collision only and then only subject to specified limitations. Third party liability not embraced by the collision clause, also other forms of third party liability and contractual liability, are covered by P & I insurance. Liability can embrace not only actual damage but also infringement of rights, loss of benefits and any other loss suffered by the injured party as a result of the negligence of the shipowner but it is, nevertheless, only a direct liability and does not extend to losses suffered by other parties indirectly connected with the injured party or his property. An example of the latter would be where a ship caused damage to a specially equipped loading pier whereby another vessel suffered loss of contract by reason of being unable to load. The negligent shipowner's liability would only extend to the loss occasioned by the owners of the pier, not to the loss sustained by the other vessel. (See " Collision Clause ", " Protection and Indemnity Risks ", " Protection and Indemnity Club " and " Carriers Liability to Cargo ".)

Shipowner's Liability to Cargo
See "Carrier's Liability to Cargo".

Shipowner's Lien
See "Carrier's Lien".

Shipped Bill of Lading
As opposed to a "received for shipment" bill of lading, this document acknowledges that the goods have been shipped. The person sending the goods is entitled to demand a "shipped" bill of lading.

Shipper
The consignor or sender of goods by ship.

Shipper's Interest
See "Seller's Interest".

Shipping Intelligence Service
See Lloyd's Intelligence Department.

Shipping Note
A note sometimes sent to the wharfinger or other person in charge of the wharf. The note is not always required. It gives full details of the goods and when returned signed by the wharfinger the consignor knows his goods have been received for shipment.

Shipshape Rig
A mobile drilling rig which is basically an ordinary ship adopted to allow the rig to drill over the side or through a slot in the stern.

Ship's Log
The log kept by the Master giving details of the running of the ship and of any accident or unusual occurrence. Entries may be extracted from this log to substantiate a claim for damage to the ship or cargo.

Ship's Markings
A British ship must have its name marked on either side of the bows and on the stern. The Port of Registry must also be shown on the stern. To enable the draught to be seen a scale in feet must appear on the stem and on either side of the stern post. The loadline grid must be shown on either side of the vessel. The official number must be carved in the main beam, which is inside the ship.

Ship's Material Burned as Fuel
Same principle as "Ship's Stores Burned as Fuel".

Ship's Name
The name of a British ship is registered and cannot be changed

without permission from the Ministry of Transport and a recognised procedure of advertising in newspapers showing the intention to change in order to invite objections from owners of vessels having the same name as that proposed.

Ship's Official Number
The identity number of a ship, which remains constant no matter how many times her name is changed. The number is " carved " into the main beam. This is the main girder fitted across the ship at deck level just forward of mid-ships. If the main beam is inaccessible the number is cut into the after end of the forward hatch coaming. A " Carving Note " is issued certifying that the number has been cut into the ship.

Ship's Papers
Certificate of Registry, Log Books, Articles and Muster Roll. If under charter, the Charterparty. If carrying cargo, the Bills of Lading and Manifest. If required, a Bill of Health.

Ship's Register
See " Certificate of Registry ".

Ship's Stores Burned as Fuel
A claim may be made in general average for ship's stores burned as fuel, but it is only allowable where there was ample fuel on board to enable the ship to complete the voyage under normal circumstances. The ship must rebunker if it is possible, but, in any case, any allowance in general average must be credited by the shipowner with the current price of fuel equal to the consumption of ship's stores.

Shipt.
Shipment.

Shore
A timber wedge used in drydocking or other circumstances, to shore up a vessel so that she remains upright when not afloat. (See " Drydock ".)

Short.
Shortage.

Shortage
A form of non-delivery. Non-delivery refers to the failure of a whole package to arrive at the destination without any evidence to show the cause of loss. To establish a claim it is necessary to show documentary proof that the lost property was in fact loaded. Shortage occurs when part of a package or bulk cargo fails to arrive. The

policy covers neither non-delivery nor shortage unless they are specified perils. A policy specifically covering non-delivery but not specifying either shortage or short-delivery does not cover these extra perils. Many bulk cargoes are insured against shortage, which is arrived at by comparing shipped and unloaded weights. A claim should be made by the consignee against the carrier for shortage.

Short Closing

The practice of closing a line on a policy for less than the amount written by the insurer on acceptance of the insurance. This practice is readily acceptable to the insurer because it arises from " overplacing " which is part of the system of " spreading the risk ". It may also occur on a cargo insurance when the amount shipped is less than the insured value.

Short Delivery

See " Shortage ".

" Short " Form of Indemnity

The form signed by the insurers of a vessel in order to indemnify a Surety or Bonding Company who have provided a libel bond to release a vessel threatened with arrest. In exchange for the indemnity the Surety Company will agree to reduce the rate of the bond premium. (See " Libel Bond " and " Surety Company ".)

Short Interest

Floating policies are seldom to be seen in practice today but when they were common the term " Short interest " was used to denote the outstanding balance of the amount insured by the policy when the last declaration had been made. A return of part of the deposit premium might by payable on the short interest.

Short Rate

The rate of premium on a time policy is agreed, as a rule, on an annual basis. A short premium rate, pro rota of the annual premium rate, is the rate charged for a period of less than 12 months.

Short Sea Tonnage

Vessels engaged on coastal and local voyages.

Short Shipment

A shipment where only part is loaded. The unloaded part is often termed " left out " or " shut out ". (See also " Short Closing ".)

Short Term

A period of insurance for less than 12 months.

Short Ton
Weight measurement of 2,000 lbs. (Metric ton is 2204·60 lbs.)

Shut Out
Cargo which has not been loaded on the ship when she sails. (See " Short Shipment ".)

S.I.
Sum insured *or* short interest.

S/I
Sum insured.

Side Frame
A steel girder, at the side of a ship, to which the shell plates are riveted, forming the hull of the vessel.

Sifting Clause
A clause used in insurance of flour providing that the insurer will pay the cost of sifting the flour to remove insects if so infested. The clause may also cover loss in weight due to the sifting. Additional expenses in connection with the sifting are covered, but deterioration, delay, loss of market or profit, are specifically excluded.

Sighting the Bottom
Examining the underside of a ship. The Insurer pays any expense incurred for this following stranding whether or not damage is found.

Signature on Policy
A marine policy must be signed by or on behalf of the insurer. A Corporation may use its Corporate Seal instead, but a Corporation is not compelled to use its Seal and may simply sign the policy. Where a policy is signed on behalf of several insurers (see " Combined Policy ") the contract is separate between each insurer and the assured.

Signed
A term indicating that a policy has been signed. (See also " Take Down ".)

Signed Line
The insurer's subscription signed on the policy. Where the risk is closed prior to the issue of a policy, it is the line on which the paid premium is calculated. Same as the " closed " line.

Signer
Another term for " Signing Slip ".

Signing A.P.

An endorsement attached to a Lloyd's policy to add a new syndicate to the existing risk.

Signing Number and Date

It is impracticable for L.P.S.O. to number all documents consecutively indefinitely or even over a short period. Accordingly, in general, documents are numbered in ranges that recommence daily. The date on which the number is allocated is added to the number to give it a unique quality; thus it is important when quoting an L.P.S.O. reference number to quote also the date that accompanies it. Reference numbers allocated at the I.L.U. are in ranges that recommence annually.

Signing Slip

A slip copied from the original slip together with all the underwriter's lines and references. It is used purely for presentation to the relevant policy signing office in order that the original slip may be retained in the broker's office for reference. Signing slips are used to sign policies off open covers, open slips and treaty reinsurance contracts. Sometimes called an " off slip ". A signing slip is initialled by the leading Underwriter to authorise its acceptance by the relevant signing office. Where Lloyd's and Companies appear on the same original slip it is customary for a separate signing slip to be issued, by the closing broker, for each market but when this is done it is necessary to indicate on each signing slip the proportion of the risk that is closed in other markets.

Signing Table

The list of subscribing syndicates, lines and references that Lloyd's Policy Signing Office attaches to a policy.

Simultaneous Payments Clause

A reinsurance clause. The clause provides that the reinsurer shall pay a claim at the same time as the claim is paid on the original insurance. Without this clause the reinsured must show that he has paid the claim already before he can claim on his reinsurance. The clause is used, frequently, in connection with " fronting " insurances. (See " Fronting Company ".)

Single Liability

The basis on which Admiralty Rule provides collision settlements should be made. (See " Cross Liabilities ".)

Singleton Policy

A combined Company policy form issued in respect of one Company only.

Sister Ship Clause

If a ship is involved in a collision with, or receives salvage services from, a sister ship no claim can be legally made upon the owner of the assisted vessel for liability or salvage contribution. This is because a man cannot sue himself. By the sister ship clause in a hull policy the insurer agrees to settle claims for liability or salvage charges as though the sister ship were owned by a third party.

Sk.

Sack.

Skeleton Case

A form of crate constructed of wooden slats. Earthenware and similar are carried in straw or other soft packing inside skeleton crates. This type of case while providing the necessary protection makes the fragile nature of the contents clear to those handling the cases. The case may sometimes contain one or more spars to support the contents.

Skimming

The act of removing damaged berries or beans. The cost of skimming is paid by the insurer where the damage is caused by an insured peril.

S/L

Sue and labour charges.

S.L.

Salvage loss.

Slacks

Slack packages or sacks. When packages or sacks arrive slack by reason of shortage of the contents they are referred to as "slacks". The loss is generally considered to be "shortage" and is recoverable under a policy covering this peril. Care should be exercised to ensure, however, that the slacks are not due simply to loss in weight, which is not embraced by "shortage". This can usually be ascertained by a comparison with other sacks arriving in the same consignment.

Slamming

The impact of water on the bow of a vessel as it emerges and re-enters the water in heavy seas. A blunt ended vessel, such as a barge, can suffer severe damage from "slamming".

S/L.C.

Sue and labour clause.

Sld.
Sailed.

Sld.a.p.l.
Sailed as per list.

Slinging
The act of loading or discharging by slings. The term also applies to the charge made for fitting slings.

Sling L.
Sling loss.

Sling Loss
Loss of cargo by falling from slings when being loaded or discharged. This is generally a total loss of part. Sling losses are particularly prevalent in surf ports where discharge is carried out into lighters or small craft.

Slings
Chains or metal netting enclosing cargo in order that it may be hoisted onto or discharged from the ship. In some cases heavy rope netting is used. (See " Sling Loss ".)

Slip
See " Original Slip " and " Signing Slip ".

Slip Agreement
An agreement expressed by an underwriter on a broker's slip at a date subsequent to the acceptance of risk. Such agreement has no more legal value than the slip itself and compliance is based on the principle of good faith. There is a standard form of slip agreement, used in the Lloyd's market, for attachment to the standard slip; one version of which is the honeycomb slip. (See " Honeycomb Slip ".)

Slip Policy
For years the work and expense of preparing full policies on S.G. forms for reinsurances continued even though the market found this onerous. In 1963, however, the marine insurance market in London agreed that both hull insurers and reinsurers would be satisfied that the slip should be used as the policy provided it bore a prescribed form properly stamped with a sixpenny stamp and showing the identifying details of the reinsurance. When marine stamp duty was abolished in 1970 the practice continued without the need for a revenue stamp on the slip. This form to be signed and/or sealed by the relevant signing office.
Once issued, the slip policy is retained in the broker's office and

the broker sends to the reinsured a cover note stating full details of the reinsurance and showing the reinsurer's proportions. During 1974 it was agreed to extend the slip policy procedure to embrace cargo insurances, in general, where the assured does not require a policy. In such cases the assured will rely on a certificate of insurance to replace the functions of a policy. Where a slip policy is issued it is understood that a formal policy will be issued if it is required for legal proceedings.

Slip (Shipping Term)
A berth in which a ship is constructed.

Slop Barge
A vessel designed to take waste oil and oily water from a tanker thus reducing the risk of pollution to the sea. The barge is equipped to separate oil from water, the latter being discharged into the sea. The waste oil is taken ashore for processing.

Small Additional or Return Premiums Clause
A clause applying to sterling business only which provides that an additional or return premium of £2.00 or less, as an adjustment of a deposit premium or of an alteration in coverage or rate or for any other reason, shall be waived. This clause is necessary where the cost of processing the entry is more than the advantage gained from the payment.

Small A/P or R/P Clause
See " Small Additional or Return Premiums Clause ".

Small Claims etc. Pool Scheme
Lloyd's market operates a " Small Claims and Recoveries Pool Scheme " the purpose of which is to reduce the expense of processing small entries. An entry that does not exceed £4.00 (U.S. $10.00, Canadian $10.00) per syndicate, on average, over the risk is paid into or out of a central pool which is funded by a general contribution from all syndicates. Certain business (e.g. treaties, excess of loss R/I contracts, S.C.A. bulk entries) is excepted from the scheme.

Small Craft
See entry " Boat ".

Smoke Damage
This is recoverable under the policy as damage by fire.

S/N
Shipping note.

S/O
Shipowner.

S.O.L.
Shipowner's liability. (Which see.)

Sold Vessel
See "Change of Ownership" and "Depreciation".

S.O.S.
Service of suit. (Which see.)

Sound Value
For the purpose of arriving at the amount due from the insurer in the event of partial loss of goods it is necessary to determine the sound value at the destination.

To obtain equity, it is necessary to estimate the *gross* sound value of the goods, so that a comparison can be made with the *gross* damaged value in order to apply the difference as a percentage of depreciation. In the case of hull it is not necessary to find the sound value for partial loss claims because the reasonable cost of repairs is payable without reference to the actual value of the vessel. It is usual to obtain a certificate of sound value when assessing the contributory value of the vessel with regard to general average or salvage contributions. Contributory values on cargo are calculated on net values . (See "Gross Value" and "Net Value".)

Southern Latitude Warranty
One of the Institute Warranties whereby the insured ship is prohibited from proceeding south of 50° S lat. The ship may only enter the prohibited area when it is necessary to reach her destination on a voyage from a place outside the area to another place outside the area. The warranty also prohibits Crozet and Kerguelen Islands.

Southern Range Ports
Ports U.S.A. (Atlantic Coast); Georgetown and south thereof.

Sparred
A system of packing goods for carriage. Wooden spars are used to support goods such as hollow ware and to keep them rigid during loading, transit and discharge.

Sp. chgs.
Special charges.

Spd.
Sparred.

Special Charges
See "Particular Charges", "Sue and Labour", "Sale Charges" and "Survey Fee".

Special Settlement
A procedure available to brokers in the London market whereby signing and/or accounting procedures are given priority at the relevant policy signing office. The procedure allows a claim to be paid outside the normal monthly settlement and usually within seven days.

Special Survey
Regular surveys are carried out periodically on both hull and machinery to enable a ship to maintain its class. The special survey is carried out by the Classification Society at four yearly intervals, dependent on the regulations of the Society.

Special Terms
An expression used to denote any special conditions imposed on the insurance by the insurer. Most insurances are effected on basic conditions customary to the particular type of risk. "Special terms" are in addition to the basic conditions. They may also be referred to as "special conditions".

Special Wordings Scheme
See "S.W.S.".

Specie
The term specie is used in two completely separate ways in marine insurance. The Marine Insurance Act 1906 refers to "specie" in the expression "loss of specie", (See entry "Loss of Specie"). The term "specie" is also used as a collective noun to embrace all forms of valuables carried as cargo, including precious metals, gems, money, banknotes and valuable documents.

Specification
Details of work to be carried out to repair damage to a ship. This is submitted with tenders.

Specific Exclusion
A specific exclusion is one which is printed, typed, impressed on or written into a policy. A specific exclusion need not necessarily reduce the cover afforded by the policy. It may be there merely to draw to the attention of the assured the fact that the policy does not cover the excluded peril. For this reason the deletion of a specific exclusion does not incorporate into the policy, even by implication, the peril which is the subject of the exclusion. The deletion merely

reverts the policy to the cover afforded before the exclusion was specified.

Specific Inclusion

A specific inclusion is a condition or term which is printed, typed, impressed on or written into the policy to the effect that the conditions are extended.

Speedboat Clauses

See " Institute Speedboat Clauses ".

Spontaneous Combustion

May occur when fibrous cargoes, such as jute, are loaded in a damp condition or when such cargoes contain an excessive amount of oil or grease, as may be the case with baled dirty wool. Soft coal, or lignite, is also liable to spontaneous combustion if loaded wet.

This is inherent nature and no claim is recoverable under the policy on the cargo which is subject to the spontaneous combustion. Fire damage to other cargoes or to the ship is recoverable under the policies applicable to such other cargo or ship as a loss by fire. (See " Statutory Exclusions ".)

Spotting

Mildew or staining on soft leather goods, such as gloves, due to damp. (See " Spotting Clause ".)

Spotting Clause

A clause used on policies covering soft leather goods such as gloves. The clause excludes claims due to spotting or staining unless caused by the vessel being stranded, sunk or burnt.

Spreading the Risk

One of the basic principles of insurance. An insurer is not prudent if he retains all his liability in one vessel or location because by so doing the chance of loss is greatly enhanced. It is better to accept a tenth part of ten insurances than the whole of one insurance because, although the premium income is the same, the risk is considerably lessened. It is for this reason that an insurer usually accepts only part of a slip which is offered to him, thus spreading the risk over a number of insurers. The broker furthers the spread of risk by " overplacing " and " short closing ". Spread of risk is also attained by means of reinsurance. Reciprocal reinsurance, not common in the marine market, is for this purpose.

Spudding

Bedding the legs of an off shore drilling rig in the seabed. (See " Jack Up ".)

Spt.
Lloyd's Register notation indicating that a superheater is fitted to the main boilers.

S.R. & C.C. *or* **s.r. & c.c.**
Strikes, riots and civil commotions.

S.R.C.C. & M.D.
Strikes, riots, civil commotions and malicious damage.

S.R.L. *or* **S.R. Liab.**
Ship repairer's liability.

S.S.M.U.A.
Steamship Mutual Underwriting Association Ltd. A protection and indemnity club.

s.s.o.
Struck submerged object.

S.S. or B.
Stranded, Sunk or Burnt.

s.t.
Steam trawler.

Stability
Control of pitch and roll whereby a ship remains buoyant and manoeuverable.

Stamp Duty
Prior to 1st August 1970 every marine policy had to bear a revenue stamp to conform with Stamp Act laws. Since that date stamp duty on marine policies has been abolished.

Standard
A measurement for cargoes of timber. A St. Petersburg standard is 165 cubic feet.

Standard Form
The form of marine policy normally used. This is based on the Lloyd's S.G. form.

Standard Form of Salvage Agreement
See " Lloyd's Form of Salvage Agreement ".

Standard Marine Clauses
Clauses published by the Institute of London Underwriters for use in the marine market. These clauses are acceptable to both

Lloyd's and Company underwriters. Often referred to as " Institute Clauses ".

Standard Policy Form
See " Standard Form ".

Standard Slip
A standardised form of broker's slip used by brokers placing business at Lloyd's or with Institute Companies. The slip comprises not less than two panels, each panel being exactly 4.75 inches wide and with an exact height of either 8.27 inches or 10.00 inches, at the broker's option. The slip provides pre-positioned boxes in which administrative detail is entered in a prescribed format. The positioning of placing detail is controlled also. The slip is designed to reduce the risk of error during data processing. A separate standard slip has been devised for R/I treaties.

Starboard
The right hand side of a ship facing forward. The term derives from the use of a starboard (steering board) fixed permanently to the right hand side of a sailing ship to assist steering through shallow water. A similar board (a leeboard) was used on the opposite side to prevent the ship from making too much leeway, but the leeboard was removable or hinged, to enable the ship to berth on that side. (See " Port ".)

Statistical Statement
When negotiating a long term reinsurance contract, such as a reinsurance treaty the broker has to produce certain statistical data for the reinsurer's assessment of the risk. Lloyd's publishes a standard form for this purpose under reference L.P.O. 205.

Statistics
See " Experience "

Statutory Exclusions
The Marine Insurance Act, 1906, Sect. 55, provides that certain perils are excluded from the marine policy. It emphasises that for a loss to be recoverable it must be proximately caused by an insured peril and that losses not proximately caused by an insured peril are not recoverable, thus giving practical effect to the principle of Proximate Cause (which see herein).

Further, the Act goes on to specify certain particular perils which are excluded. Loss *attributable* to the wilful misconduct of the assured is excluded. Note that the loss does not have to be *proximately caused* by misconduct to be excluded, only *attributable* to it. Since a loss attributable to wilful misconduct or negligence of master or crew could be deemed to be that of the shipowner, the Act goes on to say such losses when proximately caused by an insured peril are not excluded, though, of course, if the shipowner was directly responsible for the action of the master or crew such loss would remain excluded. Nothing in this section of the Act protects an innocent cargo owner in event of misconduct of the shipowner, but this situation is remedied in practice by the second part of the " Seaworthiness Admitted Clause " which appears in all cargo policies.

Loss proximately caused by delay, even when the delay results from an insured peril, is excluded. This exclusion may be waived by the acceptance by the insurer of a special clause in the policy to cover the risk. In the absence of such a clause deterioration of perishable goods, such as foodstuffs, is not covered by the policy.

Wear and tear, ordinary leakage and ordinary breakage are excluded, so is inherent vice or nature of the subject matter insured (each of these terms is defined elsewhere herein).

Loss proximately caused by rats or vermin is excluded, as also is injury to machinery (meaning ship's machinery which suffers mechanical breakdown) when it is not caused by maritime perils.

Std.
Standard.

Steamer
A steamer may be coal or oil burning. If the goods are likely to be carried by a motor vessel the original slip details should include " and/or M.V.".

Stem
The metal casting that is at the extreme forward end of a ship.

Stemming
Arranging bunkers for a ship.

Sterling AP/RP Waiver Scheme
A procedure designed to cut out uneconomic work in accounting very small additional and return premiums. The underwriter agrees to waive small APs and the insured agrees to waive small RPs, in sterling, where the total amount to be calculated over the whole risk does not exceed £2.00. The Small AP/RP Clause must be attached to the policy.

Stern
The end of a ship opposite to the stem.

Stern Thruster
A small propeller, positioned at the stern of the ship and at right angles to the main propellers. The stern thruster is used for manoeuvring the ship over a small area.

Stevedore
A contractor for labour at a port of loading and discharge.

Stev. Liab.
Stevedore's liability.

Stiffening
Taking on ballast or heavy cargo to give a ship stability.

Stop Loss Reinsurance
A form of treaty reinsurance. It is a type of excess of loss treaty but, in place of the normal provision of cover for excess of loss over a retention, the stop loss reinsurance covers all losses in excess of the net premium income to the ceding insurer. The treaty is on an annual basis and a deposit is paid on placing, to be adjusted at the end of the year on an agreed percentage of the reassured's net premium income. No declarations are made. This form of reinsurance protects the reassured from sustaining a loss on the year's underwriting account.

Stoppage in Transitu
When a seller of goods finds that payment is unlikely and the goods are already en route to the buyer he has the right of "stoppage in transitu". By this right the seller can stop the delivery of the goods at destination. The right is extinguished if the voyage is ended or if the goods have already been sold by the buyer to another person.

Storage of Cargo
The expense of cargo stored as part of a general average act is allowed as general average. Resultant damage is also allowed as general average. (See "Expenses at Port of Refuge".)

Stores Consumed for Removal
Ship's stores consumed for removal of the vessel for repairs, or used for repairs, are included in the reasonable cost of repairs.

Stowage Plan
Plan of ship showing how cargo is stowed. This is important when planning the unloading of the cargo.

Str.
Steamer.

Straddle Carrier

A carrier used in dock area to move containers. The carrier suspends the container between four straddling legs, a wheel being at the base of each leg. The operator sits in a cabin above the hoisting device. (See also " Transtainer ".)

Strake

A continuous course of shell plating or deck plating on the hull of a ship.

Strand

To strand. Applies to a vessel and means to be hard and fast for an appreciable period of time. " On a strand " means " stranded ".

Stranding

The term does not include bumping over a bar, a mere touch and go or a grounding by reason of the rise and fall of the tide. The vessel must be hard and fast for an appreciable period of time.

In hull insurance it is normal for a policy to contain the "Customary Strandings clause " which provides that groundings in certain specified areas shall not be deemed strandings. Thus, the cost of sighting the bottom is not covered by the policy in the case of such groundings. (See also " Grounding ".)

Strd.

Stranded.

Strikes Clauses

Institute clauses drafted specially to cover damage to or loss of the insured property caused by strikers, locked out workmen, rioters, persons acting maliciously, or in civil commotions. The clauses pay claims irrespective of percentage. The cargo clauses exclude loss due to delay, inherent vice, the withholding of labour or the absence or shortage of labour. The hull clauses exclude delay.

Strikes etc. Risks

See " Strikes, riots and civil commotions ".

Strikes Expenses

Expenses incurred by a carrier and passed on to the cargo owner when, by reason of a strike bound destination port, the goods are discharged at another port. The term also embraces expenses incurred by the cargo owner to carry the goods to the original destination from the place where the carrier terminated the adventure. The cargo policy does not cover these expenses. An insurer may be prepared to cover strikes expenses as a separate insurance, but it is usually necessary to effect this insurance on a time basis (say, all the assured's shipments over 12 months) because insurers will not readily accept the risk once a strike has commenced. This is sometimes referred to as " Additional Expenses—Strikes ".

Strikes, Riots and Civil Commotions

The plain policy form does not cover these risks, except where rioters attack a ship from the shore when they are designated as "pirates". To make the lack of cover clear to a cargo assured all cargo policies contain a strikes exclusion clause which excludes the above perils. In practice, it is usual to extend the policy to nullify the exclusion and to incorporate the risks of strikes, riots, civil commotions and malicious damage into the cargo policy by payment of a scale additional premium. The risks are usually incorporated in conjunction with war risks, the additional premium being increased to cover both sets of risks. The risks of strikes, riots, civil commotions and malicious damage are, in a like manner, incorporated in the war policies on hull and freight. Claims under any of these clauses are payable irrespective of percentage.

Stringer

A strake (see " Strake ") of deck plating that runs fore and aft at the side of the ship's deck.

Stripping Clause

A clause contained in a policy covering branded goods. In event of non-agreement regarding the percentage of depreciation assessed by a surveyor it may be necessary to sell the damaged goods to establish the actual loss by comparing the amount realised with the sound value of the goods sold.

To protect the reputation of the makers or producers the assured will usually insist on the wrappers being removed before sale. The clause provides that the insurer shall be liable for the cost of removing the wrappers. The clause is not a " standard " clause and may, therefore, be in any form which is agreed between the parties to the contract. It may also include a provision that the insurer shall pay the difference between the amount realised by the sale and the insured value of the goods sold.

Strong Lead

Expression used by a broker to indicate that the underwriter who has given the quotation of rate is one whom the broker feels has such influence in his acceptance that other insurers will readily follow his lead so that the insurance may be placed with little difficulty. This is purely the broker's opinion and in no way binds him to complete the placing, although it is unlikely that a broker would use the expression unless he were certain of completing.

Structural Alterations

When a ship is undergoing structural alterations and a claim for a " lay up " return is made she is deemed to be " under repair " for the purpose of arriving at the port risk retention.

Stuffing a Container

Filling a container with cargo. (See also " Groupage ").

Subject Approval No Risk

The insurer inserts the initials S.A.N.R. (subject approval no risk) on a slip when the terms and/or rate on the slip may not be acceptable to the assured. It is more or less a provisional placing subject to the acceptance by the assured of the terms and rate. It is obligatory on the assured not to delay in his acceptance or refusal.

Subject Matter Insured

The insured interest. In a cargo policy this would be the " goods ". In a hull policy it would be the " ship and machinery ". In a freight policy, the " freight ". In a policy the subject matter must be designated with reasonable certainty so that it is readily identifiable.

Submersible

A vessel submersed below the surface of the sea and resting on the sea bed. Submersibles are used for research on the sea bed and researchers can live in them for long periods. They are not normally movable vessels, such as a submarine is, but some can be moved to a limited degree.

Submersible Rig

An off shore drilling rig, comprising a number of pontoons that are towed into position at the drilling site then sunk to the seabed, from whence they support the drilling platform through vertical columns. (See also " Semi-Submersible Rig ".)

Subrogation

The right of the insurer to any remedies which the assured may have against third parties wholly or partly responsible for the loss in respect of which a claim has been paid. Under subrogation rights the insurer is entitled to any recovery obtained by the assured and any recovery which he himself may obtain in the assured's name. The maximum amount to which the insurer is entitled under his subrogation rights is the amount of the claim paid. Any amount in excess of the claim which the insurer may recover must be paid to the assured. This ruling does not affect any amount which the insurer may obtain by the disposal of what remains of property following a total loss claim, which amount he may retain in addition to any recovery under subrogation rights.

Subrogation Form

A form of subrogation. A standard form used to obtain the agreement of the assured to the insurer pressing a claim for recovery from a third party which claim would normally be made by the assured. The insurer automatically has rights of subrogation by statute without the form, but it is often more satisfactory to obtain the form of subrogation before pressing a claim, since it obviates the necessity of proving subrogation rights.

Subscription

The extent to which the insurer is liable under a policy which is signed on behalf of several insurers.

Substituted Charges

If any expense is incurred which reduces the liability of the insurer in respect of extra charges or enhanced ordinary charges the insurer is in a like manner liable for the substituted charges.

Substituted Expenses

In both general average and particular average, substituted expenses are allowed to replace losses or expenses that would be recoverable under general average or under a policy. In either case, however, the substituted expenses are allowable only up to the saving in ordinary loss or expenses. Reference to substituted expenses allowed in general average can be found in Rule F of the York-Antwerp Rules 1974. Substituted expenses in particular average on ship are usually removal expenses and overtime in carrying out repairs. In general average they may indicate the expense of moving the vessel to a different port to reduce the cost of G.A. repairs.

Sub. U/wrs. App.

Subject to Underwriter's approval.

Successive Losses

The Marine Insurance Act 1906 provides that the insurer under a marine policy is liable for successive losses even though the aggregate of such losses may exceed the sum insured by the policy. This does not generally apply to cargo because the damage is assessed at destination and the policy pays either a total loss or single partial loss. The principle does, however, apply to a hull time policy where the measure of indemnity for partial loss is simply the reasonable cost of repairs without any reference to the insured value. The insurer pays the cost of all repairs to make good damage from an insured peril, subject only to the limit of the insured value and the policy deductible in respect of any one accident or occurrence.

Thus, in a time policy successive claims for repairs may possibly in the aggregate exceed the insured value. If damage is not repaired and a total loss occurs the insurer is liable only for the total loss. If the total loss is proximately caused by an uninsured peril the insurer is not liable for either the unrepaired damage or the total loss.

Suction Dredger
See " Dredger ".

Sue and Labour
It is the duty of the assured to act at all times as though he were uninsured and to take such measures for the preservation of the insured property as a prudent uninsured person would take. To this end he may sue, labour and act in defence of the property without prejudice to his rights under the policy. This means that he may take any reasonable action or incur any reasonable expense to prevent or minimise a loss. Provided the loss which is minimised or prevented is proximately caused by an insured peril the insurer will reimburse the assured for such expense as he may so incur, whether or not the action taken is successful. Under this principle, the insurer is liable for sue and labour charges in addition to a subsequent total loss. Such charges can only be incurred by the assured or his servants or agents and must be incurred short of destination. They are payable under the policy without reference to the franchise, if any (e.g. in a cargo W.A. policy). In hull insurance, subject to the I.T.C., sue and labour expenses are recoverable from insurers, subject to the policy deductible. Sue and Labour charges are recoverable under a policy even if no loss occurs. Sue and labour charges can be incurred only for the benefit of the subject matter insured. If they are for the common benefit they are not sue and labour but may be recoverable as general average.

Sue and Labour Charges
Charges recoverable under a policy pursuant to the terms of the sue and labour clause. Since the sue and labour clause is a supplementary contract it is not affected by other losses to the property nor by undervaluation of the insurance, in the absence of any special agreement in the policy. The Institute Time Clauses provide, however, in clause 9 that any undervaluation shown must result in a reduction, in the same proportion, of any sue and labour charges payable under the policy. The I.T.C. also provide that Sue and Labour charges shall be subject to the policy deductible.

Sue and Labour Clause
A clause appearing in all marine policies providing that the in-

surer is liable for sue and labour charges. (See " Sue and Labour ".) The clause is supplementary to the contract so that the charges are payable whether or not there is a loss of the insured property.

Suez Canal Clause

A clause appearing in a hull policy where the insurer pays the cost of sighting the bottom following stranding. The Suez Canal Clause specifies certain geographical locations where grounding shall be deemed not to be a stranding for the purpose of cost of sighting the bottom. (See " Customary Strandings " and " Sighting the Bottom ".)

Suitcasing Anchors

The operation of lifting anchors on behalf of a lay barge which is pipe-laying on the seabed. The operation is conducted by an anchor laying tug. (See " Lay Barge ".)

Sufferance Wharf

A wharf where the loading and discharge of dutiable and other particular goods is permitted by the Customs Authorities.

Suing and Labouring Clause

See " Sue and Labour Clause ".

Sum Assured

Sum insured.

Sum Insured

The maximum amount of liability of the insurer under the policy. The measure of indemnity for total loss. The sum insured by a policy is the total of the signed lines (if more than one) in that policy. Usually the sum insured is for the same amount as the insured value but where it is for a smaller amount all claims paid by the insurer, whether partial or total loss, are reduced in the same proportion. The premium rate is applied to the sum insured to determine the policy premium. Return premiums are calculated in the same manner.

Summary Form

A form (LPO. 132) used in the procedure for collecting claims through Lloyd's American Trust Fund. The form is completed by the broker and summarises the details of the letter of credit transaction.

Sunk

If a sunken ship results in only partial loss of cargo the franchise warranty is broken even for damage not caused by the sinking.

Supercargo

A superintendent of cargo who travels with the ship.

Superintendent

A person appointed by a shipowner in connection with repairs to the ship. The expense of a superintendent is part of the reasonable cost of repairs.

Supertanker

A very large vessel (say, 100,000 tons or more) designed to carry large quantities of liquid cargo, such as oil. In 1973 such vessels, valued at U.S. $80 million, were insured in the London market and these enormous values in single vessels created many problems; not the least of which was market capacity to absorb the values. Usually the premium rate on large vessels is relatively low compared with the rates for smaller vessels, but the formula used for supertankers does not, necessarily, produce a reduction in rate as size increases.

Supplementary Contract

A supplementary contract is one where the limitations of the basic or underlying contract are repeated in the supplementary contract. A section of a marine policy which is deemed a supplementary contract has a separate limit in the sum insured under the policy so that the insurer may find himself liable up to 100% of the policy limit under the basic or underlying policy and *in addition* up to 100% of the policy limit under the supplementary section. The " Sue and Labour Clause " and the " Collision Clause " are deemed to form supplementary contracts. (See also " Further Agreed ".)

Supply Boat

The term can be applied to any vessel that supplies the needs of a larger vessel. Such vessels supply stationary drilling rigs and, on occasions, carry personnel to and from the rig.

Supra

A legal term meaning " as dealt with previously in the book or document ".

Surety Company or Bonding Company

A Company approved by the U.S. district courts which can post libel bonds to effect the release from arrest of vessels libelled " in rem ". The consideration for the company's so doing is called the bond premium. (See " Libel Bond " and " Short Form of Indemnity ".)

Surf Port

A port having a shallow approach which not only necessitates discharge into small craft but also creates a swell that makes discharge difficult. Discharge is generally by slings which must be handled expertly to avoid sling losses. (See " Overside Port ".)

Surplus Line

The amount of reinsurance required after having declared the maximum line on a treaty or cover. In the U.S.A. it also refers to risks which the producing broker is unable to place with Companies resident in his own State and for which he must therefore make arrangements outside the State. In these States it is obligatory by law that the business must be first offered to the Companies within the State. This applies mainly to non-marine business.

Surplus Line Reinsurance

Generally this is Treaty reinsurance and is the same as excess of line reinsurance. The original insurer has an agreed retained line and cedes the surplus of his acceptance to his reinsurers. The reinsurers are only prepared to take such surplus up to a fixed limit any one line. If this limit is not sufficient to take the whole surplus written or anticipated by the original insurer it may be necessary to effect a second or even third surplus line reinsurance.

Survey Before Shipment

The carrier briefly examines goods before shipment in order that he will not issue a "clean" bill of lading for goods damaged or improperly packed. This is not a survey. A survey is carried out at the insurer's request on cargoes which are insured for deterioration or where the guarantee of quality or quantity on arrival is covered. A survey certificate is issued by a surveyor approved by the insurer and this is conclusive evidence of soundness and/or full measure on loading.

Survey Clause

A clause contained in a cargo policy which specifies an amount under which claims properly recoverable will be paid without incurring the expense of a survey.

Survey Fee

The fee payable to a surveyor for his services in carrying out a survey and issuing a survey report. Primarily the payment of the survey fee is the responsiblity of the assured because it is part of the assured's expense in proving the loss. If no claim is payable by the insurer the fee is paid by the assured. If a claim is paid, however, the insurer also pays the survey fee, as it forms part of the claim. Even though the survey fee is considered as part of the claim it cannot be added to damage to reach a franchise or an excess. In hull insurance a survey fee for sighting the bottom of the vessel is payable in practice by the insurer when incurred specifically for the purpose of looking for damage following stranding.

Survey Handbook

Published by Lloyd's this book is for the guidance of surveyors and average agents in relation to damaged goods. It gives information on commodities and advice on surveys and treatment of damaged goods.

Survey of Machinery

Since the hull insurer is not liable for wear and tear or for ordinary breakdown of machinery, any claim for machinery damage warrants an immediate survey. No claim can be entertained unless the machinery is properly surveyed as soon as is practicable after the occurrence resulting in the claim.

Surveyor

A competent person with the knowledge and skill to carry out a survey on the insured property and to produce a survey report. (See " Survey Fee " for charges.) In cases of a report being needed on cargo when the insured property is overseas it is usual for the insurer to instruct, via the broker, that the nearest Lloyd's Agent be requested to arrange a survey. The surveyor is then appointed by the Lloyd's Agent, whose choice is accepted by the insurer. In some cargo insurances the insurer may require that a certain surveyor is appointed and this is usually specified in the insurance certificate in such cases.

Surveyor's Report

A claims document. The report submitted with a claim giving details of the damage to the insured property. This applies to both hull and cargo insurance although in hull insurance it is usual to have both the report of the underwriter's surveyor and of the owner's surveyor. In some cases the report of the Classification Society's surveyor is also available. A survey report need not necessarily apply only to claims as a report may be required on a sound vessel or a report of soundness and/or packing on loading may be required on cargo. A survey on arrival may not result in a claim, in which case the cost of the survey is payable by the assured. The cost of the survey is a particular charge on the policy if there is a claim, but if no claim is payable the charge falls on the assured; though, where the insurer instructs the surveyor, he usually pays the cost even if no claim arises.

Survey Report

The report made by the surveyor appointed to examine damaged goods or damage to a ship. The survey report gives the place and date of the survey. It also gives details of the cause and extent of the damage. Estimated cost of reconditioning and/or repairing, if any, will be included. In the case of cargo the report includes details of values, invoices, bills of lading, protest, packing, marks, numbers, weights, possibility of recovery in general average or from the carrier, percentage of depreciation (if necessary), sale details (if any), method of carriage (if relevant to the damage), rate of exchange on day of sale if necessary. In the case of ships it is usual to have reports from the surveyors acting for the insurer, the shipowner and the Classification Society. The report gives the estimated cost of repairs and the surveyor's recommendations. A survey report is also necessary in the case of constructive total loss of either ship or cargo.

S.V.
Sailing vessel.

S.W.
Shipper's weights.

S.W.D. *or* **s.w.d.**
Sea water damage.

Sweat Damage
Changing temperatures cause the ship's plates in the holds to "sweat". That is, condensation forms on the inside of the holds. This can cause damage to baled cargoes and to other cargoes vulnerable to water damage. Sweating is particularly likely to occur when the ship in a humid climate encounters heavy weather so that hatches are battened down and ventilators closed. It is, however, best to leave ventilators closed for cargoes which do not need ventilation, such as manufactured metal goods, because warm moist outer air drawn in through the ventilators will condense on the cold surface of the cargo in the cool hold and may result in sweat damage. This is not a peril covered by the plain policy but the insurer may agree to extend the policy to cover the risk.

S.W.S.
Special wording scheme. A scheme operated by Lloyd's Policy Signing Office whereby special wordings agreed by certain leading underwriters are coded and printed so that supplies are available for the use of brokers. This ensures uniformity in agreed conditions and saves a great deal of checking time. The term " Private Wording Scheme " may be used, also.

Sympathetic Damage
Damage caused to the insured cargo by another cargo, not by

actual contact, but because some reaction of the other cargo following damage to it taints or indirectly affects the insured cargo. The policy does not cover this peril except where it can be shown that the damage to the cargo causing the taint was proximately caused by an insured peril under the policy covering the cargo with the taint damage.

Syn. *or* **Synd.**
Syndicate.

Syndicate
A Lloyd's Syndicate is formed by a Lloyd's Underwriting Agency. It is a group of underwriting members at Lloyd's who are invited by an Underwriting Agency to offer a consolidated facility in which each member accepts his proportion of liabilities accepted on behalf of the syndicate by the active underwriter. The active underwriter, appointed by the Underwriting Agency, may be a member of the Syndicate or a salaried employee.

In the syndicate list, a copy of which is held at Lloyd's Policy Signing Office, each underwriting member is referred to as a "name" and his proportion of the syndicate's total liability is recorded. No individual member is responsible for any other member's liability but no member is permitted to limit his/her liability to any part of his/her assets, the whole of which can be called upon by the Committee of Lloyd's to satisfy his/her liability.

Although a syndicate is recognised by the pseudonym and number allocated by L.P.S.O. to that syndicate, it is referred to in practice by the name of the active underwriter, or by the top name on the list of members. It is not customary for English marine insurance Companies to form syndicates, though some Companies may form a group and use the services of a single active underwriter to accept liabilities on behalf of the group. A Lloyd's policy does not list every name in a syndicate but indicates the subscribing syndicate by listing their pseudonyms and syndicate numbers, with the appropriate proportion of liability and reference against each syndicate's pseudonym and number. (See "L.S.R." and "Lloyd's Underwriter".)

Syndicate List
A list of the syndicates subscribing a Lloyd's policy. The list shows each syndicate's signed line, pseudonym, syndicate number and reference. (See also "L.S.R.".)

Syndicate Reinsurance
See "Syndicate R/I".

Syndicate R/I

A reinsurance of liabilites written on behalf of a Lloyd's syndicate. This may be placed at Lloyd's or with an Insurance or Reinsurance Company or Companies. The procedure for debiting or crediting Lloyd's Underwriters, as reinsureds, is effected through the media of Lloyd's brokers, Lloyd's Policy Signing Office, Lloyd's Data Processing Services and Central Accounting.

Syndicate R/I Procedure

A procedure involving Lloyd's Policy Signing and Data Processing Services whereby the broker, having submitted a debit or credit note to the reinsured syndicate, submitted a copy of the debit or credit note to L.P.S.O. in order that the accounting procedure may be effected via Central Accounting. The normal signing and accounting procedures are used for settlement to the reinsurers.

Syndicate Sheet

A large sheet of flimsy paper showing the structure of each syndicate at Lloyd's. Prior to 1970 a copy of the current sheet was attached to every Lloyd's policy but the practice has been discontinued. A list of current syndicates is retained at L.P.S.O. for reference and copies of the current list are available to Lloyd's brokers.

Synopsis Sheet

A document used in Lloyd's non-marine claim settlement, though sometimes seen in the marine market where an element of non-marine risk may be written.

T

T.

Lloyd's Register notation that the ship has triple expansion engines. This letter on a loadline grid indicates the loaded water line for tropical waters. The same expression is used to indicate a twin screw ship.

Table of Limits

A list attaching to a contract of treaty reinsurance or a facultative cover detailing the maximum limit of liability of the insurer in any one category of risk. The ceding insurer (the reassured) must not declare, under the treaty, lines in excess of the expressed limits. In the case of cargoes the limits are specific for each type of cargo and means of carriage. In the case of hulls each limit is applied to a group of vessels of a certain class, tonnage, type and trade.

Tabulations

Accounting entries processed through L.P.S.O. and Central Accounting are advised to the interested syndicates on advice cards. (See " Advice Cards ".) The cards are accumulated in batches at Lloyd's Data Processing Services and the details included in each batch are listed on a tabulation for each interested syndicate. A tabulation, accompanied by the advice cards to which it refers, is despatched to the syndicate periodically (e.g. once every three days). The tabulation is a provisional advice. Settlement is effected on the figures shown on the monthly settlement statement; not on the figures shown on the tabulation. (See " Underwriters Tabulations ".)

Tacit Renewal Clauses

A clause in a long term contract whereby annual renewal is automatic unless the underwriter gives notice of his intention not to renew at the anniversary date. Usually, the notice period is not less than 30 days and, in some cases (e.g. reinsurance treaties), may be 90 days.

Tail Series

If the franchise is calculated on the damage to cargo discharged in series a fixed number of packages to each series is agreed. When the total number of packages is not an exact multiple of the fixed number each series the last packages discharged will not amount to a full series. These are treated separately as the " tail series ". In applying the franchise to the tail series it must be remembered that the franchise amount must be reduced to compare with a full series.

390

Tail Shaft

The extreme aft section of a propeller shaft.

Taint

Cargo may become tainted either by being stowed in close proximity to another cargo which is likely to taint it or by the action of damage by seawater or other cause to another cargo which in turn causes such other cargo to taint the insured cargo. The insurer is not liable for taint damage unless the policy is extended to specifically include the risk. If the taint arises through the former cause above there is probably a liability by the carrier for bad stowage. In the latter case the claim might be recoverable under the policy if it can be proved to be proximately caused by an insured peril.

Take Down

A term used in policy signing and accounting. It is the act of making an entry for accounting purposes. Thus, a signing office may " take down " a premium or additional premium; giving it a reference number (see " Number and Date "). The same term is used when accounting entries are made for claims, refunds and return premiums.

Tale Quale

As it arrives. Expression used particularly in the grain trade, agreement to which means that the buyer will accept the cargo in the condition in which it arrives without question as to quality or soundness. The terms are subject to a satisfactory certificate of quality at the port of shipment. Usually these terms are acceptable only where grain is carried in dry cargo vessels and not in tankers. (See also " Rye Terms ".)

T. & C.C.

Technical and Clauses Committee.

T & G

Tongued and grooved. Applicable to boards in timber carriage.

T and/or C.T.L.

Total and/or constructive total loss. Slip abbreviation.

t. and s.

Touch and stay.

Tanker

A vessel specially designed for the carriage of liquid cargo. Propelling machinery is aft and a tanker may be recognised by the cat-walk raised above the deck. A loaded tanker is usually low in the water with decks frequently awash in heavy weather. The sealed cargo compartments give the vessel remarkable buoyancy and since the hull is divided into numerous sealed tanks such a vessel is very unlikely to sink, even when holed. In view of the separate sealed compartments a tanker does not need to be fitted with a double bottom, except under the engine room space. (See also " V.L.C.C. " and " U.L.C.C. ".)

Tanktainer

A cylindrical container used for transporting liquid in bulk.

Tank Top

The upper plating of a double bottom in a ship.

Tare

Weight of a container. This may apply to wrapping, boxes, crates, drums or even wagons.

Target Risk

American expression denoting a large risk which is shared by most of the market.

Tariff

A system of rating used in non-marine insurance. The rating schedule is arrived at by actuarial computation and is used by tariff Companies. A non-tariff Company is one which sets its own rates and does not follow the tariff. Lloyd's underwriters are generally non-tariff and the marine market does not have a tariff.

T/Atl.

Trans-Atlantic.

Tax Clause

A clause in a policy which provides that in the event of returns of premium being paid any tax allowed by the insurer on the policy premium shall also be deducted from the return of premium. This provision does not apply if the policy is cancelled by insurers and the original tax paid is not recoverable from the Government imposing the tax.

Tax Paid Clause

A clause in a policy providing that the insurer will allow a deduction from the premium in respect of tax paid by the assured by reason of effecting the insurance.

T.B.A.

" To be advised " or " To be agreed ". (e.g. " Vessel to be advised " or " Rate to be agreed ".)

T.C.A.T.L.V.O.
Total or constructive or arranged total loss of vessel only.

T.C.I.
Time Charterers Interest.

Tcs.
Tierces.

Tdg.
Trading.

T.D.W.
Tonnage Deadweight. (See " Deadweight ".)

Tear of bags
A policy containing this expression covers shortage of the insured interest due to the bags being torn. It does not include replacing the torn bags.

T.E.C.H. Cargo
The abbreviation relates to " Toxic, Explosive, Corrosive or Hazardous Cargo " and is used in reference to a cargo possessing such hazardous properties which constitute a threat to the environment, particularly in the event that spillage occurs which may result in damage to other property or to pollution. (See "Dangerous Goods " and " Pollution ".)

Technical and Clauses Committee
A Committee formed of Lloyd's and Company Underwriters which meets to discuss and to draft clauses for the use in the marine insurance market. These clauses are known as " Institute Clauses ".

Technical Services Group
A group of individuals at L.P.S.O. whose function is to provide technical advice on insurance matters and to provide guidelines to the market on current procedures relating to L.P.S.O.

Telemotor
Part of a ship's steering gear. The telemotor operates the control valves that, in turn, control the rudder movement.

Temporary Repairs
Where a ship is in a port where repairs cannot be effected or where the insurer does not wish repairs to be carried out it is usual to effect temporary repairs to make the ship seaworthy in order to remove her to the repair port. When the cost of the final repairs is recoverable under the policy, the cost of temporary repairs is also recover-

able. The policy does not cover the cost of temporary repairs which are effected purely for the shipowner's convenience. So far as general average is concerned temporary repairs are allowed only when necessary for the common safety. Where temporary repairs of accidental damage are effected in order to enable the adventure to be completed the cost of such repairs is allowed in general average but only up to the saving in expense which would have been allowed in general average if such repairs had not been effected. New for old deductions are not applied in general average in respect of temporary repairs.

Tender Clause

A clause in a hull policy which places an obligation on the assured immediately to notify the insurer of any accident which may result in a claim under the policy. A surveyor must be appointed with the insurer's approval and the insurer reserves the right to decide the port of repair. Invitations to tender must be sent to repair firms and no tender must be accepted without the insurer's approval. Non-compliance with the clause entitles the insurer to deduct 15% from any claim. The insurer may require the assured to invite further tenders, in which case, any loss of time due to awaiting such further tenders entitles the assured to a recovery from the insurer for the time lost from the date of the sending of invitations to tender to the date of the acceptance of the successful tender. The allowance is pro rata, for the number of days lost, of 30% of the insured value of the vessel per annum.

Any recovery from elsewhere in respect of "loss of use" for the same period must be set against the allowance from the insurer which is reduced accordingly.

Tenders

Applications submitted by repair firms giving the estimate of the cost of repairs to a damaged ship. A specification of the damage and repair work accompanies the tender. (See "Tender Clause".)

Term

Period covered by the insurance.

Termination of Adventure

In a cargo voyage policy this is the place where the insurer's liability ceases because the goods have arrived at their destination or cover ceases within the terms of the transit clause. Under a contract of affreightment it is the place where the carrier's liability ceases. Under a hull voyage policy it is the place where the voyage is completed and the vessel has "arrived". Under any form of time policy it is the time when the policy expires.

Termination of Adventure Clause
A clause in a cargo policy which continues the cover where the adventure is terminated, in circumstances beyond the assured's control, short of destination. The continuance of cover is subject to prompt notice to the insurer and to payment of an additional premium if required by the insurer. The cover terminates when the goods have been sold and delivered to some other place or when the goods arrive at their original destination. If the goods are sold in circumstances other than as above cover ceases when the goods leave the port for the buyer's transit, a time limit of 60 days from midnight on the day of discharge being imposed. If the goods are forwarded to any destination within the 60 days' limit, as above, the insurance continues until it terminates within the terms of the transit clause.

Terminus a Quo
Attachment of risk. (Legal term.)

Terminus ad Quem
Place of arrival (i.e. termination of risk). A legal term.

Term Policy
Policy written for more than 12 months. A short term policy is one written for less than 12 months.

Terms
Conditions and rates to which the insurance is subject.

Terms of Credit
Periods of credit allowed for payment of premiums, claims etc. Lloyd's lays down a maximum period during which the broker must pay the premium or additional premium into Central Accounting. These terms are set out in the " Operating Scheme " which is published by L.P.S.O. and is circulated to all Lloyd's brokers and underwriters. Generally the period allowed for payment is five months from the attachment date of the risk. The leading underwriter enters the attachment date, or deemed attachment date, on the original slip. The date entered is not necessarily the actual attachment date of the risk but varies according to the type of insurance or reinsurance and the currency involved.

T.F.
Loadline grid marking indicating the loadline for tropical freshwater.

Theft
The actual breaking open of cases or theft of a whole case or

package. It does not embrace clandestine theft or pilferage by members of the crew.

Theft, Pilferage and Non-Delivery

A standard wording is applicable to these risks whereby claims by these perils under the policy are payable irrespective of percentage. (See also " Theft ", " Pilferage " and " Non-Delivery ".)

Thieves

This peril includes only assailing thieves, that is persons boarding the ship and breaking in with the intention of theft. It does not include clandestine theft, nor theft by passengers or crew.

Third Party Liability

In law, everyone has a responsibility to avoid actions which may cause damage to the property of others or loss to other persons. Legal liability to make good such damage or loss can occur where the party at fault is negligent and, where no contract exists between the parties involved, this is termed " third party liability ". The plain form of marine policy does not cover third party liability, but the assured has an insurable interest in respect of such liability and the policy may be extended to cover this. The hull policy is extended in practice to cover collision liability. Salvage contributions, general average contributions and sue and labour payments are not third party liabilities because they are for the preservation of the property and are not incurred by negligence. Third party liability, other than collision liability, is usually covered in P & I clubs although separate policies may be placed in respect of specific liabilities. The measure of indemnity for third party liability is the amount of the liability, subject to any limitation imposed by the policy. (See also " Collision Clause ", " Collision Liability " and " Omnibus Clause ".)

Thirds

" Thirds " new for old means the specified deductions by which the insurer is allowed to reduce any hull claim for the difference between the old material damaged and the new material replacing it. In practice this right is waived and hull insurers do not make such deductions.

Third Ship in a Collision

Where the insured ship incurs a collision liability not only for damage done to another ship but also for damage done to a third or further ships in the same occurrence the liability of the insurer under the collision clause extends to the liability to all the other ships. The policy limitation applies to the occurence and not to each liability so that the insurer is not liable for more than three-fourths (or four-fourths in some policies) of the insured value in respect of one occurrence. The claim is subject to the policy deductible.

Thirty Days Notice
The usual period of notice, under an open cover or open policy, required to enable the insurer or assured to cancel the contract.

Three Year Accounting System
A system by which the figures are calculated to establish the annually published accounts at Lloyd's. Each year the affairs of each syndicate are audited but the results are not published for any one year until a further two years' accounts have been recorded. This allows outstanding claims, attaching to the year of account, to be brought into the calculation so that a more accurate picture of the state of the account emerges.

Thro. B/L
Through bill of lading.

Through Bill
Through bill of lading.

Through Bill of Lading
A bill of lading which does not cease when the goods are discharged. It attaches as soon as the goods are in transit to the port of loading and continues after discharge until they arrive at the destination inland. Although the carrier usually makes all arrangements and charges freight throughout on a " through bill " he generally makes it clear that before loading and after discharge the goods are at the cargo owner's risk.

Thrust Block
A steel block situated at the forward end of the shaft tunnel to take the thrust pressure of the propeller as it is transmitted along the shaft and to transfer this pressure to the body of the ship rather than to the engine bearings.

Ticket
Master's or ship's officer's certificate. (e.g. Master's Ticket, Mate's Ticket, etc.)

Tierce
A measure of capacity of 42 gallons.

Tight, Staunch and Fit
Expression used in shipping to indicate that the ship is seaworthy.

Time Charter Hire

The money paid by a charterer to the shipowner for the hire of his ship for a period of time. The charterer has an insurable interest in time charter hire and also in the profit which he expects to earn by use of the vessel.

Time Charterparty

A contract or agreement whereby the shipowner hires out his ship for a period of time to another person.

Time Clauses

Sets of hull clauses covering periods of time. (See " Institute Time Clauses ".)

Time Hire Freight

Time charter hire.

Time on Risk

An internal arrangement at Lloyd's used for short term or voyage risks where the risk has expired before the policy is signed and there are no claims on the insurance. By this system no policy is actually signed and the slip is marked T.O.R.

Time Penalty Clause

The Marine Insurance Act 1906 provides that the insurer on ship or goods is not liable for losses proximately caused by delay but it does not mention the insurer on freight. To remedy this the time penalty clause appears in freight clauses providing that the insurer shall not be liable for losses consequent upon loss of time.

Time Policy

A policy covering a period of time. Prior to the Finance Act 1959 any marine time policy issued for a period exceeding 12 months was invalid. The relevant section in the Marine Insurance Act 1906 (Section 25. Sub Sect. 2) was repealed by the Finance Act 1959 so that this time limit no longer applies.

T.L. *or* T/L

Total loss.

T.L.O.

Total loss only.

T.L.O. excs. *or* T.L.O. & Exs.

Total loss only and excess liabilities. (See " Excess Value ".)

T.L.O. R/I Clause

Total loss only reinsurance clause. This clause incorporates into a hull reinsurance policy all the terms and conditions of the original policy; but claims under the reinsurance policy are payable only in respect of total or arranged or compromised or constructive total loss. The equivalent clause for cargo is the F.P.A. R/I clause.

There are various types of this clause used in the marine hull market. Generally, they limit the liability of the insurer to pay only for total loss of the vessel including constructive total loss and/or arranged total loss and/or compromised total loss. Without the last two types of loss being specified the reinsurance cover would be limited to actual total loss and constructive total loss. It is also customary to specify whether or not sue and labour and salvage charges shall be recoverable. The clause may, further, contain conditions regarding the application of additional premiums to follow the original policy. It is customary to exclude war risks although strikes risks may be covered as and if in the original policy.

T.L.R.
" Times " Law Reports. This ceased publication in 1952.

T.L.V.O.
Total loss of vessel only.

Tomming Off
Shipping term used in respect of stowage. The use of wedges to prevent movement of cargo in circumstances where a space is left between the cargo and the ship's side or a bulkhead.

Tonkang
A small craft used for lighterage in the Far East.

Tonnage
The capacity of a ship. (See " Gross Registered Tonnage " and " Net Registered Tonnage ".)

Tonnage Dues
Payments due from a shipowner when his ship is in ports and canals for the use of facilities such as marker buoys etc. Such payments are based on the tonnage of the ship.

Tonnage Marks
An open shelter deck, that is one with openings not permanently closed, entitles a vessel to a reduced tonnage by virtue of such openings, known as " tonnage openings ". The Merchant Shipping (Tonnage) Regulations, 1967 provide that alternative tonnages may be allocated and tonnage may be assessed by examination of the " tonnage marks " on the side of the ship. The submersion or non-

submersion of a mark will indicate the correct tonnage to apply. Thus the reduced tonnage of the ship will not be prejudiced because tonnage openings are permanently closed for safety reasons.

Tonnage Slip

A slip of paper which is one of the documents required to be lodged with Customs on clearance outwards, showing details of tonnage paid or payable.

Tonner Reinsurance

See " Tonners' Risk ".

Tonners' Risk

A form of reinsurance, covering total loss only, of vessels over a certain specified tonnage or between specified tonnages, accepted by the reinsured. The terms of the reinsurance may provide for one or more total loss, possibly in excess of one or more total loss; and probably with a maximum number of total losses overall if more than one total loss is covered by the reinsurance. For convenience it is customary to effect a " tonners' reinsurance " on P.P.I. terms so it is not a legally enforceable form of insurance. (See " P.P.I. ".)

Tons

Cubic ton (displacement)	= 33 cubic feet of sea water.
„ „ (for measuring ship tonnage—gross or net).	
	= 100 cubic feet.
Ton, laden	= 40 cubic feet.
Long ton	= 2240 lbs.
Metric ton (tonne)	= 1000 kilogrames (2204.60 lbs.)
Short ton	= 2000 lbs.

Tons Burden

The normal tonnage of a ship is measured in 100 cubic ft. per ton. Tons burden are measured in 40 cubic ft. per ton.

To Pay as Cargo

A term used in a policy covering increased value of cargo, usually insured on a P.P.I. basis. It means that where a loss is shown to be recoverable under the cargo policy the increased value policy pays in the same proportion without the need to show that the value of the cargo had, in fact, increased. (See " Increased Value (Cargo) ".)

To Pay as may be Paid Thereon

See " Pay as May be Paid ".

Top Hamper
An excess of superstructure above the weatherdeck of a ship.

T.O.R.
Time on risk.

Tort
An action in tort is a legal action arising in the absence of a contract. Claims under the collision clause come in this category.

Tortfeasor
The person against whom an action in tort is brought. The negligent shipowner or manager in a collision case would be a tortfeasor. (See "Joint Tortfeasors".)

Total Loss
Loss of the subject matter insured either as an actual total loss or a constructive total loss resulting in the payment of the total sum insured under the policy. Except where the policy states otherwise (an unlikely event), all marine policies cover total loss; though some policies may exclude partial loss. The term total loss includes a constructive total loss unless the policy specifies otherwise. A total loss claim, on a policy that covers partial loss which turns out subsequently to be only a partial loss may still be claimed as a partial loss, even though it was submitted by the assured as a total loss. (See "Actual Total Loss" and "Constructive Total Loss".)

Total Loss of a Craft Load
See "Total Loss of Part".

Total Loss of a Whole Package
See "Total Loss of Part".

Total Loss of Part
Total loss is not necessarily confined to the complete loss of the whole property insured, particularly where cargo is concerned. Where a cargo policy is on F.P.A. terms (virtually total loss only) it is customary to provide that the total loss of a whole package in loading or discharge or the loss of a whole craft load shall be recoverable under the policy as total loss of part. The same principle is applied where the franchise is concerned on a W.A. policy, such losses being treated as total losses and not subject to the franchise.

Total Loss of Vessel Only
A term usually applicable to a total loss policy on disbursements etc. It means that the sum insured by the policy will be paid as a

claim only if the vessel is a total loss. No claim is payable if the subject matter insured becomes a total loss but the vessel does not.

Total Loss Only

A term used in hull insurance and reinsurance. Strictly, the use of the word "only" implies that additional expenses such as "sue and labour charges" and "salvage charges" are not covered but to avoid argument on this point, it is customary to state in the T.L.O. Clause whether or not such charges are recoverable. (See "T.L.O. R/I Clause", "Total Loss" and "F.P.A.".)

Touch and Stay

Expression which may appear in a marine policy whereby the ship is permitted to call or stay at any customary ports on the route although they are not specified in the policy. It does not permit the ship to deviate from her route.

Tourist Floater

An American Inland Marine form covering baggage and personal effects of tourists and travellers.

T.O.V.A.L.O.P.

An abbreviation for "Tanker Owners' Voluntary Agreement Concerning Liability for Oil Pollution". This is an agreement subscribed by some 90 per cent of the world's tanker industry whereby each member agrees to remove persistent oil discharged from his tanker and to reimburse national Governments for expense incurred in cleaning up oil pollution resulting from the owner's negligence. The member is obliged to show his ability to meet such demands, usually by entry in a P & I or similar mutual Association. The agreement provides for a limit of liability which in 1971 was $10 m per ship or $100 per g.r.t., whichever was the less of the two. Some Governments have introduced laws that provide for a higher limit than the Agreement. Insurers are not, generally, prepared to accept the liability at present. (See "Amended R.D.C.", "Cristal" and "Pollution".)

Tow

The ship being towed by a tug.

Towage

The act of towing a vessel. (See "Tug and Tow", "Tower's Liability" and "Tow and Assist".)

Towage Bill

Account in respect of costs of towage of the insured ship.

Towage by the Insured Vessel
See " Leave to Tow ".

Towage of the Insured Vessel
The ship may be towed when in need of assistance or when it is customary for her to be towed, such as in a port or harbour. It is a breach of warranty under the " tow and assist " clause if the ship is towed for any other reason.

Tow and Assist Clause
A clause, in a hull policy, whereby towage is restricted. The clause in the I.T.C. (Number 3) is in two parts (a) and (b).

Part (a) allows the insured vessel to sail and navigate at all times with or without pilots, to go on trial trips and to assist and tow vessels or craft in distress. Nevertheless, there is an express warranty that the insured vessel must not be towed except (i) where towage is customary (e.g. when manoeuvering in a port area for loading and discharge) or (ii) when in need of assistance and then only to the nearest safe port. The second part of the clause (b) excludes claims for damage to the insured ship or liability to the other ship arising from loading or discharging operations which take place at sea (See " Ranging "); this latter not applying to such operations between the insured ship and a barge or lighter or similar craft normally used for offshore loading and discharge. The insurer may agree to waive the restriction in the second part of the clause subject to prior notice, an amended deductible (or other terms) and and additional premium. It should be noted that breach of warranty as regards towage and trade is held covered by the Breach of Warranty Clause (which see).

Towers
Persons engaged in the towage of vessels.

Tower's Liability
The main liability which a tower may incur is in respect of damage caused by a collision between another vessel and the tug or the tow, or contact by the tug or tow with a pier or other object. A tower's liability clause is, therefore, a form of collision clause covering liability for damage to other vessels and objects.

Tow. liab.
Tower's liability.

T.P. *or* **T.P. liab.**
Third party liability.

T.P.N.D. *or* **T.P. & N.D.**
Theft, pilferage and non-delivery.

T.P.N.S.D.
Theft, pilferage, non and/or short delivery.

T.Q.
Tale quale.

Tr.
Lloyd's Register notation indicating a triple screw ship.

Trade Association Clauses
See " Trade Clauses ".

Trade Clauses
Cargo clauses used on policies for specific trades, e.g.
Corn Trade F.P.A. Clauses.
Timber Trade Federation Clauses.
Coal Clauses.
Flour " All Risks " Clauses.
Rubber Trade Clauses.
Sugar " All Risks " Clauses.
Jute Clauses.

Trade Losses
Losses incurred by cargo without the operation of an insured peril, being losses which are common to a particular trade. Examples would be evaporation of oil or breakage of glass. (See " Ullage " and " Breakage ".)

Trade Ullage
See "Ullage ".

Trading Warranties
See " Institute Warranties ".

Tramp
Vessel not engaged on a regular run. A vessel engaged on a regular run is called a " Liner ". Tramps are mainly engaged in carriage of bulk cargo. Passenger accommodation, if any, is limited in tramps.

Transfer to New Management
See " Change of Ownership ".

Transhipment
Taking goods off one vessel and loading them onto another. Where transhipment is beyond the control of the cargo assured the policy continues under the " transit clause " without additional

premium, unless the insurer has stipulated an additional premium to be paid in the event of transhipment or the assured was aware of the intended transhipment when the insurance was effected and the insurer was not. If the assured is aware of the intention to tranship he must advise the insurer at the time of effecting the insurance or there is non-disclosure of a material fact, unless transhipment is customary for the particular voyage and should be known already to the insurer. There is more danger of partial loss during loading and discharge than during the voyage. It follows that transhipment increases this danger and calls for an additional premium.

In the event of transhipment due to the operation of an insured peril the insurer's liability continues, by the provisions of the Marine Insurance Act 1906, whether or not the "transit clause" is incorporated into the policy.

Cargo insured against war risks is subject to the Waterborne Agreement but, where goods are transhipped to another overseas vessel, limited cover is allowed on land during transhipment provided the goods do not leave the area of the transhipment port. The limited period is 15 days from the date of arrival at the transhipping port; following the expiry of which, cover against war risks is suspended until the goods are loaded onto the on carrying overseas vessel.

Transhipment Bond Note
A document required by Customs in respect of dutiable goods during transhipment. It is evidence of security given for the duty payable in the event of the goods remaining in the Country instead of being transhipped.

Transhipment Entry
Customs entry in respect of dutiable goods in transhipment.

Transire
A coastal shipping document detailing goods taken on board.

Transit
Movement. Goods are in transit when they are en route between the place where the adventure started and the destination, including customary periods of hold up for Customs, loading, discharging etc. This is the normal course of transit. If there is unreasonable delay the goods are no longer in the normal course of transit. The expression covers all customary forms of transport, but if the means of transport is not customary for the particular voyage or journey then this is not considered the normal course of transit.

Transit Clause

The transit clause was incorporated into the Institute Cargo Clauses as from 1st January 1963 following the decision of the case "Martin v Russell 1960". It has always been the intention of the insurer that cover continued only during the normal course of transit. When the goods were placed in a warehouse prior to delivery at the destination named in the policy with the intention of not sending them on to their destination it was always contended by the insurer that this was outside the normal course of transit and that the insurance should cease on delivery to such warehouse, unless the insurer agreed to continue cover. The warehouse to warehouse clause was designed with this principle in mind but in the case of "Martin v Russell 1960" it was held that the clause did not interpret the insurer's intention, which caused insurers to redesign clause 1 of the Institute Cargo Clauses and name it the "Transit Clause (incorporating the warehouse to warehouse clause)".

The transit clause states that the cover attaches when the goods commence transit by leaving the warehouse or place of storage at the place named in the policy and continues during the ordinary course of transit until it terminates on delivery at the final warehouse or place of storage at the place named in the policy. If, however, prior to or at destination the goods are delivered to any other warehouse or place of storage which the assured elects to use, other than in the ordinary course of transit, or for allocation or distribution, then cover terminates upon delivery of the goods at such alternative place. In the event of the final delivery not taking place within 60 days cover ceases on expiry of such 60 days, dating from completion of discharge overside of the goods from the oversea vessel at the final port of discharge. If, the goods, after discharge, are to be sent to another destination the insurance terminates, other than as above, when the transit commences to such destination.

The above definition relates to the Transit Clause in the standard Institute Cargo Clauses which are intended for marine sendings. From 15th June, 1965 a new set of clauses was issued for air sendings. This new set is entitled "Institute Air Cargo Clauses (All Risks)" and contains a transit clause similar to the marine clause. In the Air clauses, however, the words "incorporating the warehouse to warehouse clause" are omitted from Clause 1 and the limit of sixty days in the marine clauses is reduced to thirty days in the Air clauses.

Translocation Policy

This is an American form of policy covering the output of a factory. It applies from the raw material to the finished article. All

MARINE INSURANCE TERMS 407

risks of inward and outward transit, storage and location risk at depots are incorporated in the policy. Processing and manufacturing risks are not covered.

Transom
A transverse side frame situated at the extreme aft of the ship.

Transtainer
A transporter for containers. A transtainer is used during loading and discharge or for transit of containers within port or terminal areas. (See also " Straddle Carrier ".)

Transverse
At right angles to the fore and aft centre line. (A term used in ship construction.)

Transverse Metacentre
See " Metacentre, Transverse ".

Trawler
Fishing vessel which uses a conical shaped net, kept open by a trawl beam, and towed by the trawler just above the seabed. Such vessels stay at sea for long periods.

Treaty
See " Treaty Reinsurance ".

Treaty Balance
The balance between debits and credits in a treaty statement.

Treaty Number
A reference number allocated by a signing office to a reinsurance treaty. L.P.S.O. allocates such a number when the first accounting entry is processed. The number remains constant throughout the life of the treaty; being carried forward with each year.

Treaty Reinsurance
The insurer has an insurable interest in respect of his liability for the risks he has written and he may reinsure this liability. Many Companies, particularly foreign Companies, find that it is prudent to accept large lines and to reinsure, rather than to accept only small lines. They do not wish to run the risk of inability to reinsure, nor do they want the work involved in obtaining individual reinsurances. It is the practice, therefore, for them to effect a form of open cover reinsurance to take a proportion of all or a particular branch of their business. A contractual agreement is made and this is called a reinsurance treaty. Periodically, usually monthly or quarterly, bordereaux are issued showing the lines closed on the original insurances

written by the reassured and these are sent to the broker operating the treaty. It is usual for the reinsurers to agree to accept the original rates charged by the reassured, less original discounts and an overriding commission to cover the reassured's overheads. An agreed discount on the net premium is allowed by the reinsurers to the operating broker as brokerage. To encourage good underwriting a profit commission is allowed to the reassured on the treaty's annual profits. The main types of reinsurance treaty are:— (1) Flat Line (2) Quota Share (3) Excess of Line (4) Excess of Loss (5) Stop Loss. In practice, Excess of Loss is usually handled as an annual reinsurance rather than on a treaty basis.

Treaty Wording

The detailed conditions applicable to a reinsurance treaty contract. Most treaty wordings follow a standard pattern; incorporating clauses relating to advices, settlement, claims procedures and limits, reserve provisions, arbitration, etc. The wording contains consecutively numbered articles and must be signed by both parties to the agreement. L.P.S.O. may be authorised to sign the wording on behalf of Lloyd's underwriters. It is customary for two originals of the wording to be signed, with copies, as required, for use by L.P.S.O., I.L.U., brokers, etc.

Tret

Depreciation and/or wear and tear allowance.

Triatic Stay

A wire stay fitted between two masts, on the fore side of the aft mast and on the aft side of the foremast. (See also "Forestay" and "Backstay".)

Tribs

Tributories.

Trim

The difference of draught forward and aft of a ship. If the ship has a deeper draught aft she is said to be "trimmed by the stern" and vice versa "trimmed by the head". (See "Metacentre, Longitudinal".)

Trinity House

The Organisation responsible for lighthouses, light ships, beacons, buoys, lifeboat services, pilots and other aids to navigation around the coasts of the British Isles.

Trip Insurance

American expression denoting an insurance on a single journey as opposed to a period insurance. Mainly applies to non-marine.

True Sterling
The correct sterling equivalent of a convertible currency entry. When an insurance entry was closed at Lloyd's in the Category 3 procedure (now abolished) the currency was exchanged at L.P.S.O. to notional sterling and advised as such to the relevant Lloyd's Syndicates. In due course when the correct rate of exchange was known the broker would advise the true sterling amount to L.P.S.O. who would advise the underwriters of the difference if, on average, the entry difference exceeded £7.50 per syndicate. This procedure exists today only in the E.S.A. procedure.

Truss
A bale of hay, of approximately 56 lb., or of straw of approximately 36 lb.

Trustees in General Average
Persons appointed to look after the general average fund. There are two trustees, being appointed respectively by the shipowner and the cargo owners.

T/S
Transhipment.

" T " Scheme
A procedure operated at L.P.S.O. whereby a broker is not required to submit L.S.R. details with an entry advised under the scheme. The signed lines, syndicates and references (L.S.R.) are registered at L.P.S.O. before any declarations, under a long term contract, are made and a reference number is allocated. The detail is stored in a computer from which it can be extracted when an item is processed.

T.T.
Telegraphic transfer.

T.T.F. Clauses
Timber Trade Federation clauses.

TTY *or* **Tty**
Treaty.

" T " Type Tankers
The most numerous of the " T " type tankers from wartime U.S.A. were those designated the " T2 " type—over 500 being built between 1943 and 1945.
There were several differing T2 variations, but all had the same

dimensions. They were of approximately 10,400 g.r.t., and were the first vessels to adopt mass-produced turbo-electric propelling machinery. With some vessels such machinery was more powerful than in the majority, and so gave a greater speed.

These vessels were preceded by a series of fast tankers for Oil Company account—but most were absorbed into naval service. They were joined by other similar vessels and later many were released for commercial trading. Certain of these faster were known as the "T3" type.

In post-war times many "T" type ships survived to serve in their original form. Others have been converted or "jumbo-ised" into bulk carriers, container ships, liquified gas carriers and other specialised types and in the process may have been given "the full treatment" of lengthening, widening and deepening; of new or not so new bows, midbodies and sterns. They have been renewed, rejoined and rebuilt until now a converted "T" type hull may contain sections from three or four different vessels.

Of the coastal tankers from this wartime period, the largest were of the T1 design. These, generally, were diesel-driven ships of similar appearance and were of approximately 3,100 g.r.t. (Further details may be obtained from "Wartime Standard Ships" the forthcoming Volume 5 by W. H. Mitchell and L. A. Sawyer, published by the Journal of Commerce and Shipping Telegraph Limited.)

Tug

The vessel engaged in towing another vessel or craft. Same as "Tower". The other vessel is called the "Tow".

Tug and Tow

The "Tug" is the vessel which is towing. The "Tow" is the vessel which is being towed. The principles of tug and tow are complicated, but basically it may be said that the tug is responsible for the tow. (See "Tower's Liability".)

Tugs

Small craft with powerful engines used in ports to assist vessels moving in confined spaces. Large tugs are employed in deep sea salvage work. Generally highly valued for their size.

Tugmaster

A small motorised vehicle used in dock precincts for pulling trailers.

Tug Supply Vessel

A supply vessel that is powerful enough to act as a tug, when required. Used in offshore drilling operations, the vessel can lift the rig's anchors and assist in re-positioning the rig in addition to maintaining supplies. A modern vessel may have engines developing 6,700 b.h.p. and have a static bollard pull of more than 90 tons.

Tween Decker
Tween deck ship.

Tween Deck Ship
A ship having another deck below the main deck.

Twenty Four Hours Clause
A clause attached to a cargo policy, usually on refrigerated goods, where delay is an insured peril and which includes the risk of breakdown of refrigerating or propelling machinery. The effect of the clause is to make claims payable only where the breakdown of machinery lasts for not less than 24 consecutive hours.

T.W.M.C.
Transport, wages, maintenance and cure. A hull P & I term.

Typed Wording
Typed wording overrides all other wording in the policy with which it is inconsistent, other than handwriting.

U

U/A

Underwriting account.

U & O

Use and Occupancy—an American term used mostly in the non-marine market. It refers to loss of earnings due to a building, bridge, tunnel, mine or similar construction being put out of use by an insured peril.

Uberrimae Fidei

Utmost Good Faith. (Which see.)

U/C *or* **u/c**

Under construction.

U.C.B.

Unless caused by (which see).

U/D *or* **u/d**

Under-deck.

U.K.

United Kingdom.

U.K. Cont.

United Kingdom and/or the Continent of Europe. This abbreviation may be followed with B.H. (Bordeaux-Hamburg range) or H.H. (Havre-Hamburg range) or G.H. (Gibraltar-Hamburg range) or H.A.D. (Havre and/or Antwerp and/or Dunkirk).

U.K. Limits

See "United Kingdom Limits".

ul.

Unlimited during the currency of the insurance.

U.L.C.C.

Ultra Large Crude Carrier. Bulk oil carrier of approximately 470,000 d.w.t. or above. (See also "V.L.C.C.".)

Ullage

Trade ullage. Natural loss of liquid cargoes in transit. This is usually due to evaporation and occurs whether or not there is an accident. Since it is an inevitability, and not a *risk*, ullage is not covered by the policy and, therefore, the recognised percentage for ullage must be deducted from any claim based on the difference between shipped and arrived quantities. (See also " Ullage (Oil Tankers) ".)

Ullage (Oil Tankers)

The measurement from the surface of the cargo (or ballast) to the top of the tank or cargo hold. Tanks and cargo holds are rarely loaded beyond 98% full to allow 2% for expansion of the oil.

Ult.

Ultimate.

Ultimate Net Loss

A term used in reinsurance, particularly Excess of Loss reinsurance. In calculating a claim recoverable from the reinsurer it is necessary to find the ultimate net loss incurred by the reassured. The ultimate net loss is found by deducting, from the loss paid to the original assured, all recoveries by the reassured from third parties, salvage or other reinsurances. Claims collection costs and fees must also be deducted. Overheads of the reassured need not be deducted.

Unclean Bill

Unclean bill of lading.

Unclean Bill of Lading

A qualified bill of lading. (See " Dirty Bill of Lading ".)

Unconfirmed Credit

See " Confirmed Irrevocable Credit ".

Undeclared Cargo

If a shipment has not been declared under an open cover or floating policy it may be declared later, even after loss, provided the failure to declare was an error made in good faith.

If cargo is wilfully undeclared to the carrier no claim can be made by that cargo for general average, but the cargo must contribute toward any other general average payable.

Undelivered Cargo

See " Non-Delivery ".

Under-deck Shipments

Goods not customarily carried on deck are always deemed by the insurer to be shipped under-deck unless the policy states that the goods are " on deck " or " over-deck ". Shipments are carried under-deck when in holds or spaces below the main deck. Goods carried in a lighter for under-deck shipment are deemed to be carried under-deck.

Under-deck Tonnage
The capacity of a ship below the main deck, calculated at 100 cubic ft. per ton.

Underinsurance
When an insurance policy is effected for an amount which is less than the value at risk there is underinsurance. In the event of under-insurance the assured is deemed to be his own insurer for the difference between the policy sum insured and the insurable value. The valuation provisions and measure of indemnity in the Marine Insurance Act 1906 protect the insurer from being prejudiced by underinsurance in an unvalued policy. Difficulties may arise over valued policies. (See " Undervalued Policy ".)

Underlying
A term used to define the basic insurance where a supplementary insurance is effected. The term has no bearing on reinsurance, where the insurance which would otherwise be referred to as " underlying " is called the "original" insurance. It is customary for the supplementary or excess insurance to be subject to the terms of the underlying insurance, but it must not be assumed that this is automatic because in the absence of any specified agreement to follow the underlying insurance, the supplementary or excess insurance is a separate contract.

Under Repair
A vessel is "under repair", for the purpose of the "Returns Clause" in a hull policy, not only when repairs for damage are being carried out but also when structural alterations are in progress.

Undervalued Policy
The value in a valued policy is conclusive between the insurer and assured and cannot be reopened except in the case of fraud or gross overvaluation in a cargo policy. The assured gains no benefit by undervalue in a cargo policy, for the undervaluation reduces both partial and total loss claims, because the percentage of depreciation for partial loss is applied to the insured value and the maximum recoverable for total loss is the insured value. Difficulties arise for the insurer under a hull policy because the reasonable cost of repairs is payable in full whatever the insured value; limited only to the insured value in respect of any one accident. The disbursements warranty in the hull policy protects the insurer from gross under-valuation. (See, also, "Disbursements Warranty".)

Underwrite
To write a risk. An insurer writes, or underwrites, a risk when he

accepts liability for any loss to the subject matter insured from an insured peril. The term derives from the practice of the insurer to accept his proportion of the risk by initialling his name *under* the conditions stated on the slip. With the passage of time the word " underwrite " has come to be used for any action whereby a person guarantees the losses of another.

Underwriter
One who underwrites. (See " Lloyd's Underwriter " and " Company Underwriter ".)

Underwriter's Guarantee
See " General Average Guarantee ".

Underwriting Account
The record kept by an insurer to show the statistics and experience of the risks he has written. In most cases the account is run on an annual basis and the success of the underwriter's business is reflected in the balance shown in his underwriting account. Although Syndicate accounts are run on an annual basis they incorporate losses for the two succeeding years where such losses relate to business during the year of account; thus Lloyd's operates a 3 year accounting system. (See " Three Year Accounting System ".)

Underwriting Agent
An agent of an Insurance Company who underwrites business on behalf of his Company. He operates under the authority of a letter of appointment but is limited to the amount he can accept in any one class of business. Anything in excess of the prescribed limits must be submitted to the head office for approval before acceptance. The agent receives commission on the business he underwrites and profit commission on the annual net profit which his account brings to the Company. (See also " Lloyd's Underwriting Agent ".)

Underwriting Practice
The attitude of an underwriter with regard to a particular type of risk. Underwriting practice may be applied loosely to the whole market as in the case of certain cargoes which underwriters will only accept on limited terms; or it may be applied to an individual underwriter.

Underwriter's Pseudonym
A three letter pseudonym, indicating the name of the active or main underwriter in a Lloyd's syndicate. A suitable pseudonym is allocated by L.P.S.O. to each syndicate following negotiations with the syndicate concerned; thereby avoiding duplication. The pseudonym appears on the syndicate's line stamp and is quoted

in all documents to or from L.P.S.O. or L.D.P.S. relating to that syndicate. (See also " Broker's Pseudonym ".)

Underwriter's Tabulations
See " Tabulations ".

Undiscovered Loss Clause
A clause in a cargo policy which provides that the assured shall not be prejudiced because loss or damage is not discovered until the cases are opened for use. The clause includes a time limit for opening the cases, but usually contains a " held covered " provision should this time limit be exceeded.

Unearned Premium
Premium paid on risks in respect of which the property has never been exposed to peril so that the insurer could not have had any liability.

Unidentifiable Cargo
The marks and labels on cargo must be sufficient to withstand the ordinary voyage and the carrier cannot be held liable for unidentification of cargo due to lack of marks. There are limitations placed on the insurer's liability for " unidentifiable cargo ". (See " Commixture " and " Label clause ".)

Unit Carriage
Method of carrying goods. The term embraces all methods whereby a number of packages are grouped into a single unit for handling, stowage and carriage; including containerisation and palletisation.

United Kingdom and Allies Clause
A clause introduced in 1939 for use in wartime. It warrants the cargo policy free from any claim arising from capture, seizure, arrest, restraint or detainment by the U.K. Government or any of its Allies. It warrants, also, that the goods are not the property of an alien enemy even though the owner might reside in neutral territory.

United Kingdom Limits
In small craft insurance it is customary to specify the navigational limits of the vessel. When the term " U.K. limits " is used as a warranty in the insurance it is intended that the navigation of the vessel shall be restricted to the territorial waters of Great Britain and/or Northern Ireland and/or the Isle of Man and/or the Channel Islands and/or the Republic of Ireland. If the vessel proceeds outside the territorial waters of one of these countries or places the

insurance ceases from the date of the breach of warranty, even though the breach may be remedied or the vessel may be en route for the territorial waters of one of the other specified countries or places.

United Kingdom Standard Towage Conditions

Towage conditions used in the United Kingdom and Commonwealth countries. Under the terms of these conditions the master and crew of the tug become the servants of the owners or managers of the towed vessel and the tug owner accepts no liability for damage of any description whether done to or by the towed vessel or by the tug. This applies even though the damage be due to unseaworthiness or breakdown of the tug, or her gear, or by negligence of her crew, provided reasonable care was exercised by the tug owner to make the tug seaworthy.

United States Carriage of Goods By Sea Act 1936

An Act to give force of law to the rights, obligations and immunities of carriers of goods in respect of bills of lading on shipments into or out of the United States. Not applicable to Coastwise or Great Lakes shipments which are subject to the Harter Act.

Unitisation

The practice of placing several packages of goods into a single unit or container in order to expedite and make easier the loading, stowage and discharge of such goods.

U.N.L.

Ultimate net loss.

unl.

Unlimited during the currency of the insurance.

Unlawful Adventure

The adventure must be lawful and conducted in a lawful manner throughout otherwise there is a breach of warranty. (See " Legality of Adventure ".)

Unless

See " F.P.A. Unless ".

Unless caused by

Unless caused by the vessel and/or craft being stranded, sunk, on fire, in collision and/or contact with any external substance (including ice but excluding water). This term is used in cargo policies where the insurer does not wish the franchise to be broken for heavy weather damage when the ship or craft suffers a major casualty, as it would be if the words " caused by " were omitted from the clause.

Unless General

Unless general average. A term used in the average clause in a policy making it clear that the franchise does not apply to general average damage or contribution.

Unless the Policy Otherwise Provides

An expression used in the Marine Insurance Act 1906 whereby the provisions specified may be overridden by special agreement of the insurer.

Unpaid Premium

The broker is responsible to the insurer for the premium due on any insurance which he has placed, whether or not he has received it from the assured. To protect himself in this respect the broker has a lien on the policy whereby he may retain it in his possession until the premium is paid. The lien operates in respect of outstanding premiums also. The lien on outstanding insurance accounts is non-effective if the broker's client is only an agent of the assured.

Unreasonable Delay

The voyage must be prosecuted throughout without unreasonable delay or the insurer is discharged from liability under the policy from the time that the delay becomes unreasonable. (See " Excuses for Delay ".)

Unrepaired Damage

If, when the hull policy expires, damage caused by an insured peril remains unrepaired the assured is entitled to a reasonable depreciation in respect of such unrepaired damage. The depreciation allowed must not exceed the reasonable cost of repairs had they been carried out at the proper time. No claim may be recovered under the policy for depreciation in respect of unrepaired damage if the ship becomes a total loss before the expiry of the policy.

Unseaworthiness

See " Seaworthiness ".

Unstuffing

The practice of removing goods from a container.

Unvalued Policy

A policy that does not specify the value of the interest insured. In practice, only valued policies are used in marine insurance except for such interests as freight and disbursements. Calculations for measure of indemnity on an unvalued policy are based on the insurable value. The maximum amount recoverable under an unvalued policy is the insurable value of the interest subject to the limit of the sum insured or any other limit expressed in the policy.

Up and Down Clause
Another term for the Escalator Clause used in Builders' Risk insurances.

U.P. fee
Underwriters pay fee. The insurer agrees to pay the fee chargeable in respect of the insertion in the policy of the C.P.A. agreement. (See "C.P.A.".)

Uplifting
Increasing a premium by loading the rate.

U.P.S.
Underwriters pay the stamp duty on the policy. The term is obsolete since the abolition of marine stamp duty.

U.P. tax
Underwriters pay tax. The insurer agrees to reimburse the assured for any tax which he has paid by reason of effecting the insurance. (See also "Tax Clause" and "Tax Paid Clause".)

U/R *or* **u/r**
Under repair.

U/rs.
Underwriters.

U.S.A. Atl.
Ports or places on the Atlantic sea coast of the United States of America. This includes ports or places on rivers entering the Atlantic but does not embrace ports or places on the Great Lakes.

Usage
Common practice. See "Custom and Usage".

U.S.N.H.
United States north of Cape Hatteras.

U.T. *or* **u.t.**
Unlimited transhipment.

Utmost Good Faith
The Marine Insurance Act 1906 states that "Insurance is "uberrimae fidei" and, in section 17, further states that a contract of marine insurance is based upon the utmost good faith and if either party fails to observe this principle the contract may be

avoided by the other party. This is a very important principle in the practice of marine insurance and a serious view is taken by an insurer who is the victim of a breach of good faith.

A marine insurance contract is effected without the insurer seeing the property which it is proposed he shall insure and the insurer bases his decision to accept, also the rate of premium to be applied, on the material facts and representations presented to him by the insured and/or the insured's broker. If there is any misrepresentation or non-disclosure of a material fact the insurer can avoid the contract entirely and repudiate all claims. (See " Disclosure ", " Non-Disclosure ", " Material Representation " and " Representation ".)

U/W *or* **U/Wr** *or* **U/wr**
Underwriter.

V

Valuation
See "Valued Policies", "Overvaluation" and "Undervalued Policy".

Valuation Clause
The valuation clause in the Institute Time Clauses and other similar sets of hull clauses provides that the insured value is to be taken as the repaired value for constructive total loss purposes and that nothing in respect of break up value is to be taken into account. This clause is sometimes called the Constructive Total Loss Clause. (See also "Basis of Valuation".)

Valuation Form
A form completed by the cargo owner for the use of an average adjuster in a general average adjustment. The form is necessary for identification of the goods and assessment of contributory value.

Valued as Original
Valued as the original policy or policies. A reinsurance term ensuring that the reinsurance policy is a valued policy and that the value is the same as in the original policy, although the actual reinsured amount is often less than the original value.

Valued Policies
A marine policy may be valued or unvalued. A valued policy is one which specifies the value, usually with the words "valued at" or "so valued". The value in a valued policy is agreed at inception and, in the absence of fraud, is conclusive as between the insurer and assured, irrespective of whether or not it is the true value. It may only be reopened in the case of fraud or of gross over-valuation of cargo. In practice cargo policies are always valued because an unvalued policy is subject to the measure of indemnity and the valuation provisions laid down by the Marine Insurance Act, 1906, whereby the assured cannot include the profit earned by the sale of the goods. This places him in a position as though the adventure had never commenced. A valued policy allows the assured to include the profit so that in the event of loss he is placed in the position as though the adventure had been completed. In hull insurance a valued policy is used because an old vessel is as valuable a freight earner to the assured as a relatively new vessel. For this reason, the assured wishes to insure for an amount which bears some relation to the vessel's true value to him rather than its

market value. A valued policy enables him to do this. Such a valuation is acceptable to insurers, particularly as partial losses are payable in full under a valued hull policy, without reference to the true value, and over-valuation of this nature tends to increase the premium income to cover such partial losses.

Value for General Average Purposes
See "Contributory Value".

Value Increases
See "Increased Value".

Value of Cargo
If the cargo owner does not wish to include his anticipated profit in the policy value he may effect an unvalued policy whereby the measure of indemnity laid down by the Marine Insurance Act 1906 will provide the amount of cover required, subject, of course, to the amount insured being adequate. If, as in most cases, the cargo owner wishes to include his profit it is essential that he effects a "valued" policy. (See also "Gross Values" and "Net Values".)

Value of Ship
The intrinsic value of the hull, machinery, etc. of a ship is seldom sufficient to recompense the shipowner for the loss of his vessel as a freight earner. For this reason a value is compromised between the insurer and shipowner and this value is insured under a valued policy. Partial loss claims are payable in full irrespective of the policy value. (See also "Disbursements Warranty".)

Variation of Adventure
See "Termination of Adventure", "Change of Voyage", "Different Voyage" and "Deviation".

V.C.
Valuation clause.

Vd.
Valued.

Veer
To ease out a cable or anchor chain.

Vessel
A ship or any craft which is the subject of the insurance. Generally, the term includes everything that would be sold with the ship if she changed hands (e.g. boats, machinery, equipment, gear, etc.). In American policies it is customary to include stores, bunkers, etc., in the definition shown in the policy. During 1974 the American

courts held that a LASH barge is not deemed to be a vessel in its own right. In collision law this does not include craft which are not navigable.

Vessel Traffic Systems

Systems controlling the movement of vessels. Such systems are operated by the U.S. Coast Guard in San Francisco and Puget Sound. Plans are proposed to introduce similar controls in the Houston—Galveston area, New York area and other areas. Compliance with the systems is not necessarily mandatory at present, voluntary compliance being encouraged.

Verm.
Vermin.

Vermin

One of the excluded perils specified by the Marine Insurance Act 1906. The policy may be extended at the insurer's option to cover the risk of vermin, but is not the practice of insurers to cover this risk.

Vice Propre
Inherent vice.

Victory type Ships

These vessels were another of the many types built in vast numbers in the U.S.A. under the general heading of war-time tonnage.

They were successors to the earlier Liberty Ships, which had been built to be "expendable" but had proved to be considerably better than envisaged.

The Victory Ship design was a great improvement over its predecessor; it was brought about when the sight of victory allowed war-time planning to bring into service better and faster cargo carriers which would also prove of immense value in the post-war period.

The two classes of this type were similar in appearance, dimensions and tonnage (approximately 7,650 g.r.t.) but with one class the turbine propelling machinery was of greater power—giving higher speed.

All these vessels were given the suffix "Victory" when originally named.

(Further details may be obtained from "Wartime Standard Ships"—Volume 5, by W. H. Mitchell and L. A. Sawyer, published by the Journal of Commerce and Shipping Telegraph Limited.)

Voidable Policies

A policy is said to be voidable where circumstances exist that entitle one of the parties to " avoid the contract ". It is usually only the insurer who finds himself in a position where he might avoid the contract but, in law, there are only two circumstances when the insurer has the option to avoid the contract.

(1) Where the assured or his broker has been guilty of a breach of good faith prior to conclusion of the contract. (See " Conclusion of Contract ".)

(2) Where there is unreasonable delay in commencement of the voyage. That is, an unreasonable delay between the time the insurer accepts the insurance and the time risk actually commences. This does not affect a time insurance because this comes into effect automatically at a predetermined time and date. Nevertheless, if it can be shown that the insurer was aware of the circumstances leading to the delay or that he waived his right, the insurer cannot avoid the voyage insurance contract. (See " Commencement of Voyage ".)

When an insurer avoids a contract he " stands aside and treats the contract as though he never accepted it in the first place ". Accordingly, if an insurer avoids the contract he must return the whole premium to the assured except where the risk has attached (M.I.A. Act 1906 Section 84–3a). There is no statutory provision that allows an insurer to " avoid " *part* of the insurance contract; he must avoid the contract entirely from inception or waive his option. When the insurer exercises his option this does not reduce the legal validity of the contract. The assured can use the policy in a court action, to challenge the insurer's right to avoid the contract. The term " avoidance " must not be confused with the term " void ", the latter being a contract that is legally invalid. (See " Void Contracts ".) There is a common misunderstanding, in practice, that breach of a warranty entitles the insurer to avoid the contract; this is not so. (See " Breach of Warranty ".)

V.L.C.C.

This is a colloquial abbreviation which is used to indicate a very large vessel. Since this is usually a bulk oil carrier the abbreviation is interpreted, generally, as " Very Large Crude Carrier ", though it may be used in practice to indicate a very large cargo carrier or a very large container carrier. Since a V.L.C.C. is usually well in excess of 100,000 d.w.t. and has a draft of some 70 feet or more, such vessels can operate only in very deep water and are believed to be not really suitable for navigation in the English Channel, or other channels which are safe for vessels with a more shallow draft. (See also " U.L.C.C. " and " O.B.O. ".)

Void Contracts

A void policy or contract is one which is unenforceable at law. Fraud vitiates the contract and makes it of no effect. A wagering policy is void. Similarly, a P.P.I. policy or one with the term " without benefit of salvage " or " full interest admitted " are equally void at law.

Voluntary Payment to Assured

See " Ex gratia " and " Without Prejudice ".

Voluntary Stranding

This may occur in circumstances where a ship is in danger of sinking and may only be saved if she is intentionally " beached " or driven ashore. Provided the action is prudent and reasonable any resultant damage may be allowed in general average. If a ship is voluntarily stranded in circumstances where she would have stranded in any case, damage caused by the stranding would not be allowed in general average.

V.O.P.

Valued as in the original policy or policies.

Voyage

A voyage covers the period from when the ship sets sail for her destination until she arrives at her destination. In practice, the voyage in a cargo policy attaches when the goods commence transit and terminates on delivery of the goods at the final destination, subject to the terms of the " Transit Clause ", which see.

Voyage Charter Party

A contract for the hire of a ship for a voyage.

Voyage in Stages

Mainly concerned with seaworthiness of a vessel. A voyage is said to be in stages when it can be divided into clear cut sections. An example would be a ship on a voyage from Chicago to London. The first stage would be the lake risk, the second the river risk, the third the sea voyage and finally the river risk. (See " Seaworthiness ".)

Voyage Policy

A marine insurance policy covering a ship for a voyage. Most cargo policies are for a voyage but are merely referred to as " cargo policies " in practice.

Voyage Variation
See "Change of Voyage", "Different Voyage", "Deviation", "Delay" and "Transhipment".

VSL *or* **Vsl**
Vessel.

V.T.S.
Vessel Traffic Systems—U.S.A.

W

W

The mark on the side of a vessel denoting the winter loadline level.

W.A.

With average.

W.A. Clauses

Institute Cargo Clauses, with average.

W.A. Cover

Institute Cargo Clauses, W.A.

Wafering

Inserting a piece of paper in a folded policy. This does not incorporate the details on the paper in the policy. To form part of the contract the paper must be affixed permanently to the policy and be authorised by the authority that signed the policy.

Wagering Contract

A policy of marine insurance where the assured has no bona fide insurable interest and no reasonable expectation of acquiring an interest. The Marine Insurance Act 1906 (Sect. 4) provides that a wagering contract is void. It is an offence in law to effect such a policy, which contravenes the Marine Insurance (Gambling Policies) Act 1909.

Wages

The Master and crew have an insurable interest in the wages due to them but it is not necessary for them to insure since they are protected from loss of wages in the event of shipwreck by the Merchant Shipping Act. Wages and maintenance of Master, officers or crew in the event of prolongation of the voyage by reason of entering a port of refuge or returning to the loading port are allowed in general average, also when incurred whilst the ship is detained in such circumstances for repairs or for the common safety. Wages by way of overtime are not allowed in general average except up to the amount of time saved by the overtime at the ordinary rate. A Master, Officer or member of the crew has a lien on the ship for unpaid wages. (See "Wages and Maintenance Clause".)

Wages and Maintenance Clause

Clause No. 15 in the Institute Time Clauses (Hulls) 1/10/70. By this clause, underwriters do not admit in particular average wages

427

and maintenance of the Master, Officers or Crew except when incurred solely for the necessary movement of the vessel from one port to another for repairs, or for trial trips for average repairs, and then only for such wages and maintenance as are incurred whilst the vessel is under way.

Waiver Clause

A clause in the policy form which protects the rights of both the insurer and assured if either takes any action to preserve the insured property from loss. In the event of any such action the clause states that the action shall not be deemed a waiver of the rights of either under the policy. It also states that any such action by the insurer shall not be considered as an acceptance of abandonment. (See also " Reinsurance Waiver Clause ".)

Wale

A thick strake (see " strake ") designed to withstand the force of impact.

Walking Off

A peril applicable to livestock insurance which is usually excluded from the policy.

Wall Sided

A vessel having perpendicular (as opposed to curved) sides.

War and Civil War Exclusion Clause

A non-marine clause excluding war and civil war risks on land.

War Built Tonnage

Ships built during the 1939-1945 War. Generally, the term is applied to vessels approximately 7,000 to 8,000 tons built during the period 1940 to 1945 inclusive. The following are types of war built tonnage:— Liberties, "T" tankers, C type ships, Oceans, Forts, Parks, Empires, Victories, Sams.

Insurers tend to load the premium in respect of such vessels and with regard to the insurance of goods carried thereon. Definitions of the above types may be found elsewhere herein.

War Cancellation Clause

An open cover provision which permits declarations from any provides that war risks covered by the insurance are automatically cancelled on the outbreak of a major war or which allows the insurer to cancel war risks by giving the assured notice of the intention to cancel. Such a clause allows the insurer to cancel the war risk element of an insurance contract that covers other risks as well as war risks. (See " War Risk Insurance ".)

Warehouse Charges at P.O.R.
See "Costs Allowed in General Average".

Warehouse to Warehouse Clause
A clause which appeared in the Institute Cargo Clauses as a separate clause until 1st January 1963. The clause provided that the insurance attached when the goods left the warehouse at the place named in the policy for overseas transit. The insurance continued throughout all normal course of transit. The insurance terminated when the goods were delivered at the final warehouse at the destination named in the policy. A time *limit* of sixty days from midnight on the day of discharge from the ocean steamer was allowed for delivery. If the sixty days expired before delivery at the final warehouse the cover ceased on such expiry. If the goods were delivered before the expiry of the sixty day limit the insurance terminated on such delivery. The clause is now incorporated as part of the transit clause (which see.)

Warehousing Entry
When goods are to be placed in a bonded warehouse it is necessary to complete a document called a "Warehousing Entry" which is required by Customs.

Warehouse Risk
Insurance of goods whilst in warehouse. This risk generally occurs at the Customs or other warehouse at the port or place of shipment or discharge. If the warehouse period is within the "ordinary course of transit" the marine insurance cover continues and no special policy is necessary. Any warehouse period outside the marine policy cover requires either special agreement of the marine insurers or a separate policy to cover the insurance. Extension of marine policies to cover warehouse risk is customarily based on periods of thirty days or part thereof and is often restricted to Fire Risk Only.

War etc.
War, strikes, riots, civil commotions and malicious damage.

War Exclusion Clause
The F.C. & S. clause. (Free of capture and seizure etc.) By the F.C. & S. warranty war risks are excluded from the standard marine policy. In a non-marine policy or a policy covering non-marine risks the equivalent clause is the "War and Civil War Exclusion Clause".

Warp
To use ropes or cables to manoeuvre a ship.

War Perils

These embrace capture, seizure, arrest, restraint or detainment of princes or peoples, men of war, engines of war, mines, torpedoes or any hostile act. (See " War Risk Insurance ".)

Warranted

Promised by the assured. (See " Warranty ".)

Warranted Free From Average

Agreed the policy does not cover partial loss. It is usual to follow this expression with " unless general " so that the warranty applies only to particular average.

Warranted Free From Particular Average

Agreed the policy does not cover partial loss except such loss as is recoverable as general average.

Warranty

A promise by the assured that a thing will or will not be done or that a state of affairs will or will not exist. A warranty must be strictly complied with. Non-compliance is breach of warranty. In the event of breach of warranty the insurer is discharged from liability from the date of the breach, whether or not the breach is material to the loss. The insurer is still liable for insured losses occurring before the breach. Repair of the breach does not reinstate the liability of the insurer. A warranty may be " express " or " implied ". An " express warranty " is one which is specified in the policy. An " implied warranty " is one which does not appear in the policy but which is understood by both parties to be incorporated therein. An implied warranty is equally as binding as an express warranty. A breach of warranty may be waived at the option of the insurer. Non-compliance with a warranty is excused when to comply with it would involve an infringement of the law. Non-compliance is also excused when the warranty is no longer material. (See " Seaworthiness " and " Warranty of Legality ".)

Warranty of Good Safety

The Marine Insurance Act 1906 provides that where the insured property is warranted " well " or " in good safety " on a particular day, it is sufficient if it be safe at any time during that day.

Warranty of Legality

There is an implied warranty in the marine policy that the adventure is lawful, and that, so far as the assured can control it, the adventure shall be carried out in a lawful manner. (Ref. Marine Insurance Act 1906—Sect. 41.)

Warranty of Nationality
There is no implied warranty in a marine policy as to the nationality of a ship, or that her nationality shall not be changed during the risk. (Ref. Marine Insurance Act 1906—Sect. 37.)

Warranty of Neutrality
During wartime a neutral ship must observe its neutrality implicitly and it is usual to incorporate an express warranty in the policy to this effect. This means she must be properly documented, so far as the assured can control, in that she must carry the necessary papers to establish her neutrality and she must not suppress or falsify her papers nor use simulated papers. Whether on ship or goods a warranty of neutrality means that the property must have a neutral character at the commencement of the risk, which character must be preserved, so far as the assured can control it, throughout the risk.

Warranty of Seaworthiness
See " Seaworthiness ".

War Risk Cancellation
The risk of loss of, or damage to, property arising from war risks in time of a major war is greater than the insurance market is prepared to bear. By agreement, there is no war risk cover on land, other than on cargo for a limited period during transhipment. Open covers always incorporate a war cancellation clause whereby the underwriter is entitled to cancel war risk cover on all declarations where transit has not commenced before the expiry of 7 days' notice given by the underwriter. Although, in common with all other war risk clauses, the I.C.C. exclude claims arising from nuclear weapons, there is no automatic termination clause in the I.C.C. However, in hull war clauses (which also incorporate strikes risks) there is a provision that cover terminates immediately on the outbreak of a major war (i.e. a war between any of the countries U.K., U.S.A., U.S.S.R., France and/or People's Republic of China). There is, also, a provision in hull war and strikes clauses allowing either party to cancel cover by giving the other party 14 days' notice.

War Risk Insurance
The standard marine policy and all standard sets of marine clauses, other than war clauses, are subject to the F.C. & S. clause. This clause excludes the risks of war and allied perils from the insurance. In cargo insurance it is usual to reinstate the war risks into the policy, subject to the waterborne clause, and to incorporate, in addition, any hostile act, mines and torpedoes. Strikes risks are

usually incorporated into the policy at the same time. The reinstate-ment of war and incorporation of the additional risks entitles the insurer to charge an additional premium of not less than the current war and strikes scale rate at the time of sailing.

Hull war and strikes risks were and sometimes still are covered under a separate policy which at one time was limited to a period of three months and subject to 48 hours notice of cancellation. It is now customary for hull war and strikes policies to be for longer periods of up to 12 months and frequently attached to the marine policy but the war risks cover is subject to an automatic termination of cover clause whereby the policy is automatically cancelled on the outbreak of a major war and any damage by a hostile act resulting in an outbreak of major war is excluded. Further excluded is loss or damage to the insured interest or expense arising from pre-emption, requisition, also capture, arrest, restraint, detainment or confiscation by the Government of the country where the vessel is registered or owned and loss, damage or expense arising from any hostile detonation of a nuclear weapon of war. Expenses arising from delay, except in general average, are also excluded. To make it quite clear that the clauses are in respect of war cover only and, where attached to a marine policy, are deemed to form a separate insurance they specifically exclude loss damage or expense arising from arrest, detainment or restraint by reason of infringement of customs regulations or under quarantine restrictions and exclude any claim which is recoverable under the ordinary marine policy; this latter applying to both hull and cargo policies. The war cover, in a hull or freight policy, may be cancelled, also, by either party giving the other 14 days notice. Cargo policies covering war may have the war cancellation clause attached thereto providing for 48 hours notice to cancel the war cover. Open covers and similar long term contracts contain a war and strikes cancellation clause requir-ing 7 days notice, but strikes risks for shipments to and from the U.S.A. are usually subject to 48 hours notice.

Wartime Extension Clause

The earlier form of extended cover for attachment to cargo poli-cies. Now obsolete, this clause was replaced by the extended cover clause which was incorporated into the Institute Cargo Clauses. When the transit clause was introduced at 1st January 1963 the extended cover clause was removed with the warehouse to ware-house clause, but its substance is incorporated as the final part of the transit clause. (See " Transit Clause ".)

Washing Out Clause

A clause in a cargo policy covering pulp or similar in bales which may be washed out by contact with seawater. The clause provides that such washing out is deemed to constitute washing overboard and is recoverable under the policy.

Washing Overboard
An extraneous risk sometimes incorporated in the policy by agreement where deck cargo is covered. It is often the practice to cover " loss overboard " instead of " washing overboard " because it is a wider cover.

Wastage in Bulk
By the Carriage of Goods by Sea Act 1924 the carrier is absolved from responsibility for any wastage or loss of weight in bulk cargoes. This is because he cannot check the weight on loading and is obliged to accept details of weights supplied by the shipper.

Waterborne Agreement
An agreement entered into by the majority of the English Marine insurance market concerning war risk insurance. By the agreement each signatory undertakes not to insure goods against war risks except when they are on board the ocean vessel.

Waterborne Clause
A clause appearing in cargo war clauses giving effect to the Waterborne Agreement. The clause limits the war cover to the period during which the goods are on the overseas vessel. Cargo in craft to or from the ship is still covered, however, but only against the risks of derelict mines or torpedoes. A similar clause, replacing " overseas vessel " with " aircraft " appears in the Institute War Clauses (Air). A limited period (15 days) of cover is allowed on land during transhipment. (See " Institute War Clauses ".)

Water Quality Insurance Syndicate
See " W.Q.I.S. ".

w.b.
Water ballast.

W.B.S.
Without benefit of salvage to the insurer.

W.C.
West coast.

W.C.A.
Workmen's Compensation Act.

W.C.B.
With cargo on board. Now obsolete. (See N.C.B.)

W.C.S.A.
West coast South America.

W/d.
Warranted.

W.D.F.
Wireless direction finder.

Wear and Tear
The standard marine policy does not cover ordinary wear and tear and insurers never extend the policy to cover this loss because it is inevitable and not fortuitous. Nevertheless if repairs are effected to a ship under a hull policy, with the standard clauses attached thereto, no deduction is made for wear and tear when new material replaces old material. (See " New for Old ".)

Weather Working Days
Days during which work can be carried out without weather interference.

Weight Note
A document which shows the gross weight and net weight of imported goods. It is issued by the dock Authorities and also contains identification marks and dates of entry.

Well
An open space, on a ship's deck, between two superstructures or deckhouses.

Western Hemisphere
For the purposes of the cargo war and strikes risks rating schedule, used in the London market, the western hemisphere is defined as comprising U.S.A., Canada, Mexico, Central America, South America, West Indies and Bermuda.

Whale Factory Ship
A large parent ship in a whaling expedition. The whales are caught by a fleet of catchers which feed them into the factory ship. There the whales are cut up, the blubber extracted and the flesh dehydrated.

Wharf
The place where a ship moors alongside to discharge or load cargo.

Wharfage
Payment for the use of a wharf.

Wharfinger

A person having charge of a wharf.

White Label

A Lloyd's policy signing term, indicating that the policy is required urgently.

White Rust

Oxidation on metals which are treated to prevent red rust, such as galvanised metals. The insurer's liability is the same as that for "rust", which see herein under a separate entry.

Whse-whse.

Warehouse to warehouse clause.

Wider Terms

An expression used to indicate that more perils are covered than previously.

Wilful Misconduct

The insurer cannot be held liable to pay any claims under the policy which are attributable to the wilful misconduct of the assured. Misconduct or negligence on the part of the master or crew does not give the insurer the right to repudiate a claim proximately caused by an insured peril. (Marine Insurance Act, 1906, Sect. 55.)

With Average

A term which means that the policy not only covers total loss but also partial loss. The expression really refers to particular average although the policy also covers general average. A "with average" policy is subject to the franchise in the memorandum or any other specified percentage, unless the term "irrespective of percentage" is incorporated. Generally the term "with average" is used only for cargo insurance and the perils covered are limited to those printed in the policy form. The perils may be extended by agreement of the insurer and specific incorporation in the policy. (See also "Institute Cargo Clauses W.A.".)

Without Benefit of Salvage

Without benefit of salvage to the insurer. If the policy contains this term it cannot be used as a legal instrument because the Marine Insurance Act 1906 stipulates that such a policy is void. An exception may be made where there is no possibility of salvage.

Without Prejudice

In cases where the insurer is presented with a claim for which he feels he is not strictly liable under the terms of the policy he may agree to pay this "without prejudice". This means he is paying without argument on this particular occasion but it is not to be used as a basis for demanding settlement of similar future claims.

With Particular Average
Same as "With Average".

W/M
Weight and/or measurement.

W.M. fees
Winter mooring fees.

W.N.A.
Loadline marking showing Winter North Atlantic loadline level.

w.o. *or* **w.o.b.**
Washing overboard.

W.O.L.
Wharf-owner's liability.

W.Q.I.A.
Water Quality Improvement Act (1970). This was superseded by the "Federal Water Pollution Control Act Amendments of 1972". (U.S.A. Law.)

W.Q.I.S.
Water Quality Insurance Syndicate. A combined facility introduced in 1972 and subscribed by American insurance companies. W.Q.I.S. exists to offer insurance protection to shipowners and operators against legal liabilities imposed by U.S. law. The cover offers limited indemnity in respect of legal liability of the assured arising out of oil "clean up" costs. Further, within limits the cover indemnifies the shipowner or operator for reasonable expenses (for which he is legally liable) incurred in efforts to reduce or eliminate oil pollution in the navigable waters of the USA. (See also "Pollution".)

Workmen's Compensation Act
All Acts under the above heading between 1925 and 1945 were repealed before 1950, but remained in force for cases still before the courts or to come before the courts at the time of the repeal.

World to World
An open cover provision which permits declarations from any port or place in the world to any destination in the world.

W.P. *or* **w.p.**
Without prejudice *or* weather permitting.

W.P.A.
With particular average.

Wreck
Wreck or wreckage is any property which is or was part of a maritime adventure and which is no longer a thing of the kind which ventured upon the adventure, that is it is no longer of any use for the purpose for which it was intended. An insurer who has paid a total loss on the wreck is entitled, though not obliged to take over the wreck, and can, if he takes it over, dispose of it and retain the proceeds, if any. (See also " Removal of Wreck " and " Wreck Sacrificed ".)

Wreckage
See " Wreck ".

Wreck Sacrificed
When part of a ship is wrecked and in time of peril the wreckage is sacrificed, no recovery is allowed in general average because the wreckage was already virtually lost. The same applies to sacrificed cargo which was so damaged before the sacrifice that it was virtually a total loss.

W.R.I.O.
War Risks Insurance Office. The Government insurance department concerned with covering war risks in time of war.

Write
To underwrite a risk. An insurer writes a risk when he accepts liability under an insurance contract.

Written Line
The amount of liability which the insurer has agreed to accept when writing a risk. Also referred to as his " line ". The written line is the original acceptance. The line " closed " when signing the policy, called the " signed line ", may be less the written line. In no circumstance may a line be closed for more than the written line without prior agreement of the insurer.

W.R.O.
War risks only.

Wrongful Declaration of Cargo
Wrongful declaration means erroneous declaration. If any error is made in the declaration of cargo on an open cover or open policy, this has no effect on the cover, provided the error is in good faith and

is remedied immediately it is discovered.

Wrongful declaration of cargo to the carrier, where it has not been wilfully misdescribed, does not defeat the right to claim general average, but if the error is one of declaring a lower value than the true value, any recovery in general average is based on the declared value but contributions to general average are based on the true value.

Wt.
Weight.

Wtd.
Warranted.

W.T.E. Cl.
Wartime extension clause (now obsolete).

W'ties
Warranties.

Wty.
Warranty.

W/W
Warehouse to warehouse.

W.W.D.
Weather working days.

X

xs.
Excess.

XS Loss
Excess Loss Reinsurance.

Y

Yacht

Pleasure craft. Most yachts are relatively small and range from small sailing dinghies to sizeable steam yachts. There are some very large ocean going yachts. In view of the non-professional nature of the purpose of yachts premium rates are rather on the high side. Yacht conditions generally apply navigational limits and further warrant that the vessel be laid up for six months of the year (see also " Boat ").

Yacht Clause

See " Institute Yacht Clauses ".

Yacht Policies

There are several types of yacht policy in use because many insurers who specialise in yacht insurance prefer to use their own forms. If the insurance is placed with insurers at Lloyd's it is customary to use the ordinary S.G. form with the Institute Yacht Clauses attached thereto. All yacht policies follow the same basic pattern. It is usual to warrant that the vessel be laid up for six months of the year and that, whilst navigating, the vessel will be limited to within a specified navigating area and used for private pleasure purposes only. The policy covers third party liability in addition to damage to the yacht. Racing risks are subject to an additional premium under the Institute Yacht Clauses and limitations are applied regarding theft of tackle and damage to machinery and engines.

Y.A.R.

York-Antwerp Rules.

Y/A Rules

York-Antwerp Rules.

Yaw

A ship " yaws " when her bow moves from side to side, usually causing her to maintain a zig zag course. In most cases, it is caused by lack of steerage control.

Yawl

A small boat with four or more oars *or* a small fishing boat.

Year of Account

The year in which the insurance contract attaches. For practical purposes, this is usually established by the year in which the policy signing number is issued. Future APs, RPs, claims, etc. are entered in the year of account so established so that a true picture of profit or loss in any one year can be established. This is particularly important where long term contracts, such as open covers or reinsurance treaties, are concerned. Under the Separation Procedure the signing number is allocated in Stage 1, not when the policy is subsequently signed.

York-Antwerp Rules

A set of rules to enable uniformity to be obtained in adjustment of general average. The 1950 rules contain a Rule of Interpretation which provides that the specific circumstances detailed in the numbered rules shall be considered first. If the situation does not fit any of the numbered rules the lettered rules must be applied. Most general average is settled in accordance with the York-Antwerp Rules, but if the contract does not provide for these rules, the adjustment will either be made on Foreign adjustment or on English Law and Practice. Whichever set of rules is used the marine insurer agrees to abide by the decisions of the adjuster where the policy is involved.

Yt.
Yacht.

Z

Zabra
Spanish coastal vessel.